D0138179

Handbook For Developing Competency-Based Training Programs

William E. Blank

University of South Florida
Tampa, Florida

PRENTICE-HALL, Inc., Englewood Cliffs, New Jersey 07632

Library of Congress Cataloging in Publication Data

Blank, William E. (date)
Handbook for developing competency-based training programs.
Includes index.
1. Competency based education.
2. Occupational training. I. Title.
LC1031.B56 371.3 81-21102
ISBN 0-13-377416-3 AACR2

To Ivonne, Ben, and Alex who have made my life complete

Editorial/Production Supervision
and Interior Design: *Lynn S. Frankel*
Manufacturing Buyer: *Joyce Levatino*
Cover Design: *Tony Ferrara Studio* (Ray Lundgren)

Printed in the United States of America

10 9 8 7 6 5 4 3 2 1

ISBN 0-13-377416-3

Prentice-Hall International, Inc., *London*
Prentice-Hall of Australia Pty. Limited, *Sydney*
Prentice-Hall of Canada, Ltd., *Toronto*
Prentice-Hall of India Private Limited, *New Delhi*
Prentice-Hall of Japan, Inc., *Tokyo*
Prentice-Hall of Southeast Asia Pte. Ltd., *Singapore*
Whitehall Books Limited, *Wellington, New Zealand*

Contents

Preface

This book will help you develop occupational training programs that can lead as many as nine out of ten trainees to a high level of mastery (90 - 100%) in most any learning task. Although aimed primarily at instructors, trainers, curriculum/media specialists, supervisors, and others involved in job-related training in business, industry, vocational-technical education, agencies and institutions, anyone interested in developing education or training materials that lead to *results* would benefit from this book. It describes how to develop programs that:

- are based on clearly stated trainee outcomes,
- use carefully developed, mediated, and packaged learning materials,
- focus on learning—not teaching,
- insure that trainees master each task well before going on to the next,
- are individualized and personalized,
- can be self-paced, open-entry and open-exit, and
- evaluate each trainee on his or her performance.

In short, the goal of this book is to provide help in developing education and training programs that *work*.

Our whole system of education in general and vocational-technical education and industrial training in particular have come under increasing pressures lately to improve results. Often heard criticisms include: too many dropouts, lack of relevance, inability to meet the needs of special learners, outdated curricula, lack of response to the needs of business and industry, and too little concern for individual trainees. The *competency-based* approach to training has emerged as a viable alternative. This systematic approach—which goes by many names including personalized instruction, mastery learning, individualized instruction, and others—is establishing an impressive track record in responding to many of the shortcomings of today's education and training programs.

As more and more companies, agencies, and institutions have moved toward the competency-based approach, the need has arisen for practical, easy to follow reference material to aid instructors in developing and implementing programs. This handbook is designed to meet this need. It describes an approach to developing training programs that has been used successfully in many settings. Each chapter includes many samples and examples to aid the reader.

Two basic philosophies underlie the concepts presented here. First is the notion that "human competence" is the ability to actually *perform*. Knowledge, attitudes, and effort are of little value without results. The second philosophy—"mastery learning"—holds that most anyone can learn most anything well if given quality instruction and sufficient time. These two ideas are woven throughout the seven chapters.

Few books are the result of the author's ideas alone. This book is no exception. It reflects the thinking and hard work of many. The author has relied heavily on the writings of several pioneers in the field—particularly Benjamin Bloom. Much of the sample program materials described in the book are adaptations of material developed at the 916 Area Vo-Tech Institute in White Bear Lake, Minnesota. The superintendent of 916, William C. Knaak, and his staff have been most helpful and uncommonly generous in their sharing of materials and ideas.

A special word of thanks is in order to the faculty, staff, and students of Ridge Vo-Tech Center in Winter Haven, Florida for their invaluable help in developing and refining many of the concepts presented here. Under the leadership of director Bill Hampton, they have demonstrated that the competency-based approach works and works well.

I've had the good fortune of being influenced by the thinking of my colleagues at the University of South Florida and in the local schools we serve. My thanks to Raymond Hill, Robert Andreyka, Sonia Parmer, Warren Laux, Tom O'Brien, Janice Case, and the many others who have shared their ideas and opinions.

My thanks to Phyllis Whipple for her help with the section on computers, to Sonia Parmer for reviewing the original manuscript, and to Gail Vincent and Judy Williams for their typing assistance. Finally, I'd like to recognize the many instructors who so willingly implemented and refined the approach to training presented here and who, in turn, taught me so much about the competency-based approach to training.

WILLIAM E. BLANK

1

The Competency-Based Approach to Education and Training

Is This Book for Me?

A good place to begin might be to help you determine if this book is really for you. If it is not, perhaps I have saved you the time and effort required to read it and maybe I stopped you early enough so that you can return the book for a refund. To find out if you might benefit from reading it, take a few minutes to answer the 12 following questions. If you are an instructor or trainer, answer them in light of your own training program. If you are a director, dean, supervisor, manager, training director, or other administrator, answer them in light of the training programs under your supervision. For the questions to be of any value, you must answer each of them honestly after taking a long, hard look at what is actually happening—*today*—in your program—not what you *wish* were happening:

	YES	NO
1. Do you hand each trainee or student, on the first day he or she is enrolled, a list of *specific* "tasks" or "competencies" that spells out *exactly* what they will be able to *do* as a result of the training program, and *not* just a list of topics or units to be covered?		
2. Is your program based *entirely* on the actual job skills (tasks) performed by competent workers in the occupation and *not* on a textbook or course outline?		
3. Have the tasks upon which your program is based been verified during the last *12 months* as being complete, accurate, up to date, and essential for employment?		
4. Are you *certain* that the skills you teach in your training program are the *same* skills that successful workers actually perform on the job today?		
5. Can students *skip* instruction and receive *full credit* for any task in your training program for which they can demonstrate mastery based on *previous* learning?		
6. For each task students are to learn, are they provided with *carefully designed*, *high-quality* learning experiences and materials *appropriate* for both the student and the task?		
7. Are your student learning materials effectively organized or "packaged" in such a way that each individual student can *begin* a new task when ready and *slow down*, *speed up*, or *repeat* any part of the instruction as needed to learn?		

8. Is each individual student *helped* and *required* to master each task at a *very high level* of proficiency (95 to 100%) *before* being allowed or forced to move on to the next task?		
9. Is *each* individual trainee required to *perform* each task to a *high level* of proficiency in a joblike setting before being given credit for mastery?		
10. Do you document to students and employers *exactly* what specific tasks each student has or has *not yet* mastered when each student leaves your program?		
11. If grades are assigned, are they an accurate reflection of the actual *competence* of each trainee and not based on a norm or curve, attendance, attitudes, effort, or paper-and-pencil tests?		
12. Does the instructor spend *most* of his or her day helping students learn by reinforcing, giving feedback, evaluating, questioning, answering questions, and managing learning and *not* in front of the classroom "teaching"?		

If you answered "no" to one or more of these 12 questions, chances are this book has something to offer you. Its purpose is to help you put your training programs together so that you can answer "yes" for each question.

What Is Competency-Based Training?

Whether your involvement in training is through public vocational-technical education, business or industrial training, a public agency, the military, or through some other field, no doubt, you have heard the virtues of the "competency-based" approach expressed. In your particular setting, this approach to training may be called individualized instruction, learning for mastery, programmed instruction, or perhaps something else. Unfortunately, there is a lot of confusion, misinformation, myths, half-truths, and preconceived notions about the competency-based approach floating around today in the education and training field.

Just what is competency-based training, anyway? Why competency-based? Where did it come from? Is it really any different from what good instructors have been doing all along? Is it any better? How can a competency-based program be developed? These and other questions are being asked more and more by instructors and trainers as institutions, schools, and companies begin exploring and adopting the competency-based approach for their training programs. The remainder of this first chapter takes a look at this nonconventional approach to training—what it is, the philosophy upon which it is based, and why it is superior to more conventional approaches to training.

When is a program competency-based? During the past few decades the competency-based approach has emerged as a means of addressing many of the criticisms leveled against the educational system. After the early years of heated debate, experimentation, and trial and error, the dust is beginning to settle.

Many of the leaders in the competency-based movement have reached general agreement on what makes an educational program "competency-based."

I have sifted through many of the published lists of essential, desirable, and related elements that distinguish "traditional" programs from competency-based programs. An attempt has been made to condense these elements into a basic few and to express them in terms of training individuals for employment. After eliminating much of the educationese and the duplication, there seem to be four characteristics that distinguish between training programs that might be considered to be genuinely competency-based and those that are not. These characteristics are listed in Table 1-1 along with a brief explanation of the fundamental differences between traditional and competency-based training programs.

As you can see from Table 1-1, competency-based and more traditional training programs seem to differ in at least four primary ways: *What* it is trainees learn, *how* they learn each task, *when* they proceed from task to task, and, finally, how we determine and report *if* students learned each task. At first glance, these differences may appear minor but once you think about them, you will realize that these two approaches to training are as different as day and night.

Perhaps the most fundamental difference between these two approaches is that the competency-based approach is a very *systematic* approach to training while the more traditional approach is not. Each component of a competency-based training program is designed, monitored, and adjusted with one thing in mind—results. A competency-based training program is a lot like the thermostat on your air conditioner. When you put the thermostat on a certain setting, you decide then, exactly what temperature you want the room or house to be. The thermostat constantly monitors the temperature and either turns the air conditioner on or off to maintain the desired setting. If the room needs more or less cooling, the thermostat senses this and turns the unit on or off accordingly. The room gets enough, but only enough, cooling to maintain the desired level of comfort.

An air conditioner without a thermostat is somewhat like more conventional training programs that have not been designed systematically. Without a thermostat, the air conditioner would continue to cool as long as the switch was on, regardless of how cool the room became. When the switch is

TABLE 1-1 Basic Characteristics that Distinguish Between Competency-Based and Traditional Training Programs

Characteristic	*Competency-Based Programs*	*Traditional Programs*
1. *WHAT* Students Learn	1. Are based *solely* on specific, precisely stated student outcomes (usually called competencies or tasks) that have been recently verified as being essential for successful employment in the occupation for which the student is being trained. These competencies are made available to all concerned and describe *exactly* what the student will be able to *do* upon completing the training program.	1. Are usually based on textbooks, reference material, course outlines or other sources removed from the occupation itself. Students rarely know *exactly* what they will learn in each successive part of the program. The program is usually built around chapters, units, blocks, and other segments that have little meaning within the occupation—instructors focus on "covering material."
2. *HOW* Students Learn	2. Provide trainees with high quality, carefully designed, student-centered learning activities, media and materials designed to help them master each task. Materials are organized so that each individual trainee can stop, slow down, speed up or repeat instruction as needed to learn effectively. An integral part of this instruction is periodic feedback throughout the learning process with opportunities for trainees to correct their performance as they go.	2. Rely primarily on the instructor to personally deliver most of the instruction through live demonstrations, lectures, discussions and other instructor-centered learning activities. Students have little control over the pace of instruction. Usually, little periodic feedback on progress is given.
3. *WHEN* Students Proceed from Task to Task	3. Provide each trainee with enough time (within reason) to *fully* master one task before being allowed or forced to move on to the next.	3. Usually require a group of students to spend the same amount of time on each unit of instruction. The group then moves on to the next unit after a fixed amount of time which may be too soon or not soon enough for many individual trainees.
4. *IF* Students Learned Each Task	4. Require each individual trainee to perform each task to a high level of proficiency in a joblike setting before receiving credit for attaining each task. Performance is compared to a preset, fixed standard.	4. Rely heavily on paper and pencil tests and each student's performance is usually compared to the group norm. Students are allowed (and usually forced) to move on to the next unit after only marginally mastering or even "failing" the current unit.

turned off, the unit no longer cools, no matter how hot the room becomes. In conventional training programs, instruction is often turned on and turned off based solely on the clock or the calendar with little regard for how much instruction each student really needs. Instruction may be delivered in fifty-minute periods, three-hour blocks, or sixteen-week semesters regardless of how much or how little instruction each trainee may need to fully master each learning task. A competency-based program, on the other hand, allows each student's own learning "thermostat" to adjust the level and pace of instruction as needed. Each learning outcome or "setting" is established up front. Each trainee can then turn on or turn off instruction as needed to reach the desired outcome.

Recently, we have learned a great deal about the learning process. We know what promotes and inhibits learning. We understand what events must take place during any learning activity for effective and efficient learning to happen. Unfortunately, our whole system of education in general and the fields of vocational education and industrial training in particular, have been slow to capitalize on what we have learned. In essence, that is what the competency-based approach to training is all about. It is an attempt to put into practice what has been learned recently about improving the quality of what takes place in the classroom and shop.

Desirable or not? Before going any further, you probably need to decide whether or not you find the competency-based approach more desirable than the traditional approach. Basically, if you believe that training programs should (1) spell out exactly what it is that trainees should learn, (2) provide high quality instruction, (3) help students learn one thing well before going on to the next and then, (4) require each trainee to demonstrate competency, then you buy into the competency-based approach.

On the other hand, if you genuinely believe that (1) very general statements of student outcomes are sufficient, (2) instructors personally lecturing and demonstrating to the group is the best approach to instruction, (3) all students should spend about the same amount of time on each task and should move on when the group is ready, and (4) students should be evaluated based on how well they did compared with other students, then you probably don't find the competency-based approach very appealing. This is a very personal decision that only you can make for yourself.

Why "competency-based"? The term "competency-based" has been selected for the approach to training described in this book more for convenience than for accuracy or some other reason. There are almost as many names for the approach floating around as there are "experts." Everyone seems to be pushing his or her own acronym or title. Don't get confused or turned off by what this or any other author *calls* the concept. Focus on the concept itself, why it is different, why it is better, and how to do it—don't worry about what it is called. Let your school or state or corporation come up with its own label for this systematic approach to training; the real key is to get about the business of doing it.

Some of the more common labels given to this approach to training include:

- Competency-Based Instruction (CBI)
- Mastery Learning
- Systems Approach to Education
- Personalized System of Instruction (PSI)
- Performance-Based Instruction
- Criterion-Referenced Instruction (CRI)
- Learning for Mastery (LFM)
- Objective-Referenced Learning
- Individualized Instruction (II)
- Programmed Instruction (PI)
- Self-Paced Learning
- Instructional System Development (ISD)

Although all these terms are not entirely synonymous, they are similar enough that they can just about be used interchangeably. If a particular approach to training has the four basic characteristics mentioned earlier, we might consider it to be competency-based or individualized or personalized—regardless of what it is called.

Is it new? One of the ironies surrounding the competency-based movement is that many educators reject the idea as just the latest fad in a long series of "fix-it" cures for the problems we are faced with in education and training. Ironically, the *idea* behind the competency-based approach not only isn't new, it is ancient. Keep the basic elements of competency-based instruction in mind (what, how, when, if) as we look back at how job training was carried out hundreds of years ago.

> *When an apprentice blacksmith was ready to learn a new task, he was told exactly what it was he was going to learn. The master blacksmith did not introduce a new unit or enroll the apprentice in a new course. He probably said something like "Today I'm going to show you how to make a nail" (What). The apprentice, of course, was not assigned a chapter to read on the history of nails.*
>
> *The master craftsman showed the apprentice very slowly and very carefully exactly how to make a nail—how to cut the blank, how to pound the head into shape, how to shape the point, and how to heat-treat it for hardness.*

> *When the apprentice needed to know something to be more skillful*—that was *when he was told. Next, the apprentice tried his hand at making a nail—under the direct supervision of the master. When he made a mistake he was stopped and helped to correct the error—right then. When he did well he was rewarded with a pat on the back or a few reassuring words from the master (How).*
>
> *After sufficient practice, the apprentice hammered out nail after nail on his own until they were as good as those made by the master (If).*
>
> *Only then did the master blacksmith show the apprentice how to make horseshoes, or hinges. It never entered his mind to move the apprentice on to some other task until the apprentice had convinced him through his performance that the current task had been mastered (When).*

In a sense, the competency-based movement is a way of returning to this same personalized, individualized approach to transmitting skills from a master to a novice. Throughout the last several hundred years we have continued to use the same basic approach to instruction—the master personally showing apprentices how to perform skills. There are two recent developments, however, that have rendered this method of instruction *ineffective* for most trainees. These two developments are the greatly increased *numbers* of trainees assigned to the master craftsman (instructor) and the increased *complexity* of what must be learned.

No longer are one or two apprentices assigned to one master craftsman. Today, education and training are demanded and deserved by the entire population—not just by an elite few. Instructors today find themselves faced with classes of 20, 30, or more students. It is no wonder, then, that teaching methods that worked perfectly well several hundred years ago when only a handful of trainees were involved just do not work very well for many of the students in today's diverse and expanding student population. Never before in history have education and training opportunities been so abundant.

Standing before one or two apprentices and personally demonstrating, showing, and explaining how to do something worked well enough in years past. Recent evidence, however, shows very clearly that such instructor-centered teaching methods work well for only about 10 to 20% of the students enrolled in today's large classes. We have expanded the *reach* of job training a hundredfold, but the *effectiveness* of that training has not kept pace.

The *complexity* of what today's trainees must learn is also causing problems. As long as apprentices were mastering tasks that were largely skill-oriented (such as making boots, binding books, making furniture, laying cobblestones, and making candles), the "instructor" could do all the teaching—personally. Today's highly technological society dictates that trainees master not only a great many skills, but highly complex skills involving very expensive, dangerous and sophisticated equipment, instruments, devices, and processes.

In addition, most jobs require an ever-increasing amount of highly technical knowledge and decision-making ability. No longer can the teaching methods of several hundred years ago be expected to serve the demanding training needs of today and tomorrow. It is just not reasonable to expect the same instructional method used in the 1700s for a master to teach an apprentice how to tan leather, to be effective for an instructor today to teach 15 or 20 students how to insert nuclear reactor control rods or how to service catalytic converters. The competency-based training movement is an attempt to bring vocational, technical, and industrial training out of pre-industrial revolution days into the nuclear-electronic era. It is simply a means of bringing occupational training one step closer to becoming more of a science and less of an art. This systematic approach will go a long way towards helping instructors and trainers develop a "technology of training" equal to the challenge of the increasingly complex world in which we live and work.

What's Wrong with the Traditional Approach?

Although vocational education and industrial training programs have adequately served business and industry's need for trained workers in the past, they have come under increasing criticism recently. Taxpayers, policy makers, and training directors are more reluctant to spend larger and larger sums of money for sometimes questionable results. Both public vocational-technical education and business and industry training have been caught in the squeeze of public and corporate accountability and retrenchment.

Listed below are some of the more often heard criticisms of training programs in operation today:

- Very few trainees who begin training programs ever complete them. Drop-out rates in some formal programs run as high as 75%.
- A small percentage of students (typically 10% or so) really master the training tasks at a high level of proficiency. Up to 90% of students graduating may be only minimally competent.
- Heavy reliance on lectures (sometimes several hours long) as a teaching method leads to student dissatisfaction, absenteeism, and discipline problems.
- There seems to be a lack of well developed, appropriate curriculum materials and instructional media in use today. Many instructors tend to teach "off the top" with little planning.
- Students receive little or no immediate, periodic feedback throughout the learning process so they can correct their learning mistakes as they go. Often a final grade in a course or unit is a student's only indication of how he or she is doing.
- Many trainees who are only marginally competent but who show up regularly and stay out of trouble receive a certificate or diploma. As long as a

"C" average or "satisfactory" progress is maintained, students remain in good standing and the next thing the instructor knows, the student graduates.

- Employers have little indication of exactly what it is successful graduates can actually do. Transcripts and course titles are of little help.
- There is an over emphasis on theory, memorizing facts and terms, nice-to-know knowledge and background information and not enough emphasis on learning how to actually perform tasks needed on the job.
- There seem to be tremendous variations in quality from one program to the next—even in the same school or department. This quality seems to be determined primarily by the instructor. Efforts to improve quality many times meet with disappointing results.
- Programs are many times unable to respond to the unique learning requirements of students with special needs such as the educationally disadvantaged, the handicapped, and others.
- Many programs are somewhat rigid in their operation and fail to meet the real needs of students and the world of work. Most programs only allow enrollment once or twice a year, may discourage or prohibit early exit, sometimes poorly match trainees with programs, and usually will not allow students to repeat portions of the program if needed.
- In many programs, students are unable to test out of and receive credit for those competencies already mastered. Students must sit through instruction in those competencies just like everyone else.

While certainly not all inclusive, these criticisms do draw attention to some of the serious shortcomings of many training programs in operation today. This is certainly not intended as a general indictment of today's training. There are many excellent programs in operation all around us—in corporations, vocational centers, technical institutes, the military, and in other settings. Regretfully, the percentage of programs that are outstanding is disappointing. It has been said that perhaps one or two per cent of teachers are creative geniuses who will excel based on their own ability, imagination, and hard work. You might look at the competency-based approach as a systematic, well thought out approach to training to help the other 98% of us be more successful than perhaps we are now.

The competency-based approach or any other approach will not cure all the problems we face in training individuals for employment, but it will help. It is being proven around the country as a viable method of training that attacks—head on—many of the shortcomings of present training programs both in the public and private sector. Major corporations, governmental agencies, and the military began shifting towards competency-based training some years ago. It is encouraging to note that, recently, many state departments of education, local school districts, boards of education, and school-level administrators and instructors are actively exploring competency-based systems of instruction as a means of improving the quality of vocational and technical education at the local level.

Principles Behind the Competency-Based Approach

To fully appreciate the fundamental differences between the competency-based and the "traditional" approach to training, we need to examine the basic principles and assumptions that underlie the competency-based philosophy. First, a word of caution. Many of the assumptions and beliefs upon which this approach is based may at first glance appear to be very idealistic, perhaps revolutionary, or even impossible. Let me say very quickly that every principle underlying the competency-based approach presented here has been shown to be valid in hundreds of schools around the world. Rather than just theories or speculation, these principles and assumptions are being proven daily in programs where the competency-based approach is being successfully implemented.

Many of the principles described here are based on ideas presented earlier by several pioneers in the "mastery learning" movement. Those involved in shaping this movement during the last two or three decades are too numerous to mention; however, several leaders stand out. Among the most often quoted pioneers in this field, and perhaps their best known work, are:

John B. Carroll. A Model of School Learning. *Teachers College Record*, 64 (1963): 723–733.

James H. Block, ed. *Mastery Learning*. New York: Holt, Rinehart and Winston, Inc., 1970.

Benjamin S. Bloom. *Human Characteristics and School Learning*. New York: McGraw-Hill Book Company, 1976.

Anyone seriously interested in finding out more about the underlying philosophy behind this approach to education is urged to read these three resources. Those interested in the competency-based approach to vocational, technical, and industrial training are urged to read what was, perhaps, one of the first substantial works devoted to the subject:

David Pucel and William Knaak. *Individualizing Vocational and Technical Instruction*. Columbus, Ohio: Charles E. Merrill Publishing Co., 1975.

Listed below are some basic principles upon which the competency-based approach to education and training are based. The remaining chapters of this book describe strategies, techniques, instruments, and materials that have been used successfully to implement these principles in occupational training programs.

PRINCIPLE 1

"**Any** *student in a training program can master most* **any** *task at a* **high level** *of mastery (95 to 100% proficiency) if provided with* **high-quality instruction** *and* **sufficient time.**"

This principle is the real bedrock of the competency-based philosophy. Just think of the implications this has—not only for occupational training programs—but for the entire spectrum of education. You don't believe it? Think about it for a minute. Pick any task from a training program, no matter how complex. Think back on all the students you have had over the years. Could not perhaps 98% of them have successfully mastered—at a *high level*—even the most complicated task if you could have provided them with *high quality* instructional materials and *enough time* to spend on learning the task as they needed (assuming that they wanted to and had the necessary prerequisites)?

This book is based on the notion that students enrolled in our training programs cannot only learn what we have to teach, but they can learn it *well* if we simply provide them with carefully developed learning materials and a little extra time if needed.

PRINCIPLE 2

A student's **ability** *for learning a task need not predict how well the student* **learns** *the task.*

Many studies have shown that in the traditional system of education an individual's "ability" for learning is highly predictive of how well the student actually learns. Students of higher ability have typically done better in school; students of lower ability have done worse. The second principle, however, says that when provided with *favorable learning conditions*, a student's ability going into a learning situation will have *no* bearing on how well the student learns.

Let's look at an example. If we have 30 typical students in a training program who vary in ability from low to high in a normal way, their ability plotted on a graph might look like this:

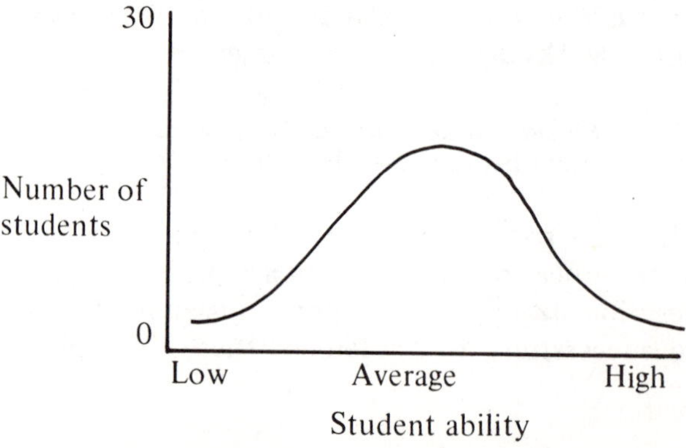

As you can see, a few students are of quite low ability, a few are of high ability, and the rest are in between—most being of "average" ability.

Now, if we have these 30 students experience a "traditional" learning activity that is of some *fixed time length* (say 50 minutes or three hours) and is *instructor-centered* (say, a live demonstration or lecture), let's see what their *test scores* would look like:

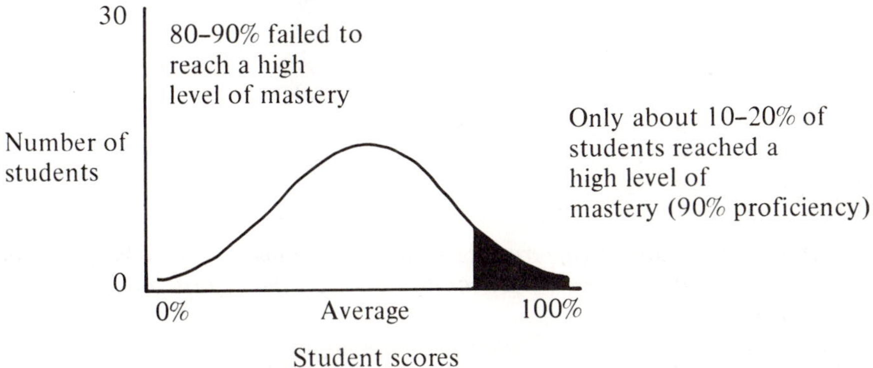

A few students would probably score at the low end on the test, a few would score at the high end, and everyone else would fall in between with most students scoring about "average." If you recognize this little scenario it is because it has been played out in virtually every school for the last 200 years. A select few excel (typically about 10 to 20%) and get A's, a few fail, and the majority simply "slide by." Not only that, but the students of *low* ability are invariably the *same* students who reach only a low level of mastery. Students of high ability are the *same* students who reach high levels of mastery. This is usually repeated year after year until many of the low ability/low mastery students drop out, flunk out, or are pushed out of the system or, even worse, remain in the system, causing disruption, crime, vandalism, and a host of related problems.

Now let's see what might have happened if the same 30 students had been provided with a competency-based "mastery learning" kind of learning experience that provided *high-quality*, *student-centered* learning experiences and *enough time* and *help* to reach mastery. (See next page for graph.)

By giving students the right kind of instruction and enough time, most can reach mastery. Each student's ability coming into the learning experience need not have any bearing on performance. Lower-ability students may simply need some additional time and help to learn, but they can learn *as much* and retain it just *as long* as students of higher ability who needed less time and help. Student ability should only predict *how long* it takes to learn—not how much is learned!

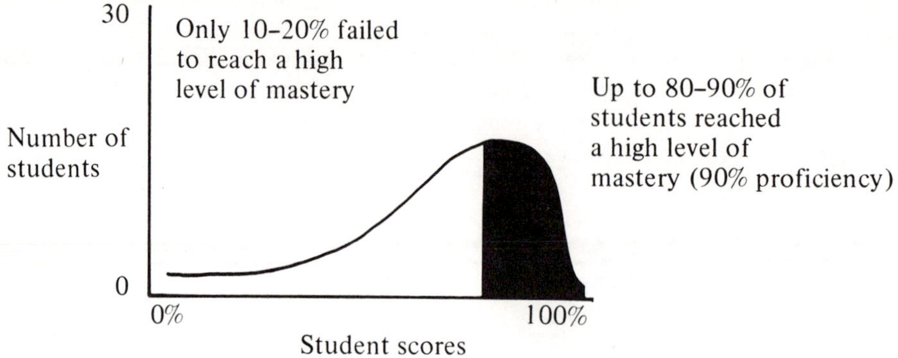

PRINCIPLE 3

Individual student differences in levels of mastery of a task are caused primarily by **errors** *in the training environment,* **not** *by characteristics of the students.*

Studies by Bloom and others have shown that many of the differences in how much students learn are caused *not* by an innate quality possessed by the student but by "errors" in the educational system. The more "ideal" an educational system becomes, the fewer differences that occur in learning. The further from ideal an educational system becomes, the greater the differences in learning among students.

Three factors that have been shown to have a lot of influence on how much students learn are (1) how many of the necessary learning prerequisites a student already has, (2) what kinds of feelings or attitudes the student has about the learning experience, and (3) the quality and length of instruction. The competency-based approach addresses all three of these elements in a positive way. Later chapters explain how the use of carefully developed "learning packages" with supportive media can provide the quality and length of instruction students need to reach mastery. By successfully mastering early, basic tasks at a high level of mastery, students will tackle later, more complex tasks with the necessary prerequisite learning well in hand and with a positive attitude about the learning experience.

PRINCIPLE 4

Rather than being **fast** *or* **slow** *learners, or* **good** *or* **poor** *learners, most students become* **very similar** *to one another in learning* **ability**, **rate** *of learning, and motivation for further learning when provided with favorable learning conditions.*

This principle, on which Bloom's book *Human Characteristics and School Learning* is based, challenges the way in which students have been viewed for many years. We can only guess at the number of students who have been tracked, channeled, turned away, or otherwise not been given the educational opportunity that was rightfully theirs simply because they were labeled as slow learners or poor students. In the competency-based approach we assume and fully *expect* that each and every trainee cannot only make it, but can excel. We focus our efforts on systematically developing and adjusting the training program to come closer to making this goal a reality.

PRINCIPLE 5

We should focus more on differences in **learning** *and less on differences in* **learners**.

We focus so much of our attention these days on differences among *learners*. We categorize, pigeonhole, stereotype, and group students based on outward characteristics that often have little if anything to do with how well they learn. When one student succeeds and another fails, we are quick to look at differences in the learners to explain it. One student was old, the other was young, one was motivated, one was not, one was a minority-group member, the other was not. Very seldom do we critically examine the *instructional process* as the source of these differences in learning outcomes and systematically try to correct it. The competency-based approach focuses less on the learner's characteristics and more on adjusting the learning process to maximize the outcomes for each student.

PRINCIPLE 6

What is worth teaching is worth learning.

Many educators and trainers take the position: "Here it is; I'm going to present it to you. If you get it fine, if not, fine—it's up to you." Incredibly, dropout rates of 25 to 50%, failure rates of up to one-half, and excellence achieved by only a handful of students does not bother some instructors. Some have the attitude that it is not my problem–it is their problem. "If they drop out or fail, that's their problem—not mine. I'm doing what I'm paid to do—teach!" Attitudes such as this (conscious or unconscious) prevent any real progress in significantly improving the quality of education and training on a large scale.

The competency-based school of thought, on the other hand, says that when a student fails to reach mastery, it is *our* problem. This approach to training is based on the notion that if it is important enough to be included in the training program, it is important enough for each and every student to learn it and learn it well. When a trainee fails to learn, we are seriously concerned—concerned enough to do everything in our power to correct the situation. Those involved in successful competency-based programs view themselves as concerned professionals who have been highly trained to operate a very complex training technology successfully. They consider themselves far more than just teachers or instructors.

PRINCIPLE 7

> *The most important element in the teaching-learning process is the* **kind** *and* **quality** *of instruction experienced by students.*

This area of concern, perhaps, is where the conventional and the competency-based approaches are furthest apart. In traditional programs, instruction is viewed as just another one of the elements affecting what students learn—just as the facility, tools, and materials are. Instruction is usually handled in a very informal, unstructured, "spray and pray" manner. In contrast, the instruction given to students in the competency-based approach is viewed as extremely critical to learning. The actual delivery of instruction is very, very carefully designed, developed, tried out, and constantly revised based on results.

Instruction is systematically designed around several essential elements. Bloom described four basic elements: First, the student is presented with some sort of cue, which might be audio or visual or in some other form. Next, the student *participates* by actually practicing, applying, responding, or in some other way doing something with the cues that were presented. As the learner participates, he or she is periodically *reinforced* to ensure that correct performance will continue and incorrect performance will not. Finally, *feedback* and *correctives* help students find out how well they are doing and what they need to improve to reach mastery.

Competency-Based Myths Debunked

As with any innovation in education (or any other field) that has the far-reaching implications that the competency-based approach has, there are many misconceptions, myths, and preconceived ideas about what it is and what impact it will have on those that will be affected by it. Let's take a few minutes to address some of the popular myths associated with competency-based training.

MYTH 1

> *The competency-based approach to training is an attempt to eventually phase out instructors.*

Absolutely false; by now you should have a pretty good idea of the tremendous amount of time and effort that will be required to develop and implement competency-based programs on a wide scale. If anything, this will take more instructors—not fewer. Once a program is fully developed and is running smoothly, it is absurd to fear that the instructor will be let go so that the program can be run by a lower paid assistant. Only a highly experienced, competent professional can adequately answer students' questions, devise testing situations and evaluate student competence. Furthermore, once learning packages and media are finally well-developed it will be just about time to begin making major revisions. If you are concerned about being replaced by a clerk or a computer—relax; it won't happen. You must, however, be willing to assume a *new role* within the training program and become less and less a presenter of information and more and more a manager of learning. You will find that helping students *learn* is far more challenging and rewarding than simply *teaching.*

MYTH 2

This approach works well only with better students.

Quite the opposite is true! It is the *traditional* approach that works well only for the better students. Any system that results in only 10 to 20% of the students reaching a high level of mastery should be suspect. The more capable students will probably succeed in most any system—it is the *less* able student who stands to benefit the most from the competency-based approach. In later chapters you will see how high risk, special needs, handicapped, disadvantaged, and other students can benefit significantly from this approach. When instruction is carefully designed and broken down task by task, and when time is made flexible, far more students can learn and learn well—far more than under the lock-step, fixed-time approach.

MYTH 3

It is mechanical and inhumane and students don't really like it.

Ridiculous! Study after study has shown that students overwhelmingly prefer the personalized, self-paced approach. They enjoy the challenge, the freedom, and the lack of pressure to keep up with the group. Being shown exactly what must be learned, being provided with high-quality learning materials and enough time and help to master each task at a high level is just about as humane as you can get. It is difficult to imagine a system of education any more *inhumane* than one that keeps students in the dark about what is to be learned, that requires students to endure two- and three-hour lectures on "theory" that will not be applied until months later, and that assigns grades to each student based on how other students perform.

Students get more individual attention from the instructor in a competency-based program than in a traditional program in which the instructor is busy "teaching" all day.

MYTH 4

It stifles instructor creativity.

Nothing could be further from the truth. A tremendous amount of creativity, resourcefulness, and imagination are needed to successfully develop, operate, and manage a truly self-paced, individualized instructional program. Assisting 20 students who may be working on 20 different tasks takes a certain amount of creativity. If standing in front of students lecturing and demonstrating, sending them out into the shop, and then giving them a test that reveals that only *one* out of ten really learned is *creative*, I think we need to redefine the word.

MYTH 5

Cramming the same competencies and objectives down every student's throat is not treating students as individuals.

Nowhere is it written that every student enrolled in a competency-based program must learn identical competencies. Competency-based training programs are usually built upon the specific tasks that have been verified as being essential for entering one of *several* closely related occupations. For example, in a competency-based secretarial program, students may be given the option of mastering only those tasks that are needed to become a receptionist or a file clerk, or if they prefer, they can master all the competencies in the program to become a well-rounded general secretary. Not requiring a student to learn tasks such as "file alphabetically" or "take incoming telephone calls" that have been verified as essential to employment in the occupation for which the student is training is certainly not meeting the individual needs of the student. The real tragedy in the conventional approach is that usually all students are "exposed" to the same tasks, with only a select few really mastering any of them well.

MYTH 6

Competency-based programs are much more expensive than conventional programs.

This just is not so. Although initial costs may be somewhat higher, over the long run, effective, competency-based, highly mediated programs are not necessarily any more costly than conventional programs. If costs vs. benefits are looked at, many feel that competency-based programs are actually *less* costly. This is due to lower dropout rates, lower failure rates, higher average daily attendance, students being allowed to exit early and then being replaced by new students, and other factors. Even when only startup and operating costs are compared, competency-based programs compare favorably with traditional programs. In conventional programs, new instructional media and related learning materials are usually purchased every few years, with much of it collecting dust. Also, multiple (sometimes one for each student) tools and equipment are purchased. It is not unusual in many traditional programs to find 20 of this tool and 10 of this instrument, since most students are working on the same task at the same time. However, in competency-based programs, since students are usually working on different tasks, the same resources can be used to purchase a greater variety of higher quality tools, instruments, and equipment.

MYTH 7

The competency-based approach might work all right for some programs, but it just won't work in mine because . . . .

This is the old "other program" myth that dies hard. I have talked to instructors and trainers from virtually every occupational area who say with great authority: "It works great in industrial occupations, but the health occupations area is too complicated" or "I've seen it work well in health-related areas, but it would never work very well in the electronics field because . . . ." It goes on and on. Everyone seems to think it might work well in most areas *except their own*. I suppose that this is a natural defense mechanism we all have. What they are really saying is, "I really don't know if it would work in my occupational area and I just don't know enough about the competency-based approach to try it. So rather than admit my lack of understanding of the concept and to eliminate the risk of failure, the easiest way out is to simply say that it won't work."

The competency-based approach will work equally well in *any* occupational training area: business, agricultural, health, industrial, marketing and distributive, public service, or home economics. It works just as well at any level: exploratory, vocational, technical, or professional. It can work equally well in any setting: military, agency, public school, private institutions, business and industry, or elsewhere. The difference must be in *how* the program is designed, developed, implemented, and operated. Obviously, a training program for preparing cashiers to operate a new optical scanning cash register in a retail store chain would be put together a little differently than a program to train neurosurgeons or seamstresses. The basic approach, however, would be very similar with similar, positive results—a far higher percentage of trainees reaching higher levels of mastery.

MYTH 8

Competency-based instruction is not appropriate for my area because my students need actual hands-on work.

Unfortunately, this is one of the more widespread myths; many believe that competency-based instruction involves learning only theory or facts and not skills. The exact opposite is true: As you will see in a later chapter, the competency-based approach downplays theory for theory's sake and focuses on the actual job skills needed by trainees to become successfully employed. Theory is only taught if and when it is needed to support the competent performance of tasks. It is based on the philosophy that workers get paid on the job for what they can *do*—not what they know.

MYTH 9

It sounds good, but it just won't work in real life, because I would need two aides, a photographer, two typists and a computer to develop and keep up with all the materials and media.

It is true that competency-based learning requires packaged and mediated learning materials that are appropriate for students and for the tasks being learned. Nobody said all the competency-based materials you might need for your program must be developed overnight. You can create a little here and a little there without putting an undue strain on your time or budget. The typing and photographing help you will need are already available in most schools and training departments. As for keeping up with all the materials once developed, this will be no more or less of a problem than it is now—only a different *kind* of problem.

MYTH 10

Instructors in other occupations may be able to put their competencies down on paper, but not me, because my students need to be able to solve problems, make judgments, and things beyond just performing basic tasks.

This argument just does not hold water. If an instructor is unable (or unwilling, maybe) to put down on paper, in black and white, *exactly* what it is the student should learn, how can the instructor develop good learning materials to help students get there or develop valid tests to see if they arrived? Any desired outcome of a program, no matter how lofty, complex, or hard to teach can be specified in terms of exactly what it is the trainee must be able to do for you to conclude that the outcome has been met. It is simply not true that the competencies that make up competency-based training programs have to be low level or basic skills. If the trainee needs to be able to "solve quadratic equations," or "diagnose the patient's condition," or "land a 747 without power," or "leap tall buildings in a single bound," then it is simply a matter of saying so.

MYTH 11

Competency-based instruction is not any different from what good instructors have been doing for years and years.

There is a lot of truth to that statement: Effective instructors are, in fact, practicing many of the principles underlying the competency-based approach. Unfortunately, many "effective" instructors only become effective after years of trial and error, and finally settle on a system that seems to work. Many times they really don't know why something works or doesn't work well—only that it does or doesn't. Usually, nobody except that instructor understands the instructional system finally developed, and when that instructor leaves, the "effective" program leaves also. Using a competency-based system of learning allows instructors to make some deliberate changes in their current programs for very definite reasons. It helps get the program "on paper" so fellow instructors, supervisors, substitutes (and yes, even students) can see and follow what is going on.

MYTH 12

I don't need this competency-based business, because my program is running smoothly right now and all of my graduates are getting jobs.

This is a touchy area. It is natural to resist any new approach, particularly when the approach implies that what you have been doing all these years might not be the best approach for students. Instructors who might be tempted to reject competency-based instruction outright because their present program seems to be doing all right, might want to ask themselves:

- How many years of tinkering and experimenting with students did it take for your program to begin working well?
- If you get run over tomorrow, would your program run just as smoothly for your successor or would he or she fumble for several years to get where you are?
- What percentage of the students who enroll in your program ever complete it? Sixty per cent, fifty per cent, twenty-five per cent, maybe less? Maybe there is a reason for losing so many students.
- Of all the students who begin your training program, what percentage graduate with a *high level* of proficiency in your learning tasks? Five per cent, two per cent, maybe even less? Are you satisfied with that? Are you satisfied with possibly 95 per cent of your beginning students leaving at some point with less than an "A" level of learning?

MYTH 13

It looks like a good idea, but it would take a hundred years for me to sit down and identify specific competencies and write all those learning packages.

It will take time to put together a competency-based program, but because it is going to take some time and effort is just not a good enough reason for not doing it. Just think, if you had begun developing competency-based materials a few years ago, you would probably be finished now. Remember that singing "ain't it awful" and complaining won't bring you any nearer to developing a more effective program than you are now. Only one thing will—action.

MYTH 14

The competency-based approach sounds good on the surface, but it only lowers standards so most students can pass!

Absolutely false: Please don't confuse competency-based instruction with "minimum competency testing." The real tragedy of the minimum competency testing movement that is sweeping the country is that it only deals with *measuring* competence—not *bringing it about*. Since our educational system is organized around the traditional, fixed-time, instructor-centered approach, most students proceed from subject to subject and grade to grade largely *incompetent* in most tasks. It is no wonder, then, that functional literacy exams for high school seniors must be written at the eighth grade level!

Minimum competency testing without "maximum competency learning" is one of the greatest tragedies to occur in American education. The competency-based approach to instruction not only insists that each student demonstrate competency, but the minimum acceptable level of competency can be set at an extremely high level and attained, because students are given the time and help needed to get there.

MYTH 15

I'm sorry, but my students just wouldn't be able to learn well from media and learning packages. They need me right there to help them and answer their questions.

Many instructors genuinely feel this way. The facts, however, just don't support the belief. Instructors who have successfully implemented competency-based programs have found just the opposite to be true. They find that the majority of students can learn well from packaged and mediated learning materials. Many instructors are shocked to find that not only can students learn a great deal without the instructor doing all the teaching, but they can often learn better and faster. "What about the unmotivated student or the one who is not self-directed?," you say. The fact is, you will have more time during the day to work individually and in small groups with students who have difficulties than you ever would if you spent the entire day teaching.

Is It Any Better?

That question is foremost in the minds of many instructors, supervisors, trainers, and others involved in vocational-technical and industrial training. Is the competency-based approach (by whatever name it may go by) really any better than the traditional approach? Is it worth all the effort and expense required to develop packaged, structured, mediated learning materials? Do the benefits justify going through the pain and agony sometimes required to promote change in individuals and institutions?

In a nutshell the answer is "yes." Ten or twenty years ago the answer would have been "probably." There has been enough hard data collected lately to warrant making a general statement about competency-based versus traditional training:

When carefully developed and implemented, the competency-based approach to training is generally superior to the traditional approach in terms of student outcomes and in several other important ways.

There has been enough evidence gathered in business, industry, the military, agencies, unions, public vocational education, and other settings to support this statement. Study after study has been conducted comparing the two approaches. The competency-based approach usually results in more trainees mastering more competencies at a higher level of proficiency than in the traditional approach.

A word of caution is in order here. Many studies reported in the professional literature compared "conventional" instructional methods with the "individualized" approach and found neither approach superior to the other. Studies reporting "no significant difference in learning" between the two approaches usually have one thing in common: a less than carefully designed and implemented approach to the individualized method. The potential benefits of competency-based training will not be realized by simply writing objectives and video-taping lectures or using workbooks. It must be a total, systematic effort—all four of the major characteristics of competency-based training programs mentioned earlier must be included if dramatic improvement is expected.

When the competency-based approach is meticulously designed, developed, and implemented, however, improvement in the training program can be seen in several areas. Below are some of the typical improvements reported by others who have successfully incorporated the competency-based approach into their programs:

- Students seem to learn more; higher scores on tests are reported.
- Students appear to remember what they learn longer; retesting over time often shows higher test scores.
- There is much less "prediction" of how well a particular student will do based on his or her previous grades in school.
- Many more students excel; rather than only a handful of students earning A's, most students reach high levels of proficiency.
- Students experience success very early in the program, providing important motivation, a better feeling about the program, and an improved self-concept.
- More can be learned in the same length of time. Many instructors report that packaged and mediated materials eliminate much of the time students usually waste—waiting for instruction; wading through reading assignments; or receiving instruction in tasks they can already perform.
- Lower test scores improve dramatically. Students typically at the low end of the achievement scale benefit greatly. Since they can now get the time and help they need, they are no longer doomed to failure.
- Dropout rates are usually lowered. Students get hands-on experience the first few days; they no longer must sit through weeks or months of theory classes and can experience a high level of success without the pressure of competing with other students for grades.
- Students learn to take more responsibility for their own learning. After some initial adjustment, most students respond well to the added responsibilities the competency-based approach places on them.
- Instructors have more time to help students who genuinely need it.
- The program can almost "run itself" when the instructor must be called away for a phone call, a day's absence, or when a substitute may be needed for several days.
- Students usually stay busier, longer. When students become "task-oriented" they spend less of their time goofing off and getting into trouble.
- Overall, the training program takes on a more professional, businesslike atmosphere which seems to contribute toward higher morale for instructors, students, and administrators.

You may not realize all these improvements in your training program; it will depend on how effective your program is now and how hard you are willing to work toward developing and implementing a truly competency-based, personalized program.

A few observations are worth sharing here. I have had the opportunity to work closely with many instructors in developing and implementing competency-based training programs. Almost without exception, instructors who give the competency-based approach an honest try rarely return to the traditional, instructor-centered approach. Once they experience the thrill of helping nearly all students learn well, they are very reluctant to settle for only a few students succeeding.

Finally, instructors who have successfully implemented competency-based learning seem to have at least one trait in common—they *wanted* it to work. Although many of these instructors were suspicious, skeptical, or outright hostile at first, once they became convinced, they found ways to make it work.

Obstacles became challenges to meet rather than excuses why it would not work. If you believe the competency-based approach will work for you, the chances are excellent that it will. If you think it won't work—you're right, it won't!

Developing a Competency-Based Training Program

One of the challenges in putting together a book like this is to try to make it equally beneficial for the several different groups at which it is aimed. If only a narrow readership were intended, whether vocational educators in the public educational system, or trainers in business and industry, or human resource specialists in agencies, this section (and the rest of the book for that matter) could have focused on one set of terminology, examples of one kind, and one very specific approach.

Since the author is convinced that virtually anyone involved in the entire spectrum of developing human resources through education and training can benefit significantly from applying the principles presented in this book, its approach had to be somewhat broad. An attempt has been made to describe an overall plan for designing, developing, implementing, and managing competency-based instructional programs regardless of the level or area. Hopefully, the plan is general enough to apply to a wide range of local training situations and yet specific enough to be truly helpful. Only time will tell if this goal has been met.

In Table 1-2 you see the overall plan for developing competency-based training programs presented in this book. There is certainly nothing magical about this *particular* plan. It is based on 12 specific tasks that should be accomplished to implement a competency-based training program successfully. This plan could just as easily have included 6 tasks or 26 tasks, depending on how finely or broadly they had been developed.

In most books dealing with curriculum development and instructional design, the reader is overwhelmed with complicated flowcharts, complex

TABLE 1-2
Twelve Tasks To Be Accomplished To Develop a Competency-Based Training Program

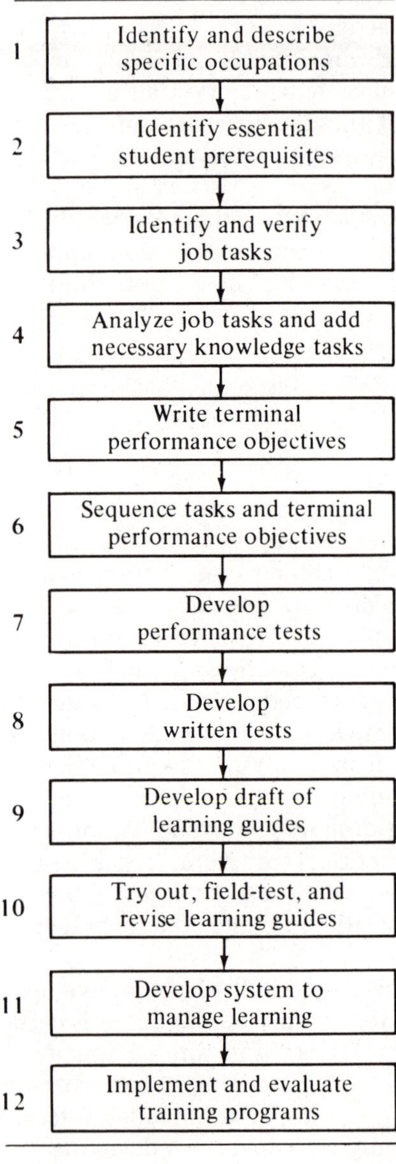
1
Identify and describe specific occupations
2
Identify essential student prerequisites
3
Identify and verify job tasks
4
Analyze job tasks and add necessary knowledge tasks
5
Write terminal performance objectives
6
Sequence tasks and terminal performance objectives
7
Develop performance tests
8
Develop written tests
9
Develop draft of learning guides
10
Try out, field-test, and revise learning guides
11
Develop system to manage learning
12
Implement and evaluate training programs

"models," and sophisticated systems analysis mumbo-jumbo that appears to be included more to impress than to inform. This tendency has been consciously avoided. If the plan shown in Table 1-2 represented by the 12 tasks looks kind of simplistic, I'm delighted.

Of course, this particular plan will not work for every local training situation. No doubt, you will find it necessary to skip over some parts and go more deeply into others. You may need to alter several of the strategies, forms, instruments, and formats presented. Some of the tips and suggestions will be helpful, whereas others will not apply to you or your situation.

The approach for developing competency-based training presented in this handbook is, of course, not *the* approach but *one* approach. It has been used with positive results in one form or another in several local settings. The main reason for presenting the plan as you see it in Table 1-2 is that it works. Try it, change it, adapt it, or redesign it to fit your needs.

Format of the Book

Since it is a little out of the ordinary, we need to spend a minute looking at the organization of the rest of the book. Chapters 2 through 7 each include two of the 12 program development tasks, so each chapter following this one has two major sections, each covering one of the 12 tasks. The format of these chapters is somewhat different from most books. In an effort to practice what I am preaching, each section has been put together as a somewhat self-contained, competency-based "learning package" designed to help you master one specific task. Each of these 12 sections contains the following components:

- *TASK*: This describes exactly what you will be able to do upon successfully completing that section. Each section covers one of the 12 tasks required to develop a competency-based program.
- *INTRODUCTION*: This is a very brief paragraph that explains why it is important to learn the particular task covered by that section.
- *TERMINAL PERFORMANCE OBJECTIVE*: This is simply a description of what you must be able to do to demonstrate that you have actually acquired that particular task.
- *ENABLING OBJECTIVES*: There will be two to four enabling objectives for each task. These are used to break the section covering each task into a few major parts. By completing the self-check, you will have an opportunity to find out if you successfully mastered each enabling objective before going on to the next.
- *SELF-CHECK*: For each enabling objective there is a self-check that will provide you with an opportunity to practice or apply what was presented. There may be questions to answer, samples to critique, or products to develop.

- *ANSWER KEY*: To provide you with immediate feedback so that you can make a decision about whether to go on or perhaps go back over something, you will be comparing your responses to each self-check with an answer key. Model responses for each self-check are given in the corresponding answer key in the appendix at the end of the book. Your responses don't have to agree with those in the answer key exactly, but they should agree in concept.
- *PERFORMANCE TEST*: For each task, there is a detailed performance test at the end of that particular section. On each performance test are instructions for demonstrating mastery of the task and a list of detailed, objective evaluation criteria by which mastery can be judged.

2

Identifying Specific Occupations and Prerequisites

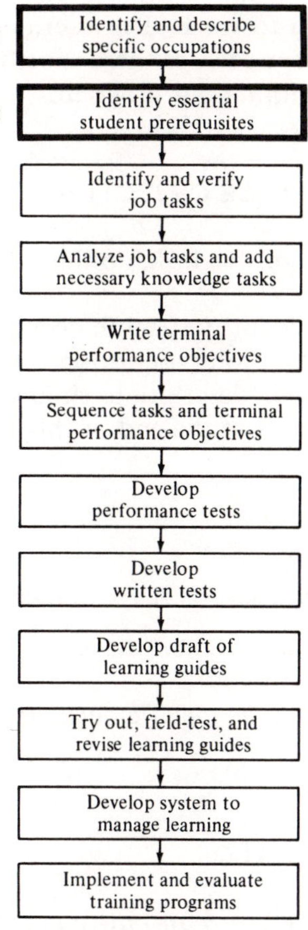

1
Identify and describe specific occupations
2
Identify essential student prerequisites
Identify and verify job tasks
Analyze job tasks and add necessary knowledge tasks
Write terminal performance objectives
Sequence tasks and terminal performance objectives
Develop performance tests
Develop written tests
Develop draft of learning guides
Try out, field-test, and revise learning guides
Develop system to manage learning
Implement and evaluate training programs

When you complete this section, you will be able to:

TASK 1: Identify and Describe Specific Occupations

INTRODUCTION

One of the shortcomings of conventional training programs is the requirement that every trainee master the same complete list of tasks to be considered a successful program graduate. Requiring all students to complete the entire, broad training program may not meet the employment needs of individual students. This section shows you how to *identify* several *specific occupations* or jobs within your overall training program. Then, students who want to master only those skills for one specific occupation within the broad program area can do so, can exit the program, and can go to work. This section also shows you how to write a *job description* for each of these specific occupations for which you will offer training within your program.

TERMINAL PERFORMANCE OBJECTIVE

To demonstrate mastery of this task, do the following:

For a training program, identify specific occupations for which training will be offered and write a job description for each. The list of specific occupations and each job description should conform to *all* criteria listed in Performance Test 1 at the end of this section.

ENABLING OBJECTIVES

This section is divided into several parts to help you:

[1] *Identify specific occupational titles for which training will be offered.*
[2] *Write job descriptions for specific occupations.*

ENABLING OBJECTIVE [1]

Identify Specific Occupational Titles for Which Training Will Be Offered

What Is an Occupational Title?

An occupational title is just what the name implies; it is a descriptive label for a *specific* occupation that exists in the world of work. Below are some examples of occupational titles for which some sort of formal vocational-technical or on-the-job training would probably be needed:

EXAMPLES

- *Finish carpenter*
- *Data-entry operator*
- *Electronics technician*
- *Short-order cook*
- *Ranch hand*
- *Surgical salesperson*
- *Cashier*
- *Medical lab technician*
- *Plumber*
- *Television installer*
- *Tool and die maker*
- *Child-care worker*

Specific occupational titles are the *actual* occupations (or jobs) for which people are hired. A good cross section of occupational titles (I will use the term "job title" interchangeably here) can be seen in the want ads of any major newspaper or by looking at job titles for employees of any large company.

The reason we want to look at *specific* job titles is because specific jobs, such as cable splicer, boat rigger, and motorcycle mechanic, are the actual slots people are hired to fill.

> Since our trainees will be recruited, hired, and paid for *specific* occupations or jobs, that is how we should organize our training programs—not solely on *broad* occupational or program areas.

Unless you are developing a highly specialized program to train workers to use a particular piece of equipment or to follow some new procedure, chances are that you will be training them to enter one of several specific jobs within a broad occupational area. Since business and industry will *hire* your students for specific occupations, perhaps you should *train* them for specific occupations.

Forcing *every* student who is enrolled in a particular training program to master the *same* list of skills and to complete the entire program is a questionable practice. Let us look at an example.

EXAMPLE

At Central Valley Vo-Tech Institute the 18-month auto mechanics program was a very comprehensive program and included instruction in all major areas of the automobile, including transmissions, brakes, tune-up, suspension, exhaust system, and major engine overhaul. Program graduates were doing well on the job.

At Central Valley, a student must successfully complete the entire 18-month training program to be considered a successful completer and receive a certificate. Instructors at Central were very concerned about the high number of students who were leaving the program early—as high as 30% during the first year.

A study was done of many of these early leavers and to the surprise of some, it was found that many of these "dropouts" were actually gainfully employed in the auto-mechanics field (one even owned his own brake shop and a second was manager at a local muffler franchise). After talking with many of these former students, it became clear that some of them had no real need to complete the entire auto mechanics training program. Some even reported that it was their original intention when enrolling to leave the program early—after learning only what they needed to get a job in a specific occupation they had selected. Other dropouts reported the reason for their leaving was the frustration of having to keep up with the group and go through the entire 18-month program to get a certificate.

Had the auto mechanics program at Central Valley offered training in several specific occupations within the field of auto mechanics, those students who wished to would have been able to enter the program, select one or more specific job titles to pursue training in, and then leave—as a successful program completer—when their training needs had been met.

Student needs might have been met better if Central had structured its auto mechanics program something like this:

EXAMPLE

Program Attempted to Train All Students for:	Restructured Program Might Train Students as:
• *Auto mechanics*	• *General auto mechanic*
	• *Tune-up specialist*
	• *Brake technician*
	• *Tire changer*
	• *Exhaust system specialist*
	• *Front-end mechanic*

Advantages of Offering Training in Specific Occupations

Offering training in several specific occupational titles within a broad program area offers several advantages:

1. The training program can focus on training students for *actual* jobs that exist in the world of work.
2. Students who have limited time, resources, or ability may choose to master only a major portion of the tasks within a program area, successfully complete that specialized training program, and go to work.
3. Students who wish to master only the tasks needed for a specific occupation are not forced to struggle through the entire program, portions of which they may be ill-prepared for and uninterested in.
4. The dropout rate may be reduced because students will be required to master only the tasks required to become employable in an occupation they select.
5. Employed students can *return* to the program and add to their employability by mastering the tasks in one or more additional occupations within the overall training program.
6. Students with handicaps, certain disadvantages, or other special needs can enter a specialized program for a specific occupation for which they are qualified. An "all or nothing" situation is avoided.
7. Programs can respond more quickly to changes in technology and the job market. A new option in "Pipe Welding," for example, could be added to a welding program simply by adding some additional learning activities for welding pipe.
8. Programs can meet the specialized training needs of specific employers while still meeting the broader training needs of students who do not yet know where they will go to work.
9. Student recruitment might be enhanced when *several* training options are available, ranging perhaps from several weeks or months in duration to maybe a year or two.
10. Some specialized training programs might be made portable and taken directly to a new company, agency, or group of students.

I am pleased to report that Central Valley Vo-Tech Institute did, in fact, decide to offer training in the following specific occupations within the field of auto mechanics:

EXAMPLES

- *General auto mechanic (two years)*
- *Tire changer (four weeks)*
- *Exhaust specialist (four months)*
- *Brake specialist (three months)*
- *Tune-up specialist (six months)*

Here is what several employers and present and former students had to say about this new structure:

"I like it; I want to be a brake specialist so I can enroll for about three months, master those tasks dealing with brakes, and go to work."

"I wasn't as happy as I thought I would be working at the muffler shop, so I *reenrolled* at Central at night and completed the entire training program; I didn't have to repeat the part on mufflers. I've landed a good job at the local dealership as a line mechanic."

"It's great; when I expanded my muffler shop to include brakes, I sent three of my mechanics down to Central for several weeks of training *just in brakes.* When I get into auto air conditioning I'm going to see if I can't get the folks at Central to add that as yet another specialty in their auto mechanics curriculum."

"It helped me a lot. I was a high school dropout with a rotten attitude about school. One of the counselors talked me into taking a crack at the training program. During the orientation, I found that tune-up was an area that I had an interest in. Since the training program for tune-up specialist was only six months, I was able to stick it out. I'm making a pretty good living now."

A Word of Caution

Do not get the idea that we should train *all* students very narrowly by having them focus their efforts only in one specific occupation. Usually, students should be encouraged to remain enrolled in your program *as long as they can* and master the skills needed for *all* the specific job titles for which you offer training. Certainly, being competent in brakes, the exhaust system and tune-up makes a program graduate more employable than only knowing how to change tires. All we are saying here is that we should provide each individual student with the *option* of completing the entire program *or* mastering only those competencies required for a specialized job within the occupational field. If a student has the *ability* or *desire* or *money* to enroll in a clerical program and master *only* those skills that will land him or her a job as a receptionist, why force the student to "endure" the entire program? If we do, we are only forcing that student to fail and probably drop out.

Keep in mind that your goal is to meet the employment goals of each *individual* trainee. After counseling with each student and determining his or her interests, abilities, goals, maturity level, and other important facts, try to steer each student in the direction that seems to best suit his or her needs, remembering that the ideal, perhaps, is to have each student complete the *entire* training program but that some students may not wish to or be able to.

Identifying Specific Occupations

Now that we have explored the rationale for offering training in several specific occupational titles within a program area, let us look at how we might go about identifying what those occupational titles might be. The following are some steps you might follow in doing this:

STEP 1: Identify possible occupational titles for which training *might* be offered.

A good place to start is to identify several possible occupational titles for which you might reasonably expect to offer training within your program. For some programs only two or three possibilities may exist, whereas in others there may be dozens. Here are some sources you may find helpful in generating a tentative list of possible occupations within your program:

- *Dictionary of Occupational Titles.*[1] This book, published by the Department of Labor, lists all recognized occupations by code number, together with a description of each.
- Your program advisory committee.
- Talking with employers, employees, labor, and management within the occupational area.
- Help-wanted ads.
- Your own knowledge of the field.
- Other instructors.
- Career education, exploratory, and related materials.
- Other sources, documents, and individuals in business, industry, education, agencies, and the military.

Below are some examples of specific occupational titles for which training *might* be offered in typical program areas:

EXAMPLES

Drafting Program	Secretarial Program	Commercial Foods Program
• Tracer	• General secretary	• Short-order cook
• General drafter	• Legal secretary	• Chef
• Civil drafter	• Medical secretary	• Salad maker
• Mechanical drafter	• Executive secretary	• Sandwich maker
• Architectural drafter	• Typist	• Waiter/waitress
• Structural drafter		
• Design drafter		

STEP 2: Narrow the list down to those occupations for which you *will* offer training.

Once you have developed a tentative listing of specific occupations for which you might offer training, you should narrow the list down to those specific titles that you will actually offer within your program. To do this,

[1] U.S. Department of Labor, *Dictionary of Occupational Titles* (Washington, D.C.: Bureau of Labor Statistics, U.S. Department of Labor, 1977).

you need to establish some sort of criteria by which you will evaluate each tentative occupation and arrive at a decision about offering it as an option. Some criteria you may consider using in examining each tentative occupation are listed below.

EXAMPLES

1. *Is formal training required for entry into the occupation?*
2. *Am I allowed or authorized by law, regulations, rules, or policies to offer training in the occupation?*
3. *Are reliable data available indicating present and future employment demand in the occupation?*
4. *Is there evidence that students are likely to enroll for training in the occupation?*
5. *Is the occupation at entry level and not a level of advancement for which workers are typically trained on the job?*
6. *Is the instructor(s) qualified and experienced in the occupation?*
7. *Is the facility, including tools, materials, and equipment, adequate or readily obtainable?*
8. *Would the demand for additional graduates be adequate to justify offering training in the occupation if other training programs exist nearby?*

A form such as Sample 2-1 might be helpful in developing a tentative list of titles and in narrowing it down to the specific job titles for which you will actually offer training. On this form the tentative titles are listed in the blanks, then the criteria you will evaluate each title by (you may want to use different criteria) are listed. Each tentative occupational title is then evaluated using the criteria. The number of "yes" responses is recorded for each tentative occupational title; the more "yes's" a specific occupation receives, the more likely you might be to offer it as a specialized option within your training program.

Look at the example shown in Sample 2-1 and notice how the original program title was expanded into eight possible occupational titles and how this list was finally narrowed down to three for which training will be offered (circled).

Tips

You may want to keep the following tips in mind as you go about the process of identifying specific occupations within your training program:

1. Do not overdo it; it is much easier to begin with a single occupational title the first year or so, then gradually add others. Do not offer too many options too quickly; you will get bogged down.

SAMPLE 2-1	FORM FOR IDENTIFYING SPECIFIC OCCUPATIONS

Occupational/Program Area: Masonry-Bricklaying

INSTRUCTIONS:

Below is a listing of possible occupational titles for which training might be offered. For each occupation carefully review the questions listed to the right. For each yes response place a (✓) in the appropriate box.

		1. Is formal training required to enter?	2. Are we authorized or allowed to offer training?	3. Is there present and future employment demand?	4. Are students likely to enroll?	5. Is occupation at entry level?	6. Is instructor(s) qualified in occupation?	7. Are facility, equipment, etc., adequate?	8. Would demand warrant offering training?	Number of YES responses:
1.	Bricklayer	✓	✓	✓	✓	✓	✓	✓	✓	8
2.	Marble setter	✓	✓			✓	✓	✓		5
3.	Stonemason	✓	✓	✓	✓	✓	✓	✓	✓	8
4.	Terrazzo worker	✓				✓				2
5.	Tile setter	✓	✓		✓	✓				4
6.	Bricklayer helper				✓	✓	✓	✓		4
7.	Block mason	✓	✓	✓	✓	✓	✓	✓		7
8.	Concrete finisher	✓	✓	✓	✓	✓	✓			6
9.										
10.										
11.										
12.										
13.										
14.										

2. If very few students choose to specialize in or are not placed in a specific occupation you offer, drop it. There may be insufficient demand or student interest.
3. Encourage students to remain enrolled as long as possible and complete the training required for *all* (or the broadest occupation) in your program. This will greatly enhance their present and future employability.
4. Sometimes, specific occupational titles will be specialized areas within a single broad occupational title. For example, tune-up specialist and front-end mechanic could both be considered specialized areas within the occupation of general auto mechanic. In other programs, specific occupations will be separate and distinct and each can stand alone. An example might be cattle herdsman and swineherdsman, or produce clerk and vegetable clerk.
5. Keep in mind that you will soon be identifying the specific competencies or tasks required for your graduates to enter each of these specific occupations successfully.
6. Training programs offered at the "technical education" level—particularly in community colleges and technical institutes—may encompass many possible specific occupational titles. For example, an electronics technology program may prepare students for several dozen possible jobs, such as bench technician, troubleshooter, equipment test technician, and so on. Since most of these occupations are highly interrelated and since most students will not know exactly which specific job they are being hired for until they are actually hired, most students should follow a very similar training program (or at least a common core) so they will be adequately prepared for a wide variety of employment possibilities.
7. Do not split hairs. If the tasks required for two specific occupations are almost identical, do not use both titles as options. Combine them into one title (such as waiter/waitress) or use only the more common of the two.
8. Work closely with your director, dean, supervisor, or other responsible person to make sure that you are in line with all rules, regulations, guidelines, laws, and so on, in offering each specific occupation within your program.
9. Make sure that the specific occupational titles you offer are related to your overall program area—do not roam too far afield.
10. Do not force it. If your program should offer training in only one specific occupational title to meet the needs of your students, do not add others.

Before you go on to the next section, complete the following Self-Check.

SELF-CHECK [1]

Check your mastery of ENABLING OBJECTIVE [1] by completing this SELF-CHECK.

1. List at least three reasons for offering training in several specific occupational titles instead of requiring all students to go through an entire training program.

(a) ______________________________

(b) ______________________________

(c) ______________________________

2. List at least four criteria that would be appropriate for evaluating tentative occupational titles when selecting those for which training will actually be offered.

(a) ______________________________

(b) ______________________________

(c) ______________________________

(d) ______________________________

3. For each of the broad occupational areas listed below, identify at least two *specific* occupational titles within each. Consult the *Dictionary of Occupational Titles* or other source if needed.

(a) *Commercial sewing* (1) ______________________________

(2) ______________________________

(b) *Carpentry* (1) ______________________________

(2) ______________________________

(c) *Clerical* (1) ______________________________

(2) ______________________________

Compare your responses with those in the Answer Key in the appendix.

ENABLING OBJECTIVE [2]

Write Job Descriptions for Specific Occupations

What Is a Job Description?

Once the specific occupations have been identified, each needs to be fully *described*. A well-written job description paints a clear picture of the occupation as it exists *in the world of work* and is of benefit to:

- Anyone developing a competency-based program
- Prospective and actual students
- Guidance personnel
- New instructors
- Parents and the public
- Advisory committee members
- The administration or supervisors
- State, local, and other governing bodies
- Employers

A typical job description is quite brief—usually several paragraphs—and describes the major activities performed by the worker in the occupation. Additional information in the description might be:

- General working conditions—particularly if extreme or unusual
- Equipment or instruments the workers operates
- Special abilities, aptitudes, or traits needed to work successfully in the occupation
- Level of training needed
- Opportunities for advancement
- Any special restrictions or license needed

Table 2-1 shows examples of two job descriptions. Notice that each occupation—cosmetologist and manicurist, is a *specific* occupational title in a cosmetology program. Also notice that, in this example, one occupation—manicurist—is a specialized area within a broader occupation—cosmetologist.

It is important to note that the job description is concerned *only* with describing the job "out there" in the factory or business, not with how the occupation will be taught. Job descriptions should not mention anything about what the worker should know or how the training program should be set up. By beginning your program planning efforts with an accurate, up-to-date and comprehensive job description, you can make sure that your training program addresses the skills students will need to successfully function on the job.

A valuable source in writing job descriptions is the *Dictionary of Occupational Titles* as well as other resources, including previously developed job

TABLE 2-1 Sample Job Descriptions[a]

Occupational Title: Cosmetologist

Provides beauty care for customers: analyzes hair to determine condition; applies bleach, dye, or tint to color hair; shampoos and rinses hair; massages scalp and gives other hair and scalp conditioning treatments for hygenic or remedial purposes; styles hair by blowing, cutting, trimming, and tapering using clippers, scissors, razors, and blow dryer; suggests styles according to features of patron; applies waving solutions; winds hair on rollers or pin curls and finger-waves hair; sets hair by blow-dry or natural set; presses hair with straightening comb; suggests cosmetics for special conditions; applies lotions and creams; massages face or neck; shapes and colors eyebrows and eyelashes; straightens hair; retains curls or waves; cleans, shapes, and polishes fingernails and toenails.

Must stand for long periods of time; daytime hours most common; must be able to relate well to public; should be well groomed; positions open to males and females; license required.

Occupational Title: Manicurist

Cleans, shapes, and polishes customers' fingernails and toenails; removes old polish; shapes and smooths ends of nails using scissors, files, and emery boards. Cleans customers' nails; softens nail cuticles; pushes back cuticles; trims cuticles; whitens underside of nails with white paste or pencil; polishes nails using powdered polish and buffer or applies clear or colored liquid polish; may perform other beauty services, such as facials, shampooing, tinting, and coloring hair. Performs most duties sitting; keeps hands in solutions, water, etc.; daytime hours common; license usually required.

[a]Adapted from *Dictionary of Occupational Titles* (Washington, D.C.: Bureau of Labor Statistics, U.S. Department of Labor, 1977).

descriptions. If you can find already written descriptions, use them as they are or modify them so that they accurately describe the specific occupations for which you offer training.

Tips

1. Make sure that each job description describes the occupation as it exists in the world of work. If there are some unpleasant conditions associated with a job, it is better for a student to find out about them now and not the first day on the job.
2. If there are two very similar occupational titles for which you offer training (such as medical secretary and dental secretary) you may be able to cover both with a single description. If two occupations are quite different, you need a description of each.
3. Make sure that the guidance department has a copy of your descriptions. Prospective students can get a good picture of an occupation by reading a description of it.

Before going on, see if you can answer the questions in the following Self-Check.

SELF-CHECK [2]

Check your mastery of ENABLING OBJECTIVE [2] by completing this SELF-CHECK.

1. List at least five groups who might benefit from having well-written job descriptions for each specific occupation in a training program.

   (a) ____________________

   (b) ____________________

   (c) ____________________

   (d) ____________________

   (e) ____________________

2. List at least four items that are typically included in a job description.

   (a) ____________________

   (b) ____________________

   (c) ____________________

   (d) ____________________

3. Select one specific occupational title and write a complete description for it. Consult the job descriptions in the *Dictionary of Occupational Titles* or other sources if needed.

Compare your responses with those in the Answer Key in the appendix.

Continue with the following performance test.

PERFORMANCE TEST FOR TASK 1

TASK 1: Identify and Describe Specific Occupations

DIRECTIONS

When ready, demonstrate your ability to identify and describe specific occupations by doing the following:

For an actual or a hypothetical training program:

1. List tentative occupations for which training might be offered.
2. Develop criteria to evaluate the tentative occupations.
3. Identify occupations for which training will be offered (use a form similar to Sample 2-1).
4. Write a job description for each occupation for which training will be offered in the program.

No.	Criteria for evaluating performance; 100% mastery required	YES	NO
	List of Tentative Occupational Titles		
1.	Is each occupation related to the program area?		
2.	Is each occupational title specific?		
	Specific Occupations for Which Training Will Be Offered		
3.	Did each occupation meet the test of valid criteria?		
4.	Is the final number of specific occupations that will be offered realistic considering the situation?		
	Job Descriptions		
5.	Is there a job description for each specific occupation for which training will be offered?		
6.	Do descriptions describe occupations as they exist?		
7.	Does each description mention major activities performed by workers on the job?		
8.	If appropriate, does each description mention:		
	(a) Working conditions if extreme or unusual?		
	(b) Equipment or instruments used?		
	(c) Special abilities or skills needed?		
	(d) Level of training needed?		
	(e) Opportunities for advancement?		
	(f) Special restrictions or licenses required?		

When you complete this section, you will be able to:

TASK 2: Identify Essential Student Prerequisites

INTRODUCTION

One way to help maximize students' chances for success in your training program and on the job is to make sure that they already possess or perhaps can acquire *essential prerequisites* before entering the training program. These prerequisites are specific traits, abilities, or previous learning that are essential to successful performance on the job but ones not usually learned while in the training program. This section will show you how to identify essential student prerequisites for entry into your training program that will enhance each student's chances for success.

TERMINAL PERFORMANCE OBJECTIVE

To demonstrate mastery of this task, do the following:

Given a list of specific occupational titles for which training will be offered, identify essential student prerequisites for entry into the training program(s). The student prerequisites should conform to *all* criteria listed in Performance Test 2 at the end of this section.

ENABLING OBJECTIVES

This section is divided into several parts to help you:

[1] *Identify types of and reasons for identifying essential student prerequisites.*
[2] *Select tentative prerequisites for a training program.*

ENABLING OBJECTIVE [1]

Identify Types of and Reasons for Identifying Essential Student Prerequisites

What Are Student Prerequisites?

A student prerequisite is simply a characteristic, trait, or ability that your students should possess to be successful on the job—but one that they will *not* get as a result of your training program. You might see it like this:

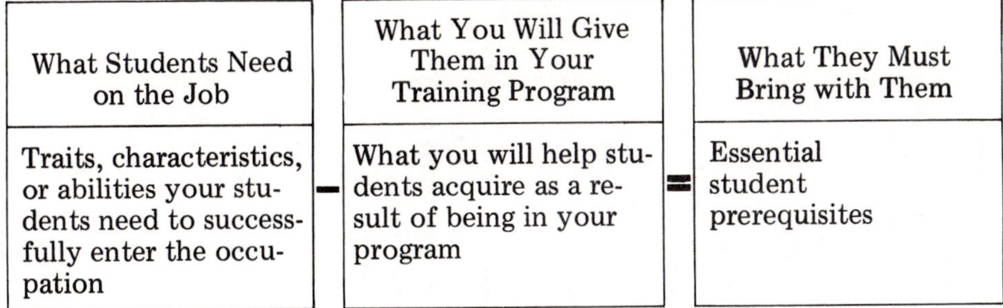

What Students Need on the Job
Traits, characteristics, or abilities your students need to successfully enter the occupation
–
What You Will Give Them in Your Training Program
What you will help students acquire as a result of being in your program
=
What They Must Bring with Them
Essential student prerequisites

Here is an example of how this works:

EXAMPLE: Drafting

On the Job Students Need:		*You Will Help Them Learn:*		*Essential Prerequisites*
• *Good eyesight* • *Visual perception* • *Ability to use basic and specialized drafting instruments* • *Ability to complete a variety of types of drawings* • *Ability to work cooperatively with others*	–	• *Ability to use basic and specialized drafting instruments* • *Ability to complete a variety of types of drawings* • *Ability to work cooperatively with others*	=	• *Good eyesight* • *Visual perception*

Since students in this hypothetical drafting program need *good eyesight* and since you do not plan to help them acquire this characteristic while in your training program (if you can, you are in the wrong profession), good eyesight is a student *prerequisite* for entry into the drafting program. They need to be able to use drafting instruments, but since you will help them learn this, it should not be a prerequisite.

> The philosophy here is not a *negative* one of barring students from entry into training programs, but a *positive* one of trying to maximize each student's chances of success! Look at prerequisites as "predictors of success"—not as obstacles to entry.

If an electrician must have at least average eye-hand coordination and must be able to lift 20 pounds overhead in order to function successfully *on*

TABLE 2-2 Sample Student Prerequisites

Physical Traits or Abilities	*Previously Learned Skills*	*Previously Learned Knowledge*	*Previously Acquired Attitudes*
• Average dexterity • Eye–hand–foot coordination • Grip strength of 20 lb • Lift 50 lb chest high • 20/20 vision • Average hearing ability • Tolerance of heat and loud noises • At least one arm • Within acceptable weight range for size • Between 5 ft 2 in. and 6 ft 2 in. • Good balance • Tolerance of heights • Absence of allergies • Stamina • Disease free • Ability to move about freely in cramped quarters	• Use of hammer, screwdriver, pliers, and other basic hand tools • Use of oscilloscope • Interpret drawings and sketches • Use drill press • Hold a driver's license • Tenth-grade reading level • Type 30 wpm • Take shorthand • Run a bead • Safe use of firearms • Fly a single-engine plane • Use an adding machine • Write a sales slip	• Add, subtract, multiply, and divide • Basic algebra • Ohm's law • Basic grammar • Basic chemistry • Metric system • Measure with architect's or engineer's scale • Measure precision parts with micrometer and calipers • Basic medical terminology • Basic anatomy and physiology • Basic principles of physics • Basic knowledge of plumbing code	• Punctuality • Courtesy • Honesty • Respect for authority • Observance of safety rules • Respect for fellow workers • Nonprejudiced in dealing with public • Tolerance of verbal abuse by irate customers • Professional attitude and demeanor • Well-groomed

the job as an electrician, you are not doing a student a favor by allowing him or her to enter the electrician program if these prerequisite abilities are seriously lacking.

Types of Prerequisites

You might look at student prerequisites as falling into several broad categories. Examples of typical prerequisites in each category are shown in Table 2-2.

Some programs may require prerequisites in only one of these categories, whereas other programs may have prerequisites in several or even all of them.

Why Identify Prerequisites?

Identifying valid prerequisites for entry into training programs has several benefits:

1. When essential prerequisites are identified and *written down*, guidance personnel and instructors are better able to steer prospective students to programs for which they are qualified.
2. Students' chances of success in the training program and on the job are maximized when they possess certain traits and characteristics essential to completing the training and working sucessfully in the occupation.

How Many?

We used the term "essential" in the heading of this section for a reason. Only absolutely essential prerequisites needed for successful performance should be used to screen students. If too many prerequisites are required or if prerequisite abilities are set at too high a level, otherwise-qualified students might be discouraged or even denied access to a program. If, on the other hand, too few prerequisites are identified or prerequisite abilities are set too low, unqualified students may enter and even complete the training program and yet be unsuccessful on the job. Make sure that prerequisites selected for a program are *essential* and not just desired. If in doubt—leave it out!

Before going on, see if you can identify student prerequisites by completing the following Self-Check.

SELF-CHECK [1]

Check your mastery of ENABLING OBJECTIVE [1] by completing this SELF-CHECK.

1. Identify three *specific* examples of student prerequisites in each of the four areas below. Each prerequisite should be precise enough to be measured.

   (a) Physical traits or abilities:
   (1) ______
   (2) ______
   (3) ______

   (b) Previously learned skills:
   (1) ______
   (2) ______
   (3) ______

   (c) Previously learned knowledge:
   (1) ______
   (2) ______
   (3) ______

   (d) Previously learned attitudes:
   (1) ______
   (2) ______
   (3) ______

2. Identify at least two benefits of identifying essential student prerequisites.

   (a) ______

   (b) ______

Compare your responses with those in the Answer Key in the appendix.

ENABLING OBJECTIVE [2]

Select Tentative Prerequisites for a Training Program

Selecting Prerequisites

One place to start is by looking closely at the target population you serve. Ask yourself: What abilities, attitudes, skills, and previous education do typical students usually bring with them? Any of the characteristics or traits that are *essential* to performing in the training program or on the job, and that you do *not* plan to help students acquire while in your program, might be good candidates for prerequisites.

EXAMPLE

Ms. Margaret O'Niel was a nursing instructor at a community college. Her target population consisted of all high school graduates. Her program enjoyed a high level of student demand. Ms. O'Niel determined that one year of high school chemistry and one year of high school math would be considered to be minimum essential prerequisites for entry into the nursing program. Students needed the chemistry to master certain competencies and they needed basic math on the job. She was probably on safe ground, here, because virtually all of her applicants were high school graduates and most have had a course in chemistry and math. Since her target population usually possessed some basics in math and chemistry, it would not make much sense for Ms. O'Niel's nursing program to waste time teaching basic math and chemistry even though both are essential to success in the program and on the job.

If students in your target population usually come to you *without* a particular skill that is needed for success in the occupation, chances are you will need to teach that skill in your training program and *not* treat it as an essential prerequisite.

Remember that one of the groups of students who stand to benefit most from the competency-based approach to training are students with special needs, particularly students with physical handicaps and certain disadvantaged learners. Keep your prerequisites to an absolute minimum and, if possible, let a particularly well motivated or determined student enter your program even though he or she may lack one or more prerequisite. Caution such students that their chances of success—both in the training program and on the job—might be less than if they had all the prerequisites.

Overcoming Lack of Prerequisites

Another thing to keep in mind is that lack of some prerequisites can be overcome. If a student without high school chemistry wanted to enter Ms. O'Niel's nursing program, for example, and was otherwise qualified, that prerequisite could be overcome by simply enrolling in a basic chemistry course then reapplying.

Lack of prerequisites in some basic skills such as reading and math skills can sometimes be overcome—sometimes with dramatic results. Some highly developed remedial programs can raise a student's reading or math skills several grade levels, but sometimes results of remediation are disappointing. Lack of other prerequisites, however, cannot be overcome. All the remediation in the world cannot replace a missing limb or give a student tolerance for working in high places. Since lack of most physical abilities cannot be overcome easily, using physical characteristics as prerequisites should be kept to a minimum.

Try to set the *level* of essential student prerequisites, particularly for physical abilities and reading and math skills, *no higher* than that required on the job. A typical violation of this usually occurs for reading ability.

EXAMPLE
Mr. Ashmore was a plumbing instructor who was having difficulty recruiting enough students to keep his program filled. When asked why he was accepting only those students with a twelfth-grade reading level, he replied: "I've found that students with any lower reading level than twelfth grade have a tough time reading my textbook." A little further investigation revealed that plumbers in the local area needed to read at about an eighth-grade level on the job. *When he located training materials written at about the eighth-grade level, he could then accept more students.*

Clearly, Mr. Ashmore was basing one of his program prerequisites on a requirement dictated by his *training program* (his textbook), *not* based on what is required *on the job*. Avoid this practice. It places artificial barriers in the way of prospective students. Sample 2-2 shows student prerequisites for a hypothetical training program. You may find a form similar to this helpful in listing prerequisites, especially in communicating prerequisites to guidance personnel and prospective students.

It is important to remember that your list of prerequisites cannot be developed at one sitting. You cannot really be sure what prerequisites you should require until your entire training program is fully developed and actually tried out with students. At this point, you are making an educated guess; you will be refining, adding to, and deleting as you go.

Tips

Some things to keep in mind as you identify the minimum, essential prerequisites for each occupation in your program include:

1. Keep your prerequisites to a minimum—do not exclude students who would otherwise be qualified.
2. Keep your target population in mind. If students typically lack a skill or ability you think is important, you will probably have to teach it (if it can be learned). You cannot realistically expect students to bring it with them.
3. Setting the level of prerequisites *too high* unfairly restricts student access to programs.
4. Setting the level of prerequisites *too low* may be doing students an injustice since lack of certain traits and characteristics may hurt their chances of getting and holding a job in the occupation.

SAMPLE 2-2	ESSENTIAL STUDENT PREREQUISITES

Occupation/Program: Diesel Mechanic

Below are the recommended minimum student prerequisites for entry into this training program. These prerequisites have been verified as essential to successful performance in the program and on the job. Entry into the program without one or more of these prerequisites may affect a student's chances of success in the training program and on the job.

A. Physical Abilities, Traits, or Characteristics

1. Full use and range of both arms and hands
2. Lift 25 pounds overhead
3. Able to stand for two hours at a time
4. Reach and work in tight spaces

B. Previously Learned Skills

None

C. Previously Learned Knowledge

1. Eighth-grade reading level
2. Add, subtract, multiply, and divide whole numbers

D. Previously Acquired Attitudes

None

5. Do not base prerequisites solely on your curriculum—try to base them on job requirements.
6. Lack of certain prerequisites can be resolved through remediation or additional training.
7. Little can be done about the lack of certain prerequisites—particularly physical traits.
8. Do not forget to include any legal or other mandated prerequisite, such as a health card, driver's license, no felony convictions, and so on.
9. Review your prerequisites periodically. Delete any prerequisites that students seem to be able to function successfully without or any that you decide to help students acquire in your training program.
10. Work closely with recruitment, guidance, and counseling personnel. Explain why your prerequisites are, in fact, prerequisites and how much better off a student's chances of success are if these prerequisites are met. Emphasize that essential prerequisites are "predictors of success" and should be viewed as a positive element in the student selection process rather than a negative one.
11. You may be able to use a single list of student prerequisites for *all* the specific occupational titles for which you offer training. For example, the prerequisites for entry into specialized training programs for residential electrician and industrial electrician might be very similar or even identical, since the requirements on the job are similar. Sometimes, however, a separate list of prerequisites might be needed for two or more specific occupations, such as tire changer and general auto mechanic. In this example, students choosing the general auto mechanic option would probably need a somewhat higher reading and math level than someone entering the tire changer area.
12. State each prerequisite as precisely as possible so that each can be objectively assessed. "20/30 vision"—not "good eyesight"; "lift 40 pounds overhead," not "better than average strength"; avoid listing prerequisites such as Math 101 or other "fuzzy" prerequisites.
13. Usually, desirable student attitudes are not appropriate to use as essential prerequisites. Many *desirable* attitudes can be *learned* while in the training program.
14. In programs where power equipment, hazardous materials, or dangerous conditions exist, be cautious about accepting students who lack prerequisites that might make them unsafe.
15. You may want to enroll certain students on a "provisional" basis if they lack particular prerequisites that can be overcome through remediation or outside work.
16. Have your list of prerequisites verified by your advisory committee for their validity as requirements for successful job performance.

17. Work with guidance, work evaluation, or related personnel to find valid instruments for quickly and accurately evaluating mastery of certain prerequisites, such as reading level or dexterity.
18. Make sure that someone has the responsibility of verifying whether a student possesses prerequisites such as previously learned knowledge or skills.
19. If you cannot find any reliable method to evaluate whether a student possesses a particular prerequisite (especially attitudes), you might consider dropping it.
20. If a student or someone in authority challenges you on a prerequisite, be prepared to show evidence (such as advisory committee meeting minutes) showing why the prerequisite is required for entry into your training program.

Before going on to the next section, see if you can answer the questions in the following Self-Check.

SELF-CHECK [2]

Check your mastery of ENABLING OBJECTIVE [2] by completing this SELF-CHECK.

1. Listed below are essential student prerequisites that were identified for entry into a high school driver's education course. Carefully review each and place a check in the column to the right of each prerequisite you believe to be valid.

	Valid
(a) Hold a learner's permit	
(b) 20/20 vision	
(c) Physically able to operate steering, brake, and accelerator	
(d) Tenth-grade reading level	

2. Select a specific occupation that you are familiar with. Tentatively identify the minimum, essential student prerequisites for entry into a training program for that occupation. Make some assumptions about the student population served, such as previous education, age, maturity level, and so on. You may want to use a form like Sample 2-2.

Compare your responses with those in the Answer Key in the appendix.

PERFORMANCE TEST FOR TASK 2

TASK 2: Identify Essential Student Prerequisites

DIRECTIONS

When ready, demonstrate your ability to identify student prerequisites by doing the following:

For specific occupations that will be offered:

1. Make needed assumptions about the student population served.
2. Tentatively identify essential student prerequisites for entry into the program for each occupation.
3. Verify the prerequisites using an advisory committee or other means.
4. Compile a final list of essential student prerequisites for each occupation on a form similar to Sample 2-2.

No.	Criteria for evaluating performance; 100% mastery required	YES	NO
1.	Is the number of essential prerequisites for each occupation held to a minimum?		
2.	Is each prerequisite stated precisely?		
3.	Is each prerequisite absolutely essential to successful performance in the training program or on the job?		
4.	Is each prerequisite set at a level *low* enough so that qualified students may enroll but *high* enough to match job requirements?		
5.	Has each prerequisite been verified by appropriate individuals within the occupation as being essential to successful performance in the training program or the occupation?		

3

Identifying and Analyzing Student Competencies

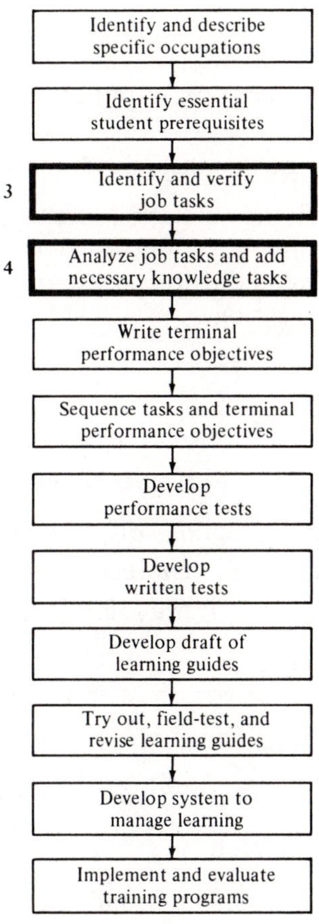
Identify and describe specific occupations
Identify essential student prerequisites
3
Identify and verify job tasks
4
Analyze job tasks and add necessary knowledge tasks
Write terminal performance objectives
Sequence tasks and terminal performance objectives
Develop performance tests
Develop written tests
Develop draft of learning guides
Try out, field-test, and revise learning guides
Develop system to manage learning
Implement and evaluate training programs

When you complete this section, you will be able to:

TASK 3: Identify and Verify Job Tasks

INTRODUCTION

A competency-based training program is based on the actual tasks successful workers perform on the job rather than on textbooks, course outlines or other such sources removed from the job itself. Basing a training program on the actual job tasks performed in the occupation will help ensure that students will master the skills that will make them competent workers. This section shows you how to *identify and verify these job tasks* and compile them on a task listing upon which to build your program.

TERMINAL PERFORMANCE OBJECTIVE

To demonstrate mastery of this task, do the following:

For one or more specific occupations, identify and verify specific job tasks performed by competent workers in the occupation. The completed task listing(s) should conform to *all* criteria listed in Performance Test 3 at the end of this section.

ENABLING OBJECTIVES

This section is divided into several parts to help you:

[1] *List benefits of basing programs on "competencies."*

[2] *Identify broad duties within an occupation.*

[3] *Identify tasks performed on the job.*

[4] *Verify job tasks.*

ENABLING OBJECTIVE [1]

List Benefits of Basing Programs on "Competencies"

A Look at Human Competence

Before we look at *competencies* and their role in competency-based training, let us take a minute to explore the notion of *human competence.*

Thomas Gilbert, in his thought-provoking book, *Human Competence—Engineering Worthy Performance,*[1] tells us that human competence is a function of *worthy performance.*

> Competent people, Gilbert says, are those who can render valuable or *worthy performance* without using excessively costly behaviors.

Gilbert proposes several novel ideas about human competence, which are all in harmony with the competency-based philosophy. Table 3-1 shows several of Gilbert's ideas and presents some implications of them for training.

TABLE 3-1 Training Implications of Gilbert's Human Competence "Theorem"

Gilbert's Theorem Suggests	*Implications for Training*
1. The true value of human competence is derived from actual accomplishments, *not* from behavior.	1. Our sole concern in training should be to help trainees acquire the ability to render "worthy performance" on the job. Training programs should focus more on the *outcomes* of training and less on the *process* of how trainees get there.
2. Great accomplishments are worthless if they incur great costs in terms of human behavior or activity.	2. Training programs should blaze the shortest trail possible between where each trainee is now and where he or she needs to be.
3. A system that rewards people for their *behavior*, rather than for the net *results* of their behavior, breeds incompetence.	3. Training programs should reward (grades, etc.) trainees *solely* for successfully mastering essential job skills—not for attendance, effort, good attitude, or other *behaviors.*
4. We should not confuse the "plow" (behavior) with the "crop" (accomplishment).	4. All our program planning and instructional activities should revolve around the valuable accomplishment we are after: trainees acquiring job skills and becoming employed.
5. Reducing the required behavior to reach a given performance promotes human competence	5. Trainees should be required to engage only in those activities that address skills they do not yet possess.
6. Knowledge and attitudes without worthy performance are meaningless.	6. Teaching knowledge for knowledge's sake and teaching attitudes in a vacuum are counterproductive to the human competence of trainees.

[1] Thomas F. Gilbert, *Human Competence—Engineering Worthy Performance* (New York: McGraw-Hill Book Company, 1978), pp. 18–19.

In developing training programs we should remember that the competence of our trainees will be judged by their employers based on their ability to *perform in a worthwhile manner* while keeping their costly behaviors to a minimum. Job competence is being able to produce desirable *results.*

This concept of human competence is vitally important as we develop competency-based training programs. Every task, every objective, every test item, every slide, every module, and every instruction sheet should pass the test: Will this training activity or learning resource contribute to the trainee's competence *out there* on the job? If we cannot answer affirmatively, we have no business including it in our training program.

What Are Competencies?

The worthy accomplishments Gilbert spoke of are the *student competencies* upon which we build competency-based training programs. Below are sample competencies that employers or customers might consider *worthy accomplishments.*

EXAMPLES: Competencies

- *Prepare a tax return*
- *Install a lockset*
- *Make a printing plate*
- *Rebuild an inboard engine*
- *Remove an obstruction in a drain*
- *Investigate arson fires*
- *Graft a plant*
- *Apprehend a fleeing suspect*
- *Build a footer*
- *Type envelopes*
- *Polish clinical crowns*
- *Turn a taper*
- *Fill a cavity*
- *Remove an appendix*
- *Pass a law*
- *Develop a competency-based program*

Notice that *not one* of these competencies mentions anything about what workers know, what attitudes they hold, how hard they work, how loyal they are, or how much they try. Each one of these sample competency statements is a *worthy performance* because each results in some product or service of value *for which someone is willing to pay.*

As we develop competency-based programs we should remember that competencies are those worthy accomplishments that make the employee *valuable to the employer* and that make the employer *valuable to the customer or consumer.*

You may be squirming in your chair right now and thinking: "I agree, accomplishments or competencies for which someone is willing to pay *are* important, but in *my* area, knowledge and attitudes are also very important." I couldn't agree more. Just be very careful, however, to remember that it is *results* that count. Let us look at an example to clarify the relationship between a worthy *performance* (competency) and the *knowledge* and *attitudes* that support it.

EXAMPLE

Ms. Cox was the lead trainer for a retail company. She was putting together a training program to teach new employees how to accept customers' checks. Knowing that the trainee behavior *of accepting checks has three components—*skill, knowledge, *and* attitudes*—Ms. Cox thought she would put the program together in three distinct parts, each part covering one of these three areas. During the first session, she covered all the* knowledge *needed to cash and accept checks, such as types of checks, endorsements, and so on. A week later, in the second training session, she covered the actual* steps *involved in properly accepting customer checks. Finally, during the third week, she covered the desirable employee* attitudes *critical to accepting checks in a customer-pleasing manner, such as asking for identification in a nonthreatening way. Ms. Cox was thoroughly disappointed when she learned that bad-check losses did not go down.*

Where did she go wrong? We cannot really be sure, but it looks like one mistake that she made was losing sight of the real purpose of the training program. Perhaps if Ms. Cox had been reminded that human competence is a function of *worthy performance*, she might have put the training program together a little differently. Since accepting customer checks—*correctly*—is the worthy accomplishment for which the employer is willing to pay the employee, Ms. Cox should have made this the overriding "theme" of the program.

Knowledge of the parts of a check and types of endorsements and *attitudes* that are needed to accept checks in a customer-pleasing manner should *only* have been included *if* and *when* they contributed to the performance. The training program, from beginning to end, should have focused on bringing about the *accomplishment*—accepting checks—not just the *behaviors* to get there. If knowledge or a critical attitude was needed at some point during the performance, it should have been learned *then* and only to the extent that it supported competent check cashing.

Someone may ask you: "Just what are the competencies required by successful employees in your occupation?" Keep the following thoughts in mind if you are tempted to say something like: "Well, they have to *know*... and they must have good *attitudes*, such as...":

- Employers and the public will not pay for what someone *knows or feels*—they will pay for some valuable product or service.
- *Knowing* everything there is to know about taking x-rays is useless unless the technician can *take an x-ray* properly (worthy performance) *without* too many costly behaviors (time, ruined film, overexposed patient). Having a good *attitude* and treating the patient courteously is fine, but it is *results* that count.
- Knowledges and attitudes contribute to human competence *only* insofar as they aid the worker to produce worthy performances.
- Look at knowledge and attitudes as electric power with great *potential* for doing work but absolutely useless without some means of transforming that power into useful work.

Competencies Versus Tasks

Recently, the term *task* has been used more and more to describe the desired student outcomes for competency-based programs. Several other terms in use include competency, job, procedure, activity, and others. Whether you use the term "task" or any other term is really unimportant. The key to effective program planning is *how* these outcomes are *identified, stated,* and *learned*—not what they are called. In this book, the term *task* has been selected to describe the outcomes of training programs for several reasons:

1. Training programs should be based on the actual activities performed on the job for which the worker is paid. The activities are actually "tasks."
2. Since our focus is on training and education, skills (and even knowledges) can be viewed as *learning* tasks—something to be accomplished by the learner.
3. Use of the term "task" seems to imply to learners that some *action* is necessary on their part for mastery.
4. Task appears to be gaining in usage throughout the education and training field.

So in the remainder of this book, *task* will be used to describe the student competencies upon which training programs are built.

The Role of the Task Listing

Let us look at an example to see how vitally important a "task listing" can be when developing a training program designed to lead trainees to competence in a particular field.

EXAMPLE

Mr. Ralston, assistant director at Washington Vo-Tech Center, had his hands full. The auto body repair program was criticized during an accreditation visit for lack of a well-defined curriculum. The auto body program consisted of a series of courses (these courses, by the way, are from an actual auto body repair program):

Term I
Auto Body Lab I
Auto Body Theory I
Applied Math I
Term II
Auto Body Lab II
Auto Body Theory II
Related Welding
Term III
Auto Body Lab III
Auto Body Theory III
Auto Body Painting I
Industrial Materials

Term IV
Auto Body Lab IV
Auto Body Theory IV
Auto Body Painting II
Term V
Auto Body Lab V
Auto Body Theory V
Automotive Electricity
Term VI
Auto Body Lab VI
Auto Body Theory VI

I think you can see why the visiting team had a difficult time figuring out what was being taught in this program. Looking at the descriptions for the courses helped very little either. The description of "Auto Body Theory IV," for example, said "A continuation of Auto Body Theory III." When pressed to show some kind of written document describing exactly what job skills students learn in the program, the department chairman could produce only some general topic statements, yellowed course outlines, and a red face. The department was charged with the task (how about that—a worthy instructor performance) of rewriting its curriculum.

Instructors in the program disagreed over what the badly needed curriculum should look like and even on what it should be based. One instructor wanted to base the curriculum on the units in a new textbook, whereas another felt sure the curriculum guide was the answer. Mr. Ralston, a recent competency-based convert, urged them to base their curriculum solely on the competencies (or tasks) successful auto body mechanics actually perform on the job. Their initial reply was: "Between us we have 96 years experience in the field; we darn well know what skills are needed!" Their only trouble was in not having these skills written down. Ralston held firm and insisted that they develop a "task listing" showing the competencies needed on the job.

After some trial and error and help from the auto body industry in the area, the following list of student competencies became the basis of the training program:

Task Listing for Auto Body Repair

Upon successful completion of the program, the student will be able to:

A. *Repairing Sheet-Metal Damage*:
1. Push sheet-metal damage.
2. Pull sheet metal damage.
3. Shrink metal with heat.
4. Repair damage with plastic filler.
5. Repair damage with body lead.

B. *Replacing Glass*
1. Replace windshield
2. Replace door glass
3. Replace vent window

E. *Replacing Auto Sheet Metal*:
1. Replace and align door
2. Replace and align fender
3. Replace and align hood panel
4. Replace grille panel
5. Replace bumper
6. Replace roof panel
7. Replace quarter panel
8. Replace gas tank
9. Replace valance panel
10. Replace door outer repair panel

Go back and take another look at the course titles originally listed for the auto body program at Washington Vo-Tech and then look at the task listing. I think you will agree that they are about as different as night and day. Ask yourself: Which document would have more meaning for students, for instructors, for employers, for accrediting agencies, and for other schools? They're not even close! You may think this example is a little extreme, but it is not really. Look at almost any school catalog, curriculum guide, program description, course outline, or even most lesson plans and see if you can pinpoint the actual job competencies that trainees will master. Basing a program on a *written* listing of clearly stated, validated job competencies—referred to as a *task listing* in this book—has several benefits, some of which are listed in Table 3-2.

A Word of Caution

The rest of this section outlines some specific steps you might find helpful in identifying the competencies upon which you will base your program. Before you begin that process, however, a very important word of caution is in order.

You might look at the overall process of developing a competency-based training program as having several major steps, such as identifying competencies, writing objectives, developing tests, and so on. Basically,

TABLE 3-2 Benefits of Using a Sound Task Listing

- As students are given a copy of the task listing, they immediately see exactly what will be learned in the training program.
- Advisory committee members and others can determine exactly what competencies make up a program.
- If a list of student competencies has been verified as essential for employment, a sound argument can be made to the administration to secure the media, tools, equipment, or consumable materials students must have to master them.
- Articulation among training institutions can be enhanced when specific tasks are listed for programs. When a high school student moves into a post-secondary program, he or she need not repeat instruction in those tasks identified as "mastered."
- Efforts of both the instructor and students can focus on students mastering tasks on the task listing—*not* on "covering" material, completing chapters in books, listening to lectures, or discussing topics.
- Individualized training programs can be put together for those students who do not want or need to complete an *entire* training program. Specific tasks that will lead to employment in a specialized area within the occupation can be identified and mastered.
- Job competencies, stated in black and white, serve as a common language among educators, students, and employers. The task "Grill fish, meats, and fowl" means the same to the student, the instructor, and the prospective employer.
- Development or selection of instructional media, materials, supplies, tool, equipment, and even the instructor can be made on the basis of how each contributes to aiding students master the tasks listed on the task listing.
- When the task listing becomes the central focus of the program, students become task oriented—just as on the job.
- Evaluating students and assigning grades and credit can be based on mastering tasks rather than on attendance, paper-and-pencil tests, final exams, and other such measures that have little to do with the human competence of trainees.
- Student transcripts and certificates can list the actual tasks mastered instead of only time enrolled.
- The task listing can be continually updated and revised to come ever closer to the "ideal" list of competencies that students need.
- When an instructor leaves the system, the program will not leave also. The program will be based on job competencies—*not* solely on the instructor.
- Job tasks can become the basic building block of the program's curriculum. Since occupations are made up of specific tasks for which the worker is paid, it makes far more sense to students to learn from training materials put together *task by task*. Courses, units, blocks, chapters, and other arbitrary units have absolutely no meaning on the job and it should not surprise us that they have little meaning for students.

these steps fall into *two* distinct phases, depending on *when* each is undertaken.

Look at Figure 3-1 and notice that phase II does not begin until *after* phase I is completed. Phase I involves *describing the outcomes* of training and phase II deals with developing a competency-based training program to

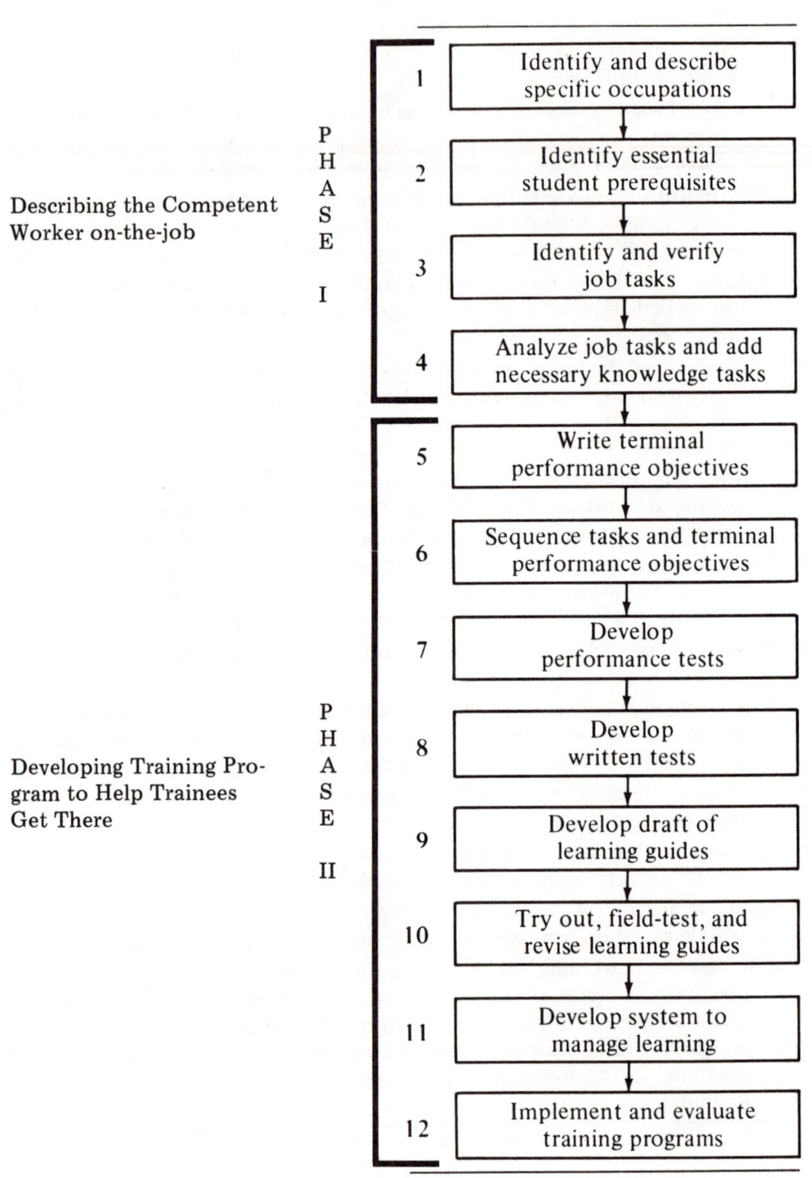
Describing the Competent Worker on-the-job
PHASE I
1 Identify and describe specific occupations
2 Identify essential student prerequisites
3 Identify and verify job tasks
4 Analyze job tasks and add necessary knowledge tasks
Developing Training Program to Help Trainees Get There
PHASE II
5 Write terminal performance objectives
6 Sequence tasks and terminal performance objectives
7 Develop performance tests
8 Develop written tests
9 Develop draft of learning guides
10 Try out, field-test, and revise learning guides
11 Develop system to manage learning
12 Implement and evaluate training programs

FIGURE 3-1 Two Phases in Developing A Competency-Based Training Program

help students *get there*. Of course, as with any complex developmental process, you will find yourself involved in many of these tasks at the same time, and as you progress you will be returning to earlier tasks for refinement. The point here is not to let the *development* of the training program influence the selection of *outcomes*.

> Do not get involved with training until *after* you have fully identified the *outcomes* of that training.

As you go through the process of developing the task listing for your program, blot out completely from your mind the fact that you will soon be involved in developing training materials and activities for students to master those competencies.

Analyzing an Occupation for Competencies

Describing the competent worker in an occupation involves identifying and listing the worthy performances or tasks the competent worker actually performs and is paid for on the job. This process is usually called *occupational analysis*. Identifying the tasks actually performed by workers on the job is essential if we want to develop a training program that will help trainees acquire the tasks that will make them successful workers. You might look at it as a "closed loop," as shown in Figure 3-2.

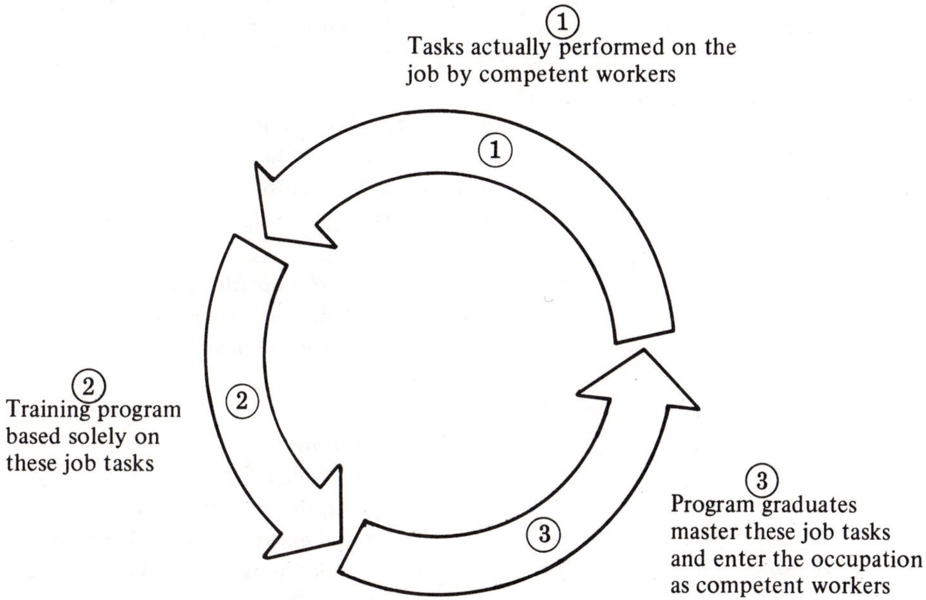
① Tasks actually performed on the job by competent workers
①
② Training program based solely on these job tasks
②
③
③ Program graduates master these job tasks and enter the occupation as competent workers

FIGURE 3-2 Relationship Among Job Competencies, Training Program and Competent Trainees

If we base training programs on anything *other* than valid job tasks (such as courses, textbooks, opinion, etc.) we may break this closed loop, and we cannot be sure if students are mastering the tasks actually needed on the job.

Occupational Analysis Terms

Before we go any further, we need to define several key terms we will be using during the analysis process. As you look at each term, also look at Table 3-3 to see how each term fits into the analysis process and for examples of each. You should go through this section very carefully, because many instructors experience some difficulty analyzing an occupation—particularly their own. Perhaps this is because the tasks performed on the job have become almost automatic over the years.

TABLE 3-3 Occupational Analysis Outline

Occupational Analysis Terms	*Examples*
Occupational area or cluster	*Carpentry*
I. *Specific job or occupation*	I. *Residential carpenter*
A. *Duty*	A. *Preparing site*
1. *Task*	1. *Establish boundary or property lines*
a. Step (and technical knowledge)	a. Check plan for reference points
	b. Check property for existing hubs
b. Step	c. Establish first property line
c. Step	d. Etc.
d. Etc.	
2. *Task*	2. *Layout building site*
a. Step	a. Establish start point on property lines
b. Step	b. Set up transit
c. Step	c. Drive stake along line of sight
d. Etc.	d. Etc.
3. *Task*	3. *Install batter boards*
a. Step	a. Set batter board stakes
b. Step	b. Make a grade pad
c. Etc.	c. Etc.
4. *Etc.*	4. *Etc.*
B. *Duty*	B. *Building Forms*
1. *Task*	1. *Design footings for soil*
a. Step	a. Set depth below frost line
b. Step	b. Extend excavation to solid ground
c. Step	c. Use side forms if needed
d. Etc.	d. Etc.

2. *Task*
   a. Step
   b. Step
   c. Etc.
3. *Etc.*

C. *Duty*
1. *Task*
   a. Step
   b. Etc.
2. *Etc.*

D. *Etc.*

II. *Specific job or occupation*

A. *Duty*
1. *Task*
   a. Step
   b. Step
   c. Step
   d. Etc.
2. *Task*
   a. Step
   b. Step
   c. Etc.
3. *Etc.*

B. *Duty*
1. *Task*
   a. Step
   b. Step
   c. Etc.

III. *Etc.*

2. *Construct square-type forms*
   a. Determine top and bottom elevations
   b. Determine size and lengths of forms
   c. Etc.
3. *Etc.*

C. *Installing rough framing*
1. *Install side plates*
   a. Put side plates in position
   b. Etc.
2. *Etc.*

D. *Installing roof components, etc.*

II. *Finish carpenter*

A. *Installing interior finish*
1. *Install metal lath*
   a. Lap sides and ends
   b. Overlap corners
   c. Apply asphalt felt
   d. Etc.
2. *Install gypsum board lath*
   a. Select nails and lath
   b. Nail lath as recommended
   c. Etc.
3. *Etc.*

B. *Construction stairs*
1. *Cut and install open rise treads*
   a. Cut tread to specs
   b. Cut and fit end nosing
   c. Etc.

III. *Etc.*

Occupational Analysis Terms

- *Occupational Analysis*: The process of analyzing or breaking down an occupation into the worthy performances or *tasks* performed by workers on the job.
- *Occupational Area or Cluster*: A group of closely related specific job titles that involve a common product, process, or service.
- *Specific Occupation or Job*: A *specific* title assigned to workers performing essentially the same tasks usually having a distinct *Dictionary of Occupational Titles* and/or a U.S. Office of Education Code Number.

- *Duty*: For instructional planning purposes, an arbitrary, convenient label given to a broad category of similar job tasks (sometimes called blocks or major units).
- *Job Task*: A complete unit of work performed on the job that results in a completed product or service for which an employer or customer would be willing to pay (sometimes called jobs, competencies, or simply tasks).
- *Task Listing*: A document listing the competencies upon which a training program is built. It is based on the actual job tasks performed by successful workers in the occupation (also called competency listing).
- *Step*: A very specific action required to carry out a task. A step is usually completed in several seconds or minutes and is of no value in itself to the employer or customer (sometimes called task detail, element, or performance guide).
- *Essential Technical Knowledge*: Knowledge such as how tight, which one, where, why, and so on, essential to performing a step in a complete and accurate manner.

Before going on, see if you can identify competencies from selected occupations and identify reasons for using a sound task listing by completing the following Self-Check.

SELF-CHECK [1]

Check your mastery of ENABLING OBJECTIVE [1] by completing this SELF-CHECK.

1. For the occupations listed below, identify one example of a worthy accomplishment or job task performed by workers on the job for which the employer or consumer would be willing to pay.

   (a) Police officer: ______________________

   (b) Mason: ______________________

   (c) Electrician: ______________________

   (d) Tailor: ______________________

   (e) Bank teller: ______________________

2. List at least five benefits of using a written task listing with precisely worded, up-to-date task statements.

   (a) ______________________

   (b) ______________________

(c) ______________________________

(d) ______________________________

(e) ______________________________

Check your responses with those in the Answer Key in the appendix.

ENABLING OBJECTIVE [2]

Identify Broad Duties Within an Occupation

Methods of Identifying Competencies

There are several ways we could go about identifying tasks performed in an occupation. We could (1) go out and observe workers on the job for a length of time and record the tasks they actually perform. We could (2) meet with a group of workers from the occupation and, together, identify tasks performed. Or we could (3) compile a tentative listing of tasks from our own knowledge of the occupation and other sources and have workers from the occupation verify them. This chapter discusses the last two methods, especially the third. The first approach observing workers in the occupation—would probably be too costly and time consuming for most of us.

Getting Started

If we want to compile a tentative list of tasks to be verified by workers from the occupation, where do we begin? We could start by just listing the tasks performed on the job that come to mind. This might work, but there is another way that might be easier. First, identify the broad *categories* or kinds of tasks performed on the job and then go back and identify the actual tasks in each category. These broad categories are usually referred to as *duties.*

Our thinking might be something like that described below.

EXAMPLE

"Let's see now, I'm trying to identify the major categories of different kinds *of tasks performed by secretaries. First there's* typing; *secretaries spend an awful lot of time behind a typewriter. There's a category of tasks dealing with* stenographic *kinds of things. Then there's* telephone-related *tasks and then there's* filing *and other clerical kinds of things. . . ."*

Below are samples of duties that fully cover the *kinds* of tasks typically performed by workers in several occupations:

EXAMPLES

Occupation:	Plumber
Broad duties performed on job	• *Roughing in plumbing* • *Topping out plumbing* • *Installing fixtures and appliances* • *Maintaining plumbing*
Occupation:	Grocery clerk
Broad duties performed on job	• *Performing checkout duties* • *Preparing meat for marketing* • *Preparing produce for marketing* • *Stocking grocery department* • *Making customer contact*
Occupation:	Livestock production worker
Broad duties performed on job	• *Tending animals* • *Maintaining facilities and equipment* • *Feeding animals* • *Keeping records* • *Producing feed* • *Marketing animals*

Relationship Between Duties and Tasks

Duties are nothing more than a means of conveniently *grouping* similar tasks that are performed on the job. We could still develop a task listing and a competency-based program *without* using duties at all. The only difference would be that, without duties, we would be working with one long list of separate tasks. Duties simply help us to *group* tasks to make our program planning efforts a little easier. Keep in mind that our aim in planning student learning activities later will be to help students master *tasks, not duties*. The samples below illustrate the relationship between duties and tasks.

EXAMPLES

	No. 1	*No. 2*
Occupation:	Parts salesperson	Emergency medical technician
Sample duty:	Selling merchandise	Treating wounds
Sample job tasks within that one duty:	*1. Conduct cash sales.* *2. Conduct charge sales.* *3. Identify replacement parts.* *4. Take phone orders.*	*1. Apply bandage to open wound on extremity.* *2. Dress wound with exposed organs.*

5. *Prepare sales displays.*
6. *Check cash register.*

3. *Apply inflatable splint.*
4. *Immobilize spine.*
5. *Give emergency treatment for eye burns.*
6. *Care for rib fracture.*

Look carefully at each sample duty statement and notice that each:

- Describes a broad, major category of work performed by the worker in the occupation. Duties are *not* the worthy accomplishments or competencies we spoke of in the previous section—only a *category* of similar kinds of tasks.
- Communicates clearly the *kind* of tasks that are included within the duty.
- Is an arbitrary label assigned to a group of tasks and has little meaning to workers in the occupation. Duties are not performed on the job—tasks are.

Tips

In identifying duties for a particular occupation, you might want to keep these tips in mind:

1. If you were writing a book describing what the worker does in the occupation, the major chapters would probably be duties. The real "meat" of each chapter would be the specific tasks that workers perform and are paid for.
2. Some occupations are made up of as many as 10 to 15 duties; others have only one or two; and some specialized occupations (such as typist) are really a single duty within a broader occupation (secretary).
3. You may want to begin duty statements with the "ing" form of an action verb to show the ongoing nature of the duty and to help separate duty and task statements (more about stating tasks later).
4. Some occupations will include duties involving activities such as supervising, training, and organizing, as well as the more common duties involving actual "hands-on" tasks.
5. If you will offer training in two or more quite different specific occupational titles, you will have a separate task listing and, therefore, separate duties for each (*some* of the duties and tasks, however, might be common).
6. If you offer training in two very closely related job titles, one list of duties may cover both even though the final task listing for each might be slightly different.
7. To identify duties, think about what different *kinds* of activities the worker *actually performs on the job* during the first year or two.

8. On any one day, a worker may be involved in performing specific tasks in several duty areas.
9. The list of duties for an occupation should fully describe the major types of tasks normally performed. Every typical task performed by the entry-level worker should fall into one of the duties.
10. A good place to look for duties is in the job description you write for each specific occupation.
11. If the duty areas seem to build upon one another, list them in the order that a typical student *might* go through them in a training program. If the duties can each stand alone and the tasks in one duty need not be learned before beginning the tasks in another, list them in alphabetical (or other) order.
12. Such topics as "using equipment," "maintaining safe environment," "mastering principles of electronics," and "maintaining professional ethics" are *not* duties. None of these examples describe *categories of tasks for which the worker would be paid.* Use of equipment, following safety, electronics principles, and ethics are all areas of *knowledge* and *attitudes* that are *worthless* to consumers or employers *by themselves.* Using knowledge and attitudes to *perform* competently is what earns a paycheck.

Identifying Duties

As you break an occupation down into duties and then go back and plug in tasks in each duty, you may want to refer to several sources to aid you. These include:

- The occupational description
- Books, pamphlets, and other information on the occupation
- State, county, federal, and other publications
- Previously developed occupational analysis data
- Course outlines, courses of study, textbooks, workbooks
- Materials from business, industry, and labor unions
- Catalogs of occupational tasks and objectives
- State departments of education
- The Task Inventory Exchange coordinated by the National Center for Research in Vocational Education[2]
- Universities and colleges
- The ERIC (Educational Resources Information Center) System[3]

[2]The National Center for Research in Vocational Education, The Ohio State University, 1960 Kenny Road, Columbus, Ohio 43210.

[3]ERIC (Educational Resources Information Center), Washington, D.C. 20202.

- The V-TECS Consortium[4]—a consortium of several states and military branches which publishes catalogs of tasks for a wide variety of occupations
- Other schools that have competency-based programs
- Professional and trade association sources
- Employee evaluation documents used by companies
- Contact with workers, employers, and supervisors from within the occupation
- Other instructors in similar programs
- Other sources from education, business, public service, and government
- Your own experience

All these sources would not be available or even useful to all program developers. Locate the material available to you and use it. Table 3-4 shows sample duties from selected occupations.

TABLE 3-4 Sample Duty Statements for Selected Occupations

Occupation	*One Sample Duty within the Occupation*
1. Auto mechanic	1. Servicing brakes and wheels
2. Flight attendant	2. Preparing and serving meals
3. Drafter	3. Developing section and cutaway views
4. Retail salesclerk	4. Stocking merchandise
5. Secretary	5. Handling mail
6. Horticulture technician	6. Applying chemicals
7. Radio-TV repairer	7. Servicing amplifiers
8. Major appliance repairer	8. Repairing dryers
9. Outboard motor repairer	9. Servicing ignition and charging system
10. Welder	10. Cutting and fabricating metal
11. Electromechanical technician	11. Constructing mechanical drive systems
12. Clerk	12. Filing
13. Seamstress	13. Making custom garments
14. Child-care worker	14. Preparing and serving meals
15. Dental assistant	15. Keeping records
16. Cashier	16. Performing customer services
17. Tractor mechanic	17. Maintaining implements
18. Hotel/motel clerk	18. Performing customer transactions
19. Machinist	19. Drilling and boring holes
20. Mortician	20. Maintaining records and documents
21. Industrial trainer	21. Developing new training programs
22. Vocational instructor	22. Managing the learning environment

[4]V-TECS (Vocational-Technical Education Consortium of States), Southern Association of Colleges and Schools, Commission on Occupational Education Institutions, Atlanta, Ga. 30308.

A Hypothetical Program

To help you follow the process of identifying student competencies for a competency-based program, throughout the remainder of this chapter, let us follow the process for a hypothetical program. Since we identified and described two specific occupations (cosmetologist and manicurist) for a cosmetology program in Chapter 2, let us continue with this example. The thinking of our hypothetical instructor for identifying duties within the occupation would probably go something like this:

EXAMPLE

"Let's see now; I know I'll be offering training for two specific occupations within my program—cosmetologist and manicurist. I guess the next step is to identify the competencies that a successful cosmetologist and manicurist actually perform on the job. I think I'll begin by tentatively identifying the broad duties performed by each. I'll start with cosmetologist. Let's see, the actual services performed seem to fall into several categories—there's cutting hair, there's conditioning and shampooing, doing wigs, coloring hair, and giving facials, manicures, and pedicures. Now let's look through these textbooks, workbooks, job descriptions, and other materials and see if I left anything out. Oh yes, I forgot curling and straightening and supervising and keeping records. Now then, it looks like the broad categories of tasks (duties) that a cosmetologist performs (and gets paid for) are:

A. Conditioning and shampooing hair

B. Cutting hair

C. Cutting wigs

D. Coloring hair

E. Curling and straightening hair

F. Giving facials

G. Giving manicures and pedicures

H. Supervising and keeping records

It's a good thing I started with the broader of the two occupations because I just noticed that manicurist is simply a subpart of cosmetologist. Basically, duties F and G describe what a manicurist does, so I don't need a separate list of duties for manicurist."

Even though this list of duties for our hypothetical program is tentative and will, no doubt, be changed somewhat as the competency identification process continues, look at these duty statements and notice:

- How each is descriptive of the tasks included in the duty.
- That, together, they fully describe the occupation of cosmetologist.
- That each is only a major category of tasks performed in the occupation.
- That there is no mention of use of equipment, following ethical practices, mastering principles of chemistry, or other areas of knowledge or attitudes that are *not* worthy performances.
- That a cosmetologist may perform one or more or no tasks from each duty on any given day.
- That someone else could have fully described the occupation of cosmetologist with a different breakdown of duties. Several duties could have been combined into one (such as B and C); one duty could have been split into two (such as G).
- There is a limited number of duties (eight). This keeps things simpler and more manageable.

Before going into the next section, see if you can recognize correctly worded duties and write several duties of your own by completing the following Self-Check.

SELF-CHECK [2]

Check your mastery of ENABLING OBJECTIVE [2] by completing this SELF-CHECK.

1. Listed below are typical duty statements for several occupations. Some are worded correctly and some are not. Read each one carefully and check the appropriate column to the right.

	Correct	Incorrect
(a) Packaging and displaying meats		
(b) Handcuff suspect		
(c) Knowing how to repair radios		
(d) Understanding terminology		
(e) Processing film		
(f) Using hand and power tools		
(g) Anatomy and physiology		

2. Select a specific occupation you are familiar with. List at least four correctly worded duties for the occupation.

(a) ______________________________

(b) ______________________________

(c) ______________________________

(d) ______________________________

Compare your responses with those in the Answer Key in the appendix.

ENABLING OBJECTIVE [3]

Identify Tasks Performed on the Job

Stating Competencies with Precision

This section focuses on the heart of the competency identification process—identifying the specific job tasks within each duty actually performed on the job. Remember, now: *forget* that you will be involved in developing materials for students to learn these tasks. At this time *all* you want to do is identify them. Also keep in mind that we only want to identify those *skills* or *tasks* performed on the job for which someone is willing to pay.

In developing a competency-based training program, *how* the tasks are stated is almost as important as the selection of the tasks themselves. Let us take a look at a typical competency or task statement as it might be written by someone in the early stages of developing a competency-based training program in photography.

Cameras

At first glance, this task appears perfectly all right. Statements just like it appear in virtually every textbook, manual, course of study, operation sheet, and other materials currently in use today in education and in industry. Look at the statement again and see if you have enough information to answer this question:

Exactly what will the learner be able to *do* upon mastering the task *as it is stated*?

The only thing we know for sure is that the trainee will be learning *something* about cameras. But is is unclear whether the trainee will learn how cameras are constructed, the different kinds of cameras, or how to take photographs with a camera.

Task statements written in vague terms such as this are useless in developing an effective program. We should be very careful to aim for *precision* in stating tasks. Precisely worded tasks communicate to all concerned (the student, the instructor, and the curriculum specialist) *exactly* what the desired performance is. When this is known precisely, it can be planned for, learned, and evaluated. The previous example would be more precise in its meaning if worded something like this:

Shoot color slides with 35mm camera

It is now quite clear *exactly* what performance we are after. We want the student to be able to shoot some color slides using a 35mm camera. It is extremely important that tasks be stated with as much precision as possible. This ensures that learning activities will be developed that focus on bringing about the precise performance stated in the task and that the student knows exactly what is expected, and it guides the evaluator in knowing precisely what performance to assess. As you begin developing separate units of instruction called "learning packages" for each task, you will quickly see the value of having precisely worded tasks.

Tasks—How Narrow and How Broad?

An important thing to keep in mind is to write tasks at an appropriate level, that is, not too specific and yet not too general. Look at the three examples below and try to identify the one written at the appropriate level for use as a task statement for which a complete unit of learning such as a module might be developed:

EXAMPLES

1. *Prepare bakery items.*
2. *Prepare and serve rolls.*
3. *Sift ingredients.*

Notice that statement 1 is very broad and general. It is really a major *duty* in commercial cooking that encompasses several different tasks (prepare breads, prepare pastries, etc.). On the other hand, statment 3 is very narrow and specific. It is a single *step* in performing one or more tasks (more about steps later). Statement 2 is stated at the proper level to be a competency statement for a training program. Statement 2 would be a bona fide competency to be included on a task listing. Look at the second statement again and notice that it is written at the most appropriate level for a task statement and that it meets the following criteria, which should be used as a guide to writing precisely worded task statements.

A Job Task

1. Is a *valuable accomplishment* for which an employer or consumer is willing to pay.
2. Is a *complete* unit of work performed *on the job*; when completed, the worker feels that something has been accomplished.
3. Has definite *beginning* and *ending* points.
4. May be broken down into several procedural *steps*, from start to finish.
5. May be a typical *assignment* given to a worker on the job.
6. Results in a *finished* product or service or change in the work environment.
7. Has *meaning* for the trainee to want to learn; results in some meaningful accomplishment.
8. Makes sense for the student to learn as a separate instructional unit.
9. Begins with an *action verb* in the present tense.
10. Is short and precise.
11. Can usually be learned in about 6 to 30 hours.

Go back and look at the three previous examples and see why the second statement ("prepare and serve rolls") is a correctly worded task statement whereas the other two are not. "Preparing bakery items" (1) is not a complete unit of work, (2) has no definite beginning and end, (3) is not a single assignment, and (4) cannot be learned in 6 to 30 hours as a single unit of instruction (it is really a *duty*).

"Sift ingredients" (1) is not a complete unit of work, (2) is not a typical assignment, (3) does not result in a *complete* finished product, and (4) has no meaning by itself for the student (it is just a *step*).

Components of Task Statements

In stating job tasks, remember that they always have at least *two* and sometimes *three* components. Table 3-5 shows each component with examples of each. First, notice that each of these examples is a correctly worded task statement. Each is a complete unit of work and each may be learned on its own. It would make sense to develop a separate instructional module or learning package for each. Now, notice from these examples that the *Performance* describes the observable activity the worker performs *on the job*

TABLE 3-5 Components of Skill Task Statements

Performance	*What is Used or Produced*	*Any Qualifiers*
Type	Letter	From dictation
Replace	Lower unit	In Mercury engine
Fabricate	Joint	Using PVC pipe
Perform	Butt weld	In the overhead position
Replace	Drive shaft	On four-wheel-drive vehicle
Cut	Grass	With power scythe
Maneuver	Vessel	For anchoring
Debug	Program	Using computer aids
Chart	Data	From information supplied
Verify	Cash amount	In cash register
Apply	Decorative trim	By hand
Record	Entries	For cash payments
Transport	Patient	By wheelchair
Make	Landing	Using instruments
Solder	Components	To printed-circuit board

and is therefore the *same* activity that the trainee will perform in the training program. Notice that each is an *action* verb in the *present* tense. The second component, *What Is Used or Produced*, describes products, tools, or things that are used or the finished product or service produced. Finally, notice that *Any Qualifiers* that may be needed serve to distinguish the task from similar tasks in the same program, such as "apply decorative trim by hand" versus "apply decorative trim by machine." It is important to note that many tasks will not always have a third component. Often, qualifiers will be unnecessary or implied; in other cases they will appear as modifiers coming before the other two components. Following are examples of tasks for which qualifiers are not needed:

EXAMPLES

- *Install windows.*
- *Replace spark plugs.*
- *Strike an arc.*
- *Lay out a building.*
- *Construct ellipses.*
- *Take inventory.*

The following tasks have qualifiers (underlined) coming *before* what is used or produced:

EXAMPLES

- *Cut mild steel.*
- *Construct wall forms.*

- *Give a cold wave.*
- *Mix practice mortar.*
- *Apply welding notes.*

Whether job tasks have all three components or just two, each task should be precisely worded and should conform to the criteria listed earlier. Table 3-6 lists some performances that appear as action verbs in typical job tasks. These may help you as you write task statements for your program.

Tips

As you write tasks, keep these additional tips in mind:

1. Each task statement should stand alone.
2. Avoid using "be able to" or "the student will" or other such beginning phrases; they just waste time and space.
3. A worker in the occupation should be able to read the task and rate it as to importance and how often it is performed.
4. Use the acceptable terminology used in the occupation.
5. Try to avoid using double verbs, such as "remove and repair." Use the more inclusive of the two (repair implies removing and replacing).
6. Do not include any phrases that have to do with the *knowledge* needed to perform the task; focus on the skill.
7. Do not include any mention of performing a skill *safely*. Safety will be learned right along with each step required to perform the skill.
8. Avoid flowery terms such as "correctly," "accurately," and so on. We assume that the student will be taught how to perform the task correctly.

Instructors and others involved in competency-based programs should become proficient in writing task statements—particularly skill-oriented task statements. In most training programs, the great majority of student competencies will be skills. This is as it should be, since we said earlier that it is not what the worker knows or feels that really determines his or her human competence—it is what they can do—*results*. Knowledge and attitudes are included only insofar as they enhance the trainee's ability to accomplish results on the job.

Identifying Tasks within Duties

Now that you know how to identify duties and how to state tasks precisely, how do you go about identifying specific tasks for each duty? Just as in identifying duties, it is helpful to look at as many sources as you can.

TABLE 3-6 Typical Learner Performances for Job Tasks

Accept	Dismiss	Hit	Order	Service
Adjust	Dispense	Hoist	Organize	Set
Align	Drag	Inspect	Originate	Set up
Alter	Drape	Install	Override	Sew
Analyze	Draw	Instill	Package	Sharpen
Answer	Dress	Instruct	Paint	Shape
Apply	Drill	Insure	Patch	Shoot
Arrange	Elevate	Involve	Perform	Sit
Assemble	Establish	Issue	Pick	Site
Assist	Evacuate	Jack	Pick out	Slice
Attach	Evaluate	Jar	Pick up	Slide
Bake	Examine	Jerk	Pin	Slip
Balance	Execute	Judge	Pinch	Solder
Bend	Expose	Kick	Place	Sort
Bleed	Fabricate	Knit	Plan	Splice
Boil	File	Knurl	Plant	Split
Bore	File down	Lable	Plot	Square
Braze	Fill	Ladle	Plow	Stand
Build	Fill in	Level	Polarize	Start
Calibrate	Fill out	Light	Pop	Sterilize
Call	Fill up	Lighten	Position	Stitch
Cast	Finalize	Listen	Post	Store
Change	Find	Locate	Pour	Straighten
Check	Fit	Loosen	Practice	String
Clean	Fix	Lube	Prep	Supervise
Cleanse	Flip	Lubricate	Prepare	Take
Climb	Flush	Maintain	Press	Tap
Collect	Follow	Make	Quarter	Tell
Comb	Follow up	Make up	Quench	Test
Combine	Free	Mark	Raise	Thin
Compensate	Free up	Mark off	Rebuild	Transfer
Complete	Freeze	Mask	Receive	Transport
Condition	Frisk	Measure	Recondition	Treat
Conduct	Fry	Measure off	Re-do	Trim
Connect	Get	Measure out	Remain	Troubleshoot
Construct	Give	Meet	Remove	Turn
Correct	Go	Mill	Repair	Turn off
Cook	Grate	Mist	Replace	Turn on
Curl	Greet	Miter	Resist	Type
Cut	Grind	Mix	Rework	Unlock
Darken	Hand	Moderate	Rinse	Untangle
Design	Handcuff	Modify	Roll	Ventilate
Determine	Handle	Mount	Run	Visit
Diagnose	Haul	Mow	Saw	Wash
Diagram	Heal	Negotiate	Scrape	Wax
Direct	Help	Obtain	Seat	Weigh
Disassemble	Hem	Open	Sell	Weld
Disinfect	Hide	Operate	Serve	Yield

SAMPLE 3-1	TASK LISTING FORM

Program/Occupation: Motorcycle Mechanics

Duty G : Servicing Electrical System

Tasks within This Duty:

1. Remove and replace wiring harness and switches.
2. Service ignition systems.
3. Troubleshoot battery ignition system.
4. Repair flywheel magneto system.
5. Repair electronic ignition system.
6. Repair half-wave charging system.
7. Repair full-wave charging system.
8. Repair three-phase charging system.
9. Repair starter.
10. Repair dc generator.
11. Troubleshoot malfunctioning electrical system.
12. __________
13. __________
14. __________
15. __________
16. __________
17. __________
18. __________
19. __________
20. __________

Developed by: H. Hitch; B. Labrie; M. Strohaber Date 8/80

Revised: 12-12-80 ; 1-10-81; ______ ; ______

Sometimes it is helpful first to generate an initial list of tasks in each duty based on your own experience and then go back and revise the initial listing. If this procedure is chosen, the following steps might be helpful:

STEP 1: Write each duty at the top of a blank sheet of paper (or use a form such as Sample 3-1)

STEP 2: Select one duty and begin mentally "walking through" that part of the occupation.

STEP 3: Begin listing the separate job activities or assignments that would correspond to tasks in that duty. At this point do not bother with knowledge or attitudes focus only on the activities or skills that the worker would be paid for performing successfully (job tasks).

STEP 4: When you can no longer think of any more tasks, begin working on the next duty.

STEP 5: As one task jogs your memory about a task in another duty, flip over to that page and jot it down.

STEP 6: Continue this process until you feel that you have fully described all the work activities normally performed by an entry-level worker in that occupation.

STEP 7: Review textbooks, curriculum guides, media, workbooks, and any resources available to see if you spot tasks that you may have overlooked.

STEP 8: Look over each sheet and see if you seem to have too many or too few tasks for any duty or perhaps tasks in two duties that are very closely related. If so, you may want to combine or reword some of your original duty statements.

STEP 9: Carefully review the tasks in each duty and see if you need to alter the list by adding, deleting, combining, or rewording any task statements. Remember the criteria for precisely stated tasks.

STEP 10: Arrange the sheets of paper (duties) into a logical sequence in which a typical student might master them.

STEP 11: Finally, when you finish editing and rewording, make a new sheet for each duty and copy the tasks for each duty onto the new sheet, this time listing tasks in logical sequence from simple to complex or basic to advanced. Be sure to list prerequisite tasks (such as "take shorthand") before later tasks that call upon the worker to use the prerequisite task (such as "type letter from shorthand").

If you go through these steps very carefully, you should end up with a pretty good tentative list of student competencies upon which to begin building a program. Remember, however:

- This is a tentative list of competencies only—it is extremely important that this tentative list be thoroughly validated and updated periodically.
- It is very important to state all tasks with great precision. Go back and review the section on stating competencies if you need to.

> Remember: what you state is what you will get. The student performance called for in the task statement is the student performance you will get—no more and no less!

How Many Tasks?

You are probably wondering: "How many tasks should I end up with in each specific occupation for which I will offer training?"

> Include *all* the tasks but *only* the tasks that will lead the trainee to entry-level employment in the specific occupation.

Do not worry about trying to fit the tasks into a year, 1080 hours, two semesters, four quarters, six weeks, or other *arbitrary* time block. You want to identify the tasks essential for gainful employment and *then* (if possible) determine how long, on the average, it will take students to master those tasks; more about competencies versus time in Chapter 7.

As a very general rule of thumb, many occupations are made up of between 50 and 150 job tasks. This is a very general guideline only. Some occupations—particularly specialized ones such as salad maker, receptionist, checker, and boat rigger—will have a limited number of tasks (and will also probably have only a few duties at most). More complex or broader occupations, such as general drafter, secretary, and cook/chef, will be comprised of many tasks (and usually more duties as well).

One last caution before we move on. Make sure you include the "higher-order" tasks performed on the job. These tasks will begin with action verbs such as evaluate, diagnose, troubleshoot, modify, construct, and analyze. Do not fall into the trap of identifying only the routine, mechanical kinds of things. You will probably want to list these higher-order tasks toward the end of the particular duty in which they fall since students will probably be mastering more basic tasks in that duty first.

Let us continue with the competency identification process for our hypothetical cosmetology program. As you recall, earlier we developed a tentative list of duties for a cosmetologist.

EXAMPLE

"Now I'm ready to begin identifying the actual job tasks performed by cosmetologists in each duty. First I'll list each duty at the top of a sheet of paper. Now I'll go through duty by duty and try to recall each service actually performed in each duty. Let's see, in conditioning and shampooing, there are plain shampoos, mild-acid rinses, dry shampoos, peroxide shampoos. . . .

"Now that I've generated a rough list of tasks in each duty from memory, I'll go through these slides and textbooks I have and see if I missed anything. Also I think I'll visit the cosmetology instructor across the county, and I also want to be sure and look at the task listing from the school in the next state that's already competency-based. Oh, I almost forgot, there's a V-TECS

catalog for cosmetology; I'll review it very carefully and make sure I'm including the V-TECS tasks that are appropriate for my local area.

"Boy, that was a job, but I think I have a pretty good tentative listing here. I changed most of the original duty statements. First, I combined "cutting wigs" and "cutting hair" since the tasks under each were almost identical. I reversed the terms "conditioning" and shampooing" to better describe the sequence of the tasks done on the job. I changed "coloring" to "tinting and bleaching" and put it after "curling and straightening." Next I combined "facials," "pedicures," and "manicures" since there were so few tasks in each one and since they all seem to belong together in light of the manicurist option in the program. Finally, I went back through the task statements I identified to make sure that each and every one was something the employer or customer was willing to pay the cosmetologist to perform. I also checked each task against the criteria listed earlier to make sure that each was written at the proper level and was precisely worded."

Before you go on, see if you can identify properly worded tasks and can write tasks by completing the following Self-Check.

SELF-CHECK [3]

Check your mastery of ENABLING OBJECTIVE [3] by completing this SELF-CHECK.

1. Below are several sample *task* statements. Some are correctly stated and some are not. Read each statement and check the appropriate column to the right. In the line below the task, indicate what is wrong with each *incorrect* task statement.

	Correct	Incorrect
(a) Install refrigerator compressor		
(b) Performing typing activities		
(c) Attach acetylene hose		
(d) Troubleshooting electromechanical devices		
(e) Meats		
(f) Attach trailer to cab		
(g) Fingerprints		
(h) Principle of electromotive force		
(i) Operate a drill press		

2. For the sample tasks below, draw *one* line under the performance, two lines under what is used or produced and three lines under any qualifiers:

   (a) Pan-fry meats

   (b) Install bumper

   (c) Remove and replace vent window

3. For one of the duty statements you wrote for Self-Check [2] list at least five job tasks within the duty.

   Duty: ______________________________

   Tasks:

   (a) ______________________________

   (b) ______________________________

   (c) ______________________________

   (d) ______________________________

   (e) ______________________________

Compare your responses with those in the Answer Key in the appendix.

ENABLING OBJECTIVE [4]

Verify Job Tasks

Why Verify Tasks?

Before the competency identification process is complete, the tentative tasks need to be *verified* to check the accuracy and need for each. A program based on out-of-date or unimportant tasks, no matter how precisely worded, would be of little benefit to the student. The aim here is to arrive at a finalized task listing that, when mastered, will lead the student to gainful employment.

The strategy for verifying our tentative tasks will be to submit the tentative task listing to qualified individuals within the occupation so that they may verify each task as being essential for entry-level employment in the occupation. If we were developing a task listing for a program that was to be adopted across an entire school district, a national company, or entire profession, we would probably want to use a more sophisticated method of verifying tasks, such as observing workers on the job. But for now, let us focus on submitting the tentative task list to qualified individuals.

What are you looking for? Basically, you want to determine which tasks on your task listing (as well as those you left off) should be included in the training program. You need to strike a good compromise between wanting to include too many because you feel "they're needed" and too few because "there's just not enough time." You might want to keep in mind that your finalized task listing should represent those job skills (you'll be adding the major units of knowledge later) that would be needed by the typical student whom you serve to enter into successfully and remain employed in the occupation(s) for which you offer training.

Now, how do you decide which tasks are worthy of inclusion in the training program? Here are some examples of criteria you and your panel of qualified individuals might use in deciding whether each tentative task should be kept or deleted (and which additional tasks to add):

EXAMPLES

- *Just how important is the task to the worker on the job?*
- *How frequently is the task performed during the first year or two of employment?*
- *How critical is the task to accomplishing the work required on the job?*
- *What percentage of workers in the occupation need the task for entry-level employment?*
- *Can the task be learned more easily after employment?*
- *Is the task a prerequisite task needed to perform others?*
- *How much time is available in the training program?*

Steps in Verifying Tasks

Following the steps outlined below might be helpful in verifying your tentative task listing using a panel of qualified individuals:

STEP 1: Make sure that you have a well-developed tentative list of duties and tasks. Go back through it one more time and make sure that the duties fully describe the different kinds of tasks performed in the occupation. See that each task statement is precisely worded, begins with an action verb, and is very clear and concise. Include only skill-oriented tasks that the worker is paid to accomplish.

STEP 2: Identify your panel of "experts" who will be involved. These should be people who have firsthand knowledge of the occupation, such as new and experienced workers, former students, supervisors, and labor. Attempt to obtain representation from a wide variety of companies and types of employers. Ten to twenty participants may be enough for some programs, whereas others may require more. Your occupational advisory committee can serve as members and perhaps help you identify others.

STEP 3: Decide if you will ask your participants to attend a general meeting to validate the tasks or if you will be mailing a list to them or making a personal visit. Each method has obvious advantages and disadvantages.

SAMPLE 3-2	TASK VERIFICATION FORM

Listed below are tasks *tentatively* identified for the welding program at Hi-Point Vo-Tech Center. Please read each task carefully and place a check mark (✓) to the right of each task that *you feel should be included as a required task to be mastered by graduates*. Base your decision on how *often* the task is performed during a welder's first year on the job or how *critical* it is to the success of a first-year welder. Please *circle* any words that you think are unclear. Add any additional tasks that you feel were omitted.

Check (✓) Tasks That Should Be Required of Graduates

A. *Cutting and Finishing Metal*

1. Drill metal using power equipment .... ______
2. Cut metal with power hacksaw .... ______
3. Shear and punch metal with iron-working machine .... ______
4. Wire brush and grind metal with power equipment .... ______
5. ______________________________
6. ______________________________

B. *Welding with Gas Welding and Burning Equipment*

1. Set up stationary and portable oxy-fuel equipment .... ______
2. Cut mild steel with oxy-acetylene equipment .... ______
3. Weld mild steel using oxy-acetylene .... ______
4. Bronze metals with oxy-acetylene equipment .... ______
5. Silver-bronze copper .... ______
6. ______________________________
7. ______________________________

C. *Welding with Shielded Metal Arc Welding Equipment*

1. Remove and replace SMAW equipment/accessories .... ______
2. Strike and control arc and run short beads .... ______
3. Build pad of beads in flat position .... ______
4. Weld single and multiple lap joints–flat position .... ______
5. Weld three- and six-pass tee joints–flat position .... ______
6. Weld outside corner joints–flat position .... ______
7. Weld butt joints–flat position .... ______
8. Weld single- and multiple-pass lap joints–horizontal .... ______
9. Weld three- and six-pass tee joints–vertical position .... ______
10. Weld outside corner joints–vertical position .... ______
11. Weld butt joints–vertical position .... ______
12. ______________________________
13. ______________________________

STEP 4: Devise an instrument on which you will type the actual tasks and on which the respondents will record their responses. An instrument such as Sample 3-2 might be used for a mailed survey. Notice that the tasks on Sample 3-2 are all "hands-on" skills which are all worthy performances. Also notice how each is worded.

STEP 5: Develop a detailed set of instructions that will make it very clear to the participant exactly what he or she is to do, upon what basis they are to rate the tasks, exactly how to respond, and what to do with the completed instrument. Mailed instruments will need more clarification than one used during a general meeting or during a personal interview.

STEP 6: Pilot-test the instrument, its instructions, and any covering letter you intend to use by having several fellow instructors, advanced students, supervisors, or workers in the occupation complete the instrument just as someone on your panel would.

STEP 7: Refine the instrument, have it duplicated, and send it to the individuals you selected.

STEP 8: Call those who failed to return the instrument by the date requested and ask them to please complete the instrument and return it at their earliest convenience. Offer to send a second copy if they lost or destroyed the first.

STEP 9: Tabulate the results on a blank copy of the instrument or by other means.

STEP 10: Carefully analyze the results of the validation process and revise the task listing by adding task statements written in by several respondents, deleting task statements rated as unimportant, and by rewording any statements marked as unclear by respondents.

Let us see how the tentative task listing was verified by our hypothetical cosmetology instructor.

EXAMPLE

"Now that I have a tentative list of duties and tasks, I'll go back through them one more time to make sure that the tasks are worded precisely.

OK, the tasks look pretty good. Now I'm ready to verfiy the tasks using a panel of experts from the field. Let's see, I'll aim for 25 participants representing small independent salons and major franchises. I'll include first-year cosmetologists and some with more experience and I'll also include several recent graduates from cosmetology programs.

"Now that I have my mailing list, I need to develop my instrument. I'll arrange the tasks in duty areas and tell respondents in the instructions to "write in the number of times they actually perform each task each week during the first two years on the job." I'll ask three or four hairdressers in the mall nearby to pilot-test my instrument to make sure that the directions and tasks are clearly worded.

"After carefully analyzing the returned instruments, I added three new tasks that were written in by several respondents; I combined two tasks into a single task, and selected better action verbs for three more. Respondents said they performed two tasks infrequently, so I eliminated them. I really feel good now about my task listing; I think I have an up-to-date list of competencies that will ensure the employment and advancement of my graduates."

The DACUM Approach

This might be a good time to mention a slightly different approach to identifying and verifying student competencies. Earlier we mentioned three different strategies: (1) observing actual workers on the job, (2) meeting with workers in the occupation, and (3) submitting a tentative task listing to workers in the occupation. The preceding section explained how the third method can be carried out.

The DACUM Approach is an example of the second method. Developed in Canada, the DACUM (*D*eveloping *A* *C*urricul*um*) process involves bringing a dozen or so workers from the occupation together for several days. With the aid of an experienced leader, the group first identifies the broad duties and then the specific tasks performed on the job. The completed DACUM chart can then serve as the task listing. Previously developed DACUM charts may be purchased by contacting the DACUM Exchange, Humber College of Applied Arts and Technology, 3199 Lakeshore Blvd. West, Toronto, Ontario M8V-1L1, Canada.

Before going on, complete the following Self-Check.

SELF-CHECK [4]

Check your mastery of ENABLING OBJECTIVE [4] by completing this SELF-CHECK.

1. List the primary reason why tasks should be verified.

2. List at least three criteria that should be used as a basis for determining whether a task should be included in a training program.

   (a) ______________________________

   (b) ______________________________

   (c) ______________________________

Compare your responses with those in the Answer Key in the appendix.

PERFORMANCE TEST FOR TASK 3

TASK 3: Identify and Verify Job Tasks

DIRECTIONS

When ready, demonstrate your ability to identify and verify job tasks by doing the following:

For one or more specific occupations:

1. Identify duties within the occupation.
2. Identify specific job tasks performed within the occupation; use any resources you have available—state tasks precisely.
3. Verify the tasks using an appropriate number of qualified individuals; use a mailed form, hold a general meeting, or conduct interviews.
4. Revise the tentative task listing based on the results of step 3.

No.	Criteria for evaluating performance; 100% mastery required	YES	NO
	Duties		
1.	Do duties describe broad categories of tasks performed on the job?		
2.	Does each begin with the "ing" form of an action verb?		
3.	Do the duties fully describe what is done in the occupation?		
	Job Tasks		
4.	Is each a worthy performance the employer or customer would pay for?		
5.	Is each task a distinct unit of work or separate activity performed on the job?		
6.	Does each have a definite beginning and ending point?		
7.	Can tasks be broken down into procedural steps from start to finish?		
8.	Is each task a job assignment or service?		
9.	Does each task result in a finished product or service or a change in the work environment?		
10.	Does each have meaning for trainees to want to learn?		
11.	Can each be taught and learned as a single unit of learning?		

12.	Does each begin with an action verb in the present tense?		
13.	Is each short and concise?		
14.	Can each be learned in approximately 6 to 30 hours?		
15.	Is each task precisely stated, describing exactly what the trainee will be able to do?		
	Task Verification Process		
16.	Were a sufficient number of people involved in the task verification process?		
17.	Were respondents representative and knowledgeable of the particular occupation?		
18.	Were tasks that were consistently rated *un*important eliminated from the tentative task listing?		
19.	Were all tasks that were consistently rated important included in the final task listing?		
20.	Were tasks written in by several respondents added to the final task listing?		
21.	Were words and phrases reworded when identified as being unclear?		
22.	Does the final list of job tasks provide a sound basis upon which to build the training program?		

Continue with the following task.

When you complete this section, you will be able to:

TASK 4: Analyze Job Tasks and Add Necessary Knowledge Tasks

INTRODUCTION

To help ensure that your students will learn the job tasks listed on your task listing as they are performed in the occupation, each task should be analyzed or broken down into the specific skills, knowledges, and attitudes required by a competent worker to perform the task. This section shows you how to *analyze job tasks* fully to identify the component parts of each so that you can more effectively select and develop learning materials to help students master each task. This section also shows you how to *add* any *knowledge tasks* that may be necessary to complete your task listing.

TERMINAL PERFORMANCE OBJECTIVE

To demonstrate mastery of this task, do the following:

Given a list of verified job tasks, fully analyze each task and add any necessary knowledge tasks to the task listing. The completed task analyses and knowledge tasks added should conform to *all* criteria listed in Performance Test 4 at the end of this section.

ENABLING OBJECTIVES

This section is divided into several parts to help you:

[1] *Analyze job tasks.*
[2] *Add necessary knowledge tasks to the task listing.*

ENABLING OBJECTIVE [1]

Analyze Job Tasks

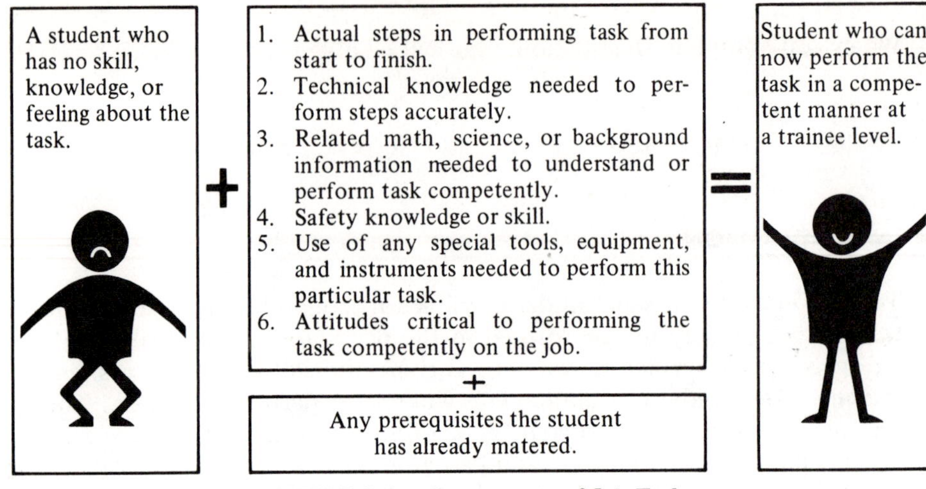

A student who has no skill, knowledge, or feeling about the task.
+
1. Actual steps in performing task from start to finish.
2. Technical knowledge needed to perform steps accurately.
3. Related math, science, or background information needed to understand or perform task competently.
4. Safety knowledge or skill.
5. Use of any special tools, equipment, and instruments needed to perform this particular task.
6. Attitudes critical to performing the task competently on the job.
+
Any prerequisites the student has already matered.
=
Student who can now perform the task in a competent manner at a trainee level.

FIGURE 3-3 Components of Job Tasks

Task Analysis

The next step in putting together a competency-based program is to *analyze* each task fully. As you recall, analyzing an occupation involves breaking it down into its component parts—*tasks*. Similarly, analyzing a *task* involves breaking it down into its component parts—*steps* and supporting *knowledge* and *attitudes*.

The result of a *task analysis* is a detailed listing of the specific *skills*, *knowledges*, and *attitudes* required by the worker to perform a specific task in a competent manner *on the job*. These component parts will then become the instructional "content" the trainee will learn.

> Task analysis is the process of identifying and writing down the specific *skills*, *knowledges*, and *attitudes* that distinguish someone who performs a task *competently* from someone who *cannot perform* the task at all.

You have *fully* analyzed a task when you have written down (1) all the distinct, procedural *steps*, (2) the facts, concepts, and other *knowledges*, and (3) the critical values and *attitudes* that, when learned by your students, will make them competent in that task at a trainee level. We might look at most job tasks as having *six* major components (for instructional planning purposes, anyway) that are essential to performing the task on the job in a competent manner. Figure 3-3 shows these six components.

Now, you might ask: "Just *how much* knowledge, skill, and attitude should be identified when analyzing a task?" A general answer to that question is: "*All* the essential skills, knowledges, and attitudes—but *only* the essential ones—that are needed by the worker to perform the task competently on the job."

Sample 3-3 shows a form that might be helpful in analyzing tasks. There is a space on the form for each of the six components of a typical task. Look at Sample 3-3 and note the following points:

1. The "backbone" of the task analysis is the actual *steps* performed by the worker on the job (remember what determines human competence).
2. The task has been fully analyzed from start to finish.
3. Any technical knowledge ("at eye level") *essential* to performing a step accurately ("Remove thermometer and read") is listed together with the step.
4. A specialized instrument (oral thermometer) needed to perform *just this task* has been identified.
5. Related information, safety knowledge, and skill and critical attitudes that *support* the competent *performance* of the task are listed.

Why Analyze Tasks?

Breaking a task down into its component parts *before* planning instruction offers several benefits:

1. Each specific step required to correctly and completely perform the task is identified and *written down* so that we can make sure that our learning activities fully teach all these steps.
2. The technical knowledge essential to performing the steps accurately and completely are identified so that we can make sure that this knowledge is learned by the student.
3. Specialized tools and materials needed to perform *just this task* can be identified so that extra care can be taken in helping the student master the use of these *as the task is being learned.*
4. Any related math, science, or background information needed to perform the task can be identified so that we can make sure that the student learns it before or perhaps during the task itself.
5. Critical safety knowledge and skills can be spotted so that we can make sure that our instructional materials address each safety point *as it occurs.*
6. Critical attitudes that are an integral part of performing the task competently can be identified and learned by the student *along with* the skills and knowledges.

SAMPLE 3-3	TASK ANALYSIS FORM	
TASK No. C-09	Take Temperature Orally	
Procedural Steps and Technical Knowledge	List each procedural step and technical knowledge required to perform task from start to finish on the job (use the back also).	
	1. Identify correct patient and explain procedure. 2. Wash hands–make sure hands are *thoroughly* cleaned. 3. Select *oral* thermometer. 4. Remove from container and shake mercury down to 95°F (35°C). 5. Wipe thermometer with tissue to remove solution. 6. Have patient sit or lie down quietly–patient should not have had hot or cold drink or smoked; if so, wait 30 minutes. 7. Place mercury tip gently under patient's tongue. 8. Keep in place 3 minutes. 9. Remove thermometer and read at eye level. 10. Shake mercury down to 95°F (35°C). 11. Clean with tissue and replace in holder. 12. Record reading on pad with patient's name, room number, time, and date. 13. Make patient comfortable. 14. Wash hands.	
Tools	List *special* tools, equipment, materials, etc., needed to perform this task:	Oral thermometer
Related	List related math, science, or background knowledge needed to perform this task competently:	1. Normal body temperature. 2. Body heat causes mercury to expand. 3. Possible results of excessive temperature. 4. Recording reading in decimals.
Safety	List critical safety knowledge and skill needed to perform this task in safe manner:	1. Washing hands. 2. Don't drop thermometer–glass. 3. Use clean thermometer.
Attitudes	List attitudes critical to performing this task in a competent manner on the job:	1. Put patient at ease. 2. Explain procedure courteously.

7. An outline of the procedural steps that might be included in a slide-tape presentation, procedure sheet, or other learning resource is now available. The *steps* will be used to plan the slides or other visuals that we may need and the technical knowledge will become the narration.
8. Particularly complex, new, or dangerous steps can be spotted so that extra care can be taken in developing learning resources to teach those steps.
9. Sequencing of tasks in a program is easier since a quick review of the six components of a task will indicate which earlier tasks might be prerequisites.
10. Developing comprehensive, objective performance tests and written tests is much easier when the specific skills, knowledges, and attitudes required to perform the task have been identified and written down.

Let us look next at how we might identify the six basic components of typical tasks. You might want to go back and refer to the task analysis form in Sample 3-3.

Identifying Steps and Technical Knowledge

The steps and technical knowledge can be identified by having someone who is competent at performing the task (such as an occupationally competent instructor) physically "walk through" the actual performance of the task, *as it would be performed on the job*. Each separate step performed is written down (or spoken into a tape recorder) as it naturally occurs; videotaping is helpful for this. As each step is identified, any technical *knowledge* that is *essential* to perform that step correctly, completely, and safely is added. This technical knowledge is commonly referred to as *directly related* knowledge, since it relates directly to performing each step.

Task Analysis Formats. For many years a *two*-column format for identifying steps and knowledge has been used—the left column for the "key steps" (doing) and the right for the "essential knowledges" (knowing) for each step. This format is fine except for one drawback. It tends to separate the steps and knowledges. Since the steps and the essential knowledges are used together on the job and should therefore be mastered *as one* during the learning process, it probably makes more sense to incorporate the steps and knowledges into a *single* list such as that in Sample 3-3.

A single-column task analysis format seems to be easier to develop and use in planning learning resources. This format keeps the steps and the knowledges tied closely together, which is how they should be learned by trainees. Whatever format is used, the goal is the same—to identify the actual steps required to perform the task on the job and the essential technical knowledge required to perform the steps correctly.

Tips

Below are several tips to keep in mind when analyzing tasks to identify the steps and technical knowledge:

1. Use a single-column format to keep the analysis simple and to keep the steps and knowledges tied together. Use a form such as the one shown in Sample 3-3.
2. Focus on describing the steps and technical knowledge involved in performing the task *on the job*—not on learning the task in the training program.
3. Fully analyze the task from start to finish. Be very careful not to skip over steps or knowledge that have become second nature to you.
4. Include implied steps that the learner will not be familiar with. Keep the level of your students in mind when deciding how much detail to include.
5. Begin each step with an action verb (place, insert, adjust, etc.).
6. Do not include trivial steps that would be common knowledge or obvious to the student, such as "pick up pliers," or "walk over to patient."
7. Do not go into great detail on complex steps in the analysis—you will do that later when you develop media or other learning resources to teach the step—right now just identify the steps and knowledges.
8. Remember that the task analysis is *not* for use by trainees (in its present form, anyway)—it is for the instructor's use in planning learning activities and resources and in developing tests.
9. Include essential knowledges needed to perform each step accurately and safely, such as how tight, why, when, how many, what happens if not, where, which one, and so on.
10. Be sure to note any cautions or danger points as they occur.
11. Try performing the task (or have someone else—preferably a student—try the task) by following the steps. Revise the steps and knowledges as needed.
12. Do not include knowledge that is really not needed to perform the steps.
13. If the task can be performed several different ways, stick to the most common or easiest method to master.
14. Keep in mind that some basic tasks (such as "wash hands using sterile techniques") may appear as a single *step* in the analysis of later more complex tasks (such as "take temperature"). In this example, "wash hands" is simply listed as a step in the more complex task without any further analysis.
15. Many steps will not require any knowledge at all—do not force it.
16. For some tasks, shop manuals, procedure sheets, equipment directions, manufacturer's technical bulletins, and other sources may already have

the steps and technical knowledges identified. V-TECS catalogs have the *steps* listed for each task under the heading "Performance Guide." If you use a source such as these, it is still a good idea to have someone try to perform the task following the steps given to make sure that the steps are accurate and complete. Also, you will need to add to the analysis the related information, safety points, special tools, and attitudes.

Special Tools and Equipment

The second section of the task analysis form provides space to list *specialized* tools and equipment unique to that task. The *routine* kinds of tools, instruments, equipment, and supplies that are used while the task is performed can be identified by simply looking at the steps. On the analysis form, we are interested primarily in *specialized* tools, equipment, or materials needed to perform *this task only*. The aim here is to have the student learn to use any specialized tool *when it is needed*. For example, to perform the task "deep-fry frozen foods," the trainee would need to know how to use the deep-fat fryer. It would make much more sense for the student to learn how to use the piece of equipment when he or she sees the *need* for it and when the equipment can be *used* immediately. Showing students how to use the fryer during a unit called "Tools and Equipment" (usually taught during the first few weeks of a program) would be a waste of both the student's and the instructor's time. Later in the program, when the student actually needed the fryer, it would have to be learned all over again.

Related Information

In some cases there may be information needed by the worker to perform a task but not *directly related* to the steps in performing the task. This knowledge can be viewed as being *generally related* and may include math skills, science concepts, background information, or other knowledge helpful to the workers as the task is performed. If this generally related knowledge is very *complex* or is required to perform *several* tasks (for example, knowledge of how a battery works would be needed to perform the tasks "Change a battery," "Service a battery," and "Install a battery") students may need to learn major units of knowledge like this as a complete, separate unit of instruction *before* beginning the tasks for which it is needed. (More about these major units of knowledge later.) Any related knowledge needed for one task only, however, should be learned right along with the task itself.

Safety

We also want to identify on the analysis form any safety-related knowledge or skill the worker needs to perform the task safely on the job. Specific

EXAMPLES: Generally Related Information

Task	Math	Science	Background Information
Estimate blocks	*Compute area*		*Size of blocks; how many blocks in a square foot*
Grind valves	*Recognize angles*	*Heat causes expansion of metal*	*How valves work; metal makeup of valve faces*
Sterilize instruments		*Certain conditions foster and inhibit bacteria growth*	
Charge a battery	*Figuring charging rate*	*Chemical process involved in battery operation*	*How battery works; basic electricity*
Treat soil to eliminate weeds	*Ratio and proportions*	*How herbicides kill weeds*	*Various kinds of weeds*

cautions are usually noted in the steps and technical knowledge listed in the first section of the task analysis form. A separate section for safety is included on the form to list any general safety needed throughout the performance of the task and to summarize any cautions and safety checkpoints identified as a part of the steps. As you plan instruction, the safety section of the form will call your attention to the safety practices that should be mastered together with the actual steps in performing the task.

Attitudes

The last section of the task analysis form is for identifying attitudes that are critical to performing the task in a competent manner on the job. The aim here is to present these attitudes to the student *when they are called for* in performing the task. A critical attitude for the task "prepare patient for major surgery" might be "assist in reducing patient's fear or anxieties."

Why List All Components on One Form?

The major advantage of listing the specific knowledges, skills, and attitudes required to perform a task competently on *one* form is so that learning activities developed for the task can treat these components as a whole—just as they are needed on the job. Let us look at some examples to see what we mean.

EXAMPLE

Ms. Woodrow, the principal at East High School, had a very efficient schedule worked out for next year. Mr. Lewis, the graphic arts instructor, hit the ceiling when he saw that the proposed schedule had his students scheduled for three hours of "theory" and three hours of "lab" each day. Ms. Woodrow thought she had done a marvelous job scheduling classrooms and labs for maximum utilization. She was quite perturbed when Mr. Lewis protested with: "My students don't need three hours of theory each day. The only time my students learn theory is when they need it while performing a job out in the shop!"

We cannot blame Ms. Woodrow totally since she probably received the same kind of professional training as most school administrators from academic backgrounds—heavy emphasis on administration and related areas with little or no exposure to vocational-technical education, especially the philosophy of training competent graduates. Ms. Woodrow violated the basic principle underlying this particular section—students should learn knowledge only *if* and *when* it is needed to ensure competence in a task.

We just looked at an example illustrating how *not* to present knowledge to students. Now let us look at how we should.

EXAMPLE

After experimenting for many years, Mrs. Perry finally came up with a system that worked. She had been having great difficulty with students mastering major units of "theory" in the hospital-based nursing program–particularly anatomy/physiology, bacteriology, and medical terms. When she began teaching she included these topics very early in the two-year training program–after all, students had to master these very important areas of theory before they could do anything. She found, however, that she was having to repeat much of it throughout the two years. The system that seemed to produce the best results was to teach the specific knowledge about anatomy/physiology, bacteriology, and medical terms when students actually needed that knowledge to learn a new nursing procedure. For example, while students were learning how to "suction a tracheostomy," Mrs. Perry taught them all the required knowledge about anatomy and physiology specifically relating to the tracheostomy procedure. Also included were facts and concepts dealing with bacteriology as they related to tracheostomy.

The medical terminology directly related to this one procedure was also taught as it came up in the process of performing the task. As Mrs. Perry continued to break her major units of "theory" up into small bits of knowledge–

teaching each bit of knowledge when it was needed to perform a task–*she soon had nothing left in her theory courses! Mrs. Perry reported that she was angry that someone did not show her how to do this sooner, since it improved student test results, reduced absenteeism, and even seemed to help reduce the first-quarter attrition rate.*

If you followed this example, you got the message that the specific concepts, facts, terms, and other knowledge needed to perform a job task should be learned together with the actual steps in performing the task. After all, that is when the knowledge is needed on the job—when the task is being performed. In a later chapter we get into developing self-contained learning packages that will present these steps and knowledges when each is needed.

Not only should the technical knowledge *directly* related to performing a task correctly be learned while the task is learned, but use of any specialized tools, instruments, equipment, and materials, as well as generally related knowledge such as math skills, science concepts, and attitudes and safety techniques, should also be incorporated into the learning activities for the task itself—when each is needed.

EXAMPLE

A large copying-machine company was putting together a comprehensive training program for its field service technician trainees. One of their trainers was writing a training module titled "Identify and Replace Malfunctioning Transistors." Luckily, this trainer was of the competency-based school of thought. After fully analyzing the task to identify the steps and technical knowledge required to perform the task on the job, he identified the specialized equipment, helpful background information, safety techniques, and math skills needed to support the competent performance of the task on the job. He decided to design the training module around the steps needed to identify and replace a malfunctioning transistor but to weave into the module when needed*:*

- *How to use a transistor tester to isolate a malfunctioning transistor*
- *Safety relating to working on transistor circuits and in soldering*
- *How transistors are constructed and how to select proper replacements*
- *Math skills needed for computing transistor circuit values*
- *How to solder transistors without heat damage*

Of course, the module focused on the actual steps a technician would perform in identifying and replacing a malfunctioning transistor (look at the task again). The module began with how a transistor operates since the technician needs that knowledge right then. *As each component of the task listed above was* needed *in performing the task on the job, that knowledge was presented* at that time, *which was the teachable moment.*

Tips

Keep these points in mind as you go about the process of breaking tasks into the basic components of each:

1. The heart of the task analysis is the actual *steps* required to perform the task from start to finish—on the job.
2. Technical knowledge should be learned right along with the actual steps required to perform the task—not in a separate "theory" class separated from the task by days or months.
3. The teachable moment for *generally* related knowledge such as math or science is *when that knowledge is most needed.*
4. Students can master concepts, facts, and terms better if they see the need for it and have something to "hang it on," such as a job-related task. Knowledge taught for knowledge's sake is of little value. Learning how to read a micrometer scale in a theory class can be boring and difficult. Learning how to read a micrometer *as a part of* learning how to "inspect machined parts" has meaning for students since they can easily see *why* they are learning it and have something to *apply* it to.
5. Not all tasks will have specialized tools, related information, safety points, or critical attitudes.
6. Use the task analysis as your blueprint for developing learning activities, evaluating new media and other resources, and developing tests.

Possible Results. I think we both agree that certain knowledges and attitudes are absolutely essential to competence. I have presented a little different philosophy in this section concerning *how* and *when* these knowledges and attitudes should be learned. Basically I am saying:

> While students are learning the actual hands-on skills needed to perform a task, they should *also* learn the technical knowledge, specific math skills, and related concepts, information, safety practices, critical attitudes, and the use of specialized tools and equipment needed to perform the task.

If you will follow this basic principle, I think you will see some very significant things begin to happen:

1. Discipline problems may be reduced.
2. Absenteeism and tardiness may go down.
3. Attrition usually experienced during "theory" classes may drop drastically.
4. Students will learn knowledge faster, with less complaining and to a higher level.
5. You will discover some areas of knowledge you have been teaching that, quite frankly, have no place in the program.
6. You will discover other areas of knowledge that are needed but were not included previously.
7. Students will stay busier, longer.
8. Critical attitudes will take on new meaning to students.
9. Learning to use tools, instruments, and equipment will become less of a chore for students.
10. Students will begin hands-on activities during the first few days of the training program, sharply increasing their motivation and chances of early success.

One last thought on the idea of having separate classes, courses, and units on knowledge and theory only:

> Perhaps we should give some thought to striking the word "theory" from the training vocabulary. A theory is nothing more than a very educated guess about how or why something behaves as it does. Hopefully, in training programs, the supporting knowledge we teach is more than just theory. Let us hope that we are giving trainees the *concrete* concepts, facts, principles, and information they need to be competent in performing job tasks in the occupation.

Before going on to the next section, see if you can identify uses of task analysis and if you can fully analyze a task by completing the following Self-Check.

SELF CHECK [1]

Check your mastery of ENABLING OBJECTIVE [1] by completing this SELF-CHECK.

1. List at least three practical uses of a completed task analysis form like the one shown in this section.

(a) ____________________

(b) ____________________

(c) ____________________

2. Select five typical tasks from a task listing. Fully analyze each task from start to finish using a form like Sample 3-3. Include all six components on the form that are a part of each task.

Compare your responses with those in the Answer Key in the appendix.

ENABLING OBJECTIVE [2]

Add Necessary Knowledge Tasks to the Task Listing

Major Units of Knowledge

The preceding section stressed the fact that knowledge *directly* related to performing a task in a competent manner should be learned by the student together with the procedural steps in performing the task. Because of this, *very few* knowledge-oriented task statements will appear on the task listing for a program. Occasionally, however, students may need knowledge that cannot easily be learned as a part of a *single* task. These major units of knowledge usually cut across many tasks.

The distinction should be made between the *major* unit of knowledge and technical knowledge needed to perform specific skills. For a worker in a commercial cooking program to correctly perform the task "prepare a meat loaf," he or she would need to know how to perform the actual steps *as well* as a certain amount of *technical* knowledge *directly related* to preparing a meat loaf, such as temperature setting, which ingredients to use, how long to bake, and so on.

> *Major* units of knowledge, however, are *not* directly related to one task, but cut across many tasks and are listed as separate competency (task) statements on the program task listing.

For example, knowledge of how bacteria grow would not be directly related to a *single* task in a health occupations program, but would be a major unit of knowledge that would contribute to the correct performance of *many* tasks, such as washing hands, giving medication, and so on. In this example, a knowledge task might be added to the program task listing worded something like: "Describe conditions that promote and inhibit bacteria growth." It is *not* a worthy accomplishment performed on the job for which the employee is paid but, rather, is a major unit of knowledge supporting the competent performance of *many* tasks, therefore not lending itself well to being learned as a part of any *one* task. These major units of knowledge stand alone and are listed on the task listing with the job tasks.

You will develop complete units of instruction for these knowledge tasks just as you will for the job tasks. Most programs will have only a very limited number of knowledge tasks; many programs will have none.

Identifying Major Units of Knowledge

Keep in mind that knowledge tasks *cannot* be identified by asking "What does the worker *do* on the job" like job tasks can. Actually, the knowledge tasks cannot be identified until *after* the job tasks have been identified and analyzed. Once the skills have been identified and analyzed, you can review the completed task analyses and ask: "What *broad* major units of knowledge does the student need that seem to be common to many tasks and would therefore not make sense to learn along with any one task?" A good place to look is the generally related area of the task analysis form. These broad areas of basic principles, concepts, facts, or other information cutting across many tasks may be the knowledge tasks for a competency-based program.

Stating Knowledge Tasks Precisely

It is somewhat more difficult to write precisely worded knowledge tasks than to write skill tasks. Let us look at a typical statement that might be found in a more traditional course of study:

Electrical resistance

Although this statement does describe a major unit of knowledge that cuts across many job tasks in an electronics program, it does not pin down *what* we want the student to know about electrical resistance. Do we want the student to *define* the term, *explain* how it happens, *compute* some values for resistance, or what? We simply cannot tell from the statement as it is worded. The statement would be much more precise if worded something like this:

Compute values of electrical resistance

Now we know what behavior we want the trainee to exhibit when completing this particular part of the training program. Equally important, we know precisely what we have to teach and what we should test. So you can see that just as for job tasks, precision is important for knowledge tasks. The following general criteria should be helpful in stating knowledge competencies for programs.

Knowledge Tasks:

1. Describe broad, major units of knowledge not directly related to a single skill task.
2. Contribute to the worker's overall safety, efficiency, or background knowledge within the occupation.
3. Can be learned as a separate unit of instruction.
4. Should begin with an action verb in the present tense.
5. Should describe *exactly* what the student will do as evidence that he or she possesses the desired knowledge.
6. Are listed right together with the skill tasks on the task listing for a training program.
7. Vary in number from none to a "handful."

Components of Knowledge Tasks. You saw earlier that skill tasks have three components: the *performance*, *what is used or produced*, and sometimes, *qualifiers*. Knowledge tasks usually have only the first two of these components, as shown in Table 3-7. Notice that each of these examples covers a broad unit of knowledge that cuts across several other tasks in the particular program.

Levels of Knowledge Tasks. Knowledge tasks can be viewed as having several *levels*. At the very lowest level we are interested only in students mastering basic facts, terms, and other specifics. One way to look at this lowest level is that students can sometimes memorize these. From this lowest level, we can go higher up into levels where we want students to do more than just demonstrate basic knowledge.

These higher levels include:

- *Comprehension* of true meanings
- *Applying* principles

TABLE 3-7 Components of "Knowledge" Task Statements

Performance	*Area of Knowledge*
Describe	Structure and characteristics of teeth
Explain	Operation of a cooling system
Trace	Major steps in the refrigeration system
Describe	Operation of a four-stroke engine
Identify	Violations warranting arrest
Trace	Flow of blood through the cardiovascular system
Explain	Basic operation of a digital computer
Identify	Markings and notations on a navigational chart

- *Analyzing* or breaking down ideas or concepts
- *Synthesizing* parts into a meaningful whole
- *Evaluating* methods, procedures, and so on, by applying appropriate criteria

The important thing to remember here is to make sure to state knowledge tasks at the *appropriate* level. If we have a knowledge task stated:

Identify methods of reproducing copies

then *all* we can expect the student to be able to do is just that—identify a certain number of copying methods. But is that *all* we really want the student to learn? Perhaps the student really needs to be able to

Select the best copying method for a situation

You can see that the ability to *select* the best method from several alternatives is a higher-level knowledge task than simply being able to *identify* the methods. Of course, as a part of learning to select the best method, the student would first learn what the various methods are. So keep in mind as you write task statements for major units of knowledge to specify the actual

TABLE 3-8 Typical Learner Performances for Knowledge Tasks

Accept	Convert	Explain	Mention	Resolve
Adapt	Copy	Express	Name	Respond
Adopt	Correct	Figure	Order	Restate
Allow	Correlate	Find	Organize	Review
Analyze	Create	Follow	Pick	Revise
Answer	Decide	Form	Place	Say
Apply	Define	Formulate	Plan	Schedule
Appraise	Demonstrate	Generalize	Predict	Select
Arrange	Describe	Give	Prepare	Set up
Assemble	Design	Grade	Propose	Sketch
Assess	Determine	Group	Punctuate	Solve
Associate	Develop	Identify	Question	Specify
Calculate	Devise	Illustrate	Quiz	Synthesize
Categorize	Diagram	Indicate	Quote	Tabulate
Choose	Differentiate	Infer	Rank	Talk
Cite	Discuss	Inspect	Rate	Test
Classify	Distinguish	Interpret	Realize	Trace
Compare	Divide	Isolate	Reason	Transcribe
Compile	Draw	Itemize	Recall	Translate
Complete	Employ	Judge	Recognize	Underline
Compose	Enumerate	Label	Record	Use
Compute	Equate	List	Relate	Utilize
Conclude	Estimate	Locate	Repeat	Validate
Construct	Evaluate	Match	Reply	Verify
Contrast	Examine	Measure	Report	Write

behavior you really want the learner to be able to demonstrate. If the job requires the ability to *analyze* a situation, do not use an action verb like *describe*! If the ability to *evaluate* is called for, do not settle for *explain*! Table 3-8 lists typical action verbs that may help you write knowledge tasks.

How Are Knowledge Tasks Analyzed?

Analyzing knowledge tasks is somewhat different from analyzing job tasks. It is fairly easy to identify the steps in performing job tasks since all we do is list each step involved in performing the task on the job. Most knowledge tasks, however, really do not have a set procedure or step-by-step process that is followed. The goal in analyzing knowledge tasks is to identify the key points, facts, concepts, and so on, that the trainee needs to master to be able to demonstrate competence in the knowledge task as it is stated.

Let us look at Table 3-9 to see how a knowledge task might be analyzed. Notice that this analysis looks like an *outline* rather than a step-by-step sequence of events. That is really what the task analysis for a knowledge task is—a content outline.

Tips

Here are some tips to remember in analyzing knowledge tasks:

1. The analysis or outline should fully cover the major unit of knowledge described by the task statement.
2. The content identified in the analysis should be sufficient to allow the learner to perform the knowledge task at the *level* stated in the task. If the performance component of the knowledge task says "evaluate, differentiate, or select," the analysis must go beyond just listing facts.

TABLE 3-9 Typical Task Analysis for a Knowledge Task

Task: Describe Basic Elements of Accounting

I. *Assets*: anything of monetary value owned by a business.
   A. *Physical items*—supplies, furniture, etc.
   B. *Rights or claim*—notes, etc.
   C. *Accounts receivable*—money owed the business.
   D. *Cash*—money, checks, money orders, bank accounts, etc.
   E. *Goods*—raw material or inventory on hand.
   F. *Equipment*—tools, equipment, machinery, etc.

II. *Liabilities*—debts that a business owes.
   A. *Loans*—money still owed from loans.
   B. *Accounts payable*—credit extended to the business for purchases.

III. *Owner's Equity*—claims that the owner has against the assets of the business (total assets minus total liabilities). Also called partner's equity, stockholder's equity or capital, or net worth.

IV. *The accounting equation*: assets = liabilities + owner's equity.

3. Do not worry about how the student will learn the facts of concepts in the analysis—at this point you just want to make sure you identify them.
4. Avoid the temptation to include more in the analysis than students actually need to know to function effectively on the job. Such things as historical aspects and nice-to-know things are luxuries the student usually does not have time for.

Tasks in General Areas

Some program planners may wish to add selected tasks to the task listing in general areas.

EXAMPLES

- *Orientation and shop procedures*
- *Employability skills (job-keeping skills)*
- *Math skills*
- *Employment skills (job-seeking skills)*
- *Communication skills*
- *Other areas*

Remember that, for example, specific math or communications skills that are needed for a *single* task should be learned as an integral part of the task and would *not* be listed as a separate task on the task listing.

Whether particular tasks are added in these or other general areas depends on factors such as:

- The philosophy and goals of the training program
- How much training time is available
- Whether a large number of students are lacking in these areas
- What age level and educational background typical students represent
- Whether qualified instructors are available
- Feedback from employers of previous program completers
- Other considerations

Table 3-10 lists typical task statements in general areas that might appear on task listings—notice that they are stated with precision, just as job and knowledge tasks are.

Developing the Final Task Listing

The ultimate goal is to arrive at a finalized, verified, precisely worded task listing that spells out the specific job tasks and the few major units of knowledge students will need to attain their employment goals. The resulting finalized task listing can now become the foundation upon which to build the competency-based training program. Keep in mind that the additional time and effort required to arrive at a valid, precisely worded task listing will yield great dividends as the program planning process continues. Selection of

TABLE 3-10 Typical Task Statements in General Areas

Communication Skills
Spell and define selected words in the occupation
Construct basic sentences
Construct complex sentences
Write a technical report
Write a summary of an oral message
Write a summary of a written message
Improve listening skills
Write a letter and memo
Prepare and deliver an oral report
Identify nonverbal communication techniques
Apply the problem-solving approach to job-related problems
Employment Skills
Describe employment opportunities in the occupation
Identify job openings through ads, agencies, etc.
Prepare a résumé and letter of application
Apply for a job
Participate in a job interview
Identify employee characteristics that lead to dismissal and advancement
Math Skills
Perform basic operations using whole numbers (+ − × ÷)
Perform basic operations using fractions
Perform basic operations using decimals
Convert English units to metric
Solve problems using ratio and proportion
Solve problems using an electronic calculator
Solve basic algebraic equations
Compute volume and area of basic shapes and solids
Use basic measuring devices
Solve problems involving triangles
Interpret graphic data, tables, and charts
Employability Skills
Work without unnecessary supervision
Work cooperatively with others
Accept supervision with a positive attitude
Follow accepted safety practices
Leave work area clean and orderly
Keep accurate records
Dress as required on the job
Return tools and equipment in ready-to-use condition
Avoid wasting materials and supplies
Attend daily and on time
Avoid distracting others
Avoid horseplay

learning experiences, development of learning materials and media, and the development of tests will all be greatly enhanced if a sound task listing is developed first!

Back to our cosmetology example. Our instructor is now ready to add any major units of knowledge that would be difficult to learn as an integral part of specific tasks. As we look in, we hear our instructor thinking aloud:

> *EXAMPLE*
>
> *"OK, now that I have the job tasks identified and verified, I know that I'm on target. Since I have each task fully analyzed into its component skills, knowledge, and attitudes, I can be fairly confident of selecting or developing learning materials that will teach each. I can also develop written and performance tests that fully assess mastery of what the student must know and be able to do to be competent.*
>
> *Now then, let's look through my task analyses and see what knowledge seems to show up in many of the tasks. Let's see, here's one: the structure of hair seems to be pretty important for many of the tasks. How hair is structured and behaves is important for cutting, shaping, bleaching, curling, and other tasks. Another major unit of knowledge I might need to develop a separate learning package for is. . . ."*

Our instructor tentatively identified three major units of knowledge for which separate units of instruction would be needed:

A-01: Describe structure and characteristics of hair.
A-03: Describe principles of chemistry relating to cosmetology.
E-01: Describe structure and characteristics of skin and nails.

After much thought and after discussing it with several instructors and salon owners, our cosmetology instructor decided to include several tasks in general areas that are critical to success in cosmetology. They were added as tasks on the task listing to call the students' attention to the importance of each and to the fact that the student would be evaluated on each, and to call the employer's attention to the fact that the student had been through a formal learning activity on each. The tasks in general areas added to the program task listing included:

G-01: Display appropriate grooming and personal hygiene practices.
G-02: Apply for a job.

The finalized version of the task listing looked as shown in Sample 3-4.

Revising Tasks

As mentioned earlier, the program task listing should be revised periodically. During the first year or two of operation of the program the listing will

SAMPLE 3-4	OCCUPATION: Cosmetologist	TASK LISTING

DUTY A: Shampooing and Conditioning the Hair and Scalp

01. Describe structure and characteristics of hair.
02. Set up a wet and dry sanitizer.
03. Describe principles of chemistry relating to cosmetology.
04. Mix hair solutions and colors.
05. Give a plain shampoo.
06. Give a conditioning shampoo.
07. Give a mild-acid rinse.
08. Give a dry shampoo.
09. Give a peroxide shampoo.
10. Assess hair damage and apply appropriate conditioner.
11. Give scalp treatment using manipulations.
12. Give scalp treatment using heat cap.

DUTY B: Shaping and Styling Hair, Wigs, and Hairpieces

01. Select hairstyle for patron.
02. Give a basic scissor cut.
03. Give a razor cut.
04. Layer-cut hair.
05. Create a finger-wave style.
06. Create a hairstyle using sculpture curls.
07. Create a hairstyle using rollers.
08. Thin hair.
09. Blow-wave hair.
10. Clean wig or hairpiece.
11. Cut, set, and style wig or hairpiece.
12. Tint wig or hairpiece.

DUTY C: Curling and Straightening Hair

01. Give a cold wave.
02. Straighten hair chemically.
03. Straighten hair with a pressing comb.

SAMPLE 3-4 (cont'd)	OCCUPATION: Cosmetologist	TASK LISTING

DUTY D: Tinting and Bleaching Hair

01. Select and apply temporary hair color.
02. Select and apply semipermanent hair color.
03. Determine skin sensitivity of patron.
04. Select and apply virgin permanent hair color.
05. Apply a virgin bleach.
06. Frost the hair.
07. Remove artificial hair color.

DUTY E: Giving Facials, Manicures, and Pedicures

01. Describe structure and characteristics of skin and nails.
02. Give a facial.
03. Apply makeup.
04. Give a plain manicure.
05. Give an oil manicure.
06. Repair nails.

DUTY F: Keeping Records

01. Order supplies.
02. Maintain appointment records.
03. Record patron's chemical treatments.
04. Obtain and renew license.

DUTY G: Employability and Related Skills

01. Display appropriate grooming and personal hygiene practices.
02. Apply for a job.

be revised numerous times as learning materials are developed. You will find some tasks too specific, and some too broad; some may be combined and others broken down further into two or more tasks. After this initial period of development, the task listing should be reviewed at least annually by advisory committee members, former students, workers and supervisors in the occupation, and others. Tasks in new and emerging areas should be added, obsolete tasks should be dropped, and those task statements that may have been fuzzy or difficult to develop instructional materials for should be reworded. Conscientious revision of the task listing will result in a training program based on job competencies that will allow graduates to enter the job market smoothly as productive workers.

See if you can identify and write correctly worded knowledge tasks by completing the following Self-Check.

SELF-CHECK [2]

Check your mastery of ENABLING OBJECTIVE [2] by completing this SELF-CHECK.

1. Below are listed several major units of knowledge that might appear as knowledge tasks on typical task listings. Some are worded correctly and some are not. Read each carefully and check in the column to the right those you feel are worded correctly:

	Correct
(a) Understand operation of x-ray machine	
(b) Demonstrate the ability to solve problems with right triangles	
(c) Identify and describe operation of components of electrical system	
(d) Marketing principles	
(e) Evaluate typical building designs	

2. Identify and state precisely two major units of knowledge that might be included on the task listing for a program you are familiar with.

   (a) ______________________________

   (b) ______________________________

Compare your responses with those in the Answer Key in the appendix.

PERFORMANCE TEST FOR TASK 4

TASK 4: Analyze Job Tasks and Add Necessary Knowledge Tasks

DIRECTIONS

When ready, demonstrate your ability to analyze job tasks and add necessary knowledge tasks by doing the following:

For a list of job tasks that have been verified:

1. Fully analyze each job task using a task analysis form similar to Sample 3-3.
2. Review the analysis of each job task and then add any necessary knowledge tasks to the task listing at appropriate points.
3. Fully analyze each knowledge task.

No.	Criteria for evaluating performance; 100% mastery required	YES	NO
	Analysis of Job Tasks		
1.	Are steps in performing each task listed as they would be performed on the job?		
2.	Is each task analyzed from start to finish?		
3.	Does each step begin with an action verb?		
4.	Are trivial or obvious steps omitted?		
5.	Is great detail avoided on complex steps?		
6.	Is all essential technical knowledge needed to correctly and safely perform each step included?		
7.	Is all nonessential knowledge omitted?		
8.	Are all cautions and danger points noted?		
9.	Is only one method of performing each task included in the analysis?		
10.	Has each analysis avoided mention of how the task should be taught or learned?		
11.	Is any required background knowledge such as math, science, etc., noted?		
12.	Is any special tool, instrument, or equipment needed for this particular task noted?		

13.	Are any attitudes critical to performing task competently on the job noted?		
	Any Knowledge Tasks Added		
14.	Is each knowledge task a broad, major unit of knowledge cutting across several skill tasks?		
15.	Can each be learned as a separate unit of learning?		
16.	Does each begin with an action verb in the present tense?		
17.	Is each action verb at the appropriate level needed by the trainee on the job?		
18.	Is each statement clear and concise, describing exactly what trainees will do to demonstrate mastery of the knowledge?		
	Analysis of Knowledge Tasks		
19.	Does content outline fully cover the scope of the major unit of knowledge?		
20.	Is the content appropriate for students to master the task at the level stated?		
21.	Does the analysis avoid any mention of learning or teaching activities?		
22.	Does the analysis include only the facts, concepts, etc., essential for mastery of the knowledge task as stated?		

4

Writing and Sequencing Terminal Performance Objectives

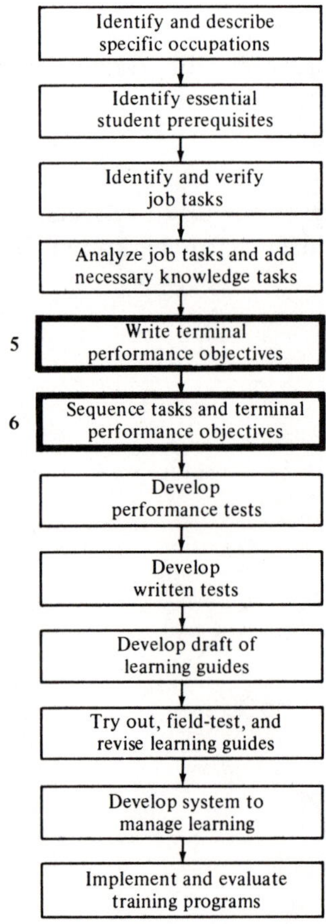

Identify and describe specific occupations
Identify essential student prerequisites
Identify and verify job tasks
Analyze job tasks and add necessary knowledge tasks
5
Write terminal performance objectives
6
Sequence tasks and terminal performance objectives
Develop performance tests
Develop written tests
Develop draft of learning guides
Try out, field-test, and revise learning guides
Develop system to manage learning
Implement and evaluate training programs

When you complete this section, you will be able to:

TASK 5: Write Terminal Performance Objectives

INTRODUCTION

Before learning materials are developed, a *terminal performance objective* for each task on the task listing should be written. A terminal performance objective (TPO) is a very brief statement describing exactly what the trainee must do to show that the task has been mastered. The terminal objective describes the situation under which performance must be demonstrated, exactly what performance is required, and how well the trainee must perform to reach mastery. Having a well-written objective for each task will help you develop appropriate learning materials to aid students in mastering the tasks on the task listing and will help you develop tests to determine if each task has been mastered.

To demonstrate mastery of this task, do the following:

TERMINAL PERFORMANCE OBJECTIVE

Given skill and knowledge task statements for a training program, write a terminal performance objective for each task. Each objective should conform to *all* criteria listed in Performance Test 5 at the end of this section.

This section is divided into several parts to help you:

ENABLING OBJECTIVES

[1] *List reasons for using terminal performance objectives in training programs.*

[2] *Correct poorly stated performance objectives.*

[3] *Write terminal performance objectives for tasks.*

ENABLING OBJECTIVE [1]

List Reasons for Using Terminal Performance Objectives in Training Programs

Begin Phase II

As mentioned in Chapter 3, the overall process of developing a competency-based training program might be viewed as having two distinct phases. Phase I, which we have been working on in the first three chapters, focused on describing the occupation and the competent worker. Tasks in phase I included identifying the specific occupations for which training will be offered, developing the task listing, and several other tasks. We want to be very careful to complete this first phase—at least in a preliminary way—*before* we get involved in the second phase.

Phase II, which we begin in this chapter, involves planning and developing the actual learning materials and activities that trainees will use to master the competencies identified during phase I. Look at this this way: Phase I pinned down *where it is* we want successful trainees to be at the end of the overall training program, and phase II involves the development of the materials, media, activities, and related learning resources to help trainees *get there*.

Terminal Performance Objectives

As you develop learning resources and activities for your training program, remember that your primary goal is to assist trainees in mastering the tasks on the task listing. The *tasks* then become the central focus of the second phase of the program planning process. Now that you have finished Phase I and are ready to put the training program together, how do you begin to develop student learning materials for each task? Before any materials or learning activities are actually developed, you *first* need to develop a *terminal performance objective* for each task.

A terminal performance objective or *TPO* is a brief statement that describes *exactly* what the trainee should be able to *do* while in your training program to demonstrate mastery of a task *after* the learning activities have been completed. By knowing precisely where it is you wish trainees to go, it becomes far easier to develop appropriate learning resources to help them get there. You will develop *one* terminal performance objective for *each* task on the task listing. Let us look at a typical task and the terminal performance objective written for that task:

EXAMPLE

Task	Terminal Performance Objective
Roll coins.	*Given loose pennies, nickels, dimes, and quarters and coin tubes for each, roll the coins so that each roll has the correct number of coins and is firmly packed.*

Look at this sample TPO and notice that:

1. It is based on the *task* itself and actually includes the task statement almost word for word (roll the coins) as the performance required of the student.
2. In addition to the performance required, the objective describes what will be *given* to the learner *during the testing situation* (loose coins and tubes) so that the learner may demonstrate mastery of the task.
3. Also included is a statement of *how well* the task must be performed for the learner to be considered competent in the task (correct number of coins and firmly packed).
4. The objective indicates what materials students will need in learning the task (coins and tubes) as well as the materials needed in testing the student.
5. We also have a pretty good idea of what instructional resources we need to locate or develop to help students learn the task. We need a book, filmstrip, slides, or other resource that will actually show the trainee how to perform the task as stated in the objective (how to roll coins in paper tubes).
6. By looking closely at the objective, we also know how we should test students (actually have them roll some loose coins).

Role of objectives. Performance objectives have been with us for a number of years, but there are still instructors, trainers, curriculum specialists, and others who question their importance and even refuse to use them.

Developing training materials without using well-written performance objectives for each task is like:

- A pilot taking off without a flight plan
- A builder erecting a house without blueprints
- A farmer plowing land not knowing what will be grown
- A tailor making a suit without having the customer's measurements

> Without clear objectives to tell us where learners are *going*, it is difficult for us to develop learning activities to help them *get there* or to assess whether or not they *arrived*!

Just as a blueprint tells a builder where he is going and also if he got there, performance objectives help us plan appropriate learning activities that will lead students to attainment of the task and also help us to develop evaluation instruments and testing situations that will assess whether or not learners have mastered the task. We might offer advice about performance objectives similar to advice given to long-distance travelers about road maps:

Do not leave without them!

You might be wondering why we chose the term "terminal" to describe the objective written for each task. All it means is that the *terminal* performance objective, as stated, describes what the trainee should be able to do *at the end* (terminal point) of the learning activity. Of course, you may have trainees who can successfully perform the task as described in the objective *before* they begin the learning process. This brings up another good use for objectives. Students who feel they can already perform a task may look at the objective for that task and tell pretty quickly whether or not they can perform the task as called for in the TPO. So remember to make your TPOs focus on the desired student performance at the *end* of the instructional process. A later chapter explores the use of *enabling objectives* that may be used along the way. For many years, objectives have been called "behavioral" objectives. We chose the term "performance" objective to keep our attention focused on the worthy performance we want trainees to accomplish, not just the "behavior" they display.

TPOs for knowledge tasks. Now let us take a look at a terminal performance objective for a *knowledge* task from a typical task listing.

EXAMPLE

Task	Terminal Performance Objective
Identify and describe various grasses	*Given samples of bluegrasses, bentgrasses, ryegrasses, and fescues, identify and list the major characteristics and uses of each with 100% accuracy.*

Again, just as in the previous example for a skill task, this TPO for a knowledge task describes exactly what the student must be able to *do* (identify and list the characteristics and uses of grasses), under what *conditions* (when given samples of grasses), and *how well* (with 100% accuracy) at the end of the learning activity to be considered competent.

The use of well-developed objectives is just as important for knowledge tasks as it is for skill tasks. TPOs for knowledge tasks should focus on the terminal performance we want the student to accomplish. Keep in mind that a performance objective is needed for each task on the task listing. Develop a well-stated terminal performance objective for each knowledge and each skill task. Do not worry about getting bogged down with unit objectives, course objectives, main objectives, intermediate objectives, global objectives, and other such confusing "educationese." At this point just remember: *one* task—*one* terminal performance objective!

Benefits of using TPOs. Listed below are some of the benefits of using a well-developed terminal performance objective for each task on the task listing.

1. In writing the objective, the wording of the task itself can be double-checked and refined if the trainee performance called for is not quite on target.
2. When learners are provided with well-stated objectives, they know exactly what performance they are going to master, under what conditions they will be assessed, and how well they must perform to be judged competent.
3. The instructor or curriculum planner can examine the objective (if written properly) and determine what kinds of learning activities might be appropriate for learning the task.
4. Also evident from the objective is how the testing situation should be set up and what kinds of evaluation instruments are needed.
5. The objective also reveals the major learning materials and resources (tools, equipment, supplies, etc.) needed for learning the task and for testing the learner over mastery of the task.
6. If examined carefully, the performance objective may give some indication of what prerequisite tasks are needed before the learner begins mastering a task.
7. A sound argument for additional tools, equipment, media, and related resources can be made when objectives clearly indicate that these additional resources are needed to learn a task.
8. Well-stated objectives tend to help keep everyone involved in the teaching–learning process "on task," including trainees, instructors, media specialists, evaluators, and others.
9. Valid objectives can provide an excellent means of looking at program effectiveness.
10. Educational research indicates that simply by informing learners of the objectives to be mastered, learning is enhanced.
11. Using well-stated objectives adds a great deal of precision to the instructional process. By writing down the *conditions* under which the trainee must perform, exactly what *performance* is required, and the specific *criteria* for mastery takes much of the fuzziness out of both the *teaching* and the *learning* process.
12. Once objectives have been used, they can be fine-tuned to enhance the efficiency and effectiveness of learning.

Flip through this book and look at the terminal performance objective written for each task in designing a competency-based training program shown on the first page of each new section. Notice how each TPO answers the question for the reader: "Just what do I have to be able to *do* to be considered competent in this particular task?"

Before going on to the next section, see if you can identify benefits of using terminal performance objectives by completing the following Self-Check.

SELF-CHECK [1]

Check your mastery of ENABLING OBJECTIVE [1] by completing this SELF-CHECK.

1. What two major steps in the overall program planning process do well-stated terminal performance objectives help us with?

   (a) ______________________________

   (b) ______________________________

2. List at least five benefits of using terminal performance objectives in training programs.

   (a) ______________________________

   (b) ______________________________

   (c) ______________________________

   (d) ______________________________

   (e) ______________________________

Compare your responses with those in the Answer Key in the appendix.

ENABLING OBJECTIVE [2]

Correct Poorly Stated Performance Objectives

Components of Performance Objectives

As you saw from the previous examples, a well-written terminal performance objective has three major components. Below are examples:

EXAMPLES

Components of Performance Objectives	Knowledge Task	Skill Task
1. Conditions *under which learner must perform the task to demonstrate competence*	*Given data about a field and crop . . .*	*Given an underground feeder wire and tools*
2. Performance *learner must actually demonstrate*	*estimate crop yield . . .*	*install wire . . .*
3. Criteria *by which learner will be judged competent*	*within 10% of actual yield.*	*according to the* National Electrical Code.

Let us take a closer look at each of these three components.

The condition. The first component, the *Condition*, basically describes to all concerned the setting in which the trainee will be required to perform the task to demonstrate mastery. Sometimes the condition is referred to as the *given* or the *situation*. Remember that the condition should be written just as carefully for knowledge objectives as skill objectives. Included in the condition may be words or phrases relating to:

EXAMPLES

- Things

  Given certain tools

  Given consumable supplies or materials

  Using test instruments

  Using manuals, specifications, etc.

  Given a lathe, sterilizer, or other major piece of equipment

  Provided with mockups, devices, etc.

  Given objects encountered on the job–soil, broken belt, patron, recipe, etc.

- Situations

  Using actual customer's car or other live work

  Under some simulated situation

  Presented with picture, problems, case study

  Given a work order, verbal instructions, blueprint, etc.

  Provided with results of a diagnostic test

  Provided with the data, measurements, parameters, map, schematics

  Given lists of terms, parts, tools, etc.

  Given a field situation

  Given numbers, figures, or problems

- Restrictions

  Without the use of references, texts, books, manuals

  Without help

  Without calculator, special tools, tables, charts, etc.

The following tips might be helpful in writing the *condition* component of objectives:

1. Avoid a long list of specific tools, equipment, and so on; the objective may become quite lengthy and of little use.
2. Do not include any thing, situation, or restriction that is obvious to all concerned, such as "given a work station, welding rods, and torch"—it might be obvious that a welding student would have these things during the performance testing situation.
3. Be careful *not* to include anything in the condition that the learner should *not* be given during the testing situation. If the student must determine what tools are needed or must locate the correct replacement parts before performing a service, *do not* list these tools and parts in the condition. Mention any special restrictions under which the students will have to perform.
4. Avoid specifying any reference to how the student will learn the task. Do not use phrases such as "given a lecture on," "given the required reading material," and so on. The condition focuses on the *testing* situation—not the *learning* situation. Remember, a student may be able to perform as called for in the objective *without* ever going through any of the learning activities.
5. Avoid making the condition too specific. For example, "given two pieces of polyester 4 inches by 4 inches" might be too restrictive. "Given two pieces of material" would probably be sufficient. Do not pin yourself down unnecessarily.
6. For some knowledge objectives, no condition may be needed since, in the testing situation, the student will be given nothing except a test containing questions. Other knowledge objectives may describe a problem-solving situation for the condition such as "given values of resistance and voltage," "given a list of terms," "given a series of problems," and so on.
7. The condition stated in the objective should resemble as closely as possible the condition under which the trainee must perform the task *on the job*. If the worker must be able to type a manuscript on the job when given a handwritten draft, then "given a handwritten draft . . ." should be the condition specified in the objective.

The performance. Remember that the *Performance* component is the heart of the objective and is based on the task statement. In some instances, the performance component will be an exact or almost exact restatement of the task itself. Other times the task statement may be expanded, additional qualifiers added or the task may be altered somewhat to describe the performance you will accept in the *training setting* to be confident that the student can perform the task in the *job setting*. Below are examples of performance components of objectives that might have been used in TPOs written for typical task statements. Notice how the task statements have been expanded or made more specific.

EXAMPLES

Tasks	Performance Component of Objective for That Task
1. *Lay a diamond pattern*	*. . . lay an 8-inch diamond pattern . . .*
2. *Clean, gap, and test spark plugs*	*. . . remove, clean, and gap the plugs and replace in engine*
3. *Prepare checks for payment*	*. . . prepare the checks and stubs . . .*
4. *Measure radial pulse*	*. . . measure and record radial pulse rate . . .*
5. *Take and store cuttings*	*. . . take cuttings and bundle . . .*
6. *Identify electrical components*	*. . . match pictures of components with their names . . .*

Here are some tips to remember when writing the performance component of performance objectives:

1. Remember that the performance is the heart of the objective—develop it with care.
2. Base the performance on the task and keep it precise.
3. If clearly worded, someone else should be able to read the performance component of your objective and describe exactly what the trainee should be able to *do* to demonstrate mastery of the task.
4. Remember that the performance component will describe what performance will be required of the trainee in the final (terminal) testing situation to be considered competent.
5. Do not confuse *instructor* performance with *student* performance. Never use "will teach," "will demonstrate," "will present," or other instructor behaviors. TPOs describe what the trainee should be able to do.
6. Avoid vague terms such as "demonstrate knowledge of," "understand," "show mastery of," "be familiar with," "know," "learn," or other such phrases that are not clearly observable.
7. Don't waste time and space by using repetitive, meaningless phrases such as "the student will be able to."

8. Avoid flowery terms such as "fully," "completely," "really," and so on.
9. Avoid words relating to positive behavior, such as "good," "well," "correct," "right," and so on. We can assume that the student will learn to perform the task in the "correct" manner.
10. Sometimes, the performance component of a TPO can only *sample* the many specific ways in which the trainee may have to perform the task on the job. Require a performance(s) that is representative of how the task is typically performed on the job.

The criteria. The third component of a terminal performance objective—the *Criteria*—describes *how well* the learner must perform the task for you to conclude that the task has been mastered. By *mastered*, we mean at a *trainee* level—not at the level of a master craftsman with years of experience. We might conclude that a trainee has mastered a task in the *training* setting when all key indicators of competence can be displayed except perhaps one—speed. Criteria should be set to ensure that each task can be performed competently but somewhat slower, perhaps, than an experienced worker could. Without definite criteria of acceptable performance, objectives are really of little value. Criteria generally specify minimum acceptable performance in two areas:

EXAMPLES

Process Criteria *(how the student performs the task)*

- *Following manufacturer's maintenance procedure*
- *Within 30 minutes*
- *Not exceeding flat-rate time by more than 25%*
- *Performing all steps in sequence*
- *Following safety practices*
- *Using proper tools and equipment*

Product Criteria *(how the finished product turned out)*

- *±0.005 inch, ±2 mm, ±4 degrees*
- *According to manufacturer's specs*
- *Within 10% of actual reading*
- *Within 100% accuracy*
- *With 90% accuracy*
- *With no errors*
- *Must agree with instructor's measurements*
- *To customer's satisfaction*
- *Salable*
- *Engine must run smoothly*
- *No visible cracks or pits*
- *Conforms to local building code*

Of course, the criteria component for a single objective may refer to the student's process *and* the finished product. The key is to specify criteria that will determine if the trainee is, in fact, competent in performing the task *as it should be performed on the job.*

Below are some tips that may be helpful in developing the criteria component of objectives:

1. Keep the criteria at a level high enough to ensure entry-level employment by the trainee. Remember that the competency-based approach will allow each trainee to continue working on a task until a high level of mastery is attained; do not settle for minimal competence.
2. Do not make criteria dealing with speed quite as high as would be required for an experienced worker performing the task on the job. Remember, the main thing that should distinguish your graduates from experienced workers is *practice.*
3. Avoid vague criteria such as "to instructor's satisfaction," "to industry standards," "correctly," and so on.
4. Avoid tying the criteria to instruction. Do not use phrases such as "following criteria in textbook" or "according to specs in handout." These resources will change—criteria should not.
5. Make the criteria comprehensive enough to include all the important indicators of competence. Include criteria covering typical errors made by trainees.
6. Do not make the criteria too restrictive. For example, if the process a student uses is of no consequence on the job, do not include the process in the criteria.
7. The minimum acceptable criteria for an objective should be the same for each student in the training program. Remember, you are holding *proficiency* constant and letting *learning time* vary.
8. If speed is particularly important on the job, you might want to mention a reasonable time limit in the criteria (or include time as an item on the performance test—more about that later).

Rather than spend a great deal of time developing detailed criteria to be included in terminal performance objectives, you may wish to simply specify a minimum score on a performance test as the criteria component. An example illustrates:

EXAMPLE

Task: Feed Infant Patient.

Objective 1: *Given patient assignment sheet and infant patient, feed the infant. Infant must be held securely, fed appropriate formula, and placed in crib to avoid aspiration.*

Objective 2: *Given patient assignment sheet and infant patient, feed the infant. All items on the performance test must receive an acceptable rating.*

Although objective 1 is perfectly all right, perhaps you can see the advantages of using objective 2. Students using the second objective would simply refer to a copy of the performance test and would be able to see the, perhaps, 10 or 15 *specific* criteria that will be used to evaluate their performance—not just the three broad criteria mentioned in objective 1.

Referring to a minimum score on a performance test for the criteria component as shown in objective 2 above offers several advantages:

1. Objectives can be written more quickly.
2. The use of a detailed performance test is "forced."
3. Skipping over essential criteria might be avoided.
4. Objectives do not become quite so lengthy.
5. Performance tests can be constantly improved and updated without having to alter the objectives.
6. Students can see exactly how they will be assessed when they can refer to a detailed performance test.

This approach can also be used for knowledge objectives by inserting a statement such as "the written test must be completed with 100% accuracy" for the criteria component of the objective. Of course, the student would *not* have access to the written test until taking it.

Now, see if you can correct poorly worded terminal performance objectives by completing the following Self-Check.

SELF-CHECK [2]

Check your mastery of ENABLING OBJECTIVE [2] by completing this SELF-CHECK.

Below are listed several terminal performance objectives. Some are correctly worded and some are not. Read each objective and check the appropriate column to the right. In the line below the objective, indicate what is wrong with each *incorrect* objective.

	Incorrect	Correct
1. Given a damaged vehicle, paper, pencil, and proper manuals, estimate the cost of repair within 10% of actual cost.		
2. Given a bed occupied by a patient and necessary linen, the student will be able to make the bed.		
3. Given a demonstration on inductive reactance, learn the concept to the instructor's satisfaction.		
4. Given a written draft of a letter, type and proofread the letter so that it is mailable and contains no errors.		
5. Provided with a General Motors engine having worn valves, correctly locate, remove, grind, and replace valves (100% mastery on test is required).		
6. Without the use of a tax chart, compute without error sales tax for purchases ranging from $10 to $500.		

Compare your responses with those in the Answer Key in the appendix.

ENABLING OBJECTIVE [3]

Write Terminal Performance Objectives for Tasks

Writing Objectives

As you begin writing terminal performance objectives for the tasks on your task listing, remember to keep the *task* itself in mind as each objective is written. The TPO is simply an extension of the task statement and describes what the trainee must do, under what conditions, and how well for you to feel confident that the task has been attained in the training setting.

Whether you write them all at once or one at a time over a period of months, you should eventually develop one TPO for each task. Do not yield to the temptation to skip over this very important step in developing an effective competency-based training program. *You* may know exactly what performance you want students to perform and how well they must perform it to attain each task, but your *students* do not. Tell them with well-written objectives and your job and theirs will be a lot easier.

Tips

When writing terminal performance objectives, you might want to keep the following tips in mind:

1. Base each terminal performance objective on a single task statement, whether it is knowledge or skill. If the objective looks too broad, the task may be too broad.
2. Someone else knowledgeable in the area should be able to read your TPO and agree with you on what you intended students to be able to do, under what conditions they must do it, and how well. If not, your objective is not clear enough.
3. There are excellent sources available from which you can locate already developed objectives and adapt them to your needs. These include V-TECS catalogs, ERIC documents, textbooks, curriculum guides, instructors, and others.
4. If written properly, someone else knowledgeable in the area should be able to *teach* from your objectives and a third person should be able to *test* students on the objectives—all in basic agreement with your original intent.
5. Keep the reading, education, age, and maturity levels of your intended students in mind as you develop objectives. Lower-level students may need objectives with more detail than those needed by higher-level students.
6. An objective cannot require the student to perform the task under *all* possible conditions or demonstrate *all* possible performances inherent in the task. It should, however, include all critical indicators of competence. The task may say "test metal for hardness," but of course you cannot have the student test *all* metals using *all* methods. Lack of time, money, and other resources forces you to *sample* the performances normally called for on the job. Your objective might say: "Given samples of mild, soft-tempered, and stainless steel, use the Rockwell Hardness Test to determine the hardness of each. Readings must agree with actual hardness of samples ±5%."
7. Do not be afraid to revise your objectives if students find them confusing or if you find it difficult to develop appropriate tests and learning resources for them as they are stated.

8. Have your TPOs reviewed by advisory committee members and others from the occupation. Ask them to determine if the conditions specified by the objectives match the conditions found on the job. Also ask them if the criteria are realistic—difficult enough to promote competence, yet attainable by trainees.
9. Make sure that your terminal objectives very closely simulate the job setting. The condition that calls for the student to respond should be a replica (identical if possible) of the setting on the job in which the worker will be called upon to perform. The performance called for in the TPO should be as close as possible to the actual performance required to perform the task competently on the job. Finally, the criteria should include the critical things that distinguish between competent and incompetent performance on the job.
10. Be sure to write the TPO for a task *before* you attempt to develop media, handouts, or other learning materials to teach the task.

Look carefully at the sample TPOs in Table 4-1 that were written for selected task statements from typical training programs. Notice how each is based on the task and answers the question for the student: "Just what do I have to do, under what conditions, and how well for me to get credit for mastering this task?"

See if you can write terminal performance objectives for tasks by completing the following Self-Check.

SELF-CHECK [3]

Check your mastery of ENABLING OBJECTIVE [3] by completing this SELF-CHECK.

1. Based on the instructor's "thoughts" shown below, write a correctly worded TPO for each task; include the criteria in the objective.

   (a) *Task: Pressure-test water system (plumbing).*
   "Let's see now, to find out if students really mastered this task, I'll provide them with the needed tools, materials, and a pump. I'll require them to test the water supply lines in a building for leaks. They have mastered the task if they detect all leaks and if their pressure readings agree with mine."

   (b) *Task: Set up window display (floral merchandising).*
   "The final testing situation for this task should probably look some-

TABLE 4-1 Sample Terminal Performance Objectives

Tasks	*Sample TPOs for Skill Tasks (Including Criteria Component)*
• Apply ice bag to wound	• Given an ice bag and cover, apply ice bag to affected area of patient. Ice bag must cover affected area and remain in place a specified length of time.
• Cut wigs	• Given a wig and patron's instructions for cutting, cut the wig into the style specified. Cut must meet with patron's satisfaction and be completed within 30 minutes.
• Repair window mechanism	• Provided with an automobile with damaged window mechanism, repair or replace mechanism so that it operates smoothly.
• Divide line into equal parts with instruments	• Using only a compass and straightedge, divide a straight line into a specified number of segments. Segments must be equal within ±1/64 inch.

Tasks	*Sample TPOs for Skill Tasks (Referring to Performance Test for Criteria)*
• Make chest x-ray	• Given a patient, an x-ray unit, and the necessary materials, make a chest x-ray. All items on the performance test should receive a "yes" rating.
• Add cuffs	• Provided with a garment and verbal instructions, add cuffs as instructed. 100% mastery is required on the performance checklist.
• Calm pediatric patient	• When confronted with an excited pediatric patient, calm the patient. All items on the instructor's checklist must have a satisfactory response.

Tasks	*Sample TPOs for Knowledge Tasks (in Ascending Level of Knowledge Required)*
• Identify and describe fittings.	• When shown actual or photos of typical cast-iron and PVC fittings, identify each by name and describe the purpose of each with 100% accuracy.
• Estimate project costs	• Given a sketch of a typical field project, estimate the cost of the finished product using current prices. The estimate must be within 5% of the actual cost.
• Diagnose problem(s) and recommend service(s) for typical engine malfunctions	• Given specific symptoms of malfunctioning engines, indicate the most likely cause(s) and the appropriate service called for. Your responses should match the answer key with 100% accuracy.

thing like this: I'll give students some merchandise, props, and materials. They must set up an actual display in a window. I want the display to show successful application of all the basic elements of design (shape, color, etc.) and be structurally and electrically safe. It shouldn't have any fire hazards either."

(c) *Task: Identify and describe the use of various nails (carpentry).* "What I'm after here is for students to be able to tell me the name of the 15 most common types of nails and to tell me how each is used in carpentry. I want them to be able to do this when I show them a picture of each nail or the nail itself. I'd like for them to be able to get 13 out of 15 correct."

2. Select *five* skill and *two* knowledge tasks from your task listing. Write a correctly worded terminal performance objective for each. Include the criteria in the TPO for *two* of the skill tasks and one of the knowledge tasks. In the TPOs for the remaining tasks, mention a minimum score on a written or performance test as the criteria.

Compare your responses with those in the Answer Key in the appendix.

Continue with the following performance test.

PERFORMANCE TEST FOR TASK 5

TASK 5: Write Terminal Performance Objectives

DIRECTIONS

When you feel you are ready, demonstrate your ability to write terminal performance objectives by doing the following:

For a list of tasks that have been fully analyzed:

1. Write a terminal performance objective for each skill task.
2. Write a terminal performance objective for each knowledge task.

No.	Criteria for evaluating performance; 100% mastery required	YES	NO
	Each TPO for Skill Tasks		
1.	Does the *condition* describe what the student will be provided with during the testing situation?		
2.	Is a long list of, or obvious tools, equipment, etc., avoided in the condition?		
3.	Is the condition general enough to avoid being too restrictive?		
4.	Are things the student should *not* be given *not* listed in the condition?		
5.	Does the condition closely resemble the setting in which the task is performed on the job?		
6.	Are references to learning resources avoided in the condition?		
7.	Does the *performance* tell *exactly* what the trainee should be able to do at the *end* of the learning process?		
8.	Is instructor performance *not* mentioned?		
9.	Is the performance based on the task statement?		
10.	Are phrases such as "the student will," "fully," "correctly," etc., avoided?		
11.	Does the *criteria* component specify how well the task must be performed?		

12.	Are criteria at a high-enough level to ensure competence but still be attainable?		
13.	Are the major indicators of competence included in the criteria?		
14.	Are vague criteria such as "to instructor's satisfaction" avoided?		
15.	Is mention of learning resources avoided in the criteria?		
16.	If criteria are not included in the TPO, is a minimum score on a performance test included?		
	Each TPO for Knowledge Tasks		
17.	If the objective has a condition, does it describe a problem or testing situation?		
18.	Does performance indicate exactly what the student must do to demonstrate mastery of the task?		
19.	Do criteria (if included) specify a minimum acceptable level of performance?		
20.	If criteria are not included, is a minimum score on a written test included?		

Continue with the following task.

When you complete this section, you will be able to:

TASK 6: Sequence Tasks and Terminal Performance Objectives

INTRODUCTION

After terminal performance objectives for the tasks on the task listing are written, they should be *sequenced* to ensure a smooth transition from one task to another. The goal in sequencing the tasks and terminal performance objectives for a training program is to avoid imposing a rigid sequence on students unless absolutely necessary. The only places in the training program where students should follow a definite sequence is where one task is an essential prerequisite for learning another task. Where tasks are independent of one another, however, students should be given the choice about which tasks to begin next. Students will usually select tasks they are most interested in—greatly increasing their chances of success.

To demonstrate mastery of this task, do the following:

TERMINAL PERFORMANCE OBJECTIVE

Given a task listing for a training program and terminal performance objectives for each task, sequence the duties and tasks. The sequence of duties and tasks should conform to *all* criteria listed in Performance Test 6 at the end of this section.

This section is divided into several parts to help you:

ENABLING OBJECTIVES

[1] *Sequence broad duties.*

[2] *Sequence tasks and terminal performance objectives.*

ENABLING OBJECTIVE [1]

Sequence Broad Duties

Why Sequence Tasks and Objectives?

Once you finalize the task listing and write a terminal performance objective for each task, you are faced with the question: "In what *order* should students tackle the tasks on the task listing?" Looking at a typical task listing, you will notice that the major duties are listed in some sort of order and the specific tasks in each duty are listed one after another.

> It is important to realize that students should *not* be *forced* to begin the major duties and to master the specific tasks within each duty in the sequence in which they are listed on the task listing *simply because they are listed that way*!

Of course, if anyone sits down and lists the specific tasks to be mastered in a competency-based training program, some task must appear on the list *first*, another task must be *last*, and all the rest will fall in between. This might not be the *best* sequence, however, in which students should master the tasks. In fact, for many of the duties and for many tasks within any given duty, there may very well be *no* particular sequence that students should follow.

One of the major shortcomings of traditional instruction is the rigid sequence of instruction forced upon students. Often, the sequence in which students encounter units of instruction is determined by:

- The sequence in which the current textbook being used happens to be written
- Past history—"That's the way we've always done it"
- The instructor's best guess as to which unit should come first, which one next, and so on
- The course outline, curriculum guide, or other instructional plan in use at the time
- By accident—which film, guest speaker, piece of equipment, or other particular learning resource happens to be available on a given day

Two major problems result from this kind of sequencing:

1. Tasks that are essential prerequisites for mastering other tasks do not always come right before the tasks for which they are prerequisite. Many

times these prerequisite tasks will come weeks or months before the tasks they are prerequisite for. Worse still, they may even come *after* these tasks. Without these prerequisites being recently mastered, students have great difficulty mastering later, more complex tasks.

2. Individual students have little or no choice about which task they will begin working on next. Many students react negatively to having the sequence for an entire training program rigidly laid out from start to finish. The approach to sequencing described in this section is aimed at addressing these two shortcomings.

How Much Sequence?

The position taken by this author is to *avoid* imposing a definite sequence of learning on students unless there is a sound educational reason to do so. The only justifiable reason for *forcing* a particular sequence on students is if a task happens to be an essential prerequisite that is needed to master another task. If learning how to "write shorthand symbols" is a prerequisite task for learning how to "take shorthand," obviously it should come first. However, if learning how to "make a felony arrest" is *not* needed to successfully learn how to "complete a suicide report," why force every law-enforcement trainee to master one before the other? Why not give the trainee (if possible) a choice as to which task will be begun next?

> When given a choice, students tend to select tasks to work on that they are *most interested in*!

This may not seem like much at first glance, but look carefully at what happens when learners are given the freedom to concentrate their current efforts where their interests lie. If students are working on tasks *they* select (within reason), some desirable things occur:

- Attendance and tardiness problems decrease.
- Student motivation is much easier to develop and maintain.
- Students take a more positive attitude.
- Students have more incentive for success.
- Students' chances of successfully completing the task are greatly enhanced.
- Fewer duplicate tools or pieces of equipment will be needed since fewer students will be working on the same tasks at the same time.
- Students can begin the next task with a success experience behind them and with a positive feeling about themselves and the program.

Giving students a choice about what they will learn next is certainly not a cure-all, but it will help in dealing with many of the problems faced by instructors—especially those dealing with student attitudes. Of course, students must still master *all* the required competencies for the training program, but they should, whenever possible, have some choice in which task they learn next.

Some programs will allow for much greater student choice than others. The goal is to keep the rigid structure to a minimum. As we increase the student's options, we also increase the student's chances for early success in the training program. Chapter 6 explains how to provide students with the necessary learning materials to work on various tasks in the program.

Sequencing Duties

The first step in sequencing your training program is to sequence the major duties. Remember that you want to avoid imposing a rigid sequence on students unless absolutely necessary. Let us look again at the duties for our hypothetical cosmetology program.

EXAMPLE: Duties in Hypothetical Cosmetology Program

A. *Shampooing and conditioning the hair and scalp*

B. *Shaping and styling hair, wigs, and hairpieces*

C. *Curling and straightening hair*

D. *Tinting and bleaching hair*

E. *Giving facials, manicures, and pedicures*

F. *Keeping records*

G. *Employability and related skills*

In deciding on the most efficient sequence in which students should tackle these duties, the instructor should ask:

> Are the tasks in a duty essential prerequisite tasks for successfully mastering the tasks in another duty? If so, that duty should come first in the sequence. If not, students should be allowed to begin working on the duties in the sequence *they* choose.

Sample 4-1 shows the sequence of duties that might have been developed for our cosmetology program. Our hypothetical instructor's thinking went something like this:

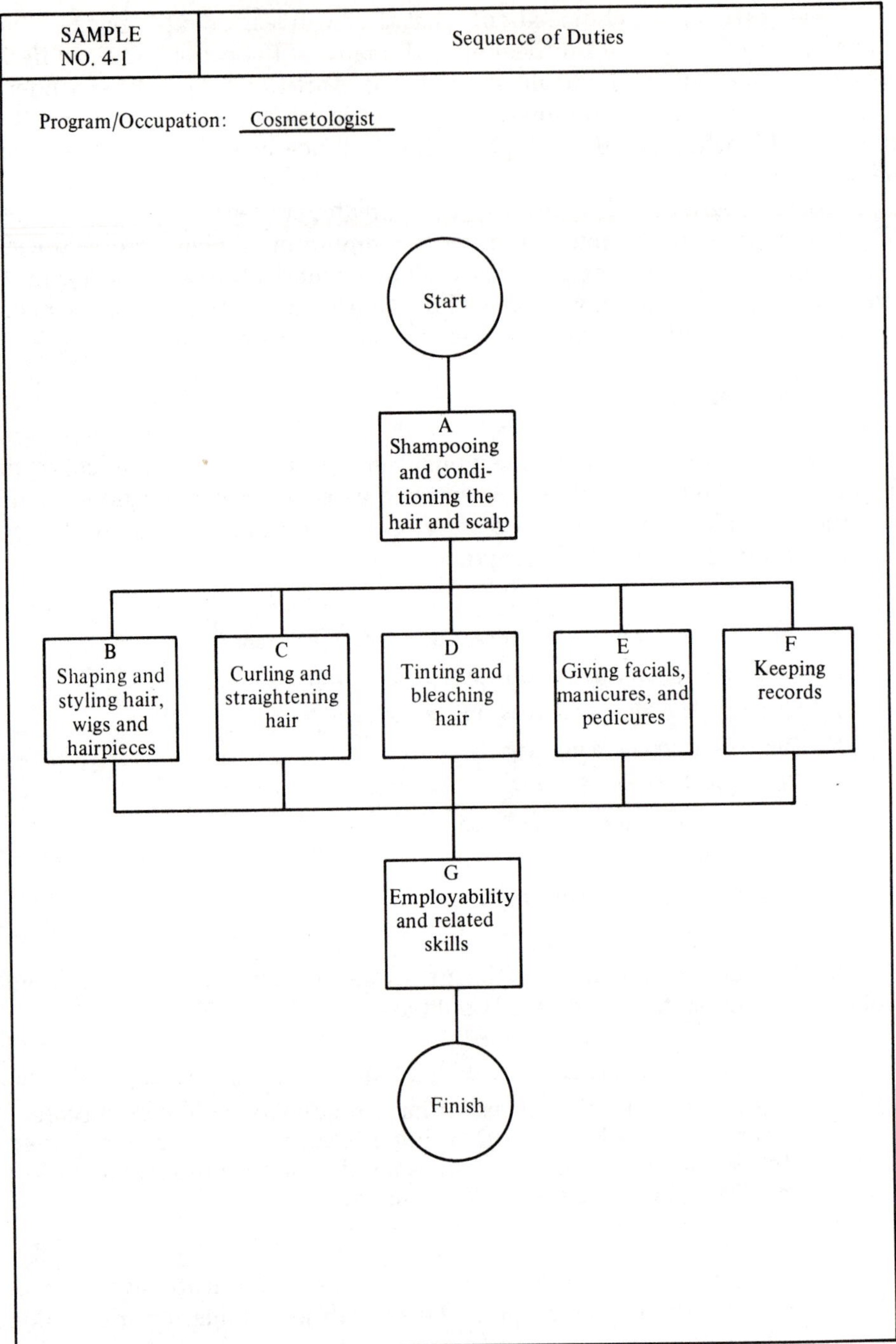
SAMPLE
NO. 4-1
Sequence of Duties
Program/Occupation: Cosmetologist
Start
A
Shampooing and conditioning the hair and scalp
B
Shaping and styling hair, wigs and hairpieces
C
Curling and straightening hair
D
Tinting and bleaching hair
E
Giving facials, manicures, and pedicures
F
Keeping records
G
Employability and related skills
Finish

EXAMPLE

Now I'm ready to pin down the best sequence for my students to go through the training program. I'll start by sequencing the seven duties. After looking at the kinds of tasks in each duty, I think the only duty that includes tasks that are prerequisite for other tasks is duty A. Tasks such as "describe structure and characteristics of hair," "describe principles of chemistry relating to cosmetology," "mix hair solutions," and one or two others are needed to master other tasks in the program. Therefore, I'll have each new student begin with duty A. The tasks in the other six duties seem to be independent of one another, so students should be able to choose the order in which they begin these duty areas.

Look at Sample 4-1 and notice that students should begin the training program by mastering the tasks in duty A. Once A is completed, the student has a great deal of choice about which duty will be begun next. Students may select duties B through F. When duties A through F are completed, duty G is completed. Notice that the student must master the tasks in *all* the duty areas to complete the program successfully. In this example, duties appearing above another duty should be completed first. Also notice in Sample 4-1 how "wide" the sequence is *horizontally*. A straight *vertical* sequence with one duty under the other eliminates student choice and is nothing more than the traditional lock-step approach. You may wish to use a form something like Sample 4-1 for students to use to help them determine which duty to begin next. Finally, notice that Sample 4-1 shows the sequence of duties for those students pursuing the cosmetologist option within the program. Students interested in specializing in the manicurist area would work only on duty E.

Tips

These tips might be helpful in sequencing duties:

1. Include as much choice as you can in sequencing duties.
2. "High-risk" students should perhaps be encouraged to begin on the least difficult duty or on a duty that might lead to basic employment if the student exits early.
3. A form such as Sample 4-1, enlarged and posted on a wall, may be useful.
4. If your program provides training in two or more specific occupations that are quite different, you probably need a separate sequence of duties for each.
5. You may want to encourage trainees to master fully all tasks in the duty they have selected to work on first before beginning tasks in another duty.

This provides a little more continuity, makes your record keeping somewhat easier, and cuts down on the variety of different kinds of materials, supplies, and tools that must be readied. Completing all the tasks successfully in a duty gives the student a sense of accomplishment that is not possible if the student randomly skips around from duty to duty. There may be times, of course, when a student may need a task in another duty before all the tasks in one duty are completed.

6. In sequencing duties, do not concern yourself with the sequence in which the tasks making up each duty are performed on the job. Your concern here is to develop an efficient *learning* sequence.
7. Use boxes or large circles to represent duties and write in the name and identifying information for each duty. Use lines to show the relationship among duties. Show a "start" and a "finish" point.

Before going on to the next section, see if you can sequence duties by completing the following Self-Check.

SELF-CHECK [1]

Check your mastery of ENABLING OBJECTIVE [1] by completing this SELF-CHECK.

1. List three benefits of allowing students to decide which task they will work on next.

   (a) ____

   (b) ____

   (c) ____

2. Below are duties for two occupations listed in alphabetical order. Based on the tasks implied to be in each duty, develop a sequence of duties for each occupation similar to Sample 4-1. Remember to keep the sequence as wide as possible horizontally. Focus only on the sequence needed to enhance learning—*not* the sequence performed on the job.

   (a) *Homemaker*
   Caring for children
   Cleaning and caring for clothes
   Cleaning and sanitizing the home
   Managing finances
   Planning, preparing, and serving meals

(b) *Nurse's Aide*
Assisting patients in physical movement and transport
Assisting with medical treatments
Assisting with nutrition and elimination needs of patients
Caring for personal needs of patients
Maintaining a clean, safe environment

Compare your responses with those in the Answer Key in the appendix.

ENABLING OBJECTIVE [2]

Sequence Tasks and Terminal Performance Objectives

Sequence Tasks to Enhance Learning

Just as in establishing the sequence for the major duties within a program, the sequence of specific tasks within each duty should allow for as much student choice as possible. Simply because the tasks are listed on the task listing in a particular sequence is no reason to require students to master the tasks in that sequence. The only tasks that students should be required to attain before others are those tasks that are prerequisite for successfully mastering other tasks. Keep in mind that since there will be one terminal performance objective for each task, sequencing the tasks also sequences the terminal objectives.

Once the duties have been sequenced, you should then look at the tasks in each duty and establish a sequence that will enhance learning. Let us look at an example.

EXAMPLE: Small Engine Mechanics Program
Duty C: Maintaining Fuel System
Tasks: C-01: Identify and explain operation of fuel system components.
C-02: Service fuel tank and hoses.
C-03: Service carburetors.
C-04: Service fuel pumps.
C-05: Diagnose and repair malfunctioning fuel system.

Sample 4-2 shows the sequence of tasks for this example. Notice that when students begin duty C they must begin with task C-01, since it is at the very top. Apparently, C-01 is prerequisite for the other tasks in that duty. Upon mastering C-01, however, notice that students have a choice about which task will be begun next—either C-02, C-03, or C-04. Notice also that these three tasks, as well as C-01, must be mastered before C-05 is begun. In developing this sequence of tasks for this particular duty we tried to keep two points in mind.

SAMPLE 4-2	SEQUENCE OF TASKS

Program/Occupation: Small Engine Mechanic

Duty: C : Maintaining Fuel System

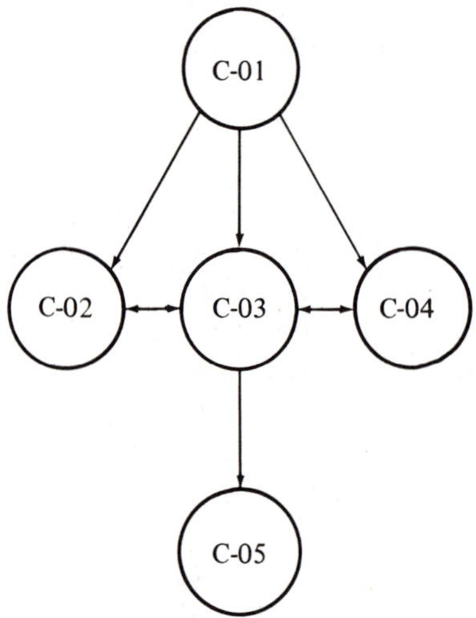

C-01: Identify and explain operation of fuel system components.

C-02: Service fuel tank and hoses.

C-03: Service carburetors.

C-04: Service fuel pumps.

C-05: Diagnose and repair malfunctioning fuel system.

> When sequencing tasks, sequence prerequisite tasks immediately prior to tasks for which they are prerequisites. Also remember to give students as much choice as possible in determining the sequence in which they will master independent tasks.

Tips

The following tips should prove helpful as you sequence the tasks within each duty:

1. If the tasks in a duty are independent of one another and the tasks can be learned in any sequence, avoid imposing a sequence on students. The sequence of eight independent tasks, for example, would look like this:

EXAMPLE: Sequence for Eight Independent Tasks

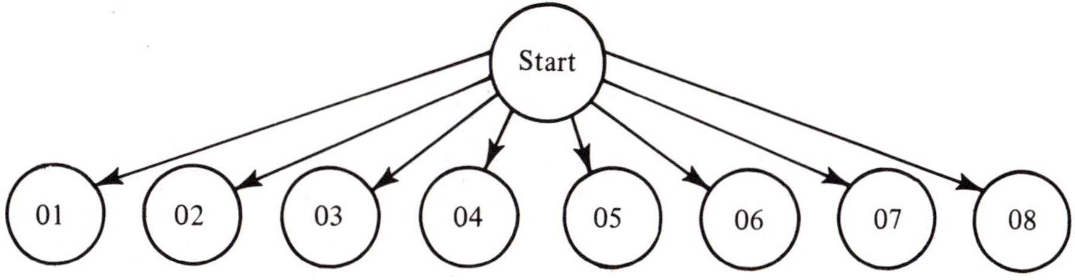

2. If one task is dependent on another, it should appear *below* that task in the sequence. For example, if task 06 should be learned before task 07, task 07 should come below task 06 in the sequence of tasks.

EXAMPLE: Sequence for Two Tasks, One Dependent on the Other

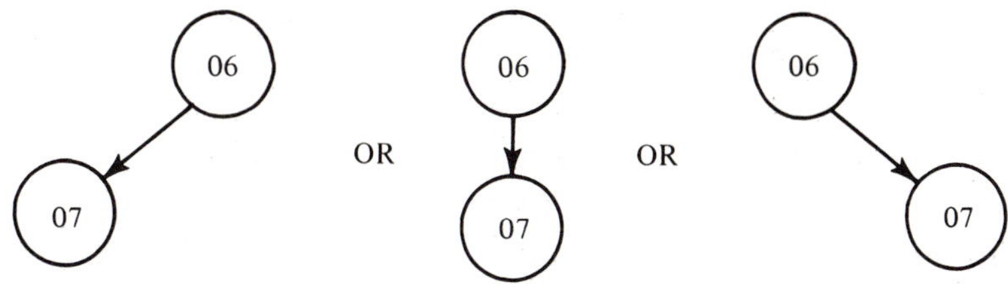

3. When there is a combination of dependent and independent tasks, be careful to sequence the tasks to give students a choice in choosing the sequence for the independent tasks while ensuring that dependent tasks appear in the sequence at the appropriate point. If a task appears *above*

other tasks in the sequence of tasks, it is a prerequisite for the tasks below it. Tasks on the *same* level are independent tasks which may be completed in *any* sequence. They are usually connected by lines with arrows on both ends.

EXAMPLE: Combination of Independent and Dependent Tasks in a Particular Duty

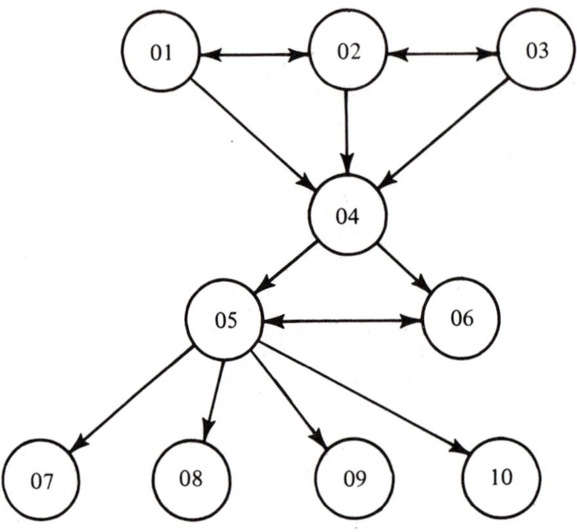

4. If you are unsure whether a particular task (task 15) is prerequisite for another (task 16), ask yourself: "Could a typical trainee master task 16 without the benefit of having mastered task 15?" If the answer is yes, the two tasks are independent and 15 is *not* prerequisite for 16.
5. Avoid imposing any "artificial" sequence on students. Sequences based on any of the following should be avoided:
   a. This is the sequence we have always followed.
   b. This seems to *me* to be the logical sequence.
   c. This closely matches the sequence followed in our textbook.
   d. This is the sequence in which I learned it.
6. Do not concern yourself with the sequence in which tasks are normally performed *on the job*. Just because carpenters will normally "build a wall" before they "install windows" does not mean they must be *learned* in that order.
7. Look closely at the terminal performance objective and the task analysis you develop for each task. These will assist you in spotting tasks that may be prerequisite for others.

8. Be willing to revise your task sequence as needed. If students seem to be having difficulty mastering task 14 without first mastering task 13, you may want to establish 13 as a prerequisite for 14.
9. You may want to prepare one overall sequence chart for your entire training program. You might do this by completing a sequence of tasks for each duty similar to Sample 4-2 and then photographically reducing each sequence of tasks and pasting them up on a single sheet along with a sequence of duties.
10. Give students a copy of the sequence of tasks you develop for each duty immediately when they begin each new duty. If you have the sequence of tasks for each duty all on the same sheet, give the student a copy the first day. Encourage each student to check off, color in, or otherwise keep track of each task as it is mastered. This can serve as a valuable motivator as well as an excellent management tool.
11. Have other instructors, students, advisory committee members, or others review your sequence of tasks to help you spot problem areas.
12. Closely observe the first several students who follow your sequence of tasks. Be prepared to adjust the sequence if needed.

See if you can sequence tasks by completing the following Self-Check.

SELF-CHECK [2]

Check your mastery of ENABLING OBJECTIVE [2] by completing this SELF-CHECK.

1. For the sequence of tasks shown below, answer the following questions.

   (a) On which task(s) may a student begin this duty?

   ____

   (b) In what order must tasks 03, 04, and 05 be completed?

   ____

   (c) Which tasks must be completed before 06 is begun?

   ____

   (d) Which tasks must be completed before task 09 is begun?

   ____

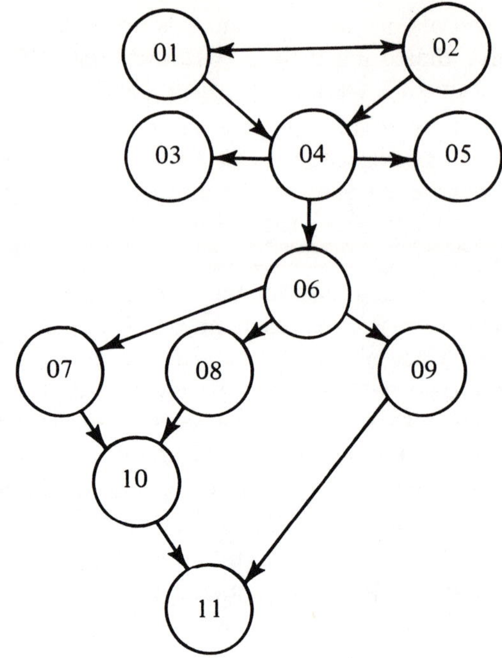

2. Based on the description given below of the relationship among tasks in a hypothetical duty, develop a sequence of tasks similar to the one shown above. "Students must begin with task 01, proceed to task 02, and then to task 03. They can then begin 04 or 05, but both must be completed before going any further. After 04 and 05 are finished, 06, 07, 08, or 09 may be begun. Task 10 can be started only after 09 is completed."

Compare your responses with those in the Answer Key in the appendix.

Continue with the following performance test.

PERFORMANCE TEST FOR TASK 6

TASK 6: Sequence Tasks and Terminal Performance Objectives

DIRECTIONS

When you feel you are ready, demonstrate your ability to sequence tasks and terminal performance objectives by doing the following:

For a task listing for which task analyses and terminal performance objectives has been developed:

1. Sequence the duties included on the task listing (use a form like Sample 4-1)
2. Develop a sequence of tasks for the tasks in each duty (use a form like Sample 4-2).

No.	Criteria for evaluating performance; 100% mastery required	YES	NO
	Sequence of Duties		
1.	Is the starting point clearly shown?		
2.	Is the sequence of duties clearly shown?		
3.	Do prerequisite duties appear in the sequence *above* other duties for which they are prerequisite?		
4.	Is the sequence as wide as possible horizontally with an absolute minimum of prerequisites?		
5.	Is each duty labeled for easy identification?		
6.	Is the sequence based on learning sequence and *not* the sequence performed on the job?		
7.	Is the finishing point clearly shown?		
	Each Sequence of Tasks		
8.	Are prerequisite tasks listed above tasks for which they are prerequisites?		
9.	Are tasks labeled in some way for easy reading?		
10.	Is each sequence of tasks as wide as possible horizontally with a minimum of prerequisites?		
11.	Is the sequence of tasks in each duty clearly shown?		
12.	Is the sequence of tasks based on learning sequence and *not* the sequence performed on the job?		

5

Developing Performance and Written Tests

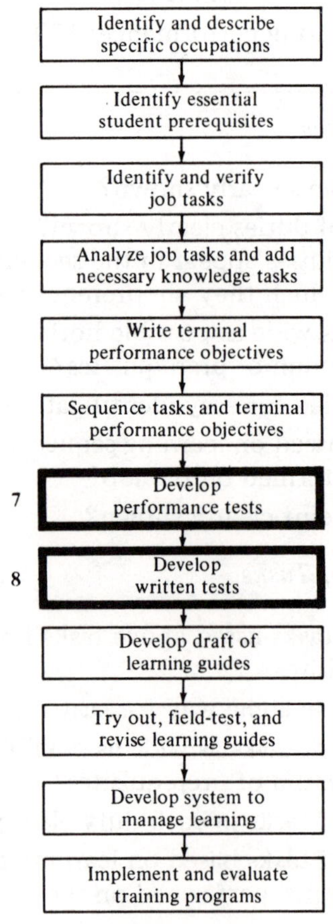
Identify and describe specific occupations
Identify essential student prerequisites
Identify and verify job tasks
Analyze job tasks and add necessary knowledge tasks
Write terminal performance objectives
Sequence tasks and terminal performance objectives
7
Develop performance tests
8
Develop written tests
Develop draft of learning guides
Try out, field-test, and revise learning guides
Develop system to manage learning
Implement and evaluate training programs

When you complete this section, you will be able to:

TASK 7: Develop Performance Tests

INTRODUCTION

The only way to be confident that your students have acquired the tasks in your program is to have them perform each task so that you can evaluate their performance for mastery. Since most of the tasks in your training program will be skills, you will find yourself developing and administering many *performance tests*. This section shows you how to construct and try out performance tests that are appropriate for the task, are objective, and measure the students' competence in performing the task.

TERMINAL PERFORMANCE OBJECTIVE

To demonstrate mastery of this task, do the following:

Given tasks for which task analyses and terminal performance objectives have been developed, develop appropriate performance tests to assess mastery of each task. The completed performance tests should conform to *all* criteria listed in Performance Test 7 at the end of this section.

ENABLING OBJECTIVES

This section is divided into several parts to help you:

[1] *Describe the role of testing.*
[2] *Describe criterion-referenced testing and match tests with tasks.*
[3] *Construct and try out performance tests.*

ENABLING OBJECTIVE [1]

Describe the Role of Testing

A Quick Review

Let us take a moment to review how far we have come in the program planning process so far. Up to this point, we have (1) identified and described the specific occupations for which we will offer training within the program, (2) identified any essential student prerequisites, (3) identified and verified the tasks that will make up the training program, (4) analyzed the tasks, (5) developed performance objectives, and (6) sequenced the tasks. Now we are ready to develop instructional materials, media, and other learning resources for students to use. Right? *Wrong*!

We are still not quite ready to get involved with teaching the tasks. There is one more very important step that comes next—developing instruments or tests to assess students' mastery of tasks. It is important for this step to come next in our program planning process—*before* we concern ourselves with how students will learn the tasks.

Why Develop Tests before Instruction?

You might ask: "How can we test a trainee on a task if we haven't taught the task yet?" Of course, we cannot actually test a learner on a task until the task has been mastered, but we can *construct* the test *before* we develop the materials trainees will use to learn the task. The point here is that assessment of the task should be *independent* of how the task is learned. Developing the test *first* helps "keep us honest" as we develop learning materials. Let us say that we have a task that looks something like

EXAMPLE
Take x-ray of pelvis

Let us assume that we have fully analyzed the task and identified the steps to perform the task along with essential knowledges. We have also developed the following terminal performance objective (TPO):

EXAMPLE
Given a patient, x-ray machine, and cassette, position the patient and radiograph the pelvis. Performance test must be completed with 100% accuracy.

What next? The next step should be to develop the test or tests that will be used to assess mastery of the task—*before* developing learning packages, media, or other learning materials. For this example, a detailed *performance* test *based on the step-by-step analysis* of the task would be developed next. Keep in mind that a *written* test based on the knowledge, facts, concepts, and principles underlying the task may also be needed. The performance test would list the specific criteria by which the trainee's actual performance of the task will be judged. Some of the items on the performance test might look like this.

EXAMPLE

	Yes	*No*
1. *Was x-ray requisition for the patient read?*		
2. *Was patient identified by ID bracelet?*		

Only *after* developing the test for assessing the trainee's mastery of the task should we get involved in worrying about how we might teach the task. Developing assessment instruments *before* learning activities are planned offers several advantages:

1. Developing tests *before* planning instruction does not require a student to have learned from a particular book, audiovisual unit, demonstration, or other resource to pass the test. The test can focus on evaluating the task *as it should be performed on the job*—not as it was presented in a particular learning resource.
2. Once the test is developed, we can then select learning resources that will teach the specific steps covered in the task analysis and assessed on the performance test.
3. The temptation to select the first instructional materials we may run across might be avoided. If we know the test is *comprehensive*, we are forced to locate or develop appropriate resources that will *fully* teach the task *as it will be tested.*
4. Several learning options (reading, viewing, etc.) may be developed for students to use—as long as each fully prepares the student to master the task as evaluated on the test. Student assessment should be *independent* of the method or materials a student may have used to learn the task.
5. You may have students entering your training program who have already mastered certain tasks. If your tests have been based solely on how the tasks *should* be performed and *not* on how students learn them, when a student successfully "tests out" of selected tasks you can be more confident that the student is competent.
6. After developing a *comprehensive* written and/or performance test for a task, you have a clear picture of what the student must *know* and be able to *do* to be competent, therefore increasing the likelihood that learning materials selected or developed will fully teach what should be taught—no *more* and no *less.*

The Role of Testing

Testing plays a very crucial role in the competency-based approach to training. Four of the most important uses of tests include:

- Diagnosing entry-level competence of new trainees
- Providing immediate feedback to students during the learning process
- Assessing trainees' mastery of each task
- Evaluating effectiveness of training materials

Let us look at these four major uses of tests:

Diagnostic. Often, trainees already possess some of the knowledges and skills included in training programs. In the traditional system of education and training, these students usually end up going through the learning activities for these tasks just like everyone else. This wastes instructor and trainee time and leaves these trainees with a negative feeling about the program. In the instructor-centered, group-paced approach, there usually is not sufficient time or the necessary instruments to assess each trainee's entry-level skills—particularly when all trainees begin at the same time.

In the competency-based approach, separate objective tests are developed for *each* task on the task listing. Students who have already mastered certain tasks can take the written or performance tests for those tasks and, if successful, can be granted full credit for those tasks. Their learning efforts can focus on those tasks *not yet* mastered.

Tests can also be used to diagnose weaknesses of new students, particularly in the area of essential prerequisite skills and knowledge. Just as you may have some students who already possess many of the tasks in your training program, you will also have some students who have very little entry-level competence. Well-developed tests will provide a tool for the instructor or trainer to assess where an individual trainee is *now* so that an appropriate training plan can be developed.

> Providing *all* trainees (especially adults who enter programs with a wide variety of previous experiences) with identical training plans and learning experiences is like a physician writing all patients the same prescription.

Without valid tests to assess where students are *now*, we can only guess at what learning experiences they need to get where they *want to be.*

Providing feedback. Educational research tells us that learning is greatly enhanced when the trainee is given *immediate* and *continuous* feedback about progress. Remember the course you took where the professor's only test was the final exam? It was a little too late to *do* anything about your performance then. If the professor has provided you with *periodic feedback* about how you were doing in the course, you could have either *continued* to do what you were doing or you could have changed your behavior if the feedback on your progress was unsatisfactory.

You can provide this necessary feedback to trainees in competency-based programs by using *informal* written and performance tests as an *integral part of the learning process*. As each major concept is covered, a short informal written test can be provided so that the *student* can determine if the concept was fully mastered *before going on*. Similarly, as each major portion of a task is presented and practiced, a short informal performance test should be provided to aid the student in determining if that part of the task has been mastered correctly.

These informal instruments are usually referred to as *self-checks*, check-points, or other term which refers to their use to *aid* learning rather than to *evaluate* learning. Self-checks are typically scored *by the student* and the results are *not* recorded. If any portion of the self-check is not completed successfully, the student simply goes back through the necessary learning resources until successful. The self-checks used in this book are included for the same reason.

As you can see, self-checks are an essential part of the learning process.

> Students should be spending a substantial percentage of their time gaining feedback about their progress.

This regular feedback allows the student to "adjust" course if needed to keep on track toward mastery. Heavy use of self-checks for knowledge and skills should be incorporated into competency-based training programs. Students should be encouraged to check their own progress. The temptation to cheat on self-checks will diminish when the trainee realizes that they are there to *aid* learning.

Assessing mastery. A third use of tests is to assess whether or not each trainee has mastered the tasks included in the training program. Mastery of skills, of course, are assessed by performance tests and mastery of major units of knowledge are assessed by written tests. These *formal* tests are administered by the instructor and the results are recorded. Keep in mind that the same written and/or performance test used to assess mastery *after* students have completed the learning experience (post-test) may be administered to a student *before* any learning experiences are attempted if the student feels that he or she is already competent in a particular task (pretest).

Basically, each task on a task listing requires a *written* test if the task is knowledge, a *performance* test if the task is a skill, and both a written *and* performance test for skill tasks involving a great many concepts or principles, or a great deal of knowledge. The thinking here is that no matter how good a performance test may be, it cannot always assess the student's mastery of the why, why not, and other technical information underlying the successful and safe performance of the task. Of course, those skill tasks involving little knowledge will require only a performance test.

The trainee should successfully complete the required test or tests for each task *before going on to the next task*. For particularly complex, basic, or critical tasks (especially skills) you may require the student to perform several times for mastery as well as require additional performance later in the program for reinforcement.

Since tests will be used to certify the competence of each trainee, it is extremely important to have well-developed tests. In a sense, your training program is no better than your assessment instruments. Weak or poorly constructed tests will allow partially competent trainees to complete your training program successfully. Rigid, comprehensive, well-developed tests, on the other hand, will allow only *competent* trainees to proceed to the next task and to complete the program successfully.

> Requiring *each* trainee to demonstrate mastery of *each* task before successfully completing a training program is probably the *single* most significant difference between the competency-based and the more traditional approach to training.

Evaluating training materials. In addition to assessing each individual trainee's performance, tests can also be used to evaluate the effectiveness of the *instruction* trainees are receiving. If you have an unusually high number of students who fail to reach mastery for certain tasks, the problem might lie with the materials and learning experiences students are using.

> If trainees *want* to learn and possess the necessary *prerequisites* and still fail to reach mastery as measured by valid tests, something is obviously wrong with the learning activities, materials, media, or other learning resources used.

Only by using valid, well-developed tests will you be able to evalute accurately the effectiveness of your training materials and overall learning system used and be able to continually improve the quality of instruction.

See if you can identify the role played by various testing situations by completing the following Self-Check.

SELF-CHECK [1]

Check your mastery of ENABLING OBJECTIVE [1] by completing this SELF-CHECK.

1. List at least four benefits of developing tests for assessing mastery of tasks *before* developing instructional materials.

   (a) ____

   (b) ____

   (c) ____

   (d) ____

2. Below are four case studies describing ways in which tests were used. Read each case study and identify the role served by testing in each (diagnostic, providing feedback, assessing mastery, or evaluating training materials).

   (a) Ms. Hinton was a firm believer in students taking an active part in their own instruction. She had her drafting program broken down into short, self-instructional units. After each section in a unit, students were directed to evaluate their own progress by using a self-check.

   (b) A military branch was in the process of developing a training program to be used by thousands of recruits during the next several years. To be confident that they had the most effective training program possible, three separate programs were developed by three different design teams. Each of the three programs was judged largely on the basis of how well three groups of recruits scored on a proficiency test after going through one of the three programs.

   (c) A large electronics firm developed a formal training program for quality control inspectors. Since this was the first training program developed for this group of workers, the training staff was not sure exactly what skills the QC technicians already had. A comprehensive test was developed covering the overall skills desired of successful quality control inspectors. The results were used to establish the beginning point of the training program.

   (d) Most states utilize a two-part examination to certify the competence of licensed drivers. This test is usually composed of a written portion covering mastery of laws, road signs, and so on, and a driving portion covering basic driving skills. Usually, a driver must successfully complete both portions to get a license.

Compare your responses with those in the Answer Key in the appendix.

ENABLING OBJECTIVE [2]

Describe Criterion-Referenced Testing and Match Tests with Tasks

The Criterion-Referenced Approach

Take a look at the scores that trainees earned on a hypothetical test:

EXAMPLE

Trainee No.	Score
1	94
2	93
3	90
4	90
5	87
6	86
7	86
8	84
9	84
10	81
11	74
12	73
13	62
14	30

Now, what *grade* should be assigned to each score in this hypothetical situation? If we assign grades as they usually are in our educational system, they might very well look like this:

EXAMPLE

Trainee No.	Score	Grade
1.	94	A's
2.	93	
3.	90	B's
4.	90	
5.	87	
6.	86	C's
7.	86	
8.	84	
9.	84	
10.	81	
11.	74	D's
12.	73	
13.	62	F's
14.	30	

Now, you might say: "What's wrong with this, the better students got the A's, the worst students got the F's, and everyone else was somewhere in between?" Well, there may very well be nothing wrong with this—it depends on *what was being assessed* and *what the grades mean*. Assume for a moment that this test was the final exam (if there is such a thing) for trainees preparing to be pilots of jet airliners. I think you get the message. I don't know about you, but I would not feel too comfortable flying with any of these pilots—not even the two who got A's.

I think you can see that the kind of grading used in this example is subjective and quite *relative*; each trainee's grade depends somewhat upon *how all the other trainees scored*. This is especially true when we establish—up front—that we will give a small number of A's, a small number of F's, and that everyone else's grade will be somewhere in between. This approach to assessing student performance is referred to as *norm-referenced* testing, since each student's individual score is compared to the norm.

> The norm-referenced approach is *inappropriate* in competency-based training because it does not really reflect whether or not each *individual* trainee is competent in a task at some *predetermined minimum level of acceptability*.

If you were going to hire a pool of typists, would you rather look at their final grades as determined by how each student scored compared to the group norm or would you want to know which ones could type, say, 60 words a minute? If these typists were graded using the *norm-referenced* approach, only the top few typing students would have gotten A's, the bottom students the F's, and the others the B's, C's, and D's. However, if a *criterion-referenced* approach is used, it is possible that *all* students could have gotten A's (or passed, etc.) if they all could actually type at some minimum prespecified criterion level! By the same token, they could *all* have failed had they all scored below that level. Grades in the criterion-referenced approach are determined by how each trainee scores compared to a *predetermined* criterion level. Table 5-1 summarizes some of the major differences between the norm-referenced and criterion-referenced approaches to student assessment.

Making the Test Match the Task

Let us go back to our hypothetical task for which a test is needed:

> Take x-ray of pelvis

TABLE 5-1 Characteristics of Norm-Referenced and Criterion-Referenced Testing

Characteristic	*Norm-referenced*	*Criterion-referenced*
• Goal	To report how student scores varied from one another	To report which students scored at minimum criterion level
• Criteria	Relative; depends on how the group scores	Fixed
• When criteria determined	Usually *after* scores are reviewed	Determined *before* test is administered
• Promotes	Varying levels of proficiencey because time is usually held constant	Varying times for reaching task mastery because proficiency is held constant
• Average performance of group	Usually moderate—few score high, a few low, and most average	Can be quite high; students are encouraged to reach mastery
• Fosters	*Incompetence* of a large percentage of trainees (sometimes as high as 70-80%)	*Competence* at high level of mastery for a large number of students (may reach 90-95%)
• Encourages	Competition among trainees	Competition against criterion level
• Classifies students	In relation to how each scored as compared to the norm	Into two groups—mastery and nonmastery
• Re-testing	Discouraged	Encouraged after student "recycles" through learning activities
• Separates students	Along a line of varying levels of proficiency	Along a line of time when proficiency was attained

What kind of test or tests might be needed to assess mastery of this task *as stated*? Below are some possible testing situations that might be selected:

1. Have the student explain from memory the step-by-step procedure in taking a pelvic x-ray.
2. Have the student take an x-ray of a mannequin's pelvis.
3. Require the student to pass a detailed, comprehensive written test covering the anatomical structure of the pelvic area, how the patient should be positioned, and the correct procedure for taking an x-ray of the pelvis.
4. Require the student to take a pelvic x-ray of a patient.
5. Have the student take a simulated pelvic x-ray of a fellow student.

Look at each of these possible tests and ask yourself:

> Which testing situation requires the trainee to perform the task as it should be performed on the job?

I think you can see that testing situation 4 is the only one of the five choices that requires the student to perform the task as it should be performed on the job. The other four choices "test at" the task but not the task itself—as it is stated. Students who talk a good story could pass test 1. A student could pass test 2 and could have gone unnoticed in pushing the wrong button or turning the wrong dial and may have zapped the mannequin with enough radiation to have killed a real patient. Test 3 tests only the knowledge behind giving a pelvic x-ray. Finally, test 5 just does not come close enough to the real job situation to assess student competence fully. Number 4 is the *only* choice that affirmatively answers the question just posed. Keep in mind that the other four testing situations would be necessary checkpoints to use along the way but only test 4 is appropriate to assess the terminal behavior of the trainee.

Written tests should also be carefully devised to ensure that the *test matches the task*. Here is a typical knowledge task that might be found on a program task listing:

Determine nutritional needs of horses

Here are several possible testing situations to assess mastery of the task:

1. Require the student to list all the factors that should be considered in determining the nutritional needs of horses.
2. Provide the student with typical data for several hypothetical horses and have the student determine each horse's nutritional needs.
3. Have students explain in writing the process of determining nutritional needs of horses.

As in the previous example, only one of these testing situations, number 2, can assess the task as it is stated. Students good at memorizing could pass test 1, and some could struggle through test 3. Only those students who actually *know how* to determine the nutritional needs for a particular horse could pass test 2. Before devising the testing situation for a task, look at the task statement and the terminal performance objective to see what behavior the trainee is being called upon to demonstrate.

Before going any further, complete the following Self-Check to make sure that you can match the test with the task.

SELF-CHECK [2]

Check your mastery of ENABLING OBJECTIVE [2] by completing this SELF-CHECK.

1. Listed below are several characteristics of tests. For each characteristic, define or further explain the characteristic as it relates to the "criterion-referenced" approach to testing.

   (a) Basic goal of the test: ______________________

   (b) How criteria are set: ______________________

   (c) Re-testing: ______________________

   (d) Competition among students: ______________________

   (e) Separates students as to: ______________________

2. Below are sample task statements. In the line below each task, describe the testing situation required to fully assess the trainee's mastery of the task as it is stated.

   (a) Type a manuscript:

   ____

   (b) Troubleshoot a cooling system:

   ____

   (c) Set up and operate an M-S-A Model 2A explosimeter:

   ____

   (d) Test urine for sugar and acetone:

   ____

   (e) Describe the operating principles of a four-cycle engine:

   ____

Check your responses with those in the Answer Key in the appendix.

ENABLING OBJECTIVE [3]

Construct and Try Out Performance Tests

Developing Performance Tests

Basically, there are *two* kinds of tests used to assess trainees' mastery of tasks: written and performance. It is easier to keep these two tests separate in your mind if you remember there are two basic kinds of competencies or tasks upon which we build training programs: *skills* and *knowledges.*

> Assessment of skills calls for a performance-testing situation, whereas assessment of a knowledge can be handled with a written test.

Two basic kinds of tasks—two kinds of tests. Remember that attitudes can be assessed only by assessing the *knowledge* required to exhibit the attitude and the voluntary *performance* of the desired behavior.

Let us take a look first at developing performance tests. Remember from our discussion of human competence in Chapter 3 that we are interested primarily in what the trainee or student can *do*, so in most training programs you will be more involved with developing and administering performance tests. Essentially, a performance test does just what the term implies—it is an instrument to help the instructor judge whether or not the student can actually *perform* the task in a job-like setting to some minimum level of acceptability. How are performance tests developed? Let us walk through the construction of a typical performance test, step by step. Before we begin, remember that we are developing the test *before* we worry about how students are going to learn it. We simply want the performance test to evaluate each student's performance of the task and not be dependent on a particular resource that students may have used to learn it.

STEP 1: Determine exactly what should be tested.

Remember from an earlier section that the test should match the task. Look at the task statement itself very carefully and ask yourself:

> Exactly what should the trainee be required to do to demonstrate competence in the task, as it is stated?

The answer to this question describes the testing situation called for. To find out even more about the specifics, look at the terminal performance objective for the task. An example of a TPO for the task "wash hands following aseptic techniques" might be:

EXAMPLE
Provided with sink and soap, wash hands following aseptic techniques. Performance test must be completed with 100% accuracy.

By examining the task statement we can see that the students' ability to wash hands following accepted aseptic techniques is what is being tested. Looking at the TPO, we also notice the following:

1. All the student will have during the test is a sink and soap (remember the *condition* component of performance objectives).
2. The student will actually be required to go through the entire process of washing hands.

3. To be judged competent, all items on the performance test must receive an acceptable rating.

I think you can see now how critical it is for the task statement and TPO to be worded very precisely. Sloppy wording in either may result in a confusing test or, even worse, a test that does not measure what it is supposed to measure, or a test that is not *valid*.

Keep in mind that you cannot have the student perform the task in all possible settings, so you may have to "sample" typical situations or require the student to perform under the more common or perhaps difficult of typical situations that will arise on the job.

So in the first step we carefully reviewed the task and TPO and determine that washing of hands be tested; therefore students must actually wash their hands during the performance test. Now what?

STEP 2: Determine whether *process*, *product*, or *both* is critical.

The *process* is *how* the student performs the task; the *product* is, of course, the end *result*. Sometimes, *how* the task is performed is critical to attaining competence; other times, the finished *product* is what we are interested in, and in some cases we need to evaluate both process *and* product.

Essentially, it boils down to deciding which is required for job competency and, therefore, which should be assessed. Let us look again at our hand-washing example. Which is more important—process or product? Most of us would agree that probably the finished product (clean hands) is really all that we are worried about—regardless of *how* the student got them clean. Although this is perhaps a valid point, we cannot tell by looking exactly how clean the completed product is (unless we do a bacteria culture). So in this case the product is important, but we must evaluate the student's *process* to infer that the hands are, in fact, clean. Items on the performance test for this task might look as follows:

EXAMPLE

	Yes	*No*
1. *Avoided touching clothing to edge of sink?*		
2. *Used towels to adjust flow and temperature?*		
3. *Wet hands thoroughly?*		
4. *Applied sufficient soap to cover hands completely?*		
5. *Washed:*		
a. *Palms?*		
b. *Backs of hands?*		
c. *Wrists?*		
d. *Forearms?*		
6. *Used sufficient friction to loosen dirt and bacteria?*		

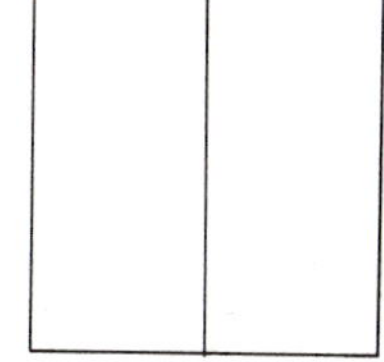

7. *Rinsed all soap from hands?*
8. *Rinsed so that water ran from forearms to fingers?*
9. *Repeated steps 4 through 6 at least once?*
10. *Dried hands with sterile towel from fingers to forearms?*
11. *Turned off water with towel?*

Notice that all 11 items on the test refer to *how* the student performed the task, or the *process*. Next let us look at the performance test for the task "make biscuits":

EXAMPLE

	Yes	*No*
1. *Is the shape uniform, with straight sides and level tops?*		
2. *Is the finished size approximately double the size of unbaked biscuits?*		
3. *Is the color a uniform golden brown and free from yellow or brown spots?*		
4. *Is the crust tender and free of excess flour?*		
5. *Is the inside free from yellow or brown spots?*		
6. *Is the inside flaky–pulls off in thin sheets?*		
7. *Is texture tender and slightly moist?*		
8. *Is flavor pleasing?*		

This time we are interested only in the finished *product*. We have assumed that if a student's biscuits measure up to these eight criteria, the process must have been correct (or there may be several ways of doing it—each acceptable). Of course, many performance tests will include items assessing process as well as product. A close look at the steps and knowledges identified during an analysis of a task will help.

STEP 3: **Construct the items to be included on the test.**

The heart of the performance test is the specific items for which some sort of rating will be given. Where do these items come from? Where *process* is important, the test items will be based on the procedural *steps* identified during the task analysis process.

EXAMPLE

Steps from Analysis of Task	Performance Test Items
1. *Always disconnect power cord before removing chasis.*	1. *Was cord disconnected* before *chasis was removed?*

2. Press the altered area.

3. Dispense cash to customer—coins first, then currency.

2. Was the altered area pressed?

3. Were coins dispensed before currency?

If process is important, only include *critical* steps as items on the performance test—do not overdo it.

> Include only those process-related items that will distinguish between someone who can perform the task competently and someone who cannot.

If process is really not important, do not include in the test any process-related items. If time is important, include this as an item. One caution: including process test items means that you will have to actually observe the student as he or she performs the task.

If the *product* is critical, your test items will describe desirable characteristics of the completed product, such as size, shape, color, condition, and so on. These will not always be obvious by looking at the steps identified during analysis of the task. It may be helpful to look at a sample of the finished product and ask the question:

> What essential characteristics must the finished product have for the student to be judged occupationally competent in producing the product?

Here are some sample product-related test items:

EXAMPLES

1. *Is the door plumb?*
2. *Is the weld free of visible cracks or pits?*
3. *Is the inside diameter accurate ± 0.010 inch?*
4. *Does the bandage cover the entire affected area?*
5. *Does the engine start easily and run smoothly?*

Now the question arises: How many items are enough for a performance test?

> Include as many items (and the right kind of items) as necessary to *assess mastery of the task.*

Here are some tips to keep in mind as you develop items for performance tests:

Items Relating to Process

- Base the items on the steps identified during the task analysis.
- Begin each item with a verb in the *past* tense (was, did, were, used, removed, etc.) since each step can be rated only *after* it takes place.
- Each item should be observable and objectively assessed.
- Avoid subjective words such as "properly," "correctly," "enough," "well," and so on.
- Word items so that they can be rated as *yes* or *no*, with *yes* being the desired response.
- Anyone competent in the task should be able to evaluate a student accurately using your performance test.
- Include only one distinct step per item—do not combine several procedural steps into one test item.
- Each item should be clear, concise, and be able to stand alone.
- Items should be broken down into subitems to avoid repetitious wording:
    2. Stored grinding wheels in a place that:
        a. Was dry?
        b. Had no excessive heat?
        c. Had no excessive humidity?
- Do not begin items with a phrase such as "Did the student . . ." It is obvious who is being assessed.
- List process items in sequential order as they would be performed and observed.
- If only a few steps are critical in a lengthy process, you might want to warn the student beforehand when to stop and have his or her process checked. Your instructions to the student might include a statement such as: "Check with instructor before installing head." This may be useful for "hidden" steps or procedures that are no longer visible when the process is completed and will also conserve the evaluator's time.

Items Relating to Product

- Include only *critical* characteristics of the finished product—items that would indicate competence or lack of competence.

- Begin items with a verb in the *present* tense (does, is, are, etc.), since product characteristics are fixed and can be evaluated now.
- Do not use repetitious words or phrases in succeeding items.
- Include exact indication of how competence will be determined for each characteristic (±0.001 inch; within 2 degrees; at least three stiches; etc.)
- Do not settle for unreasonably low standards because you are dealing with trainees. Students should still be able to write loan contracts, locate parts, operate lathes, and pack parachutes *as well as experienced workers*—it will simply take them more *time* to do it.

STEP 4: Determine how items will be rated.

The specific items included on the performance test will have to be rated by the instructor or whoever is evaluating the student. Two common methods are use of the *rating scale* and *checklist.*

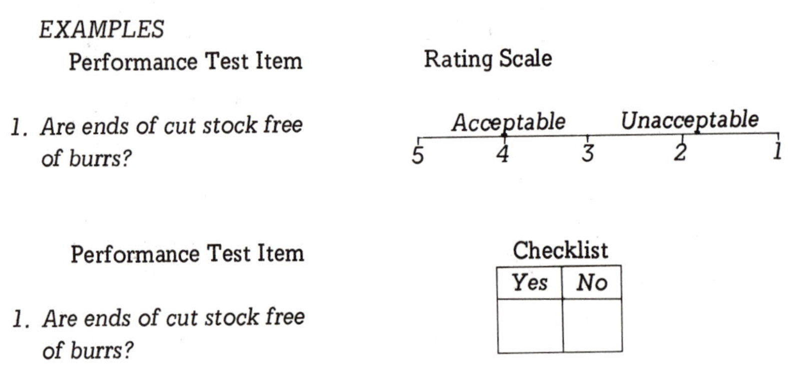

EXAMPLES
Performance Test Item
Rating Scale
1. Are ends of cut stock free of burrs?
Acceptable
Unacceptable
5
4
3
2
1
Performance Test Item
Checklist
Yes
No
1. Are ends of cut stock free of burrs?

Either method or rating the student's performance will get the job done, but the *checklist* offers one key advantage over the rating scale—it is much less subjective. Look at the two examples and note that the rating scale has *five* possible ratings that the evaluator could have circled to rate the finished product. Some scales in use have as many as nine or ten possible choices. You can probably see the major drawback of rating scales. For the example above, you might ask: "What is the difference between a 5 and a 4 or between a 2 and a 1?"

With the *checklist*, on the other hand, the test item is rated either *yes* or *no*. The ends of the cut stock were either free of burrs or they were not. It is recommended that *checklists* be used for performance tests. You may want to use satisfactory/unsatisfactory, pass/fail, yes/no, acceptable/unacceptable, or other such terms. One note of caution when using a yes/no type of checklist as recommended here: word the items so that they can be observed and rated objectively as yes or no. Our previous example could not be rated simply yes or no if worded "ends of stock," "finish of metal," and so on. The item must be detailed enough to be readily observable.

STEP 5: Determine the minimum acceptable score for mastery.

Establishing the minimum cutoff score for mastery of performance tests is a difficult task for many instructors and trainers. Percentages varying from 80% or lower up to 100% are common. How many of the items on the performance test must a student accomplish before being considered competent?

Although certainly not accepted universally, this author proposes that:

> Only *essential* process- and product-related items be included on performance tests, and the student should complete the test with 100% accuracy to be considered competent!

This relieves the evaluator of the burden of wrestling with the question of whether 80, 85, 90, 96, or 98% is sufficient. One instructor may require 90%, whereas another may require 100% for the same task. The same instructor may require 85% mastery on one test and 95% on another. By requiring 100% mastery, this problem is avoided.

Can students consistently score 100% mastery? By including only *essential*, critical items on the test and providing well-planned learning experiences, *most* students will be able to reach 100% mastery. You must ask yourself: "If only 10 essential items are included on a performance test and a student misses one for 90% accuracy, has the student mastered the task?" Not really; the student is only 90% competent. (You've heard the one about the neurosurgeon performing a procedure with 90% accuracy.) Of course, if only one or two items are missed, the student may not have to repeat the entire performance test. It may be a matter of correcting a problem when it occurs or questioning the student so that you are satisfied that he or she can perform the task competently.

If you are still not quite sold on the 100% mastery philosophy, take a look at this performance test for the task "take a picture with a 35mm camera." The minimum score for mastery in this example is *90%*.

EXAMPLE

	Yes	*No*
1. *Was the proper film selected for the subject?*	X	
2. *Was the film loaded in a dark area?*	X	
3. *Were the manufacturer's instructions followed in loading the film?*	X	
4. *Was the dial set to the proper ASA setting?*	X	
5. *Was the camera held in the dominant hand and settings made with the other hand?*	X	

6. *Were the shot and angle chosen to maximize scenery and background?*	X	
7. *Was the lens cap removed?*		X
8. *Was the exposure set for light conditions?*	X	
9. *Was the shutter squeezed without shaking the camera?*	X	
10. *Was the film advanced immediately?*	X	

Our hypothetical student was judged "competent" in this task because a score of 90% was achieved. However, the one item missed resulted in 36 completely black pictures. I would not want to pay this 90% competent photographer to shoot pictures at my daughter's wedding!

STEP 6: Write directions for the student.

The directions to the student should be worded carefully so that they explain:

- The purpose of the test
- The general testing situation
- Exactly what the student is to do
- Any special restrictions, cautions, and so on
- Any time limit
- How mastery will be determined
- Anything else the student needs to know

Here is what a typical set of directions for taking a performance test might look like for the task "replace windshield":

EXAMPLE: Directions
The purpose of this test is to assess your ability to replace damaged glass in a vehicle. You will be provided with a vehicle with a cracked or broken front or rear windshield. Remove the damaged glass, and locate and install the correct replacement. All the items on the performance test must receive a "yes" response, and you must complete the job within the flat-rate time plus 25%.

STEP 7: Assemble the test and try it out.

Now that you have all components of the test constructed, you are ready to assemble them into the actual performance test that you'll be using with students. Keep in mind that the test should be made available to the student throughout the entire learning process—up to the time when the test is actually administered. At this point, of course, the student should have had sufficient instruction and practice to be able to perform the task *unaided*. The instructor may use a copy of the test on a clipboard to rate each item yes or no while the student performs the task if the process is being evaluated, or while examining the finished job if the product is being evaluated.

It is a good idea to try out the test with a fellow instructor and one or two students before using it to evaluate students. Have them look at the directions and each test item for clarity, then revise as needed. Remember: several evaluators competent in the task should be able to use copies of your test to evaluate a student and arrive at ratings that are very much similar. If not, the items may be vague, poorly worded, and open to several interpretations. To summarize this section, here are some tips to use in developing performance tests:

- The test should assess the task *as it is stated*.
- The actual behavior called for in the task statement and TPO should also be required for the performance test (sampling may be required).
- If a process is critical to performing the task competently on the job, items must be included that assess *how* the student performs the task. Someone must actually observe the student, at least during key steps.
- If producing a completed product is important to be competent, *product*-related items must be included and the finished product must be evaluated critically.
- If process *and* product are important, include items to assess both.
- The actual test items on the performance test should:
  - Be sufficient to cover the major areas of competency in performing the task
  - Begin with a verb, be short and concise, and be ratable as yes or no
  - Be observable
- Several evaluators using a well-developed performance test should rate a single student's performance very similarly.
- You may want students to repeat the task several times, perhaps each time under different conditions or separated by time, or both.
- Each individual student should be required to perform the task independently. Administering performance tests to groups only assesses the competence of the group.

Sample 5-1 shows a sample performance test that might be used in a competency-based training program. Notice how the directions tell the student exactly what is about to take place and notice how the items to be evaluated are precise, observable, and clearly worded. Also notice that items 1 through 13 are process items, whereas items 14 and 15 evaluate the product.

AVTI	PERFORMANCE TEST	Task No. C-12
TASK	Charge vehicle battery	
DIRECTIONS	Demonstrate mastery of this task by doing the following:	

This test evaluates your ability to slow-charge a vehicle battery. You will be assigned a customer's vehicle. Clean and check the battery and slow-charge it to full charge. Write down the temperature and specific gravity *each hour*.

Caution: Have the instructor check your connections before turning on the battery charger.

No.	Your performance will be evaluated using the items below; all must be "yes"	YES	NO
1.	Were any external defects in the battery detected during inspection?	✓	
2.	If needed, were cells filled?	✓	
3.	Was the battery cleaned and dried?	✓	
4.	Was the battery removed from the vehicle *or* cable clamps disconnected (ground first) before charging?	✓	
5.	Was the charger switch in the *OFF* position before being connected to the terminals?	✓	
6.	If the battery was removed, was it placed on an insulating surface?	✓	
7.	Was the charger connected to battery + to + and – to –?	✓	
8.	Was the charger turned on?	✓	
9.	Was the charging rate appropriate for the vehicle's battery?	✓	
10.	Were the temperature and specific gravity checked every hour?	✓	
11.	Was the charger turned off before being disconnected?	✓	
12.	Was the battery reinstalled in the vehicle securely?	✓	
13.	Were the cables reconnected + to + and – to –?	✓	
14.	Is the battery fully charged?	✓	
15.	Will the battery start the vehicle?	✓	

Student	Date	Attempt	Instructor's Signature	Page
Janice Brown	Oct 11	(1) 2 3 4	S. L. Crozier	1 of 1

SAMPLE 5-1

Before going on, complete the following Self-Check.

SELF-CHECK [3]

Check your mastery of ENABLING OBJECTIVE [3] by completing this SELF-CHECK.

Below are typical items that might appear on performance tests. For each item, determine whether it is a *process*-related or *product*-related item by checking the correct column to the right. *Also*, in the lines below each item, indicate how *incorrectly* worded items could be improved.

	Process	Product
1. The student watered only those plants needing it?		
2. Shut off emergency shutoff valve?		
3. Were holes located correctly?		
4. Clean oil and sterilize at 320°?		
5. Used enough lubricant?		

Check your responses with those in the Answer-Key in the appendix.

Continue with the following performance test.

PERFORMANCE TEST FOR TASK 7

TASK 7: Develop Performance Tests

DIRECTIONS

When ready, demonstrate your ability to develop performance tests by doing the following:

For tasks for which TPOs and task analyses have been developed:

1. Develop performance tests.
2. Try out performance tests and revise.

No.	Criteria for evaluating performance; 100% mastery required	YES	NO
	Directions		
1.	Are the directions clear and concise?		
2.	Is the purpose of the test mentioned?		
3.	Is the testing situation described for the student?		
4.	Is the student told exactly what to do?		
5.	Are any special restrictions mentioned?		
6.	Is any time limit mentioned?		
	Test Items Relating to Process		
7.	Are process items included if the process is important for competence on the job?		
8.	Are only critical process items included?		
9.	Do items begin with a verb in the *past* tense?		
10.	Are items based on the procedural steps in the task analysis?		
11.	Is each item objective and observable?		
12.	Can each be rated *yes* or *no* and worded so that *yes* is the desired response?		
13.	Are words such as "good" and "well" avoided?		
14.	Is only one step included per item?		

15.	Are subitems used if needed?		
16.	Are items listed in the order in which they occur?		
	Items Relating to Product		
17.	Are product-related items included if the quality of a finished product is critical for competence?		
18.	Are only critical characteristics of the finished product included?		
19.	Do test items begin with a verb in the present tense?		
20.	Are items objective and observable?		
21.	Are criteria for acceptability spelled out clearly (size, location, precise dimensions, etc.)?		
22.	Can each be rated *yes* or *no*, with *yes* the desired response?		
23.	Is only one product characteristic included per test item?		
24.	Are subitems used if needed?		
25.	Are items written at a high-enough level to ensure the job competence of those passing the test?		

Continue with the following task.

When you complete this section, you will be able to:

TASK 8: Develop Written Tests

INTRODUCTION

Although most of the tests you will develop and administer will be performance tests, you may often be faced with the need to evaluate the student's mastery of concepts, principles, and other knowledge underlying the competent performance of various job tasks. Also, you may have added several knowledge tasks to your task listing for which performance tests would not be appropriate. *Written tests* can be used to evaluate the student's mastery of knowledge ranging from recall of basic terms and facts to evaluation of complex situations. This section explains how to select the best type of test item to use and how to construct and try out written tests.

TERMINAL PERFORMANCE OBJECTIVE

To demonstrate mastery of this task, do the following:

Given both skill and knowledge tasks for which task analyses and terminal performance objectives have been developed, develop appropriate written tests to evaluate mastery of the knowledge tasks and the knowledge components of the skill tasks. The written tests should conform to *all* criteria listed in Performance Test 8 listed at the end of this section.

ENABLING OBJECTIVES

This section is divided into several parts to help you:

[1] *Identify advantages of recognition test items.*
[2] *Construct and try out written tests.*

ENABLING OBJECTIVE [1]

Identify Advantages of Recognition Test Items

Developing Written Tests

Written tests are used to assess a student's mastery of knowledge tasks and to assess mastery of complex or critical concepts or facts underlying skill tasks. The term *written* test is being used more for convenience since most often the test questions are written and the student responds in writing. Of course, the test could be administered and responded to verbally, and in some cases this may be desirable. Although written tests are a valuable part of assessing mastery of competencies, a word of caution may be in order about the *overuse* of written tests. Many times we use written tests out of convenience rather than appropriateness. After all, it is far easier to give a student a written test over the procedure "alter a dress pattern" than to have the student actually do it. Do not fall into the trap of using "paper-and-pencil" tests when performance tests are called for.

> If the task says do something, the test should require the student to *do* it. Remember that written tests have a place in competency-based training but should not be used for convenience.

Since we cannot look into the student's mind and tell whether he or she possesses the particular knowledge we are after, we use results of written tests to *infer* that the student does, in fact, possess the knowledge. Just as required for performance tests, a written test should match the task. Remember that "knowledge" has been described as having various *levels*, ranging from basic knowledge to comprehension, application, analysis, synthesis, and evaluation. If the task and TPO call for the student to be able to evaluate something, the written test must include test items that require the student to do just that. Knowledge tasks beginning with verbs such as explain, differentiate, evaluate, describe, construct, solve, and so on, require written tests that assess more than mastery of facts. Also, written tests assessing the knowledge components of skill tasks often call for questions beyond recall of terms and facts.

Types of Written Test Items

What kinds of test items are there and which ones are most appropriate for criterion-referenced tests in competency-based training programs? Basically, there are two kinds of written test items:

Recall Items	*Recognition Items*
Short answer	Multiple choice
Completion	True–false
Essay	Matching

Recall (sometimes called supply) items, as you might suspect, require the student to *recall* from memory the correct answer to the question. Recognition (sometimes called selection) items, on the other hand, call for the student to *recognize* the correct answer from a list of alternatives provided. Table 5-2 shows examples of the more common recall and recognition types of test items.

Although any type of item may be used on a written test for a training program, one of these two basic types is *more suited* for use in competency-based training programs. Let us look at the major advantages and disadvantages of each type and see if we can determine whether *recall* or *recognition* items are best suited for use in competency-based programs (see Table 5-3).

In training programs where students are at various points and testing is more or less a *continuous process requiring immediate feedback*, the use of *recognition* items is advantageous. Tests using recognition items can be taken quickly, scored easily, and graded objectively. Many people think that recognition items can test only rote memorization of facts. Take a look at the two items below and see for yourself which is assessing a *higher level* of learning.

TABLE 5-2 Examples of Common Types of Written Test Items

	Recall Items
• Short answer	• What function does compost serve?
• Completion	• There are__ columns on a standard punched card.
• Essay	• Describe factors to be considered when selecting a dress pattern for a customer.
	Recognition Items
• Multiple choice	• The pitch of a roof is the: a. Ratio of the rise to the span b. Unit length divided by number of feet in run c. Ratio of rise to run d. Number of inches in rise for every foot of run
• True-false	• T F One ampere of current is defined as 6.25×10^{18} electrons flowing past a given point per second.
• Matching	• Column A lists primary *uses* of tools; column B lists *names* of tools. Match each tool with its proper use by placing the *letter* of the proper tool in the blank to the left of each use.

TABLE 5-3 Advantages and Disadvantages of Recall and Recognition Test Items

Type	*Advantages*	*Disadvantages*
Recall Items • Short answer • Completion • Essay	1. Can be constructed quickly. 2. Can test broad areas of knowledge.	1. Many possible answers to most questions. 2. Grading is open to subjectivity. 3. Grading is quite time consuming. 4. Encourages memorization of fact. 5. Time consuming to take.
Recognition Items • Multiple choice • True–false • Matching	1. Students can respond quickly. 2. Only one correct answer. 3. Can be graded very quickly. 4. Can be graded by a proctor or clerk. 5. Grading is very objective. 6. Items can test ability to make judgments and evaluate alternatives.	1. Good items are sometimes difficult to construct. 2. If items not worded properly, guessing may become a problem.

EXAMPLE

Item 1 *(Recall): Metals are __________ in their makeup.*

Item 2 *(Recognition): What is the minimum size of fuse that should be used for a water heater with 8 ohms resistance:*

A. 5 A
B. 10 A
C. 15 A
D. 20 A

Item 1, a *recall*-type item (completion), simply requires the student to "spit back" the bit of information needed to correctly complete the statement. The correct answer, "crystalline," could have been memorized or guessed at and the student would have gotten the item right and still might not *understand* what "crystalline" means. To compound the problem, if a student had responded with "solid, metallic or magnetic," they really would not be *wrong*—their answer, however, would not be *right*. The argument might go on and on to no one's satisfaction. (You have probably heard about the essay question that asked the student to "define the universe and give three examples.")

For item 2, on the other hand (multiple choice), there is only *one correct answer*. Even though the student only had to recognize the correct answer (c) from four alternatives, he or she had to master the concept being tested (use of Ohm's law) to respond correctly. Furthermore, the way the item is worded actually simulates the situation on the job. The worker is confronted with a water heater of 8 ohms resistance and must know that Ohm's law is required to determine the proper fuse size and must be able to calculate the proper size of fuse for the heater.

So you can see that there is a strong case for using *recognition*-type items on tests in competency-based training programs. Of the three recognition items, the *multiple-choice* type has more pluses than does the matching or true-false. True-false items encourage guessing (50% chance) and are difficult to construct to test higher levels of learning. Matching items are somewhat cumbersome, the tests take quite a bit of time to take, and they are not well suited to testing a large amount of different kinds of knowledge. Matching items *are* useful for assessing mastery of lists of things, such as terms, equipment, and so on.

> All things considered, the *well-constructed* multiple-choice item is perhaps the most suitable test item to use for written tests in competency-based training programs.

Of course, there will be times, particularly in Self-Checks, when short-answer, completion, essay, true-false, matching, and other test items are appropriate, but for general use in assessing competency mastery, the multiple-choice item is highly recommended.

See if you can identify the advantages of recognition test items by completing the following Self-Check.

SELF-CHECK [1]

Check your mastery of ENABLING OBJECTIVE [1] by completing this SELF-CHECK.

1. Which kinds of test items listed below have only *one* correct answer (if constructed properly) and can be graded very objectively?

______ (a) Essay

______ (b) Completion

______ (c) Matching

______ (d) Multiple choice

______ (e) Short answer

______ (f) True–false

2. List at least four advantages of using multiple-choice test items on written tests.

   (a) ______________________________

   (b) ______________________________

   (c) ______________________________

   (d) ______________________________

3. Which test item below is assessing the highest level of knowledge?

   (a) Explain what board feet means.

   (b) The formula for board feet is ____ times ____ times ____ times divided by ____ .

   (c) T F The number of board feet in a board 1 in. x 6 in. x 10 ft. is 5.

   (d) How many board feet are needed for a project requiring the following boards: 2—2 in. x 4 in. x 8 ft., 4—4 in. x 6 in. x 4 ft., 6—1 in. x 10 in. x 12 ft.?

   A. 8.55 B. 36.6 C. 46.3 D. 102.6

Check your responses with those in the Answer-Key in the appendix.

ENABLING OBJECTIVE [2]

Construct and Try Out Written Tests

Construct Multiple-Choice Items

Since the multiple-choice item is recommended, the remainder of this section provides some tips that will help instructors and others develop good multiple-choice test items. Basically, a multiple-choice item consists of two parts: (1) the *stem*, which poses the problem or question, and (2) several *alternatives*, which include the correct response and several distractors. The trainee is instructed to choose the alternative that is the correct or most appropriate response.

The stem. The stem presents the problem and may be a question, a statement, or a phrase. Care should be taken to develop a clearly worded stem.

As you write the stem for multiple-choice items, remember:

- If you write the stem in negative terms, underline the word making the stem negative (*not*, *worst*, etc.).
- Avoid ending the stem with "a" or 'an" since some alternatives may begin with vowels and some with consonants.
- The stem should be complete enough that students who have mastered the task should be able to determine the correct answer *without* looking at the alternatives.
- The stem should present the problem in a clear and unambiguous manner. Avoid stems that are vague or too short.
- Avoid clues in the stem which give away the correct alternative.
- Punctuate the stem properly; use a question mark for a question, a period for a statement, and a colon for an incomplete sentence or phrase.
- You can refer to or include diagrams, pictures, schematics, or other types of problems in the stem.

The alternatives. As you develop alternatives for the stem, remember that the alternatives:

- May be single words, phrases, or complete sentences
- Should be written at a level appropriate for the students
- Should be very similar to one another in length, point of view, and grammatical structure
- Should all be reasonable, plausible responses
- If numerical, should be in ascending or descending order
- Should not give any hint of the correct answer through arrangement, wording, or punctuation
- Should each appear on a separate line and be labeled by capital letters or other easily identifiable means
- Should be 4 or 5 in number (fewer than four greatly increases the chances of guessing; more than five takes a lot of time)
- Should not follow any pattern of correct answers; using dice (ignoring five and six) is a good way to ensure that the correct response (A, B, C, or D) appears randomly

- Should be as short as possible—include any repetitious wording in the stem
- Should include only *one* correct answer
- Should not use "all of the above" or "none of the above" just to come up with enough alternatives
- Should each contain only one complete thought

Although each of the foregoing tips may seem minor, taken together they will result in much more valid test items that will more effectively assess a student's mastery of tasks.

Guidelines for Written Tests

Regardless of the type of test items used to make up a written test, several guidelines should be followed.

1. Make certain that the test items assess the student's mastery of the task. Do not include test items that question the learner on content outside the scope of the task and not included in the learning activities.
2. Remember: the primary purpose of testing is to assess whether or not each trainee has mastered a task.
3. "Trick" items do nothing but waste time and confuse and frustrate the student.
4. Avoid items that force the student simply to recall facts.
5. Include enough, but only enough items on a test to fully assess the student's mastery of the key concepts or facts covered in the scope of the task itself. Broader and more complex knowledge tasks will require more test items.
6. Make sure that the test items require a high level of learning on the part of the test taker if the task is written at a high level.
7. A good test should be easy to take and easy to score.
8. Tests should be fair. Questions should relate only to material the student should know and an inflexible key should be used in scoring.
9. Tests also reflect the effectiveness of the learning activities and resources students are using. When several students fail to reach mastery of a task, the trouble may lie with the learning materials.
10. Testers should keep track of how often students miss specific test items. When a higher-than-usual number of students miss a particular test item, it probably needs to be reworded.
11. Each item on a test should stand alone. Information for subsequent items should not be revealed in an earlier item.

12. Have someone review your test before administering it to make sure that the directions and test items are clear.
13. Include clearly worded directions for each test. Include the purpose of the test, how to respond to each kind of item, how many must be answered correctly for mastery, and what time limit is imposed.
14. Avoid questions from quotes, specific pages of books, or other trivial sources.
15. Shoot for a minimum mastery score of 100% if possible. Try to boil the test down to as few items as possible and word them very carefully. Another strategy is to require "corrected to 100% accuracy" as your minimum score for written tests. If you use something less than 100%, you should have a very good reason other than "students just won't score 100%."

See if you know how to construct multiple-choice test items by completing the following Self-Check.

SELF-CHECK [2]

Check your mastery of ENABLING OBJECTIVE [2] in this section by completing this SELF-CHECK.

Below are several sample multiple-choice test items. In the lines below each, indicate how the item could be improved. There may be more than one thing wrong with each.

1. Dirt and debris are attracted to hair:

   (1) Because of cosmetic treatments

   (2) Because of moisture

   (3) Because of electrical forces created by static electricity charges

   (4) Because of absence of oil

____

____

2. Electricity

   A. Is an invisible force

   B. Can produce heat, light, and motion because of electromagnetic effects

C. Is what causes a compass to point north

---

3. How many feet in 3 × 12 × 8

a. 24   b. 12   c. 16   d. 8

Check your responses with those in the Answer Key in the appendix.

Continue with the following performance test.

PERFORMANCE TEST FOR TASK 8

TASK 8: Develop Written Tests

DIRECTIONS

When ready, demonstrate your ability to develop written tests by doing the following:

For tasks for which TPOs and task analyses have been developed:

1. Develop appropriate written tests to evaluate mastery of knowledge tasks and to evaluate the knowledge component of skill tasks—use only multiple-choice test items.
2. Try out the written tests and revise.

No.	Criteria for evaluating performance; 100% mastery required	YES	NO
	Directions		
1.	Is the purpose of the test stated?		
2.	Is the student told how to respond to test items?		
3.	Is the mastery score indicated?		
4.	If applicable, is a time limit mentioned?		
	Overall Test		
5.	Is there a sufficient number of test items to assess adequately mastery of the task?		
6.	If the task involves mastery of higher-level concepts and principles, does the test evaluate this?		
7.	Do all items relate directly to the knowledge involved in the task?		
8.	Are clues avoided that may indicate the correct answer to other items?		
9.	Are trick test items avoided?		

	Multiple-Choice Stems		
10.	Is each stem complete enough for students to determine the answer without looking at the alternatives?		
11.	Is each stem a phrase, statement, or question?		
12.	Does each stem state the problem or question clearly?		
13.	Are negatives underlined if used?		
14.	Are "a" or "an" endings avoided?		
15.	Are stems punctuated appropriately?		
	Multiple-Choice Alternatives		
16.	Are alternatives constructed similar in length and point of view?		
17.	Is each alternative a reasonable, plausible choice?		
18.	If numerical, are they listed in order?		
19.	Does each appear on a separate line?		
20.	Is each identified by a capital letter or other easily recognizable means?		
21.	Are patterns of correct responses avoided?		
22.	Are there four or five alternatives for each item?		
23.	Is repetitious wording avoided in each alternative?		
24.	Is there only *one* correct answer for each question?		
25.	Does each alternative contain only one complete thought?		

6

Developing Learning Packages

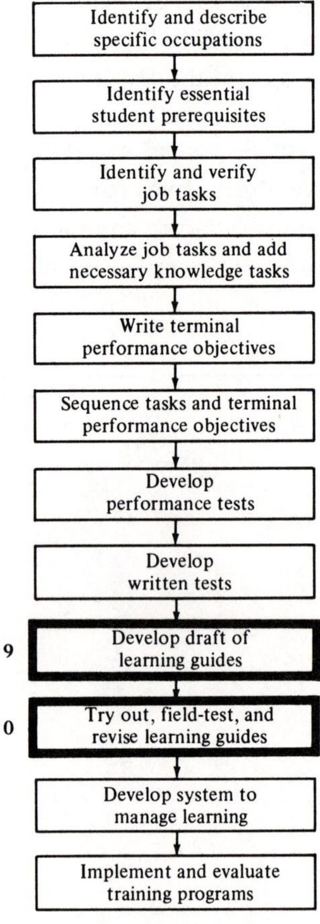
Identify and describe specific occupations
Identify essential student prerequisites
Identify and verify job tasks
Analyze job tasks and add necessary knowledge tasks
Write terminal performance objectives
Sequence tasks and terminal performance objectives
Develop performance tests
Develop written tests
9
Develop draft of learning guides
10
Try out, field-test, and revise learning guides
Develop system to manage learning
Implement and evaluate training programs

When you complete this section, you will be able to:

TASK 9: Develop Draft of Learning Guides

INTRODUCTION

One way to provide each student with the right kind of instruction and enough time to master each task fully before going on to the next is to "package" instruction so that each student has all the necessary media, materials, and other essential learning resources close at hand. If provided with a complete and well-developed "learning package," each student can begin, speed up, slow down, or repeat instruction as he or she needs to. This section shows you how to develop a *learning guide* for each task which is a learning package design that is easy and inexpensive to develop and that has been used successfully around the country.

TERMINAL PERFORMANCE OBJECTIVE

To demonstrate mastery of this task, do the following:

Given tasks for which task analyses, terminal performance objectives, and written and/or performance tests have been developed, construct a draft of a learning guide for each task. Each draft should conform to *all* criteria listed on Performance Test 9 at the end of this section.

ENABLING OBJECTIVES

This section is divided into several parts to help you:

[1] *Describe how learning packages enhance learning.*
[2] *Identify components of effective learning packages.*
[3] *Develop cover page and learning steps page for learning guides.*
[4] *Select and develop learning resources for learning guides.*

ENABLING OBJECTIVE [1]

Describe How Learning Packages Enhance Learning

Our Goal: Effective and Efficient Training

Up to this point, we have worried more about the *what* of training—identifying, analyzing, and sequencing tasks and objectives and developing tests to find out if trainees mastered the tasks. Now, we are faced with the *how* of training—how should we go about actually delivering instruction in these tasks to trainees? Let us first agree on the *basis* upon which we should compare various approaches to delivering instruction.

> The most desirable approaches to delivering instruction are those that are most *effective* in terms of *results* and most *efficient* in terms of *cost.*

A training technique or method that is not both effective *and* efficient is not of much value to us. For example, Psychology 1101 taught in a lecture hall for 250 students approaches the ultimate in *efficiency*. The only costs are the professor's salary and the upkeep of the lecture hall. But when we examine the dropout rate of Psychology 1101 students, their failure rate, final exam scores, and retention of learning over time, we are appalled by the almost nonexistence of any real *effectiveness*. On the other hand, if we hired enough psychology professors to tutor all 250 students individually, we might have a high degree of *effectiveness*, but few (especially the taxpayers) would view this arrangement as *efficient*. So, as we search for a method to deliver instruction for our tasks, we need to strike a balance between effectiveness (does it *work*?) and efficiency (how much does it *cost*?). What training strategies yield good results but have a reasonable price tag?

What Works Best?

Why don't we start by identifying training strategies that have already proven to be highly effective—in other words, let us find out what works best. Since we do not have the time to conduct careful educational research to find out which approaches to training are more effective than others, let us review the findings of those who have. Table 6-1 lists some of the characteristics that highly effective training and education programs seem to have in common. By effective, now, we mean methods or strategies that have resulted in a *high percentage of students* reaching a *high level of mastery* of the learning tasks. In Table 6-1, you are looking at common characteristics of programs that *work*.

Summarizing, we might say:

TABLE 6-1 Characteristics of Effective Training Programs

Highly effective education and training programs:

1. Keep student "mastery" as the overriding concern of the program; they focus on *learning*—not teaching.
2. Allow each trainee enough time to master each task fully *before* being forced to move on to the next.
3. Break each learning task into several smaller segments—each presented only when the student is ready.
4. Provide instruction that is appropriate for both the student and the task being learned.
5. Allow individual students to speed up or slow down their learning pace based on their needs.
6. Inform students of exactly what it is they are to learn and how well they must learn it for mastery.
7. Help individual students when and where needed during the learning process.
8. Allow students to spend most of their time actively engaged in learning—not covering material, or putting in seat time.
9. Provide some means for each student to get immediate feedback about his or her performance at critical points in each learning unit and to correct that performance if needed.
10. Help students master early learning tasks, so mastery of essential prerequisite tasks will be assured and the student will quickly develop a positive attitude about self and the program and will be adequately prepared for later, more difficult or complex tasks.

Highly effective training programs (1) spell out very clearly what it is and how well students are to learn, (2) provide carefully designed student-centered learning activities to help them get there, and (3) allow each student sufficient time to fully master each task before going on to the next.

With this in mind, I think you will agree that the "traditional" approach to training is not the way for us to go. As we look at these characteristics of effective programs it is not difficult to see why the conventional approach to education and training just does not work very well. If we visit most typical schools or training programs, here is what we will find:

The instructor gets up before the class and demonstrates or lectures on a topic, then students go out into the shop or lab or field to practice. Students are then tested, which usually results in test scores that vary widely, with only 10 to 20% reaching a high level of mastery

("A"). The group of students then moves on to the next topic without much concern for the 80 to 90% who failed to reach mastery. The process is then repeated, getting progressively worse as nonmastery students fall further behind and either drop out, withdraw, or complete the program only marginally competent.

You have probably realized by now that the traditional instructor-centered, group-paced approach to training actually *prevents* the majority of students from reaching a high level of mastery! We might say that the only way of getting 30 students from point A to point B, and making sure they all arrive, is by school bus!

Conventional education and training programs usually (1) are based on vague student outcomes that are rarely written down; (2) rely primarily on the instructor as the primary source of instruction, dictating instructor-centered, group-paced teaching methods which are ineffective for most students; and even worse, (3) force students to move on to the next task when the "group" is ready—even though many trainees have not yet fully mastered the task on which they are working.

The traditional approach does not work very well for the majority of students because it virtually eliminates the characteristics of effective training programs.

Why Learning Packages?

If the conventional approach in which the instructor does most of the teaching and the group moves from task to task is not very effective, what approach can we use that will capitalize on what we know about what works well? One approach that has proven very effective is the use of *learning packages* as the *primary* means of delivering instruction in each task. A learning package is simply a well-designed and carefully developed learning aid that gives students detailed instructions to guide them through the learning process and provides them with appropriate learning materials *when* and *how long* needed, which results in each student having as much time on a task as needed to reach mastery.

In training programs organized this way, there is usually a separate learning package for each task. An effective learning package is carefully developed and breaks the learning task down into several smaller segments. Step-by-step instruction in only one major segment of the task is presented through some appropriate resource, such as slides, tapes, films, or readings. The learning package then guides the student through hands-on practice of that segment of the task. The student then gets feedback on that performance from the instructor or other source. Instruction, practice, and feedback are then provided for each additional segment. Finally, the student demonstrates overall mastery of the entire task.

Learning packages are not new and they will not solve all the problems involved in training. But they have been successful in delivering effective and efficient training. Let us look at what learning packages are *not*:

Learning packages are *not*:

- A cure-all for training problems
- An experimental approach not yet proven
- A gimmick or fad that will fade away
- A replacement for instructors
- A cold, inhuman, mechanical means of delivering instruction
- Something to be shoved in the student's face and the student told to "come back in a week"

TABLE 6-2 Benefits of Using Learning Packages

Learning packages can help provide effective training by:

1. Providing a wide variety of learning resources and activities, such as books, media, or hands-on practice that are appropriate for the task being learned.
2. Providing learning materials that are available when students need them and that each student can use at his or her own pace.
3. Providing needed structure to the learning process by providing detailed instructions about what to do and when to do it.
4. Organizing the training program by task. Job tasks become the basic unit of the curriculum just as they are on the job. Tasks do not get lost in chapters, units, blocks, and other arbitrary divisions that have little meaning for the student.
5. Providing a means of upgrading the quality of instruction. Based on test results and input from students, learning packages can be continually improved and updated. Also, when the instructor leaves, the training program will not leave too.
6. Including built-in checkpoints for checking each student's progress toward mastering a task.
7. Providing a system of learning that students prefer. Students have expressed their overwhelming preference for this approach; students experience more success, more freedom of choice, and more active involvement in learning.
8. Ensuring that initially each student receives the same, appropriate instruction. The media and materials incorporated into learning packages do not vary every time they are used as do live demonstrations and lectures.

Using learning packages is an efficient way to provide each student with the *right kind* of instruction and *enough time* to reach mastery.

We need to point out that using learning packages is *one* approach—not *the* approach. Unfortunately, there is not one best approach to education and training. About all that we can do is to identify what has worked well and use those strategies and improve them. Perhaps we need to look at training as more of a science than an art and work to refine the technology of training constantly focusing on improving results. That is where learning packages come in. Using carefully designed and well-written learning packages as the primary means of delivering instruction allows us to incorporate many of the common elements of successful training programs mentioned earlier. Table 6-2 lists several benefits of using learning packages as the primary means of delivering instruction.

Before going on, see if you can describe how learning packages enhance learning by completing the following Self-Check.

SELF-CHECK [1]

Check your mastery of ENABLING OBJECTIVE [1] by completing this SELF-CHECK.

1. Various methods of delivering instruction to trainees should be compared on the basis of what two factors?

   (a) ____________________

   (b) ____________________

2. List at least five characteristics of highly effective training programs.

   (a) ____________________

   (b) ____________________

   (c) ____________________

   (d) ____________________

   (e) ____________________

3. List two basic reasons why the instructor-centered, group-paced, traditional approach to training does not work very well for the majority of students.

(a) ____

(b) ____

4. List at least four reasons why learning packages enhance learning.

   (a) ____

   (b) ____

   (c) ____

   (d) ____

Compare your responses with those in the Answer Key in the appendix.

ENABLING OBJECTIVE [2]

Identify Components of Effective Learning Packages

Three Approaches

If using learning packages is the way we have decided to go, what should our learning packages look like? Should they have one page or ten pages? Should they be self-contained or use outside resources? There are several approaches we might take. Figure 6-1 shows three common learning package designs and advantages and disadvantages of each. Samples 6-1 and 6-2 show examples of the *student direction sheet* and the *module*. A sample *learning guide* is included later in this section. All three designs are currently in use in occupational training programs in public vocational schools, business and industry, the military, and in agencies. One of these approaches to writing learning packages is not necessarily better than another. It is a matter of selecting a design that is both effective and efficient for the situation.

Figure 6-2 shows the relative effectiveness and efficiency of these three basic learning package designs. First, let us compare the *efficiency* of each. The one-page student direction sheet, as you might expect, is a very efficient approach. It takes very little time, energy, or funds to write, reproduce, distribute, and store them. At the other end of the efficiency curve is the more formal, self-contained "module." Modules requiring extensive writing, editing, artwork, layout, illustrations, photography, and related production work are very expensive to produce. The efficiency of professionally produced modules would be less than that of a single sheet of student directions that could be developed in a matter of hours.

Now, comparing the *effectiveness* of these three approaches to see how well each works, we see that complete, self-contained modules are perhaps

FIGURE 6-1 THREE LEARNING PACKAGE DESIGNS

DESIGN	ADVANTAGES	DISADVANTAGES
1. The *student direction sheet*: a single sheet with a list of student directions for accomplishing a learning task.	1. Can be written very quickly with little training needed. 2. Less paper to shuffle for the student. 3. Low cost to copy and store. 4. Can be revised easily.	1. Must rely almost totally on already developed learning materials, usually textbooks. 2. Difficult to incorporate checkpoints and feedback into the learning process. 3. Usually has no formal written or performance test. 4. Often directs students to group-oriented activities such as lectures or demonstrations.
2. The *learning guide*: carefully guides the student through the use of a wide variety of commercially produced and instructor-developed materials and media as well as hands-on practice. Includes selfcheck and tests.	1. Can be developed by anyone with minimal training. 2. Can take full advantage of any good resource available. 3. Commercially available mediated programs and textbooks can be easily incorporated. 4. Can incorporate materials already developed locally. 5. Easy for students to follow. 6. Ensures checkpoints and final evaluation of task. 7. Can be easily adapted for programs in other locations.	1. Some formal training needed to develop guides. 2. Every learning resource needed is not within the guide—student is referred to external resources.
3. The *self-contained module*: a more formalized complete learning package; all learning resources are within each module. Usually includes detailed instruction in performing the task, pictures, diagrams, self-tests, pretests, and post-tests.	1. Self-contained; student does not need any additional outside resources. 2. Usually carefully designed, developed and field-tested. 3. Usually has a more finished, professional look.	1. Very time consuming to develop. 2. Sometimes confusing for students to follow. 3. Very expensive to develop, reproduce, distribute, and store. 4. Relectance to revise modules when completed. 5. Does not take advantage of materials already available. 6. High level of training needed for development. 7. Sometimes relies too much on reading. 8. Sometimes locks the user into specific types or brands of tools or equipment.

FIGURE 6–1 Three Learning Package Designs

SAMPLE 6-1	STUDENT DIRECTION SHEET

Program: Industrial Arts II

Task: Make moldings using the shaper

Objective: Given rough stock, shaper, and various bits, make decorative moldings. Molding should have smooth finish and have no tool or burn marks.

LEARNING ACTIVITIES

1. Read Chapter 12, "Using the Shaper," in your textbook.
2. Take a safety test on use of the shaper.
3. Observe the instructor demonstration on the setup and proper use of the shaper.
4. Have the instructor check you on use of the shaper.
5. Make the moldings shown in Figures 12-6 through 12-10 on page 178 of your textbook.

SAMPLE 6–1 Student Direction Sheet

Figure 9-18 Adjusting point gap, using slot method

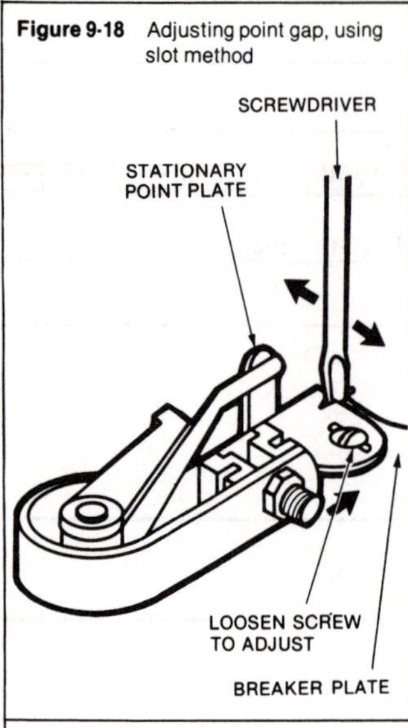

Using the slot method.

STEP 1 Loosen the base-locking screw of the stationary contact point, using a screwdriver (see Figure 9-18). Loosen it just enough so that the stationary point base can be moved.

STEP 2 Insert the screwdriver into the opening in the breaker plate assembly.

STEP 3 Slide the stationary point base in order to close or widen the gap. Check the opening with the feeler gauge.

STEP 4 Retighten the base-locking screw and check the gap opening again.

Using the eccentric method.

STEP 1 Loosen the base-locking screw of the stationary contact point just enough so that the stationary point can be moved (see Figure 9-19).

STEP 2 Using a screwdriver, turn the eccentric screw in either direction to move the stationary point base (see Figure 9-19). This closes or widens the point gap. Check the opening with a feeler gauge.

STEP 3 Retighten the base-locking screw, and check the gap opening again.

Using the allen wrench method.

STEP 1 Insert an allen wrench into the stationary contact point adjusting screw (see Figure 9-20).

Figure 9-19 Adjusting contact point gap, using eccentric method

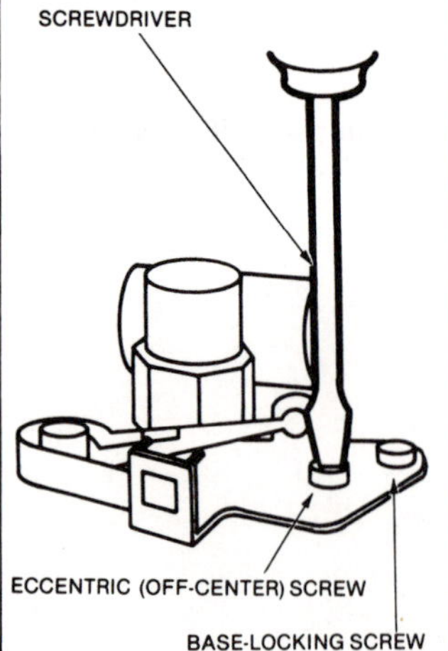

Figure 9-20 Adjusting contact point gap, using allen wrench

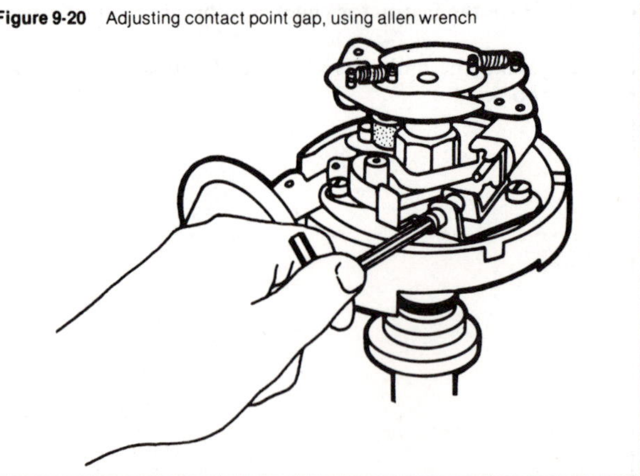

SAMPLE 6-2 Typical Page from a Professionally Produced Module (Source: Unit 3 Tire Service, Automotive Mechanics Curriculum Project, Florida State Dept. of Education, Tallahassee, Fla., 1979.)

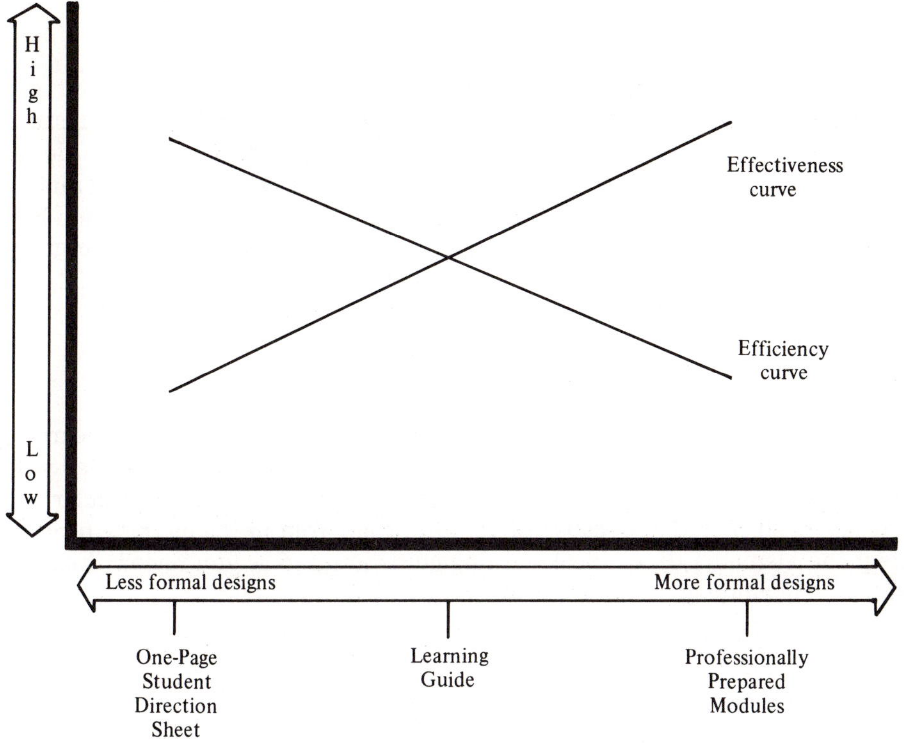

FIGURE 6-2 Effectiveness and Efficiency of Three Learning Package Designs

more effective than are less formal packages. Notice from Figure 6-2 that the *learning guide* design strikes a good compromise between the two extremes. The learning guide approach is formal enough to be effective, yet informal enough to still have a high degree of efficiency—it works and it is fairly inexpensive. For this reason, the learning guide approach to developing learning packages is recommended for most situations and is explained in detail in this chapter.

Keep in mind that this is *one* approach to delivering instruction in a training program—not *the* approach. When a training program needs to be developed very quickly, very cheaply, or perhaps on a one-shot or temporary basis, the one-page direction sheet or other highly efficient approach is the right way to proceed. When a training program is developed for a large number of trainees or is to be repeated many, many times, more formalized, highly effective modules might be the answer.

The Ideal Learning Guide

We have decided that we will use learning packages rather than instructor demonstrations or lectures as our primary means of delivering instruction. Also, we have decided that the most practical learning package design for us is probably the *learning guide*, which relies heavily on learning materials already developed, such as references and media. Now, let us decide how our learning guide should be put together. Although it is beyond our grasp, let us try to design the "ideal" learning guide.

Table 6-3 describes what an ideal learning guide might look like.

A Suggested Format

On the next several pages you will find a sample of a complete learning guide. This sample guide uses a format that has been carefully designed with the "ideal" learning guide in mind. Every component of this particular format has been included because of its important role in the learning process. Keep the elements of an ideal learning guide in mind as you review this sample learning guide.

TABLE 6-3 Characteristics of an Ideal Learning Guide

The ideal learning guide would probably:

1. Be easy to locate, handle, and use; it would probably be "free standing" and not be bound to other learning guides.
2. Be pleasing to the eye and attractively laid out.
3. Show very clearly on the first page *exactly* what task the learning guide covers.
4. Describe *exactly* what the student must do to demonstrate mastery of the task after the guide has been completed or before the guide is begun if the student can already perform the task.
5. Very early in the guide, provide some explanation or introduction that motivates the student to want to learn the task well.
6. Be divided into several major parts, each teaching a major part of the task rather than trying to teach the entire task at once.
7. For each major part of the task, present instruction in a clear, straightforward, appropriate manner, provide hands-on practice of what was presented and then provide immediate feedback.
8. Heavily involve the instructor at critical points during the learning process, such as checkpoints, problem areas, danger points, and final evaluation.
9. Be relatively easy to develop and take full advantage of a wide variety of learning materials already developed or purchased.
10. Provide detailed instructions to the student explaining exactly what to do, and why and when to do it, from beginning to end.

There is really nothing revolutionary about this particular format. About the best thing we can say for it is that it works! Several variations of this learning guide design have been in use for a number of years in training programs around the country. The format shown in this section is simply a refinement of several proven designs. One large institution that has implemented this basic learning package design very successfully is the 916 Area Vo-Tech Institute in White Bear Lake, Minnesota. At 916, thousands of learning guides have been developed and used. The evidence so far collected shows very clearly that most students can reach a high level of mastery using learning guides as the primary source of routine instruction.

The format of our sample learning guide (or some variation of this format) is recommended, at least as a starting place, perhaps, until your particular school, company, or agency adopts its own design. I highly recommend this format because:

- It has a proven track record—it works.
- It is educationally sound—students can master tasks effectively and efficiently using it.
- With a minimum of training, anyone can develop learning guides using this format.
- It relies heavily on a wide variety of already developed media and materials—this design makes most of your existing textbooks, handouts, job sheets, and media self-instructional—without any modification whatsoever.
- It is economical to develop, duplicate, and store. Following this format, most of your learning guides will be less than 5 to 10 pages long, even less if you can locate good references and audiovisuals.

Take time to review carefully the sample learning guide that follows; you may want to go through it as a student would (see Sample 6-3). Notice how the learning guide has been constructed and how it avoids many of the shortcomings of conventional group-oriented teaching methods.

SAMPLE 6-3	LEARNING GUIDE	E-02

AUTOMOTIVE MECHANICS

AVTI
ANY VO-TECH INSTITUTE
1234 MASTERY LANE
ANYTOWN, U.S.A. 98765

Program 7291 Task E-02: Replace exhaust pipe, muffler, and tail pipe.

TASK: Repair exhaust pipe, muffler, and tail pipe

INTRODUCTION:

Since the exhaust pipe, muffler, and tail pipe are on the underside of the car, they take a terrific beating. If you can spot exhaust system parts that are corroded, cracked, or broken, you may save the customer more costly and inconvenient repairs later. Often, the exhaust pipe, muffler, or tail pipe must be replaced. If not replaced properly by the mechanic, the exhaust system may rattle or may leak deadly exhaust gases into the passenger compartment, causing sickness or even death.

TERMINAL PERFORMANCE OBJECTIVE

To Demonstrate Your Master of This Task, Do the Following:

GIVEN: Automobiles needing exhaust system repair and access to tools, equipment, and replacement parts,

YOU WILL: Remove and replace defective exhaust system components.

HOW WELL: Written test and performance test must be completed with 100% mastery.

ENABLING OBJECTIVES

This Learning Guide Is Divided into Several Parts to Help You:

[1] Describe function of and inspect exhaust system components.

[2] Remove and replace tail pipe.

[3] Remove and replace muffler.

[4] Remove and replace exhaust pipe.

School	Dept.	Prog.	Duty	Task	Preqt	Avg.Hrs		Dates Revised		
AVTI	Ind.	7291	E	02	E-01	36				

SAMPLE 6-3

A V T I	Follow the LEARNING STEPS listed below:	Task E-02

EO [1]	Describe function of and inspect exhaust system components.

- ✓ 1. Read pages 171–174 in *Modern Auto Repair* describing the function of exhaust system components.
- ✓ 2. Read Instruction Sheet 1, enclosed, describing what to look for when inspecting the exhaust system.
- ✓ 3. See if you can describe parts of the exhaust system and determine which parts need replacing by completing Self-Check 1, enclosed.

EO [2]	Remove and replace tail pipe.

- ✓ 1. View slides 1–32 in slide-tape E-02, showing how to remove and replace tail pipe on automobile, all the way through.
- ✓ 2. While viewing slides 1–32 again, remove and replace the tail pipe from vehicle assigned by instructor.
- ______ 3. Check your work using Self-Check 2, enclosed.
- ______ 4. Have instructor check your work before going any further.

EO [3]	Remove and replace muffler.

- ______ 1. View slides 33–50, showing how to remove and replace muffler, all the way through.
- ______ 2. While viewing slides 33–50 again, remove and replace muffler on vehicle assigned by instructor.
- ______ 3. Check your work using Self-Check 3, enclosed.
- ______ 4. Have instructor check your work before going any further.

EO [4]	Remove and replace exhaust pipe.

- ______ 1. While viewing slides 51–64, remove and replace muffler on assigned vehicle.
- ______ 2. Check your work using Self-Check 4 enclosed, then have instructor check your work.
- ______ 3. Now, practice replacing muffler, tail pipe, and exhaust pipe on customer's car assigned by shop foreman.
- ______ 4. Have instructor check your work.
- ______ 5. When you are ready, take the Written Test for Task E-02.
- ______ 6. When ready, take the Performance Test for Task E-02.

Program 7291

SAMPLE 6-3 *(continued)*

AVTI	INSTRUCTION SHEET 1	Task E-02

Listed below are the steps to inspect the exhaust system. Make these checks both with and without the engine running. *Caution*: Exhaust system components are *hot*!

1. Identify vehicle–match car with work order–read it twice.

2. Raise vehicle on lift–be sure to follow rules for raising cars on lift. Review learning guide B-04 if needed.

3. Locate and inspect *muffler*. You will need to replace muffler if you find any of the following:

   a. Holes or cracks in body of muffler

   b. Breaks in either end of muffler where end is attached to body of muffler

   c. Excessive rust or corrosion

   d. Large dents or areas weakened by rust

   e. Loose, broken, or missing muffler clamps (check both ends–tighten or replace as needed)

4. Inspect the *exhaust pipe*. You will need to repair or replace if you find:

   a. Loose or missing nuts holding exhaust pipe to manifold (tighten)

   b. Missing or broken gasket (replace)

   c. Leaks in manifold/exhaust pipe connection. Feel for leaks with your hand (*caution*: exhaust pipe and manifold are hot!)

   d. Cracks or holes or split seams in pipe (replace)

   e. Loose connections at manifold or muffler (tighten)

   f. Dents or kinks that restrict flow of exhaust gases (replace)

5. Inspect *tail pipe*. You will need to repair or replace if you find:

   a. Loose connections (tighten)

   b. Cracks, holes, or split seams (replace)

   c. Dents or kinks (replace)

   d. Broken or frayed support brackets (replace brackets)

Program 7291

SAMPLE 6-3 *(continued)*

AVTI	SELF-CHECK 1	Task E-02

In bin 12 in shop area are actual components from the exhaust systems of foreign and domestic cars. Each part has a letter written on it which corresponds to the letters A–P below. Beside the letter for each component, write in the *name* of the component, what its *function* is (list each new function only once), and *check* (✓) those you think should be replaced if they were actually on a customer's car and *why*:

Component	Name	Function	Replace?	Why?
A				
B				
C				
D				
E				
F				
G				
H				
I				
J				
K				
L				
M				
N				
O				
P				

Check your answers with Answer Key E-02-1 in toolroom.	Program 7291

SAMPLE 6-3 *(continued)*

AVTI	SELF–CHECK 2	Task E-02

	Yes	No
1. Were safety glasses worn at all times?		
2. Is car seated securely on lift or jacks?		
3. Was penetrating oil used to loosen connectors?		
4. If the following were used, were instructions followed:		
a. Heat clamp?		
b. Hand chisel?		
c. Air hammer chisel?		
d. Pipe cutter?		
e. Pipe expander?		
f. Pipe end straighting cone?		
g. Resizer?		
5. If still good, was muffler not damaged?		
6. Were correct replacement pipe, hangers, and clamps selected?		
7. Was pipe inserted into muffler far enough to prevent leaks through end slots but not far enough to enter muffler body?		
8. Were clamps positioned approximately 1/8 inch from end and tightened securely?		
9. Was clearance between pipe and brake lines, frame, axle, shocks, and tank maintained?		
10. Was tail pipe installed to prevent gas leaks and rattles?		

All items should receive a "yes" response.	Program 7291

SAMPLE 6-3 (*continued*)

AVTI	SELF-CHECK 3	Task E-02

	Yes	No
1. Were safety glasses worn at all times?		
2. If still good, were pipes on either side of muffler *not* damaged?		
3. Were correct replacement muffler and clamps selected?		
4. Were clamps positioned 1/8 inch from end and tightened securely?		
5. Was muffler installed to prevent leaks and rattles?		

AVTI	SELF-CHECK 4	Task E-02

	Yes	No
1. Were safety glasses worn at all times?		
2. Were nuts holding exhaust pipe to manifold removed without damaging studs?		
3. Was exhaust pipe disconnected from muffler without damaging the muffler?		
4. Were proper exhaust pipe and gasket selected?		
5. Was exhaust pipe installed to prevent gas leaks and rattles?		

All items should receive a "yes" response.	Program 7291

SAMPLE 6-3 *(continued)*

AVTI	WRITTEN TEST	Task E-02
TASK	Replace exhaust pipe, muffler, and tail pipe	
DIRECTIONS		

The purpose of this test is to find out if you know how to replace the exhaust pipe, muffler, and tail pipe on an automobile. The test contains 18 multiple-choice questions. Circle the letter on the answer sheet for each question—DO NOT write on this test; 100% mastery is required.

1. Parts A on the attached drawing of the exhaust system of an automobile are:
   A. Screws
   B. Bolts
   C. Studs
   D. Clamps
2. The purpose of part B on the attached drawing is to:
   A. Filter emmissions before going through the exhaust system
   B. Prevent part E from rattling
   C. Provide proper spacing
   D. Provide a seal against escaping gases
3. Part E on the attached drawing is the:
   A. Tail pipe
   B. Exhaust pipe
   C. Extension pipe
   D. Resonator pipe
4. When replacing a tail pipe, you should use an extension jack to support the:
   A. Tail pipe
   B. Exhaust pipe
   C. Converter
   D. Muffler
5. What may happen if the clamps are not secured approximately 1/8 inch from the end of the pipe?
   A. The clamp may rattle
   B. The pipe may extend too far into the muffler
   C. Exhaust gases may leak from the slot in the pipe
   D. The clamp cannot be tightened securely

Program 7291

SAMPLE 6-3 *(continued)*

AVTI	PERFORMANCE TEST	Task E-02
TASK	Replace exhaust pipe, muffler, and tail pipe	
DIRECTIONS	Demonstrate mastery of this task by doing the following:	

1. Tell instructor you are ready to take the performance test.
2. Get work order for car(s) needing exhaust system repair.
3. Inspect entire exhaust system and select replacement parts needed.
4. Remove defective parts; you must use the following tools: (a) air hammer chisel, (b) pipe expander, (c) heat clamp.
5. Install replacement parts, check for leaks, and road test.

No.	Items to be evaluated; 100% mastery is required:	Yes	No
1.	Were safety glasses worn at all times?		
2.	Was car raised on lift safely and securely?		
3.	Were all damaged exhaust system parts replaced?		
4.	Were correct replacement parts used?		
5.	Were all clamps positioned 1/8 inch from end and tightened securely?		
6.	Were all parts installed to avoid gas leaks and rattles?		
	When replacing tail pipe:		
7.	If good, was muffler not damaged?		
8.	Was pipe inserted into muffler far enough to cover slots but not into muffler body?		
9.	Was clearance maintained around lines, frame, axle, shocks, and tank?		
	When replacing muffler:		
10.	If good, were pipes on either side of muffler not damaged?		
11.	Was muffler damage avoided during installation?		
	When replacing exhaust pipe:		
12.	Was manifold stud damage avoided?		
13.	Was muffler damage avoided?		

Student:	Date:	Attempt:	Instructor's Signature:	Page 1 of 1
		1 2 3 4		

SAMPLE 6-3 *(continued)*

Look over this sample learning guide once more and notice:

1. It "guided" the student through carefully selected learning activities and carefully developed learning materials that helped the student master the task.
2. It took advantage of learning materials already developed. This particular sample referred the student to a standard textbook and a commercially produced audiovisual presentation that were found to be appropriate.
3. Instead of trying to teach this rather complex task all at once, it split the task into four parts (enabling objectives)—one knowledge and three skills.
4. The student fully masters each enabling objective *before* going on to the next. For each enabling objective, instruction was *presented*, the student was told to *practice*, and then was given immediate *feedback*.
5. It could have been developed in as little as 3 or 4 hours.
6. The instructor was actively involved in the learning process, but *not* as a presenter of routine instruction. This was accomplished by the book, slides, and instruction sheet. The instructor's involvement was at critical points in the learning process: checking student progress, helping the student correct performance, answering questions, and evaluating the student's overall mastery of the task.
7. The only material needed to be developed by the instructor was an instruction sheet.
8. The learning guide is complete. Everything the student needed was either included in the guide or was referred to specifically, such as pages 171–174 or slides 33–50.
9. The guide is largely self-instructional. The student can spend most of the day actively engaged in learning the task and not asking questions like "What do I do next?" or "Where do I go from here?"
10. By looking at the performance test the student can see *precisely* how he or she will be evaluated. The criteria for mastering the task are spelled out clearly.

Let us look at why this suggested learning guide format was designed as it was. Every component of this particular learning package has been included for a good reason. The learning process has been thoroughly analyzed during the last several decades and most educational psychologists agree that any successful learning experience (whether it is a group discussion, a demonstration, or a learning package) will include several essential events. Table 6-4 lists these events in a successful learning activity and shows how each component of our recommended learning guide format addresses these events.

See if you can identify components of effective learning packages by completing the following Self-Check.

TABLE 6-4 The Learning Guide Includes Essential Events in the Learning Process

A Successful Learning Experience	*Purpose of Each Component of the Recommended Learning Guide Format*
1. *Informs* the student exactly what is to be learned and what *mastery* is.	1. The *task* statement tells the student exactly what will be learned. The *TPO* expands on this and explains how well it must be learned.
2. *Motivates* the student to want to learn.	2. The *introduction* tells the student why the task is important.
3. Either helps the recall or teaches any *prerequisite learning* needed to master the task.	3. If needed, the resources selected for the *first enabling objective* help the student master any necessary background knowledge or skill prerequisite to mastering the task.
4. Provides *guidance* and structure throughout the learning process.	4. The detailed *learning steps* tell the student exactly what to do, why and when to do it, and what learning resources to use.
5. *Presents* instruction appropriate for the task and in small enough units to promote efficient learning.	5. Carefully selected or developed *learning resources* present instruction for each enabling objective.
6. Provides appropriate application or *practice* of what was presented.	6. Usually, the second or third learning step for each enabling objective directs the student through a carefully designed activity to *practice* or apply what was presented.
7. Provides immediate *feedback* on practice.	7. Usually, the second or third learning step for each Enabling Objective directs the student to a *self-check* or to the instructor to get immediate feedback on performance.
8. *Evaluates* mastery.	8. The *written* and *performance tests* are designed to evaluate the student's overall mastery of the task.
9. Provides for *retention* and transfer.	9. Performing the task for the performance test several times and in slightly different settings each time promotes retention and transfer of learning to different situations.

SELF-CHECK [2]

Check your mastery of ENABLING OBJECTIVE [2] by completing this SELF-CHECK.

Listed below are advantages and disadvantages (a through i) of three different learning package designs. Match advantages and disadvantages with each design by placing the correct letter to the right of each design. Use each letter only once.

Learning Package Design	*Advantages*	*Disadvantages*
1. Student direction sheet		
2. Learning guide		
3. Self-contained module		

a. Very expensive and time consuming to develop

b. Easy to incorporate commercial and instructor-developed materials

c. Sometimes relies heavily on group-oriented activities

d. Difficult to revise when developed

e. Very quick and easy to write and revise

f. High level of training needed to develop

g. Completely self-contained

h. Can incorporate locally developed materials

i. Fairly easy to develop and contains checkpoints and final evaluations

Below are listed key *events* in the learning process and the *components* of the suggested learning guide format. For each event, identify the component(s) of the suggested learning guide that accomplishes that event by placing the letter(s) of the component(s) in the blank beside each event.

Events in Learning Process	*Learning Guide Component*
___ 4. Informs student of what is to be learned	a. Written test
___ 5. Motivates student	b. Performance test
___ 6. Helps recall or teaches prerequisite learning	c. Enabling objectives
___ 7. Provides guidance and structure	d. Learning steps for practice
___ 8. Breaks instruction in the task into a few major parts	e. Self-checks and answer key
___ 9. Provides application of learning	f. Task statement
___10. Provides immediate feedback	g. Terminal performance objective
___11. Evaluates mastery	h. Introduction
	i. If needed, the first enabling objective
	j. Learning steps

Compare your responses with those in the Answer Key in the appendix.

ENABLING OBJECTIVE [3]

Develop Cover Page and Learning Steps Page for Learning Guides

Construct Guides Carefully

Since we are going to rely heavily on learning guides to deliver the bulk of instruction to students, we must construct them with great care. You can adjust lectures and demonstrations as you go but you cannot do this with learning guides. What you develop is what the student gets. If students must constantly interrupt their learning to ask you where to find materials, what to do next, what pages in a book to read, or which frames of a filmstrip to view, you may as well go back to the traditional approach. To realize the full potential of learning packages, they must be complete and easy to follow.

To aid you in developing learning guides that will be as effective as possible, the remainder of this section offers suggestions, examples, and tips on how to construct each component of the learning guide recommended in this chapter. Keep in mind that this is just one format. There are several variations of this format being used successfully around the country. After some trial and error you may want to alter this format to suit your local needs better. In this section, we look at the first two pages of the guide. The *cover page* lists the task, orients the student to the task, explains what must be done for mastery and shows how the learning guide has been organized. The *learning steps* page lists some carefully developed steps for the student to go through and tells the student exactly what learning resources to use.

Cover Page

The cover page is the first page the student sees. It should be attractively laid out, easy to read, and contain at least the following information:

Learning guide number. This helps the student, the instructor, the typist, and anyone else involved in developing, using, or storing the guide to easily identify it. Each guide should carry the number of one task on the task listing.

Logo. If each instructional program has its own unique logo, learning guides can be very quickly identified. Also, instructors and students in each program like having an identity of their own. The program name is entered just below the logo on our sample guide.

Identification of ownership. This information identifies the school, district, institution, agency, or company that developed and owns the learning guide. This can be left blank and added later if several schools are jointly developing learning guides.

Task. You know, of course, what task statements are, how they are worded, and where they come from. Make sure that each learning guide covers one and only one task listed on the task listing. Also check to be certain that the wording of the task on the guide matches the wording of the task on the task listing. If you wish, a space for the duty in which the task is found can be included.

Introduction. This is one of the most important, yet most difficult parts to write. Many instructors wait and write it last after developing the rest of the guide. The introduction (sometimes called *purpose*) is a short paragraph that answers the question for the student: "Why should I learn this task?" Keep it brief and to the point. Mention such things as how often the task is performed, how critical it is to job performance, how dangerous it may be if not done correctly, or other *job-related* reasons. Avoid generalized statements such as "Data entry operators need to know how to do this task" or "This task is performed by a competent dental assistant." Tell the student specifically *why* it is important. Write the introduction so that it speaks directly to the student. The introduction should not include much instruction in the task—its purpose is motivational.

Terminal performance objective. As explained in Chapter 4, the TPO tells the student what is required at the end of the learning experience to demonstrate mastery of the task. The TPO describes the final testing situation.

Enabling objectives. The learning guide is constructed around several enabling objectives so that the student is not presented instruction in the entire task at once. Since most instructors are not accustomed to using them, enabling objectives may at first be difficult to develop. The next section explains the rationale behind using enabling objectives and how to develop them.

Identifying information. The information you see listed at the bottom of the cover page is very useful. Included on our sample is space for school, department, program, duty, task, any immediate prerequisite task, the average number of hours previous students have spent on this learning guide, and dates revised. Notice that at the very bottom of the cover page is a copyright notice to discourage someone from duplicating the guides for profit without permission. Also notice how identifying information was included at the bottom of all the other pages of the learning guide.

Before we look at the next page of our sample learning guide, we need to examine why enabling objectives are used and how to develop them.

Enabling Objectives

One of the most difficult steps in putting together a learning guide is deciding what the enabling objectives should be. If the enabling objectives are very carefully developed, the student will have little trouble reaching mastery of the task. It is important to realize why enabling objectives are so crucial to effective learning.

One of the most serious shortcomings of conventional instructional techniques is presenting too much to the student at once. Whether it is a lecture, demonstration, film, slides, or other method or media, the problem results from the student not being able to recall all that was presented when called upon to practice.

If you do not fully appreciate how frustrating it is for students to be presented several things at once, try a little experiment. First, write your name as you normally sign it. Now, raise your right foot off the floor and move it in a large circle. Now, try writing your name while circling your foot. I think you see what I mean.

Although you can perform the tasks required in your occupation while blindfolded with one arm tied behind your back, your students cannot. If they found the tasks on your task listing as "simple" as you may think they are, they would not be enrolled in the training program. Students who have never before performed a particular task may find it overwhelming and quite difficult, especially if you teach them how to perform the *entire* task at once. Using enabling objectives is an excellent way of helping students master the "name-writing" part of tasks first, then the "foot-circling" part, then putting the two together smoothly.

Think about how frustrating it must be for many of your students to watch you demonstrate a new skill requiring, perhaps, 20 or 30 complex steps together with a considerable amount of technical knowledge and perhaps even the use of a new piece of equipment. It is not hard to see why many instructors may give a well-planned and rehearsed demonstration and then shake their heads in dismay when some students practice the skill as if they never saw the demonstration.

Enabling objectives provide us with a way to break the demonstration of the task down into two or three major parts. We may still show the student the overall performance of the task, but we should then present a major part of the task step by step, help the student become proficient in that part, and then and *only* then go on to the next part.

Smaller objectives leading to mastery of a terminal objective may be called enabling objectives, learning objectives, micro-objectives, subobjectives, or anything else. The purpose is the same—to divide instruction in the job task into a few smaller bite-size pieces that will lead the student to mastery of the task. The term *enabling objective* (EO) is used by this author because mastering each EO *enables* the student to come closer and closer to performing the task. An important point to remember is that you will no longer locate or develop instructional media or materials for teaching the *entire* task. You will be selecting or developing learning materials for each enabling objective developed for a task.

Notice that enabling objectives (as presented in this book, anyway) are stated exactly as tasks are stated. Each EO begins with an action verb in the present tense and is observable. The main difference is that EOs are much more narrow than task statements. In stating enabling objectives, strive for the same precision and clarity as you do when stating tasks. Notice that enabling objectives do not include the given or criteria component as terminal objectives do. This is to save time in developing the EOs and make them easier for students to read.

Look at the enabling objectives that were developed for the sample tasks shown in Table 6-5 and notice that:

TABLE 6-5 Sample Enabling Objectives for Selected Tasks

Tasks	*Enabling Objectives*
1. Weld tee joints in flat position	[1] Set up station and tack weld tee joints [2] Make three pass welds [3] Make six pass welds
2. Give a manicure	[1] Prepare nails and cuticles [2] Apply base coat and polish
3. Inspect airframe using dye penetrate	[1] Describe principles of dye penetrant inspection [2] Perform dye penetrant inspection [3] Interpret results
4. Take arterial blood pressure	[1] Describe source of and problems resulting from abnormal blood pressure [2] Take and record blood pressure
5. Fight fires with portable extinguishers	[1] Select extinguisher for various types of fires [2] Extinguish class A, B, C, and D fires
6. Set up and calibrate a pressure transducer	[1] Describe the operation of the pressure transducer [2] Set up transducer circuit [3] Attach transducer and calibrate
7. Install moldings	[1] Install door casings and stops [2] Install baseboards [3] Cope moldings
8. Develop draft of learning guides	[1] Describe how learning packages enhance learning [2] Identify components of effective learning packages [3] Develop cover page and learning steps page [4] Select and develop learning resources

1. Each enabling objective is a major part of performing a task or something the student needs to learn before beginning the task.
2. It would be easier for a student to master each successive enabling objective than to master the entire task at once.
3. Students learn important background information and principles such as EO [1] for task 3, "Describe principles of dye penetrant inspection" in the same learning guide that teaches the task itself.
4. Each enabling objective involves something *new* the student is going to learn.
5. It is much easier for the instructor or curriculum specialist to locate or develop learning materials for each EO than for the entire task.
6. Each enabling objective is stated precisely and begins with an action verb. Each EO describes what needs to be taught by the learning materials to be located or developed.
7. Each enabling objective tells the student exactly what is to be accomplished in each part of the learning guide.

Let us look at several different situations, each requiring a slightly different approach to developing the enabling objectives for tasks.

Major segments of the task. In the first example, the enabling objectives developed for the task are each a major segment or part of the task itself. This is a typical situation in which each enabling objective is somewhat of a milestone in performing the task.

EXAMPLE
Task: Prepare and administer oral medication.
Steps *(taken from task analysis)*:

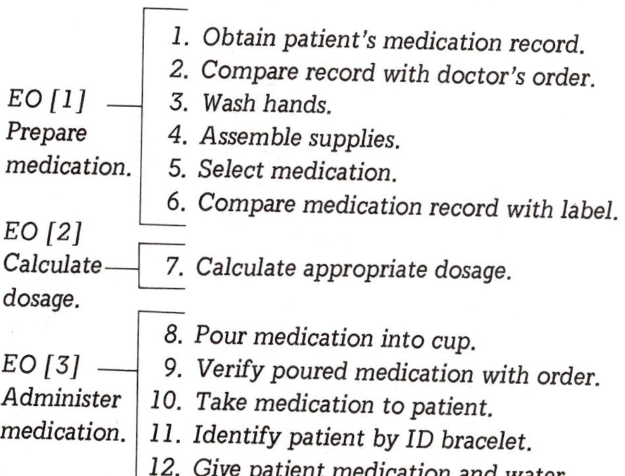

EO [1]
Prepare medication.
1. Obtain patient's medication record.
2. Compare record with doctor's order.
3. Wash hands.
4. Assemble supplies.
5. Select medication.
6. Compare medication record with label.
EO [2]
Calculate dosage.
7. Calculate appropriate dosage.
EO [3]
Administer medication.
8. Pour medication into cup.
9. Verify poured medication with order.
10. Take medication to patient.
11. Identify patient by ID bracelet.
12. Give patient medication and water.

13. *Observe patient take medication.*
14. *Discard cup.*
15. *Provide for patient's comfort.*
16. *Record medication taken.*

Look at this example and notice that the enabling objectives have been developed by carefully reviewing the steps from the task analysis and then grouping these steps. EO [1] "prepare medication" includes the first six steps actually performed by the nurse in completing the task on the job. The instructor decided that these first six steps should be presented and then practiced *before* the remainder of the steps involved are presented. Notice that EO [2], "Calculate dosage," is a *single* step. The instructor felt that step 7 in performing this task was complicated enough for students who have never done it before to be an enabling objective by itself. After mastering EO [1] the student will then be shown how to calculate dosages and will practice that until proficient. Only then will the student move on to EO [3], "Administer medication," in which steps 8 through 16 will be presented and then practiced. Of course, the student will then practice the overall task from beginning to end several times.

Look at this example again very carefully and notice that:

1. The enabling objectives were based on the actual steps required to perform the task. Fully analyzing each task to identify the steps, technical knowledge, background knowledge, special tools, safety, and attitudes involved will help you develop enabling objectives that promote efficient learning.
2. EO [1] included six steps, EO [2] only one step, and EO [3] nine steps. The number of steps that are included in an enabling objective depends on the complexity of the steps. Remember that the reason for using EOs is to avoid showing students how to perform the entire task and forcing them to remember this while practicing. Include only as much in an EO as students can remember.
3. Notice how there seems to be a natural break or resting place in the learning process between each enabling objective.
4. Each enabling objective describes what will be learned in each successive part of the learning guide. The first six steps all dealt with preparing the medication, so it was called "Prepare medication." Do not forget: we still must show the student how to perform each detailed step in preparing medication using slides, films, references, pictures, or other means. EOs simply help us organize learning a little more efficiently for the student. Try to call each EO something that is descriptive of the performance students will learn.
5. Two nursing instructors could have taken these same 16 steps in performing the task on the job and could have developed different enabling

objectives. One instructor might have decided that four EOs were needed, whereas a second instructor might have felt that two were sufficient. You will not really know how many enabling objectives are needed until you try out the learning guide.

Prerequisite knowledge. Now let us look at a slightly different situation calling for a little different approach to developing enabling objectives:

EXAMPLE

Task: Lay out and cut rafters.

EOs: *[1] Describe function and types of rafters.*

[2] Lay out rafters.

[3] Cut rafters.

Notice in this example that before the student will get involved with the task itself, some very important *prerequisite* knowledge will be mastered first—EO [1]. Many *job* tasks may require one or more *knowledge*-oriented enabling objectives.

In Chapter 3, we stressed the point that knowledge needed to perform a task should be taught together with the task itself. This example shows how this is accomplished. Although knowing the "function and types of rafters" may not be essential to being able to "lay out" and "cut" rafters, this knowledge certainly contributes to the competence of the trainee. The function and types of rafters should *not* be taught at the beginning of the carpentry program in a unit called, perhaps, "building components." The student has the most need for knowledge about what rafters are and what they do (they hold the roof up, by the way) *just prior* to learning how to layout and cut rafters. Including knowledge EOs in learning guides for job tasks is an excellent way of teaching students such things as anatomy and physiology, electronics fundamentals, and other background knowledge, *as it is needed*!

Specialized tools and equipment. The two examples below illustrate situations when the use of a specialized piece of equipment or use of a special tool may become an enabling objective.

EXAMPLES

Task 1: Replace brake shoes (drum).

EOs: *[1] Remove wheels and replace shoes.*

[2] Turn drums on lathe.

[3] Replace wheels and road test.

Task 2: Test charging system.
EOs: [1] *Describe operation of charging system.*
[2] *Hook up and interpret readings from volt-amp tester.*
[3] *Test alternator and regulator output.*
[4] *Test system, and insulated and ground circuit resistances.*

For task 1, EO [2] involves using a specialized piece of equipment—a lathe—to turn down drums. Teaching this during a unit on "use of shop equipment" or at any other time would be foolish. When the student has removed the brake drums and sees *why* the drums need turning is when the student *needs* and *wants* to learn how to operate the specialized piece of equipment for turning down drums—not before and not after; the same of task 2. The student sees the need for learning how to "hook up and interpret readings from volt-amp tester" while learning how to test the charging system. Learning how to use specialized tools, materials, and equipment will be far easier when the student sees a need for it and can apply it immediately.

Variations of the task. There may be times when the enabling objectives are each a different application or way of performing the task.

EXAMPLE
Task 1: Construct basic seams.
EOs: [1] *Construct plain seams.*
[2] *Construct top-stitched seams.*
[3] *Construct seam corners.*
Task 2: Overhaul lower unit.
EOs: [1] *Overhaul Mercury lower unit.*
[2] *Overhaul Evenrude lower unit.*

In these examples, each EO involves a slightly different application of the task. This is a way to make sure that the student can perform different variations of a task.

Preparing for the task. Sometimes, you may need to develop the first enabling objective to help the student prepare for learning the task. This may involve getting set up, collecting materials, tools, supplies, or equipment or getting other preliminaries out of the way. An example illustrates.

EXAMPLE
Task: Weld lap joints.
EOs: [1] *Set up station and clamp metal.*
[2] *Weld lap joints.*

The first enabling objective in this example involves getting set up. This includes collecting the materials and supplies, setting up the welding station, measuring and cutting the metal to be welded, and clamping it into place. For the student who has never done it before, setting up to perform this task might be difficult enough that it should be a separate enabling objective. Remember that after instruction in each EO is presented and the EO is practiced, a checkpoint is reached. Either the student or the instructor (or both) checks the accuracy of the practice for that EO. In this example, it probably makes good sense to have "set up station and clamp metal" as the first enabling objective.

The setup can then be checked—*and corrected if needed*—before expensive equipment is damaged, costly material is ruined, valuable time wasted, or, perhaps, the student is seriously injured. EOs involving preparation and set up might be called for when the preparation is very complicated, dangerous or critical to the successful performance of the task.

Combinations. Keep in mind that combinations of these previous examples will be very common. An example illustrates.

EXAMPLE

Task: Collect evidence at crime scene.

EOs: [1] Describe evidence admissible in court (knowledge).

[2] Prepare for collecting evidence (preparation).

[3] Collect evidence from crimes against people (variation).

[4] Collect evidence from crimes against property (variation).

Tips

Here are some tips you may find helpful as you develop enabling objectives:

1. Remember that the task itself is what you want trainees to master. Using enabling objectives is simply a means to help students reach that end.
2. There is no magic number of enabling objectives for a learning guide. One learning guide may need two EOs, whereas another may need four or five. Two or three is a typical number of EOs for a learning guide. You may occasionally develop a learning guide for a task that is so simple or narrow that only one enabling objective is needed; the one EO is simply the task restated.
3. Keep the level of your students in mind as you develop enabling objectives. A student population consisting of younger or less prepared students may need more enabling objectives for a given task than older, more mature, or better prepared students.

4. Make sure that each enabling objective will have some kind of meaning for the student. Avoid making EOs too narrow or trivial.
5. Knowledge tasks will, of course, have all knowledge-enabling objectives. Make knowledge EOs just as precise as skill EOs.
6. If more than 4 EOs are required for a task, a second learning steps page like the one shown in the sample learning guide can be included.

Learning Steps

Now that we know how to develop enabling objectives, let us look at the next page of the learning guide. The *learning steps* listed on the second page are the heart of the guide. If the learning steps and learning resources referred to in the steps are carefully selected, the student will be able to proceed smoothly through the learning process from beginning to end. Look back at the learning steps listed under each enabling objective on the second page of the sample learning guide and notice how they guide the student toward mastery of the task. These learning steps should not be casually developed. Great care should go into the selection and wording of them. In a sense, the learning steps page in the learning guide gives each student his or her own individual teacher's aide.

The learning steps written for each guide will vary somewhat but they will be developed following a very definite pattern. Let us look at the learning steps selected for a typical enabling objective:

EXAMPLE
Task: Monitor vital signs.
Enabling Objective [2]: Take blood pressure.

1. *View filmstrip F-12 (frames 6–20) to identify the steps in taking blood pressure.*
2. *Take and record the blood pressure of at least five fellow students.*
3. *Have your instructor verify the accuracy of at least three of these readings.*

Notice that these learning steps ensured that *three absolutely essential* events took place. Table 6-6 describes these events and lists possible activities and materials to achieve them. The learning steps for each enabling objective will be a little different, but these three events—*presentation*, *practice*, and *feedback—must* be provided for. Sometimes it may take two or three specific learning steps to accomplish any one of these events, and other times two of these events may be accomplished by a single learning step.

Let us look at some examples of how these three essential events in the learning process were handled for typical enabling objectives. In the example

TABLE 6-6 Learning Steps Provide Presentation, Practice, and Feedback

Learning Steps for Each Enabling Objective Must Ensure That:	*Activities and Materials to Achieve This:*
First, The student is presented some instruction appropriate for the enabling objective.	• Reading textbooks, references, manuals • Viewing slides, films, filmstrips • Listening to tapes • Observing an advanced student
Then, The student is provided an opportunity to practice or apply the *same* knowledge or skill that was presented.	• Solving typical problems • Critiquing case studies • Hands-on practice of a skill • Answering questions
Finally, The student is given immediate *feedback* on the success of that practice and is helped in correcting it if needed.	• Checking answers with answer key • Checking finished product or procedure with detailed checklist • Having instructor or experienced student evaluate product or critique performance.

below, *presentation* of instruction required two specific learning steps (Nos. 1 and 2):

EXAMPLE
Enabling Objective [2]: Grind valves.

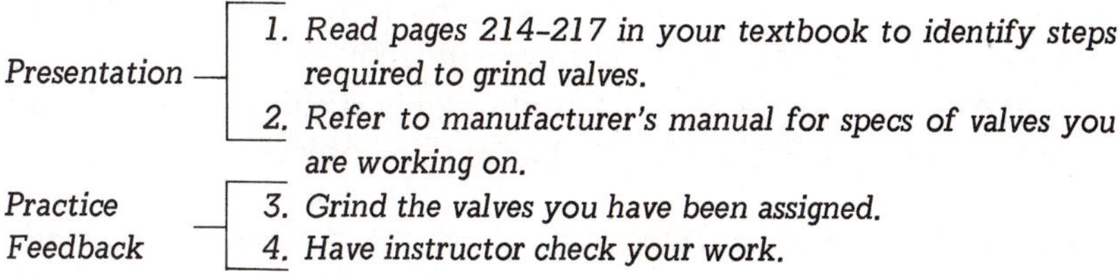

Presentation
1. Read pages 214-217 in your textbook to identify steps required to grind valves.
2. Refer to manufacturer's manual for specs of valves you are working on.
Practice
Feedback
3. Grind the valves you have been assigned.
4. Have instructor check your work.

The following example shows how the *presentation* of instruction and *practicing* of what was presented may be provided for in a single learning step (No. 1):

EXAMPLE

Enabling Objective [1]: Calibrate oscilloscope.

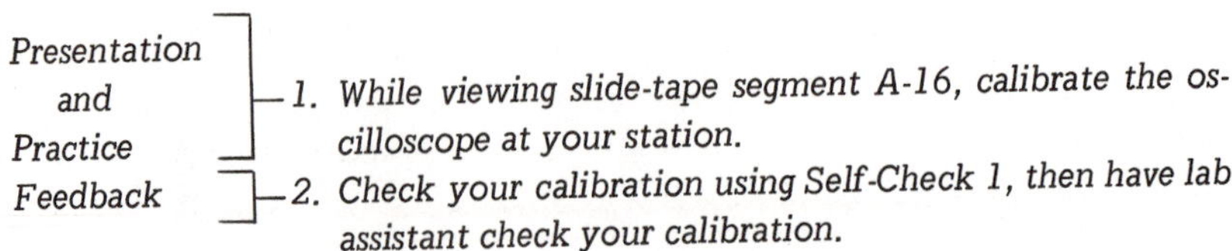

Presentation and Practice
1. While viewing slide-tape segment A-16, calibrate the oscilloscope at your station.
Feedback
2. Check your calibration using Self-Check 1, then have lab assistant check your calibration.

The example below shows how *practice* and *feedback* have been included in one step (No. 2):

EXAMPLE

Enabling Objective [3]: Spray vertical panel.

Presentation — 1. *Carefully view and listen to video tape No. 14 to identify the procedure for spraying a vertical panel.*

Practice and Feedback — 2. *With your instructor present, practice spraying vertical panels 1 and 2 set up in shop.*

In these examples, notice the following:

1. *Presentation*, *practice*, and *feedback* are included in each example, although in a little different manner each time.
2. These learning steps do *no* teaching at all; they simply tell the student what to do next.
3. Each learning step involving presentation of instruction tells the student *what to do* (read, view, etc.), exactly *what resource to use* (pages 214–217, slide tape A-016, etc.), and *what to look for* (to identify steps to grind valves, etc.). Even though each learning step is only a single sentence, it may give the student more *specific* information about what to do and why than we usually give students in traditional programs.
4. The practice called for in each example required the student to attempt the exact performance called for in the enabling objective.

It is critical that each learning step direct the student to some activity that is *appropriate*. Learning steps to accomplish the presentation of instruction must direct the student to read or view some appropriate learning resource, such as specific pages in a book or some media. Learning steps focusing on practice should tell the student exactly how to go about attempting to perform what was presented in the previous learning step or steps. Finally, learning steps you include to give students feedback must steer the student to some resource, such as a self-check, an answer key, the instructor, or an advanced student or other resource that will help the student recognize whether the practice was accurate or not and, if not, why and what to correct.

The key word here is *appropriate*. Presentation steps *must* direct the student to a resource that shows the performance called for in the EO. Practice steps *must* require the student to actually do what was presented. Immediately after practice the student *must* be helped to compare his or her performance with ideal performance.

Selection of specific resources referred to in each learning step is just as critical as the selection of the learning steps. The appropriate learning step may be to read some information or see a skill being performed. If the reading material is over the students' heads or if the visuals used to present the skill are not clear, students will have difficulty learning. The next section will help you select and develop appropriate learning resources.

Practice constructing the *cover page* and *learning steps* page for several learning guides by completing the following Self-Check.

SELF-CHECK [3]

Check your mastery of ENABLING OBJECTIVE [3] by completing this SELF-CHECK.

1. Select 12 tasks that have been analyzed. Carefully review the task analysis for each and develop enabling objectives for each task that would be appropriate for constructing learning guides around. You may want to make some assumptions about the level and previous preparation of students and where each task would appear in the sequence of tasks. Select at least *two* tasks in each category below.

    a. A job task requiring enabling objectives that are each a major part of performing the task itself.

    b. A job task requiring at least one enabling objective covering necessary prerequisite knowledge.

    c. A job task requiring at least one enabling objective covering the use of a specialized tool or piece of equipment.

    d. A task requiring an enabling objective teaching the setup or preparation for a complex or dangerous task.

    e. A knowledge task requiring all knowledge-enabling objectives.

2. Select any five tasks for which you just developed enabling objectives. Construct a draft of the *cover page* and *learning steps* page of a learning guide for each.

Follow the format shown for the sample learning guide in this section and include the following:

Cover Page:
  a. Task
  b. Introduction
  c. Terminal performance objective
  d. Enabling objectives

Learning Steps Page:
  a. Develop learning steps to accomplish the following events for each enabling objective. At this point, you can refer to ficticious learning resources:
    - *Presenting* instruction for each enabling objective
    - *Practicing* the performance called for in each enabling objective
    - Gaining *feedback* on performance for each enabling objective
    - Directing the student to take the written and/or performance test when ready (usually after practice and feedback for the *last* enabling objective in a learning guide).

Compare your responses with those in the Answer Key in the appendix.

ENABLING OBJECTIVE [4]

Select and Develop Learning Resources for Learning Guides

Role of Learning Resources

Learning resources are the books, media, tools, supplies, and other materials used in the learning process. The learning guide is only a carefully developed set of instructions telling the student what to do, when to do it, and why. The learning resources are the things the student will use when carrying out the instructions outlined in the learning guide.

In conventional instructional programs, the instructor is often the only one who uses many of the learning resources. Overhead transparencies, chalkboards, films, mockups, and actual objects are typically used by the instructor during talks and demonstrations while students sit passively and watch and listen. Even during hands-on practice, some students in traditional programs do not really get an opportunity to use the learning resources. This is especially true when small groups of students are assigned to a practice activity. Usually, one or two students do the actual practice, another few help, and the rest watch.

In the competency-based approach to training this is changed drastically. Each student must interact *personally* with the materials needed for learning. Small groups of students may still study reference material and view media together but when it comes to practice and finally demonstrating mastery of the task, students are on their own—just as they will be on the job. Learning resources to support each learning guide should be carefully selected and developed so that they will help students master each task as easily as possible.

It was mentioned earlier that the learning steps in our recommended learning guide format should accomplish three essential events for each enabling objective: present instruction, provide practice, and give feedback. Let us look at how we can select learning resources to go along with the learning steps for these three events to ensure efficient and effective learning.

Resources for Presenting Instruction

The resources referred to in the first few learning steps listed under each enabling objective on the second page of the learning guide actually do most of the presenting of instruction. Deciding what learning resources to use for these first learning steps is really not complicated.

Let us look at an example.

EXAMPLE

Instructor Ralph Taylor was in the midst of developing a learning guide for the task "Trim horse's foot." After analyzing the task and developing a terminal performance objective, he developed the following enabling objectives around which to construct the learning guide:

EO [1] *Describe growth pattern, parts, and need for trimming horse's foot.*

EO [2] *Trim horse's foot.*

Mr. Taylor knew that for each of these two EOs he needed to include learning steps and resources in the guide for presenting instruction, practicing what was presented, and giving the student feedback on practice. For EO [1], he was not sure what kind of resource to use for presenting instruction. He narrowed it down to two possible choices: purchasing a filmstrip, or having students read 12 pages in their textbook. He chose the reading. For the second EO, his possible choices were having the student read the next 6 pages in the textbook (no illustrations), purchasing a 16mm film for them to watch, or shooting about 20 slides showing a horse's foot being trimmed and narrating the slides with a cassette tape. After considering each option, he decided to shoot the slides and make the tape.

For each enabling objective, Mr. Taylor probably made the most *appropriate* selection of resources for presenting instruction. Look again at his choices for each EO and notice that he made his selection based on a very important consideration.

> Usually, the most appropriate resource to select or develop for presenting instruction for an enabling objective is one that is *effective* in presenting the skill or knowledge called for *and* the one that costs the *least* in time, money, and energy to purchase, develop, and to use.

For EO [2], Mr. Taylor ruled out the reading because it probably would not teach how to trim a horse's foot effectively—it just was not appropriate. The 16mm film and the slides would probably have both been effective in teaching the student how to trim a horse's foot. The slides, however, would cost less in terms of initial cost, cost of a projector, and the student's time and effort in setting up and using. In addition, the 16mm film did not seem to lend itself well to repeated use by individual or small groups of students.

As you select among several possible learning resources for presenting instruction, try to select one that teaches what should be taught, but one that is also cost effective. Determine exactly what student performance the enabling objective calls for and locate or develop something that "models" this performance for the student. The performance called for in the EO is your best clue about what learning resource to select.

Table 6-7 shows several different types of resources that can be selected or developed for presenting instruction for each enabling objective in your learning guide. Also listed are typical uses and advantages and disadvantages of each. You can use this as a guide in selecting resources.

Let us compare each of these three major types of resources. First, let us compare human resources with print and nonprint materials. As you can see from Table 6-7, using the instructor to present instruction has several drawbacks. Using well-developed media, instruction sheets, and related print and nonprint learning resources for presenting much of the instruction, however, has several important advantages over having the instructor do it:

1. Audiovisual presentations, well-written instruction sheets, and similar instructional resources give every student the benefit of getting the same, technically accurate instruction. Instructor presentations, no matter how well planned, always vary each time they are given. One phone call during the middle of a lecture can ruin it for everyone.
2. Media and other packaged and printed materials can be speeded up or slowed down on demand. The *student* controls the pace. Instructor presentations, on the other hand, are delivered at the instructor's pace.

3. Both print and nonprint resources can be viewed again and again by a student if needed. An instructor-delivered lecture or demonstration, once delivered, is gone forever.
4. Every student has a front-row seat. When reading an instruction sheet or viewing slides, the student does not have to compete with other students for a good view. Also, embarrassing questions need not be asked in front of the group (they usually are not, anyway).
5. Learning resources that are mediated or printed are always available. Students do not have to wait for the group to catch up to hear the next lecture or see the next demonstration.
6. When most instruction is packaged, the instructor is freed to do what instructors do best: answer questions, give feedback, check students' progress, reinforce, and evaluate. If instructors are busy most of the day lecturing and demonstrating, there is simply no time left for these other activities that are crucial to learning.

Someone once observed that live lectures and demonstrations are a lot like showers—they are not much good after 24 hours! So in most cases, having the instructor serve as the learning resource for presenting instruction is not the best way to proceed. Now let us compare print and nonprint materials.

> When faced with a choice between print and nonprint materials that both do an equally good job of presenting instruction for a particular enabling objective, select *print* over nonprint.

This statement may seem out of step with the trend during the last few decades toward mediated instruction. Remember: we said select print over nonprint when *both* would be effective. Let us look at some characteristics of these two major kinds of learning resources to see the rationale behind our statement.

Printed resources, such as books, manuals, instruction sheets, and other materials students read:

- Can be read at each individual trainee's best pace
- Are inexpensive to purchase
- Can usually provide each student with his or her own copy
- Can usually be developed locally very economically
- Are easy to store
- Can often be included inside the learning guide
- Are easy to transport

TABLE 6-7 Types of Learning Resources for Presenting Instruction

Resource	*Used to Present*	*Advantages*	*Disadvantages*
	Print Materials		
Textbooks, references, etc.	Facts, concepts, terms, background information, principles, and actual steps in performing tasks if written well and illustrated if needed.	Economical, portable, easy to use; each student may have his or her own copy.	Reading level and currency a problem; most books focus on broad topics—not tasks; difficult to alter or update.
Technical, shop, and manufacturer's manuals	Step-by-step procedure for performing task using a specific make or model of a product, tool, or equipment.	Technically accurate, economical, usually illustrated.	May assume many other tasks already mastered; may not be written at a trainee level. New editions published frequently.
Magazines, journals, pamphlets, trade publications, and periodicals	Leaders, current issues, and trends in the occupation; new advances in technology; career awareness.	Excellent link to the occupation, economical, motivational.	May be over students' heads.
Instructor-developed "Instruction sheets"	Anything for which other resources cannot be located.	Can be included right in the learning guide; can be made to fit a specific, local situation.	Take time to develop, may need illustration, tendency to be wordy and too lengthy.

		Nonprint Materials	
Still visuals (with and without sound), slides, filmstrips, flip charts, and photographs	Step-by-step procedure in performing task; interior parts or construction of devices, etc.; close-up shots; color.	Can show and explain complicated steps clearly and sequentially, can show color and detail; economical; easily updated; can be produced by instructors and students.	Need projection equipment for viewing; purchased materials sometimes technically inaccurate or incomplete; can be lost or destroyed.
Motion visuals (with and without sound)—16mm, 8mm films, film loops and cartridges, video tape, video discs	Complex tasks where motion and sequence are critical; speed up or slow down time.	Complex motion and sequence can be shown and explained; can be slowed down or stopped as needed; students seem to enjoy viewing them.	Very expensive software and projection and recording equipment needed; maintenance and security a problem; difficult to develop locally.
Casette tapes, reel-to-reel tapes, records, and language machines.	Recordings of specialized sounds or noises; pronunciation of words.	Can duplicate actual sounds encountered on the job.	Students may become easily distracted or bored.
		Human Resources	
Instructor, aide, tutor, or advanced student	Live demonstration of skills or presentation of knowledge for which no other learning resource is *yet* available.	Little or no cost, can be captured on film, slides or tape for later use as a "packaged" resource.	Instructor-paced, group-oriented, little student involvement, time consuming, does not promote high level of mastery for most students, takes up instructor's time.

- Require no batteries, outlets, extension cords, or replacement bulbs
- Can be duplicated quickly and cheaply
- Are largely "student-proof"
- Can be used under less-than-ideal field conditions
- Require no projectors, recorders, or other hardware
- Can be used at home, in the office, or at remote sites

Many nonprint resources, on the other hand:

- Require very expensive projectors, recorders, cameras, and related hardware
- Usually require quite expensive software; and already prepared software may be nonexistent, incomplete, or of poor quality
- Require batteries, outlets, or other power sources
- Require expensive and/or difficult to arrange maintenance
- May expose students to shock hazards
- Break easily
- Can be easily tampered with or stolen
- Require carrells or other space to use and store
- Are difficult or bothersome for some students to use
- Can be rendered useless by a missing slide, broken tape, and so on.

I think you will agree that the advantages of print materials over nonprint materials are numerous.

If you are concerned about the overuse of materials that students must read, do not be. Much of the reading problem students have today is caused by *what* we have them read and *how* and *when* they read it. It is no wonder many students have difficulty reading and comprehending when we move the entire group of students from one task to the next, require them to read chapter after chapter of "material," and keep them in the dark about why they are reading it and how they will ever apply what they are reading.

Remember that the learning guide format we are recommending breaks the task down into several parts. Learning steps will direct the student to read *specific*, short, carefully selected passages from books and other materials. When using learning guides, the student will rarely be given entire chapters to read. You do all the searching for the student; you wade through the "material" and find the specific passages that teach what students must know.

Of course, if a complicated skill is involved, reading about how to perform it will not do. The student must see the skill being performed. In such cases there is absolutely no substitute for well-planned, clear audiovisual learning materials. But when you do have a choice between print or nonprint resources, select print. Let us look at some of the print and nonprint resources typically referred to in learning guides.

Print Resources

There is a vast array of valuable printed materials available to you. This includes textbooks, reference books, manuals, technical literature, product releases, manufacturer's bulletins, instruction books, and instructor-developed materials. If you can locate the information you need to present instruction for a particular enabling objective, use it. Why waste your time reinventing it? By referring students to reading sources outside the learning guide, you familiarize the student with documents that are a part of the occupation. An added benefit is keeping the student active and involved. Sitting at a desk reading page after page of summarized material can be tiring. Moving around the room, locating reference books, and locating the *specific* passages called for in the learning guide can help provide much needed variety to the learning process and keep the student active. When selecting and referring the student to print materials *outside* the learning guide, keep these tips in mind:

1. Refer the student to the exact page, sections, or paragraphs to read. Searching through pages of unrelated material to find the passage needed is a waste of the student's time.
2. Have the student read only what is essential to present instruction in the particular enabling objective and no more. Try to limit each reading to a few pages. Do not assign readings that teach the entire task and do not repeat the exact same reading assignment for subsequent EOs.
3. Make sure that you read the passage first and that it is appropriate and written at your students' reading level.
4. Tell the student in the learning step to pay particular attention to certain paragraphs, terms, figures, or tables, if particularly important.
5. In the learning step, be sure to tell students what to look for. Chances are that this will help them find it.
6. Tell the student where to find the resource if it is in an out-of-the-way place.
7. If conducting research, locating materials in references, and similar "investigative" skills are what you are trying to teach, you can give less specific directions to students on where to find what they need to know.

Let us look at how printed materials *outside* the learning guide are typically referred to in learning steps:

EXAMPLES

1. *Read pages 72–74 (begin with section on "Installing Hinges") in* Carpentry Today *to identify the specific steps in installing hinges on interior doors. Pay close attention to Figure 17-2 through 17-9.*
1. *Carefully read Sections 14.1–14.3 in instruction manual for the Jarrett volt-ohm meter, showing how to hook up leads and set meter to read ohms. Do not connect leads to circuit yet!*
1. *Read "Pressing Issues in Nursing" on pages 101–112 in* Nursing Magazine *(Vol. XXI, No. 2) to identify some of the major issues facing nurses today.*
2. *Read the following describing attitudes important in handling complaints:*
   a. *Textbook paragraphs 23.2–23.5.*
   b. Your Future in Retailing, *pp. 89–91, on reserve in the library.*

Notice how each of these resources is an *external* resource located outside the learning guide and how the learning steps tell the student exactly what part of the resource to read and what to look for.

Instruction Sheets

There will be times when printed materials are appropriate, but nothing is available or, at least, you cannot locate anything, so you will have to develop your own materials. The *instruction sheet* has been included in the suggested learning guide format for this purpose. Instruction sheets are included in the learning guide and present several types of instruction, including:

1. Information such as facts, explanations, examples, discussions, concepts, or principles.
2. Specialized instruction, such as diagrams, prints, drawings, schematics, charts, graphs, maps, and illustrations.
3. Material and tool lists; if too lengthy to include in the learning steps, the student may be referred to an instruction sheet listing specific tools, instruments, equipment, supplies, parts, or material to assemble.
4. List of specific steps in performing a skill; together with these steps will be any essential technical knowledge and any necessary pictures or illustrations needed for clarification. If you have job or operation sheets already developed, this is how you can incorporate them in your learning guide.

For a particular enabling objective, you may need to develop an instruction sheet to refer the student to if you cannot locate resources outside the guide, such as a textbook or manual. Below are typical references in learning steps to instruction sheets located within the learning guide.

EXAMPLE

1. Read Instruction Sheet 1 to identify the steps for mixing potting soil.

1. Read the Instruction Sheet enclosed "Making a Club Sandwich" to identify the steps to make a club sandwich.

2. Following the steps in Instruction Sheet 2, practice changing the spark plugs on engine assigned by instructor.

1. Read Instruction Sheet 1 describing the importance of telephone courtesy on the job.

2. Locate the tools and supplies listed in Instruction Sheet 1. Check with the instructor before going any further.

Below are several tips that may help you develop better instruction sheets:

1. Use simple, easy-to-follow illustrations to clarify intricate steps or complex movements. Simple freehand line drawings can be valuable to the student. Illustrations need not be of professional quality; they should be technically accurate and easy to follow. You can cut and paste using illustrations from manuals and books and other materials (remember to get permission to use copyrighted materials). Try to put the illustration to the side of or just below the sentence(s) referring to the illustration.
2. By photographically reducing transparencies, transparency masters, or photographs (again, get permission), you can develop excellent illustrations to clarify the steps listed in performing a task.
3. Make sure that the reading level of your instruction sheets matches that of your students.
4. Make instructions simple and easy to read. List steps in performing a task sequentially (Step 1: Remove the motor housing). Avoid long paragraphs of text; leave plenty of "white space"; underline key words and define new ones as they are used; avoid instruction sheets that list definitions. Use arrows, boxes, asterisks, dots, circles, or other means to help organize and highlight the material presented.
5. Keep instruction sheets brief and number them page 1 of 2, page 2 of 2, and so on. Give them a title that is descriptive of what is taught in the instruction sheet.

Nonprint Resources

Sometimes, print resources just are not appropriate for presenting instruction for particular enabling objectives. Nonprint resources might be called for when:

1. Motion is needed.
2. Very small or intricate parts need to be seen.

3. Color or texture is important.
4. Other situations.

Nonprint resources are either *still* or *motion*, and there are various types of each. Below are examples.

EXAMPLE

Still	Motion
• *Slides*	• *16mm films*
• *Filmstrips*	• *8mm loops or reels*
• *Charts*	• *Video discs*
• *Photographs*	• *Video tapes*

Sometimes, you may be faced with a choice between still and motion nonprint resources.

> When faced with a choice between still and motion nonprint resources that both do an equally good job of presenting instruction for a particular enabling objective, select *still* over motion.

If we could purchase a complete mediated program either on video tape (motion) or slide-tape format (still), we should probably select the slide-tape format even if the initial cost of the two formats was equal. You will usually pay a premium for motion. That premium is usually in the form of:

- Higher initial cost
- Higher projector and related equipment costs
- Higher maintenance costs
- Greater amount of downtime and pilferage
- Greater difficulty updating and adapting materials
- Higher cost of software

> Very few training programs will need motion for teaching all tasks. When possible, select *print* resources; if print is not appropriate—use *still* visuals; only is absolutely essential, use *motion*.

Occasionally, you may find yourself in the lucky position of having several different types of resources on hand that effectively teach a particular skill or knowledge. When this happens, you may want to use more than one resource for presenting instruction.

EXAMPLE

1. *Read Instruction Sheet 2* or *view filmstrip B-06, describing how to pull wire through conduit.*

1. *Read one of the following to find out how to compute missing values of resistance:*
   a. *Textbook, pp. 183-194,* or
   b. *Workbook, Section E-12*

1. *View film "Completing Log Book"* or *read* FTC Bulletin 1248, *describing how to complete your daily log book.*

If you locate several resources that present basically the same instruction (especially if they are the same type), avoid *requiring* the student to view or read them all. Give the student a choice; use "or" instead of "and" in the learning step. Students who like to read will select the reading and those who do not will probably select the media. If one resource is good, two are not necessarily better. A future goal may be to develop or locate two or three different *kinds* of alternative resources to present instruction for each enabling objective. For now, however, concentrate on finding one that works; you can add more later.

Evaluating Resources

There is an ever-growing amount of commercially available learning resources available for purchase—both print and nonprint. Here are some things to keep in mind when considering materials for purchase.

1. How much do the materials cost?
2. How much do the projection and related equipment needed for using the material cost?
3. Is the material at an appropriate level for the student population?
4. Is it technically accurate and up to date?
5. How easy is the material to update, add to, or adapt?
6. How compatible is it with material already in use in the program?
7. Is it copyrighted?
8. Can it be duplicated easily?
9. Is the material "interactive"; does it require the student to become actively involved? Audiovisual programs that present a step or two and stop, require the student to perform that step, and then reactivate the program keep students more involved than presenting all steps without stopping.
10. How closely does an audiovisual program match the task listing and the enabling objectives for each task?

11. How well does it teach each enabling objective? If you follow the approach presented in this chapter, you will rarely present instruction in an entire task at once.
12. Is the technical quality high?
13. Are replacement slides, tapes, or pages available at reasonable cost?
14. How much space is required to store and use the material?
15. Has the material been thoroughly tested with students similar to yours?
16. Can small or large segments of the program be purchased separately?
17. How durable and trouble-free are the materials?
18. How easy is the material for students to locate, use, and return to storage?
19. Can the materials be used in a lighted, noisy environment?
20. Will students enrolled in the program have to continue purchasing consumable materials such as lab sheets?
21. Is it very clear exactly what task or part of a task is included in each separate component or unit?
22. Are self-checks and tests included?
23. Does the material include guide sheets or similar software that can temporarily serve as learning guides until guides are developed?

Resources for Practice and Feedback

Now that we have looked at resources for presenting instruction, let us look at resources typically used for the practice and feedback events in the learning process. Table 6-8 lists resources that are commonly used by students during practice of skills or application of knowledge and in gaining feedback.

The resources students will use for practicing the performance called for in skill-enabling objectives will usually be tools, materials, supplies, and other tangibles. Of course, while a student is practicing, he or she may wish to go back and review all or part of the resources that were used to present instruction. Resources usually used to gain feedback after practicing skills are the instructor, some form of self-check instrument, or both. After practicing how to "lay blocks to a line," for example, the student may check his or her own work using a self-check as well as call the instructor over to check the wall.

For knowledge-enabling objectives, problems or questions listed on a self-check usually serve the purpose of applying what was presented. Comparing solutions to problems or answers to questions with an answer key or with the instructor serves as a means of gaining immediate feedback. After being presented instruction on how to compute percentages, for example, the student might be directed to a self-check with percentage problems.

TABLE 6-8 Resources Used for Practice and Feedback

Practicing What Was Presented		*Getting Feedback on Practice*
	Skill-Enabling Objectives	
• Tools • Materials • Supplies • Equipment • Instruments • Live work • Customers	• Patrons • Projects • Objects • Field assignments • Trainers • Simulators • Mockups	• Instructor, advanced student, or aid to observe performance or evaluate finished product • Self-check for evaluating student's own work • Checklist or rating scale in books or other sources for checking work
	Knowledge-Enabling Objectives	
• Self-checks containing questions, problems, case studies, situations, activities, or other assignments • Review questions and problems in books • Oral quizzes • Role playing		• Answer key or solutions to compare answers with • Instructor checking answers or assignment • Instructor quizzing student or or critiquing report

Solving the problems provides appropriate practice and comparing the answers with an answer key provides feedback.

Self-Checks

We have included self-checks in this section on learning resources because that is really what they are. Self-checks are not tests—they are an integral part of the learning experience. It has been shown that students learn more and faster if they are provided with immediate feedback on how they are doing. This is the purpose of self-checks.

Since different students will be working on different tasks on any given day, self-checks can help the student get immediate feedback without having to wait for the instructor. You will be using two basic types of self-checks in your learning guides—one type for students to check mastery of knowledge and the other type for checking mastery of skills.

Knowledge self-checks. When an enabling objective covers knowledge only, that knowledge is presented to the student by means of some appropriate learning resource. After being presented with this knowledge, the student needs an opportunity to apply this knowledge and find out how well the knowledge was mastered. The student can then make an intelligent decision about going on to the next enabling objective.

Below are examples of knowledge-oriented enabling objectives and problems or questions that might appear on a self-check to help the student apply the knowledge.

EXAMPLE

Knowledge-Enabling Objectives	Problems or Questions on Self-Check
[1] Compute tax on purchases.	• *List totals of typical purchases and various tax rates and have students compute the tax.*
[1] Explain operation of four-stroke engine.	• *Give students a series of questions on the operation of the engine.*
[1] Identify parts and their function.	• *Give students a diagram with each part numbered and a list of part names and functions for them to match up.*

Notice that in these examples, the situation described in the self-check has been carefully designed to require the student to perform what is called for in the enabling objective. Of course, we would assume that the first learning step(s) under each EO has adequately presented instruction to the student so that the student is now prepared to apply what was presented.

In these examples, students would get immediate feedback on their performance by comparing their answers with some sort of *answer key*. You might feel a little uncomfortable about including the answer key in the learning guide; however, this is the only way to give the student *immediate* feedback. "What about cheating?" you ask? Students may try to look ahead to the answers on their first few self-checks, but they will soon realize that cheating on self-checks will prevent them from successfully completing the written and performance test. For particularly dangerous, complex, or basic tasks, however, you may want to have the student bring the self-check to you, an aide, or proctor for checking.

It was strongly recommended in Chapter 5 that only multiple-choice questions be included on formal written tests. On knowledge self-checks, however, any type of question or problem can be used. The disadvantages of recall-type test items for use on written tests become advantages on self-checks. Fill-in-the-blank, essay, and short-answer questions, as you recall, are *not* recommended for written tests because they are so subjective and there are many possible answers to most questions.

On self-checks, this may be an advantage. When a student answers a completion or essay question on a self-check and finds that his or her answer disagrees with the answer key, discussing this with the instructor becomes a valuable learning experience. However, arguing over the one right answer to a fill-in-the-blank question on a *formal* written test (which will be recorded) is not a very productive use of the instructor's or student's time and energy.

Skill self-checks. Most of the enabling objectives your learning guides will be constructed around will be skill-oriented. For these enabling objectives the first learning step or steps listed under them will direct the student to an appropriate learning resource that presents how to perform the skill. The next step or steps will direct the student to practice what was presented. Finally, the student will be directed to a self-check, the instructor, or other source to find out how successful that practice was.

When possible, it is a good idea to have students evaluate their own performance. This promotes responsibility, encourages decision making, and gives them the opportunity to correct their own mistakes before being embarrassed. Of course, after checking their own performance, the students may then be told to have the instructor check his or her work, especially if equipment damage, material spoilage, or student injury might result from proceeding. Again, just like knowledge self-checks, students will quickly realize that fudging on skill self-checks will only hurt their chances of completing the final performance test successfully.

Below are examples of how knowledge and skill self-checks can be referred to in learning steps on the second page of our sample learning guide.

EXAMPLE

2. *Practice typing business letters by typing the handwritten drafts found on Self-Checks 1, 2, and 3.*
2. *Practice reading the architect's scale by measuring and recording the lengths of the lines shown on Self-Check 2.*
3. *Check your setup using Self-Check 1; then have instructor check your setup* before *proceeding.*
2. *Compute sample problems found on Self-Check 1.*
2. *See if you can name and describe parts of the middle and inner ear by answering questions 1-3 and 6-10 on pages 82 and 83 in your textbook. Have instructor check your answers.*

You might find these hints helpful as you develop self-checks:

1. Make sure that each self-check covers only the knowledge or skill presented as a part of the enabling objective under which it is listed. Be especially careful about testing any knowledge or skill not yet covered in

the learning guide. You can back up in what self-checks cover but you cannot jump ahead.

2. In writing the items for skill self-checks, follow the same guidelines outlined in Chapter 5 for developing performance tests. Skill self-checks can be used to help the student assess process or product or both. Make the items very clear and go to extra care to indicate clearly the basis on which each item should be judged yes or no. Students may check "yes" to an item worded like "Was clamp installed properly?" because they believe they did. "Was clamp installed ½ inch from end of hose?" may prompt the student to realize, 'Hey, I didn't do that part correctly" and then fix it.
3. Including the answers to self-check questions and problems in the learning guide speeds up giving the student feedback. Having the answers on the back of the self-check, typed upside-down or at the very end, might discourage cheating. Having answer keys in a central location such as the toolroom may give fairly quick feedback and discourage looking at answers prematurely.
4. Oral self-checks can provide valuable instructor–student contact and can help poorer readers get feedback on performance.
5. Avoid recording scores for self-checks; emphasize to students that self-checks are to help them—not hurt them.
6. If an enabling objective involves a skill, the skill must be presented, practiced, and then checked. A skill self-check for checking the process, the finished product, or both is called for when skills are involved; a knowledge self-check is not enough. The actual skill must be compared somehow with competent performance of the skill.
7. If your students' textbooks, workbooks, or other resources already have review questions, problems, rating scales, checklists, or other devices students can use to practice or get feedback, simply refer the student to those resources. There is no need to develop a self-check and include it in the guide if you can locate some resource that serves the same purpose.
8. If your self-checks are short, you can combine several on one sheet in the guide to conserve paper. Make sure that you label each self-check so that students can identify each when needed.
9. Items on skill self-checks will be almost identical to the items on the performance test. Questions or problems on knowledge self-checks will cover the same knowledge as the written test, but the specifics will be different. Self-checks check the same knowledge and skill as final tests, but self-checks do it in *parts* and the result is *not recorded.*

A Planning Aid

The first several learning guides you develop will be the most difficult. As you get the hang of it, developing learning guides will be much easier and you will develop them faster. To help you develop your first several learning guides, you may first want to *plan* the guide. Planning the learning guide before sitting down and writing it will save you an awful lot of time and effort, especially for the first several guides you develop. You may want to use a learning guide planning form similar to Sample 6-4 to help you plan the learning guide.

Before going on, see if you can select and develop appropriate learning resources for learning guides by completing the following Self-Check.

SELF-CHECK [4]

Check your mastery of ENABLING OBJECTIVE [4] by completing this SELF-CHECK.

Listed below are typical learning activities or resources that might be referred to in learning guides. For each, indicate whether it is being used to *present* instruction, provide *practice* or give *feedback* by checking the appropriate column to the right of each.

	Present	Practice	Feedback
1. Directing the student to draw the missing view when two views are given			
2. A filmstrip-tape outlining the steps in taking inventory			
3. The student comparing his or her aircraft inspection report with the report of a certified inspector			
4. Having the instructor check the operation of reassembled mixer			
5. Listening to tape recordings of various engine noises			
6. Attempting CPR on a fellow student			
7. Instruction sheet outlining steps to charge an air-conditioning system			

<table>
<tr><td>SAMPLE 6-4</td><td colspan="2">Learning Guide Planning Form</td><td>Task B-06</td></tr>
<tr><td>TASK</td><td colspan="3">Irrigate the eye</td></tr>
<tr><td colspan="4">Terminal Performance Objective</td></tr>
<tr><td colspan="4">Given: A patient and doctor's orders,
You will: Select appropriate supplies and equipment and irrigate one or both eyes.
How well: Written and performance test to 100% Mastery.</td></tr>
<tr><td colspan="4">Key points for introduction; why should student learn task well:</td></tr>
<tr><td colspan="4">✓ Fairly common procedure
✓ Patient's severe discomfort can be relieved
✓ Serious eye injury can result from improper irrigation</td></tr>
<tr><td colspan="4">Develop enabling objectives that will lead student to mastery of the task. For each enabling objective, plan all three activities listed below:</td></tr>
<tr><td>Presentation</td><td colspan="2">Practice</td><td>Feedback</td></tr>
<tr><td>What is the most effective and cheapest way to present the performance called for in the enabling objective:</td><td colspan="2">What situation is required to have the student actually practice or apply the same performance that was presented:</td><td>How can student determine if the practice was correct and if not, what to do to correct the performance:</td></tr>
<tr><td colspan="4">Enab. Obj. [1]: Identify name and function of major parts of eye and related area</td></tr>
<tr><td>* Read pages 72-102 in <u>Anat. and Phys. for Nurses</u>
* Examine model of eye</td><td colspan="2">* Have student match name and function with parts in illustration of eye and surrounding area</td><td>* Answer Key - see instr. if questions</td></tr>
<tr><td colspan="4">Enab. Obj. [2]: Select materials and prepare irrigation solution</td></tr>
<tr><td>* Need to develop instruction sheet - need drawing of all equipment and supplies</td><td colspan="2">* Have student actually prepare solution</td><td>* Student check setup and solution with self-check
* Intructor check</td></tr>
<tr><td colspan="4">Enab. Obj. [3]: Irrigate the eye</td></tr>
<tr><td>* Need slide-tape showing draping and irrigation step by step</td><td colspan="2">* Irrigate first eye on dummy, then do self-check
* Irrigate second eye with instr. present</td><td>* Self-check
* Instr. observe</td></tr>
<tr><td colspan="4">Tests needed to evaluate mastery of the task: ✓ Written ✓ Performance</td></tr>
</table>

SAMPLE 6-4 Learning Guide Planning Form

8. Comparing solutions to descriptive geometry problems with answers in workbook
9. Having five students taste test samples of a student's yeast bread
10. Directing student to library source to determine sales volume of five largest fast-food outlets

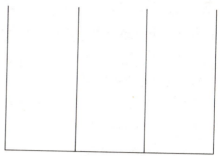

11. Refer back to the five learning guides you began for the previous self-check. Select appropriate learning resources for presenting, practicing, and getting feedback for each enabling objective. In the learning steps for presenting instruction, refer to *actual* resources; include titles, page numbers, frames, slide numbers, or other specifics. Develop at least *two* instruction sheets to serve as the resource for presenting instruction. Also develop at least *two* skill self-checks and *two* knowledge self-checks for practicing or gaining feedback.

Compare your responses with those in the Answer Key in the appendix.

Continue with the following performance test.

PERFORMANCE TEST FOR TASK 9

TASK 9: Develop Draft of Learning Guides

DIRECTIONS

When ready, demonstrate your ability to develop draft of learning guides by doing the following:

For tasks that have been analyzed and for which TPOs, written and performance tests have been developed:

1. Develop draft of learning guide for each task; include cover page, learning steps page, actual learning resources, instruction sheets, and self-checks.
2. Include written and performance tests developed previously or develop them.

No.	Criteria for evaluating performance; 100% mastery required	Yes	No
	Cover page		
1.	Is the task stated exactly as it appears on the task listing?		
2.	Does the introduction tell the student specifically why it is important to learn the task?		
3.	Does the terminal performance objective clearly describe *exactly* what the student must do to demonstrate mastery?		
4.	*Enabling Objectives*		
	a. Will mastery of the EOs enable students to perform the task competently?		
	b. Is each EO broad enough to require presentation, practice, and feedback before going on?		
	c. Is each EO narrow enough that the student can remember what was presented while practicing?		
	d. Is there a natural break in the learning process between each EO?		
	e. Is each EO numbered, specific, and observable?		

f. Does each begin with an appropriate action verb in the present tense?

g. Does each EO present something new for the student?

h. If needed, is setup, prerequisite learning, or use of a specialized tool an enabling objective(s)?

Learning Steps Page

5. Are learning steps specific and easy to follow?
6. Are learning steps directed at the student?
7. Under each enabling objective, is an appropriate learning step(s) listed to provide for:
   a. Presentation of the knowledge or skill called for in the EO?
   b. Practice or application of what was presented?
   c. Feedback on performance?
8. Is the student directed to attempt the written test (if needed) immediately prior to the performance test?
9. Is the student directed to attempt the performance test after practicing the task and completing the written test (if needed)?

Resources for Presenting Instruction

10. Does each resource actually present the student performance called for in the enabling objective?
11. Is the type of resource appropriate for the kind of performance called for in the enabling objective?
12. Is the resource appropriate for the level of students?
13. Is each resource the least costly available that will effectively teach the performance called for in the enabling objective?
14. Is each resource technically complete and accurate?
15. Is the student directed to *specific* slides, pages, frames, etc.?
16. Is each instruction sheet easy to follow and illustrated if needed?

Resources for Practice and Feedback

17. For knowledge-enabling objectives, is the student called upon to apply or use the knowledge presented?
18. Do knowledge self-checks provide an opportunity to apply what was presented?

19.	Is an answer key or some other means provided to give the student immediate feedback on how well the knowledge was mastered?		
20.	For skill-enabling objectives, is the student called upon to actually perform the skill presented?		
21.	Are any special resources needed for practice (such as materials or equipment) mentioned in the learning steps?		
22.	Is some means provided for the student to compare the practice performance with correct performance?		
23.	Do skill self-checks list specific, observable criteria by which to check the process or product?		

Continue with the following task.

When you complete this section, you will be able to:

TASK 10: Try Out, Field-Test, and Revise Learning Guides

INTRODUCTION

After you complete the rough draft of a learning guide, it is a good idea to give it an initial tryout with one or two students to see if they can easily follow the learning steps and can locate and use the resources called for. Any problems found can then be corrected very easily in the rough draft. After a new learning guide has been tried out and revised, you should then field-test it with a small number of students to see how well it actually works. This section explains how to *try out*, *field-test*, and *revise* your learning guides as you develop them.

TERMINAL PERFORMANCE OBJECTIVE

To demonstrate mastery of this task, do the following:

Given drafts of learning guides, necessary learning resources and typical students, conduct initial tryout and field-test learning guides and revise as needed. The initial tryout and field testing should conform to *all* criteria listed in Performance Test 10 at the end of this section.

ENABLING OBJECTIVES

This section is divided into several parts to help you:

[1] *Conduct initial tryout of learning guides and revise.*
[2] *Field-test learning guides and revise.*

ENABLING OBJECTIVE [1]

Conduct Initial Tryout of Learning Guides and Revise

Why Try Out Learning Guides?

As much as we may hate to admit it, even though we went to a great deal of effort to construct a learning guide carefully, it may not work very well. The only way we can find out if the learning guide is any good is to try it out. You should test your newly developed learning guides in two steps. The first step is to have a student or two sit down with the rough draft of a learning guide and go through it from beginning to end to see if it makes sense. Rough spots are ironed out, then the draft is typed.

Step two is to give this version to a small number of students for field testing to see if they can master the task. After correcting any problems, your learning guide is ready for general use. Let us first look at the initial tryout of a newly developed draft of a learning guide.

The Initial Tryout

Your goal in this initial tryout is not really to see how well the learning guide works.

> The purpose of the initial tryout of a newly developed learning guide is to see if typical students can easily follow it from start to finish; does the learning guide make efficient use of the student's time?

Here are some steps you might follow in conducting this initial tryout of a new learning guide.

STEP 1: Go back through the rough draft once more and make sure that all components are there. Check the task, TPO, introduction, EOs, and learning steps for accuracy and completeness. For this initial tryout the guide need not be typed; make sure that it is legible, though—print if possible.

STEP 2: Assemble all learning resources called for in the learning steps. Check to make sure that the external resources, such as books, are referred to accurately. Make sure that instruction sheets and self-checks referred to in the guide are included.

STEP 3: Place all learning resources where they normally would be. Place tools in their proper location, materials where they are typically stored, and reference books and media where they will be kept during general use.

STEP 4: Select one or two average or above-average students to conduct the initial tryout. Selecting a student of exceptionally high or low ability will not give you a fair test. If possible, have each student try out the guide separately.

STEP 5: Orient the student(s). Explain exactly what you are doing and why. It is very important that students understand that *they* are not being evaluated—the learning guide is. Tell them you expect them to find problems with the guide—that it why you're trying it out. Tell them to go through the guide and its resources just as a typical student would. Ask them to mark anything in the guide that it unclear.

STEP 6: Look and listen. Get out of the way and carefully observe the student go through the learning guide. Every place the student must ask you a question or get a clarification is a trouble spot. On a photocopy of the guide make notes each time a student has a problem or question.

STEP 7: Ask each student what he or she thought of the learning guide. Do not ever discourage criticism from the student; if you do, you will not get it. Encourage them to be honest. Ask them what they liked, what they did not like, and what was confusing. Find out if the resources could be located easily and if they were appropriate for each enabling objective.

STEP 8: Make the necessary changes in the learning guide and have it typed and duplicate four or five copies for the field test.

See if you can conduct the initial tryout of a newly developed learning guide by completing the following Self-Check.

SELF-CHECK [1]

Check your mastery of ENABLING OBJECTIVE [1] by completing this SELF-CHECK.

1. Briefly explain the purpose of each activity.
   (a) Initial tryout of newly developed learning guide: ______________
   (b) Field test of learning guide: ______________________________

2. During the initial tryout, the learning resources should be located:
   (a) In the library or other place where they can be monitored.
   (b) Collected and placed alongside the learning guide.
   (c) It does not matter; the guide is being tried out.
   (d) In the normal location for each resource.

3. If possible, the student(s) involved in the initial tryout should be:
   (a) Below average in ability
   (b) About average in ability
   (c) Above average in ability
   (d) b or c

4. During the initial tryout, the instructor should be:
   (a) Absent from the learning environment
   (b) Actively involved in explaining each part of the guide

(c) Observing and listening to what students do and say

(d) Present only when called upon to answer a question

5. Conduct an initial tryout of the learning guides you developed for Performance Test [9]. Use one or two students who are average in ability or above. Revise the rough draft as needed.

Compare your responses with those in the Answer Key in the appendix.

ENABLING OBJECTIVE [2]

Field-Test Learning Guides and Revise

The Field Test

The initial tryout was a very informal tryout just to find out if the learning guide was complete and could be followed easily. The field test comes next.

> The purpose of the field test is to see if the learning guide is effective in helping students master the task at a high level of mastery.

The steps below might be followed in conducting the field test:

STEP 1: Make sure that the learning guide has had an initial tryout with at least one student. If not, it may contain serious errors or omissions that will prevent students from reaching mastery. Place all learning resources in their normal locations.

STEP 2: Select a small number of students (perhaps three to five) to participate in the field test. The students do not need to participate in the field test all at once, and sometimes it is better if they do not. The students you select should be typical of the students who will eventually be using the learning guide. If the guide being field tested has a prerequisite, make sure that these students have completed it.

STEP 3: Take care *not* to say too much to the students involved in the field test. These students should think they are simply using the next learning guide in the program. This way, they will probably give the guide "typical" effort. If they know they are testing a new guide, they may exert "superhuman" effort or even try to sandbag your efforts. Also, the student who goofs off can say: "I failed because this was a new learning guide."

STEP 4: Involve yourself in the learning process only as dictated by the learning guide. Avoid involving yourself with the field-test students more or less than the guide calls for.

STEP 5: After each student has completed the guide, explain that it was new and you would like to have their honest opinion about the guide. Make notes on the guide itself as you and the student go through it. Carefully record the actual time each student spent working on the guide from start to finish. Average this time; this average becomes "standard time" for that particular learning guide. Chapter 7 explains how to use standard times for grading purposes.

STEP 6: Analyze the results of the field test. Look very carefully at the results of the written and performance test. If several students do not master the performance test, those resources may be suspect. If several students miss a particular item on a test, the item needs rewording or the knowledge or skill tested by that item is not being taught very well. If several students fail to master the written test successfully, you may need to take a look at the resources you selected for teaching the knowledge and concepts covered.

STEP 7: Make any needed changes in the learning guide itself and in the resources used. If the learning guide needed major surgery, you may want to field-test it again before using it widely.

STEP 8: Have the learning guide retyped and duplicated and placed in use.

Typical Changes

Below are typical changes made in learning guides as a result of both the initial tryout and field testing.

1. Clarifying wording—especially learning steps. You may have known exactly what you wanted to say, but students may not interpret it as you intended.
2. Not enough information; a typical problem with learning steps is not giving the student enough information to locate a reference, complete a project, or select some material.
3. Fuzzy criteria statements on self-checks and performance tests. If any of your criteria statements are not crystal clear to students, you will find this out.
4. Inappropriate learning resources; if you have the student read pages in a book or view certain film loops and they do not really help the student perform as called for in the EO, this will come out during testing.
5. Too many or too few enabling objectives.
6. Omissions—leaving out a learning step that provides feedback, for example.
7. Having students take the written test *before* they actually practice the skill called for in the last enabling objective. You may need to move the written test up in sequence when the final EO involves particularly complex or dangerous skills or when incorrect practice would waste a lot of instructor time or valuable materials.

8. Instruction sheets with too much reading or reading at too high a level. Illustrations may need to be added and the "nice-to-know" information may need to be deleted.
9. The introduction not specific enough or not clear as to why the student really needs to learn the task.
10. Needing a written test for a job task when you felt a performance test was sufficient.
11. Items on written tests that are bad items or simply too easy.
12. Lack of precision in the wording of the task, the TPO, and the EOs.
13. Inappropriate practice; not requiring the student to actually perform the skill or apply the knowledge that was presented.
14. If you have difficulty fitting all the learning steps for *four* enabling objectives on one page, such as the learning steps page shown in Sample 6-3 earlier in this chapter, you may want to modify the format and use a *separate* learning steps page for *each* enabling objective. Look at Sample 6-5 and notice how this has been done. It contains the same information as the learning steps page in Sample 6-3 but for only a *single* enabling objective. Also notice in Sample 6-5 that another change has been made. The learning steps that tell the student what to do and the resources that tell the student what to use have been separated into two separate columns.

    Separating the steps and the resources may make it a little easier for students to follow and may make the job of updating and revising resources somewhat easier, since only the right-hand column need be changed. You may wish to use a combination of these two approaches, such as developing a learning steps page format for only two or three, rather than four, enabling objectives—with or without separating the steps and resources. Using a separate learning steps page for each enabling objective will perhaps make things a little easier for less advanced students to follow, but will require considerably more typing, duplication, and storage costs.

Now, see if you can field-test learning guides by completing the following Self-Check.

SELF-CHECK [2]

Check your mastery of ENABLING OBJECTIVE [2] by completing this SELF-CHECK.

ENABLING OBJECTIVE <u>2</u>	
Type spirit masters and duplicate copies.	
Learning Steps	**Resources**
___1. Read Resource 1 to identify procedure for typing spirit masters.	1. *Modern Office Procedures*, pp. 82–86.
___2. For the original assigned by instructor, type up a spirit master.	2. a. Original—see instructor b. Spirit master c. Typewriter
___3. Evaluate your typed master using Resource 3.	3. Self-Check 2, enclosed
___4. View Resource 4a and 4b, showing how to set up and operate the spirit duplicator.	4. a. Slide-tape unit 16-a b. Operating instructions for spirit duplicator
___5. Set up the spirit duplicator for operation—have instructor check your setup before turning on machine.	5. a. Spirit duplicator b. Fluid c. Paper
___6. Run 25 copies and evaluate them using Resource 6.	6. Self-Check 3, enclosed
___7. Go on to Enabling Objective 3.	

SAMPLE 6–5 Learning Steps Page for a Single Enabling Objective

1. Students involved in field-testing a learning guide should be:
   (a) Of less-than-average ability
   (b) Of about-average ability
   (c) Of above-average ability
   (d) Typical of students who will use the guide

2. During the field testing of a learner's guide, the instructor's involvement should be:
   (a) Involved only as the guide requires
   (b) Close observation of the students involved
   (c) No involvement whatsoever
   (d) Helping students proceed through the guide

3. For the learning guides tried out for Self-Check [1], field-test them with three to five students. Make any corrections needed.

Compare your responses with those in the Answer Key in the appendix.

Continue with the following performance test.

PERFORMANCE TEST FOR TASK 10

TASK 10: Try Out, Field-Test, and Revise Learning Guides

DIRECTIONS

When ready, demonstrate your ability to try out, field-test, and revise learning guides by doing the following:

For newly developed drafts of learning guides:

1. Conduct an initial tryout of each learning guide in rough draft form using one or two average or above-average students.
2. Make necessary corrections and have guides typed.
3. Field-test each learning guide using three to five students.
4. Revise each learning guide based on results of field test.

No.	Criteria for evaluating performance; 100% mastery required	Yes	No
	Initial Tryout		
1.	Were all necessary components of each learning guide included?		
2.	Was the rough draft legible?		
3.	Were learning resources in their normal locations?		
4.	Were one or two average or above-average students used in the tryout?		
5.	Were the students oriented?		
6.	Did the instructor observe each student and make note of any problems or questions?		
7.	Was constructive criticism from students encouraged?		
8.	Was the rough draft corrected as needed?		
	Field Testing		
9.	Did each guide have an initial tryout?		
10.	Was each guide field-tested with three to five students?		
11.	Was little said to the field-test students about the guides being tested?		

12.	Was the instructor involved only as dictated by the learning guide?		
13.	Was constructive criticism encouraged from each field-test student?		
14.	Were needed changes in the learning guide made based on the results of the field test?		

7

Implementing and Managing the Training Program

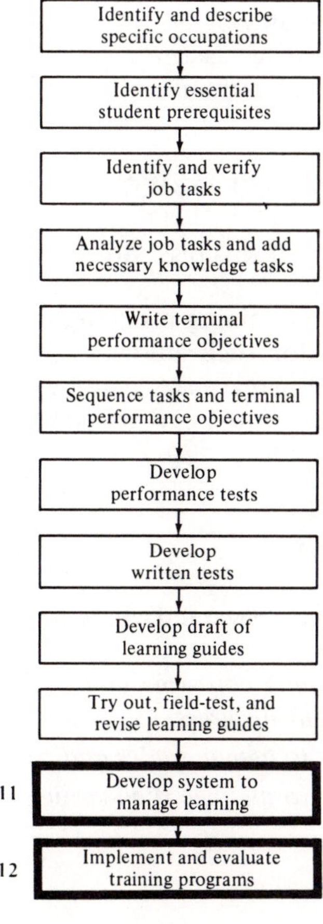

Identify and describe specific occupations
Identify essential student prerequisites
Identify and verify job tasks
Analyze job tasks and add necessary knowledge tasks
Write terminal performance objectives
Sequence tasks and terminal performance objectives
Develop performance tests
Develop written tests
Develop draft of learning guides
Try out, field-test, and revise learning guides
11 Develop system to manage learning
12 Implement and evaluate training programs

When you complete this section, you will be able to:

TASK 11: Develop System to Manage Learning

INTRODUCTION

Effectively managing instruction in more traditional training programs is not too difficult, since most students enter at the same time, go from topic to topic as a group, and the instructor does most of the teaching. In competency-based programs, however, managing learning is more challenging, since new students may arrive throughout the year, each student progresses at his or her best pace, and a wide variety of learning materials and media must be kept readily available for students. This section describes some strategies and instruments that have been used successfully in competency-based programs that should help you *develop a system to manage learning* when you implement the competency-based approach to training.

TERMINAL PERFORMANCE OBJECTIVE

To demonstrate mastery of this task, do the following:

For a competency-based training program, develop a management system to plan and monitor each student's progress, assign grades, and certify competence and manage the learning environment. The management system should conform to *all* criteria listed in Performance Test 11 at the end of this section.

ENABLING OBJECTIVES

This section is divided into several parts to help you:

[1] *Identify management concerns and develop instruments to plan and monitor student progress.*

[2] *Develop strategies to assign grades and certify competence.*

[3] *Develop strategies to manage the learning environment.*

ENABLING OBJECTIVE [1]

Identify Management Concerns and Develop Instruments to Plan and Monitor Student Progress

Managing Individualized Learning—A Challenge

Up to this point we have been involved in planning and developing the training program. In this chapter we look at some ways to manage learning in an individualized competency-based program. We also look at how you might go about implementing and improving this approach to training in your program, department, school, institution, agency, or company. Let us talk first about managing learning. It is one thing to have a valid task listing, well-written learning guides, and good learning resources. It is quite another to be able to *manage* student learning effectively after the program is implemented. Look at Table 7-1 and you will get a pretty good picture of what you are up against in managing learning in an individualized program. The major difference in managing traditional and individualized programs is *what* is being managed.

> Most management concerns in traditional programs deal with managing *instruction*. In competency-based, individualized programs, the primary concern is with managing *learning*, and there is a world of difference in the two.

When all trainees begin at the same time, go through the program at the same rate, and exit at the same point, managing instruction is not that difficult. It is a matter of staying one day ahead of the students, getting everything ready for the next day, and solving problems as they arise. When students enter at various times, work on different tasks, and progress at their own rate, managing learning becomes a little more complicated. Do not, however, let that scare you away from implementing individualized instruction. The benefits to your students make the effort worthwhile and the management challenges you will face using the competency-based approach can be solved with a little effort and ingenuity.

That is where a *management system* comes in. You cannot implement a truly competency-based, self-paced program and hope to develop management strategies as you go—at least not without getting a lot of gray hair in the process. A *plan* for effectively managing student learning is something you should develop together with the learning materials and media. Let us emphasize the word *system*. If you focus on developing an overall system

TABLE 7-1 Managing Individualized versus Traditional Programs

In Traditional Programs:	*In Indidividualized Programs:*
1. Instructors focus on managing *instruction.*	1. Instructors focus on managing *learning.*
2. Most students enter at about the same time.	2. Students enter at various times throughout the year.
3. Students all cover the same material.	3. Different students may be training for different occupations within the same program.
4. Students all proceed from one topic to the next at the same time.	4. Each student moves on to the next task only after mastering the task he or she is currently working on.
5. The instructor controls the learning pace.	5. Each student progresses at his or her own pace.
6. All students are usually tested at once.	6. Each student is tested when ready to demonstrate mastery.
7. Very little continuous feedback is given.	7. Immediate feedback is given to each student at critical points in the learning process.
8. The instructor is involved in teaching only one topic at a time.	8. The instructor must be able to answer questions on many different tasks each day.
9. Retesting is discouraged or not allowed at all.	9. Retesting is encouraged for reaching mastery.
10. Materials, tools, and supplies for only one topic are needed at a time.	10. The instructor must see that all materials needed for many tasks are readily available.
11. The number of students enrolled is maximum capacity at the beginning of the year or term and declines to half or less toward the end.	11. As vacancies are filled, student enrollment remains at maximum capacity all year long.
12. Most instruction is delivered by or dependent upon the instructor.	12. The instructor must manage the use of a wide variety of instructional media and materials each day.
13. The program is usually closed down or shortened during the summer months.	13. The program usually operates year round.
14. The evening program is usually separate and distinct from the day program.	14. Day and evening programs both have access to all learning guides and resources.
15. The instructor controls the sequence in which topics will be covered.	15. If possible, students determine the sequence of tasks.

for managing learning, you will make sure that each part of the system fits together and promotes one thing—efficient and effective learning. You really cannot throw together a grading system here and a progress record there and hope it works. You need to keep the big picture in mind and develop each part of the management system so that it enhances learning and supports all the other components.

Here are some typical questions instructors, supervisors, administrators, curriculum and media specialists, and even students have about managing things in this nontraditional approach to training and education:

- "How am I going to keep track of who's working on what task on each day?"
- "How am I going to grade students?"
- "How can I make the A B C D F grading system I have to live with compatible with the competency-based philosophy?"
- "Where can I set up the media to which my learning guides will be referring students?"
- "What about the students who can't take responsibility for their own learning?"
- "How do I give written and performance tests when needed?"
- "Where do I keep the learning guides?"
- "How can I control cheating?"
- "What about the student who can't work alone?"

No doubt, you can add to this list of questions.

Of course, this book does not have all the answers to these or other questions you may have. In this section and the next, you will find some tips, techniques, helpful suggestions, and sample forms that have worked for others. Ultimately, of course, you and those who work with you will have to develop your own management system, try it out, work out the bugs, and then use it. Anything you find in this chapter that you think you can use, do so; the parts you have trouble with—change. And those strategies or instruments that just will not work in your local situation—overlook.

Planning Each Student's Work

Planning each student's work and keeping up with his or her daily or weekly progress is one of the first problems with which you will be faced. Here are some of the elements of the problem:

- Students may be entering at different times—perhaps weekly or monthly.
- New students may begin at various points in the program. Remember: we agreed in Chapter 4 to avoid forcing a rigid sequence of tasks on students. We will try to give them a choice of where to begin. One student may begin with duty A and another with duty B.

- You need to be able to tell at a glance who is working on what task so that you can have materials, media, and testing situations ready when needed.
- Each student needs some sort of document showing what tasks he or she has chosen to work on during the next few weeks or months and in what order (if any).
- You may be called upon to submit grades, progress reports, or other information to students, parents, or VA or CETA sponsors, documenting what kind of progress is being made by each trainee.
- You need some way of keeping tabs on which task each student successfully masters and when.

On the following pages are two examples of instruments you might use in planning each student's work and keeping up with who is working on which task. The first example is rather simple, whereas the second is a little more elaborate, and of course, there could be many variations of these two approaches.

Monthly student planning form. Sample 7-1 shows an example of a short form you might find helpful in planning each student's work for the coming month. Look at Sample 7-1 as we follow through an example of the "monthly student planning form":

EXAMPLE

During the last day or so of October, the instructor sat down with student June Thompson for about 15 minutes. They discussed what was accomplished during October, any problems June was having, and together, they decided what was to be accomplished during the upcoming month. June looked over the task listing and decided what tasks she might like to tackle next month. Using the sequence of duties and sequence of tasks as a guide, Mr. Lewis recommended tasks that had no prerequisites or tasks for which the prerequisites had been met. Also, he listed the tasks on the form in a suggested sequence based on the nature and difficulty of the tasks, what he knew about the student, availability of equipment, live work and materials, and other factors. Both instructor and student initialed the form. The three-part, self-carboning form was separated—the original went into the student's file, the second was placed on the wall in Mr. Lewis' office, and Ms. Thompson kept the third.

When the student successfully completed the written and/or performance test for task D-01, she brought her copy of the form to Mr. Lewis. He placed her copy over the copy taped to his wall, entered the date mastered, and signed; this information transferred to Mr. Lewis' copy. This will be repeated each time June masters a task. At the end of November, the instructor and

STUDENT:	AVTI MONTHLY STUDENT PLANNING FORM	MONTH:	NO.:
June Thompson		Nov.	3

Listed below are tasks planned for mastery this month:

Task	Begun	Mast.	Instr. Sig.	Task	Begun	Mast.	Instr. Sig.
D-01	11-2	11-6	M. Lewis	E-12			
D-02	11-9	11-12	M. Lewis	E-13			
D-03	11-13			F-01			
D-04							
D-05							

Student No.	Program No.	Entry Date	S-initials	I-initials
481-72-9186	820	9-12	J. T.	M. L.

SAMPLE 7-1 Monthly Student Planning Form

student will make sure the form is up to date and the copy on the wall will be removed and placed in the student's folder and used for grading and record-keeping purposes. Another planning form will be completed for December. Any tasks listed on November's form and not mastered can be listed first on December's.

A form such as that shown in Sample 7-1 has several advantages:

1. It is very short, easy to fill out and read, and is very inexpensive to develop, duplicate, and store.
2. The instructor can tell at a glance what each student is planning to master this month simply by looking at the forms posted on the wall or assembled on a clipboard or other handy place.
3. Since the student gets a copy, he or she knows exactly what he or she is expected to accomplish during the coming month.
4. Mastery of each task is documented immediately, with *two* copies being made—one for the student and one for a permanent record.
5. Instructor verification (signature) is required to document mastery of each task.
6. Midway through a month, the form can be torn up and a new one developed if needed.
7. Tasks can be selected for each student to work on based on each student's individual needs and abilities.
8. A record is made of when the student began working on each task and when the task was mastered.

9. If small groups of students wish to work together, this can be accomplished by listing the same tasks on their forms.
10. The approximate time students spend on each task can be determined by comparing the date begun with the date mastered.

Adaptations of this sample form you might want to make include:

1. Expanding it to cover two or more months or reducing it to cover one or more weeks.
2. Providing space for the task name and other additional information on the form.
3. Using carbon paper to make copies or photocopying the original rather than making a pad of self-carboning forms.
4. Listing the number of *all* tasks on the task listing on a large version of the form and checking or circling each task number the student plans to master during the coming month. For each subsequent planning period, additional task numbers are checked or circled.
5. Any other change that might aid you in planning the work to be accomplished by each student during the coming months or weeks.

Student performance agreement. The "student performance agreement" is a little more elaborate form that contains the same basic information as the monthly planning form plus some additional information. It is used for planning each student's work and can also be used for computing and recording each student's grade at the end of each grading period. Sample 7-2 shows only a portion of the student performance agreement. The next section shows how the complete form is used for planning and grading. Notice that there is sufficient space for planning as many as 22 tasks.

Keeping Track of Daily Progress

In addition to knowing what tasks students plan to master and what tasks they have already mastered, in an indivdualized program you may also want to keep track of each student's *daily* progress. You may want to monitor when students attend, when they are absent, what time they arrive and leave, and what they actually accomplish each day.

Student time cards. An excellent way of doing this is by using "student time cards." Sample 7-3 shows a sample time card developed at Ridge Vo-Tech Center in Winter Haven, Florida. Let us walk through an example to see how it works. This example is based on the information on the time card shown in Sample 7-3.

1	FROM: 2-6	
	TO: 4-12	
IN SCHOOL HOURS		
ACADEMIC HOURS		
OTHER		
HOURS IN VOC. PROGRAM (HIVP)		
PLANNED		STD. HOURS ACTUALLY ATTAINED
TASK	STD. HOURS	
E-03		
E-04		
E-05		
E-07		
E-08		
E-09		
F-01		
F-02		
F-03		
F-04		
F-08		
TOTALS		
STUDENT INITIALS		

%	GRADE
%	EMP. SKILLS
ABSENCES	TARDIES

SAMPLE 7-2 Portion of Student Performance Agreement for Planning Student's Work

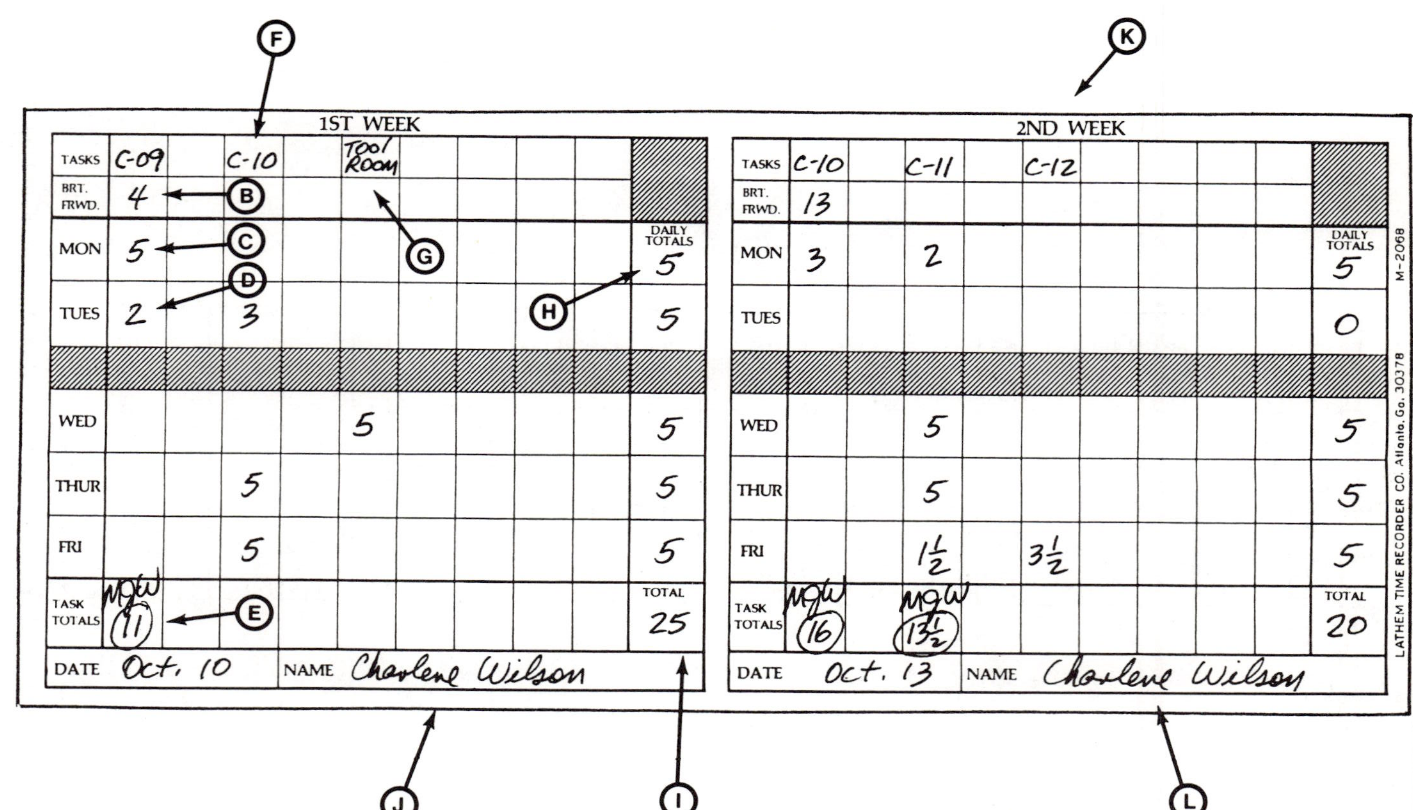

1ST WEEK

TASKS	C-09		C-10		Tool Room					
BRT. FRWD.	4									
MON	5									DAILY TOTALS 5
TUES	2		3							5
WED					5					5
THUR			5							5
FRI			5							5
TASK TOTALS	MGW (11)									TOTAL 25
DATE	Oct. 10		NAME	Charlene Wilson						

2ND WEEK

TASKS	C-10		C-11		C-12					
BRT. FRWD.	13									
MON	3		2							DAILY TOTALS 5
TUES										0
WED			5							5
THUR			5							5
FRI			1½		3½					5
TASK TOTALS	MGW (16)		MGW (13½)							TOTAL 20
DATE	Oct. 13		NAME	Charlene Wilson						

SAMPLE 7-3 Student Time Card (Developed at Ridge Vo-Tech Center, Winter Haven, Fla.)

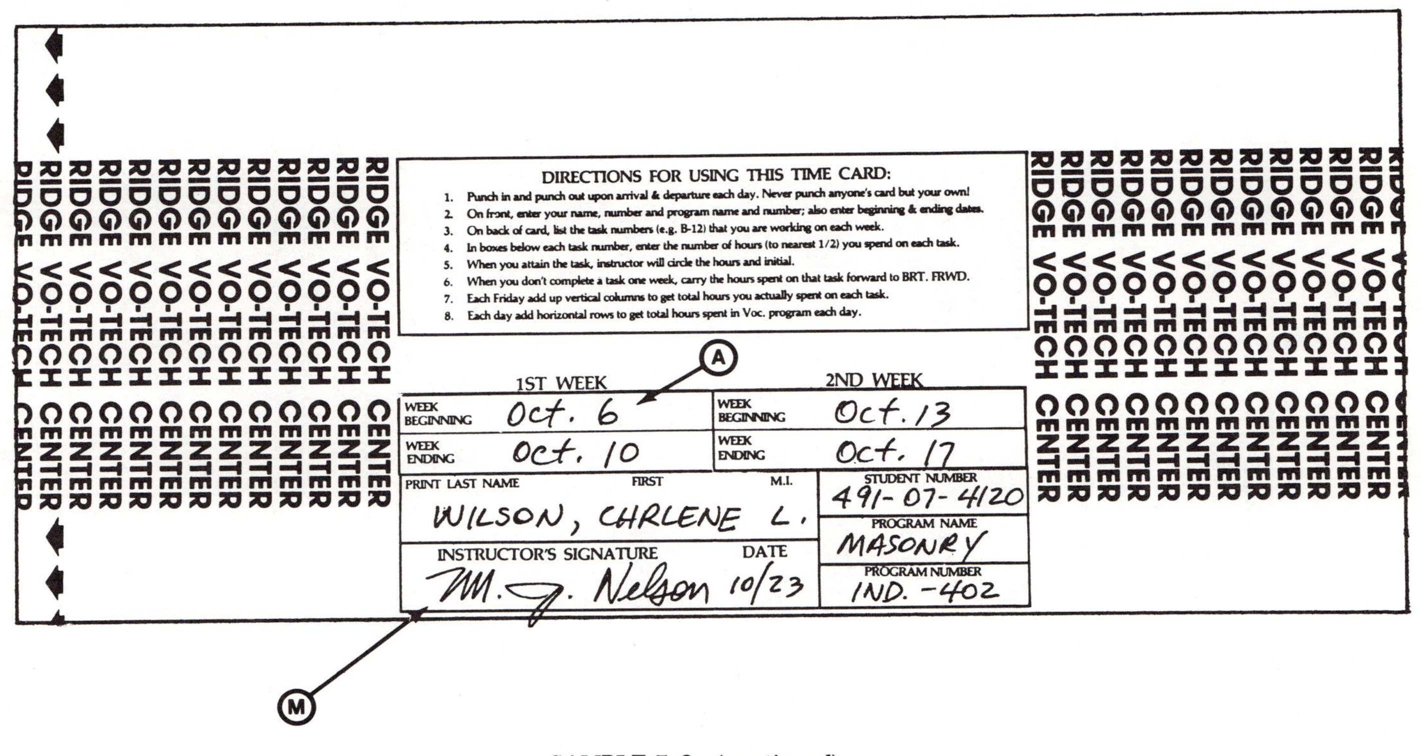

RIDGE VO-TECH CENTER

DIRECTIONS FOR USING THIS TIME CARD:

1. Punch in and punch out upon arrival & departure each day. Never punch anyone's card but your own!
2. On front, enter your name, number and program name and number; also enter beginning & ending dates.
3. On back of card, list the task numbers (e.g. B-12) that you are working on each week.
4. In boxes below each task number, enter the number of hours (to nearest 1/2) you spend on each task.
5. When you attain the task, instructor will circle the hours and initial.
6. When you don't complete a task one week, carry the hours spent on that task forward to BRT. FRWD.
7. Each Friday add up vertical columns to get total hours you actually spent on each task.
8. Each day add horizontal rows to get total hours spent in Voc. program each day.

(A)

1ST WEEK		2ND WEEK	
WEEK BEGINNING	Oct. 6	WEEK BEGINNING	Oct. 13
WEEK ENDING	Oct. 10	WEEK ENDING	Oct. 17

PRINT LAST NAME / FIRST / M.I.: WILSON, CHRLENE L.

STUDENT NUMBER: 491-07-4120

PROGRAM NAME: MASONRY

PROGRAM NUMBER: IND. -402

INSTRUCTOR'S SIGNATURE: M. J. Nelson — DATE: 10/23

(M)

SAMPLE 7-3 *(continued)*

EXAMPLE

A. *Charlene Wilson, a masonry student, filled out her time card on Friday afternoon for the coming two-week period.*

B. *On the back, the 4 hours already spent on task C-09 during the current week was brought forward (BRT. FRWD.). Charlene punched in each morning and punched out each afternoon. The blanked-out row between Tuesday and Wednesday is for the holes the time clock punches in the card each time it is used.*

C. *At the end of the day on Monday, Charlene recorded the fact that she spent all 5 hours of instructional time (breaks and lunch do not count) on task C-09.*

D. *On Tuesday, she spent 2 additional hours finishing C-09.*

E. *The total hours Charlene actually spent on C-09 was listed in the "Task Total" row (11 hours: 7 hours this week and 4 last week). Since the task was mastered, the instructor circled and initialed (MJW) the total for C-09.*

F. *Charlene listed the next task she worked on (C-10) at the top in the "Tasks" row. She spent 3 hours on C-10 on Tuesday, and all day Thursday and Friday.*

G. *Wednesday was her day in the toolroom, so she entered 5 hours under "Toolroom."*

H. *Each day, Charlene checked to make sure that she was accounting for 5 hours of instruction per day.*

I. *Charlene totaled the number of hours she was in the program during the week (25).*

J. *Friday afternoon, she checked over her card carefully to make sure that all the information was complete and accurate. She signed and dated the card, attesting to the accuracy of the information listed for the first week.*

K. *Charlene punched in and out each day of the second week and entered the daily totals just as she did for the first week. She mastered C-10 and C-11 and will bring 3½ hours forward for C-12 on next week's card. Notice that Charlene was absent on Tuesday of the second week.*

L. *Charlene signed and dated the second week after carefully checking all the information.*

M. *Her instructor checked over the time card and signed it.*

Benefits. Using a student time card like Sample 7-3 has several very important benefits, including:

1. Since each student is charged with the responsibility of filling out his or her time card each day, a tremendous record-keeping burden is taken off the instructor's shoulders.

2. The time card maintains an accurate and up-to-date record of:
   a. Exact dates of absences
   b. Exact dates of tardiness and exact time of arrival
   c. Exact time of departure each day
   d. Tasks worked on each day
   e. Actual time it takes each student to master each task
   f. Which tasks were mastered and date of mastery
3. Students gain valuable experience in punching a time clock; they learn about the consequences of forgetting to punch in or punch out, punching someone else's card, or losing their time card.
4. Students get experience in maintaining accurate records and managing their own affairs.
5. The training program is being run more like a business, which will ease student's transition from training to working.

Tips

Here are some tips on managing the use of student time cards:

1. Make absolutely sure that each new student fully understands the importance of the time card and how to fill it out. In your orientation, show students several examples of correctly filled out cards. Monitor each new student the first few days to see if the card is being filled out promptly and accurately.
2. Use time cards even if you do not have a time clock. Instead of punching in and out, an aide, the shop foreman, or you can write in the arrival and departure times.
3. When punching in each day, have students place their cards in a second time card rack or in the same rack upside down. This way, you "take roll" simply by looking at the rack.
4. Spotcheck students every so often by calling roll or checking on certain students. When students are caught punching in or out for friends, use the situation as a learning experience to impress upon students the consequences of doing this on the job.
5. Keep used time cards on file as a backup record of task mastery, absences, and tardiness.
6. Impress upon students the need to keep track of how much time they actually spend working on each task and record this on their time card. Emphasize that this has nothing to do with their grade, so fudging will not benefit them at all. Average the time students spend on each task and this average or "standard time" can be used in your grading system—more about that in the next section.

7. Once you have developed reliable standard times for all tasks, you can use a simplified time card simply for punching in and out.
8. You may want to develop a time card that covers only one week or three or four weeks.
9. A wide variety of time clocks may be used; design your time card so that it is compatible with the time clock.
10. If possible, use only one type of time clock and one time card format throughout the entire institution. This will make centralized record keeping much easier. Also, students can take their cards with them to punch in and out for a related class in another building.
11. Reserve a few minutes each Friday afternoon to assemble all students so that they can bring their time cards up to date, sign them, turn them in, and fill out a new one for the coming week.
12. On a rotating basis, advanced students might be assigned to check time cards each day or week to help students who are having trouble filling them out.

Progress record. Another way of keeping tabs on who is doing what each day is some sort of progress record. Progress charts and similar documents have been in use for many years, so this is certainly not something new. The progress record shown in Sample 7-4 has a few new wrinkles; however, that makes it usable in an individualized, competency-based program. Notice:

1. Rather than wall size, the chart is 8½ × 11 inches, so it will fit in the student's folder.
2. One copy of the progress record is used for each individual student.
3. There is sufficient space on the form for duties A through I, with up to 15 tasks in each duty.
4. Preprinted in the lower part of the box for each task is the standard time established for each task.
5. In the upper part of each box, the instructor (or student) enters the actual time spent on each task.
6. Those tasks for which actual times have been entered have been mastered; those without actual times entered have not yet been mastered.
7. Actual times could be entered each time a task is mastered or weekly, biweekly, monthly, or at other intervals.

Before going on, complete the following Self-Check.

SAMPLE 7-4	STUDENT PROGRESS RECORD

Student: Thomas Quenn Student No.: 1481 Date Entered: 2/14 Date Exited: ____

Program: Drafting Occupation: Mechanical Drafter Program No.: TI 016

Duty	Duties	TASKS 01	02	03	04	05	06	07	08	09	10	11	12	13	14	15
A	Dev. Projection Drawings	6/4	7/6	10/4	8/12	20/18	6/10	4/6								
B	Dev. Sectional Views	8/6	7.5/6	15/18	17/15	/21	/12	/6	/3							
C	Dev. Detail & Assb'ly Drawings	/4	/5	/13	/30	/24	/42	/12	/14	/27	/9	/22	/10	/17	/31	
D	Dev. Pictorial Drawings	10/8	/6	/12	/9	/14	/12	/18	/12	/19	/8	/7	/15			
E	Drawings Cams and Gears	7/4	12.5/9	/15	/18	/24	/15	/10	/8							

Actual Time → 2/4 ← Standard Time

SAMPLE 7-4 Student Progress Record

SELF-CHECK [1]

Check your mastery of ENABLING OBJECTIVE [1] by completing this SELF-CHECK.

1. In more traditional programs, instructors worry more about managing ____________________.

2. In competency-based programs, however, instructors are concerned more with managing ____________________.

3. List at least five factors that make management more of a challenge in a competency-based program than in a conventional program.

   (a) ____________________

   (b) ____________________

   (c) ____________________

   (d) ____________________

   (e) ____________________

4. Identify at least three important pieces of information that would be desirable on an instrument to be used to plan each individual student's work.

   (a) ____________________

   (b) ____________________

   (c) ____________________

5. List at least three benefits of using time cards to monitor daily student progress.

   (a) ____________________

   (b) ____________________

   (c) ____________________

Compare your responses with those in the Answer Key in the appendix.

ENABLING OBJECTIVE [2]

Develop Strategies to Assign Grades and Certify Competence

Grading—Good or Bad?

The subject of grades and grading is a touchy one, especially in individualized, competency-based instruction. Grading has been labeled as damaging, meaningless, irrelevant, subjective, and a host of other evils. Perhaps the problem has been more one of how grades are assigned than with grading itself.

> One of the greatest shortcomings of grading systems now in use in traditional education and training programs is that grades are *not* an accurate indication of what each student has learned.

In most programs it is difficult or impossible to determine exactly what an "A" on a test or a "B" for a unit or "passing" in a course really means. Often, grades are nothing more than the instructor's best estimate of how each student has performed in comparison to the group norm. As mentioned in Chapter 5, this approach to testing and grading is usually referred to as the norm-referenced approach.

> Norm-referenced grading systems, in which a student's performance is compared to the performance of other students, do not accurately reflect the human competence of the trainee and are therefore *inappropriate* for use in competency-based training programs.

In a norm-referenced system, a student who makes a "B" in a class made up of exceptionally capable students may have really learned *more* than the student who makes an "A" in a class of less able students. As Chapter 5 pointed out, test scores and grades should reflect the actual competence of each individual trainee, *not* the *relative* competence of the trainee as compared to his or her fellow trainees. The only way to keep grades from being relative is to base them on some predetermined, rigid criterion.

> A truly competency-based training program must evaluate students using a *criterion-referenced* approach, in which each individual student's performance is compared to a predetermined standard of competence.

By using a criterion-referenced grading system, you can avoid most of the pitfalls now associated with grading students.

I think we need to debunk the myth that grading is bad and that evaluating students--particularly adults—is demeaning. It is just not so. What *is* bad and demeaning is for a student to work like crazy and then receive a low grade because of a poor test, shoddy teaching, a grade curve, or other reason that has nothing to do with measuring competence.

> Giving grades is not bad; evaluating student mastery of learning tasks and reporting student progress regularly enhances learning, encourages excellence, is necessary for accountability, is the only way instruction can be evaluated, and is just good sense.

So the problem is really not with grading but with *how* we grade students. We need to devise a grading system that accurately reflects the competence of the trainee, that is fair, and that is easy to understand and use.

Let us focus on two issues involved in grading. First, how should we grade students on their mastery of *each* task in the training program? Second, how should we go about reporting student performance during a particular period of accountability such as six weeks, a quarter, or during a course? First, let us look at assigning grades for each task.

Assigning Grades for Each Task

There are basically two schools of thought on this issue. One says that various grades, such as A, B, C, D, F or 1, 2, 3, 4, should be assigned to varying levels of proficiency in demonstrating mastery of a task:

EXAMPLE

Ms. Jamieson was in the process of implementing a competency-based training program in ornamental horticulture. She knew that her grading system should not be subjective and should not compare students with one another. However, she felt that the grades she would assign to each task should reflect the varying levels of mastery that students were bound to achieve. She set up the following criteria to use in assigning grades for each learning package:

Grade	Percent of Total Items Correct on Written and/or Performance Test
A: Excellent	*90-100*
B: Good	*80-89*
C: Fair	*70-79*
D: Poor	*60-69*
F: Failing	*Below 60*

What do you think of her proposed grading system? First, it *is* a criterion-referenced grading system, as it should be. The criteria for making an A, B, C, D, and F are explicit and predetermined. No student will be compared with any other student, only with the criterion levels. If all the students score below 60, they all get F's; if they all make a 90 or better, they all get A's. So her basic philosophy is sound.

What about her assigning various grades to varying levels of proficiency? This is where Ms. Jamieson went wrong. The system she developed for grading each student's mastery of each task—although criterion-referenced—would only promote *incompetence*. An example should help you see why.

EXAMPLE

After experimenting with several ways of assigning grades for each task, Bill Knight, a trainer for a major computer firm, settled on a simple method that worked surprisingly well:

Grade	Percent of Items Correct on Final Evaluation
Mastery	*100*
Nonmastery	*Anything below 100*

What Mr. Knight did was to abandon altogether the notion of trying to assign *various* grades for each task. He took the position: "They either master a task at some minimum acceptable level or they don't—it's as simple as that. Those who master a task move on to the next; those who do not continue working on the task until they do."

If you go with a system of giving various grades for levels of task mastery like our misguided Ms. Jamieson did, you will have some major headaches, including:

- Your expectation that students will reach various levels of proficiency will materialize. What you expect of students is pretty much what you get.
- You will have many incompetent students successfully complete your training program. Students who master tasks at the "C" and "D" level will get the same certificate at the end of the program as students who master tasks at the "A" level, yet they may have demonstrated only 60 or 70% mastery for many of the tasks.
- Students will soon realize that there is no reward for excellence other than a letter grade. The *minimum* level for passing (say, 70%) may very well become the *maximum* level of performance for some students.
- When you set 70% or 80% as an acceptable level of mastery for a task, you are really saying that 20 to 30% of what you want the student to learn is not really important.

However, if you adopt Mr. Knight's philosophy and only assign a yes/no, pass/fail, S/U, or mastery/nonmastery score to each specific task and *set the cutoff score at a high level* (say 95 to 100%), you will see the following happen:

- Most students will reach a high level of proficiency in each task since the criterion for mastery has been set at a high level.
- Students will be better prepared for subsequent tasks since early tasks will be mastered at a high level of proficiency.
- The only trainees who successfully complete your training program will be those who can perform the tasks competently at a trainee level.
- Less able students may require more help but will reach the same high level of mastery as more able students.

The notion of assigning students to either mastery or nonmastery for each task is based on several important assumptions that have been shown to be valid:

- Most *any* student can master *any* task at a *high* level of proficiency if given the *right kind* of instruction and *enough time.*
- The *time* it takes a trainee to master a task has little to do with *how well* the task can be performed once it is mastered.

So, in summary, I recommend that you avoid trying to use several categories of mastery for each task, such as "3 = skilled, 2 = moderately skilled, 1 = limited skill" or "A: performs without supervision, B: performs with limited supervision, C: needs constant supervision." Do not worry at all about assigning grades for each task.

Students have either mastered a task at the minimum acceptable level for competence or they have not.

This "go/no go" approach will be much simpler to manage, is fairer, makes more sense to the student, and promotes human competence. Assume that all students can master the tasks in your program at a high level, develop high-quality learning materials for them to use, and do your best to help them get there. Letting a student go on to task 2 after earning a "C" or being rated as "partially proficient" in task 1 just does not make sense.

Grading Periodic Progress

The second issue we need to resolve is assigning grades over a period of time to reflect student progress. You may be required to assign grades each quarter, term, nine weeks, semester, or during some other marking period. There are those who feel that this requirement of assigning grades every so often is in violation of the basic philosophy behind the competency-based approach to training and education. That is not true as long as the method by which these periodic grades are computed is compatible with the competency-based philosophy. Even if giving grades was not a requirement, reporting each student's progress in the training program periodically is still a good idea.

Any grading system for reporting periodic student progress is in tune with the competency-based approach if the following are true:

1. Every student has an equal opportunity to earn each grade possible.
2. Every student knows ahead of time exactly what is required for earning each grade possible. At any point in time, a student should be able to compute his or her grade up to that point; the grade is *earned*—not *given.*
3. The grade earned by a student is a measure of competence—his or her ability to render worthy performance on the job—and is based solely on task mastery. Attendance, attitudes, and effort are not reflected in the grade.

A Recommended Grading System

Several approaches to assigning grades in competency-based programs have been tried. These include systems that base student grades on:

- The number of tasks mastered during the grading period
- The level of proficiency in mastering tasks
- The number of tasks that were mastered at a proficiency score higher than the minimum level set for mastery
- The number of "extras," such as number of other students tutored, attendance, attitudes, and other factors
- Other sytems

Although each of these approaches has its merits, the first—basing grades on *the number of tasks mastered*—is highly recommended as a very practical, manageable approach that fits in with the competency-based way of thinking.

Based on time? Assigning periodic grades based on speed or time may sound like a complete contradiction of the whole approach to training and education presented so far in this book. It is not really. There are those who contend that a truly competency-based, self-paced, individualized program should not concern itself with time. They say that as long as students are learning, that is OK. Their thinking is based on the notion that there are *fast* learners and *slow* learners and that grades should reflect the students' competence—not how long it took them to get there.

Well, that may sound good on paper, but it is just not a workable solution in practice. If we used such a "time-free" grading system proposed by the "purists," the student who mastered *one* task successfully during a grading period would get the same grade (an A or S or a gold star, perhaps) as the student who mastered 10 tasks. Now that's just not right. Obviously, one of these two students is more competent than the other and their grades should reflect it. I think the student who mastered 10 tasks would probably agree. I think prospective employers would agree. I think most reasonable people would agree that *some* kind of incentive to promote steady progress is absolutely essential in a grading system.

What we need is a grading system based on task mastery but one that takes the *number* of tasks mastered into consideration and that also does not unnecessarily penalize a student who may have difficulty learning a task or two. The rest of this section describes a grading system based on these requirements.

Learning time. Basing grades on speed or the number of tasks mastered may seem awfully punitive for the slower learner. Well, there is a growing amount of research data that leads to the conclusion that there may really be no such thing as a fast *learner* or a slow *learner*! What we have observed for the last several hundred years is fast *learning* and slow *learning* brought about by traditional teaching methods. Rather than being slow learners, some students are simply less able to "tolerate" traditional, instructor-centered, fixed-time, low-quality learning environments.

> The time it takes different students to master a learning task successfully will become very similar if (a) students desire to learn the task, (b) they have the necessary prerequisite learning, and (c) they are given high-quality instruction.

Now, before you accuse me of playing with less than a full deck for making such a rash statement like this, hear me out. This notion of equal student learning time for a task is not just a theory; it has been verified over the last several decades. You need to keep in mind, now, that I said the time it will take students to learn a task will be very similar when students are *motivated*, equipped with *prerequisites*, and provided with high-*quality* instruction. When I first heard it, this statement sounded just as far out to me as it did to you because conventional programs that we are all so familiar with allow none of these necessary conditions to exist. The competency-based system of instruction presented in this book has been developed with these three essential conditions uppermost in mind. Requiring the student to master *each* task at a *high level* of mastery helps ensure that prerequisites will be acquired and will greatly increase motivation for learning subsequent tasks. Using well-developed and thoroughly tested learning packages will provide high-quality instruction.

Although not fully attainable during the early stages when your learning packages are still rough and perhaps never attainable for a small percentage of students (perhaps 5 to 10%), you will find that the time most students spend on each task will become very similar when you make sure that they master early tasks at a high level of proficiency, thus ensuring their mastery of prerequisites and adding to their motivation, and when you develop better and better learning guides, media, and related resources.

If this is true, then, basing the grading system on the number of tasks mastered during the grading period (or essentially on time) penalizes only the following students:

- Those who goof off and clown around all day
- Those who cut class, don't show up, and leave early
- Those who waste time and engage in activities other than those for which they are there

One thing you may notice is that these students are the same employees who will be penalized on the job with reprimands, low raises, and termination—usually for the same reasons. So, hopefully, you see how basing students' periodic grades on the number of tasks successfully mastered actually promotes the competence of the trainee. Such a system rewards students' worthy performance and penalizes their unproductive behavior—just as their employer will.

Standard time. Before we get into the details of the grading system, we need to explain the concept of *standard time* or *standard hours* upon which the system is based. The standard hours assigned to each task is an indication of how complex the task is. A task that has been assigned 10 standard hours is roughly twice as complex or lengthy—from a *learning* point of view—as a 5-standard-hour task. The preceding section suggested that you keep track of the time students spend on each task by having them record this on their time card. This is how you arrive at standard time for each task.

> The standard hours assigned to each task is the average number of hours it has actually taken students to master the task in the training program and is a function of the complexity of the task.

As you get started, you will have to base standard time for each task on the average time it took students to pilot-test each new learning guide. If you base standard time on your best "guesstimate, ' you will probably be way off and nine times out of 10, you will greatly *overestimate* the time it will take students to master a task.

> You will be shocked to find out that your students can *learn* a task in less time—sometimes half or less—than it took you to *teach* them in the traditional fashion. When high-quality, self-paced learning materials are used, you will find that training time can typically be cut in half *or* trainees can master twice as many tasks in the same time.

So a task of 10 standard hours has taken—on the average—10 hours for students to complete the learning package successfully from beginning to end. Some students who completed that particular learning package may have completed it in slightly less than 10 hours and others in more than 10 hours. When these times were averaged, standard time came out to approximately 10 hours. The notion of standard hours is somewhat like the flat rate assigned to each repair job in the transportation industry. A flat-rate time of 1.75 hours for a repair job simply means that on the average, mechanics have completed that job in 1.75 hours. Therefore, mechanics are paid 1.75 times their hourly rate when performing that particular service, *regardless* of how much time they may actually spend doing it. The mechanic who does the job in 1.2 hours is ahead of the game, whereas the one who takes 2.5 hours loses. It may not seem so, but this system is very fair, since the 1.75-hour "standard" was based on the average time it actually took a large number of mechanics to do the job competently.

The grading system recommended in this section is based on the philosophy that competent trainees will make steady progress toward mastering the tasks on the task listing. If a student is enrolled in a program for 100 hours, let us say, during a grading period, he or she should be held accountable for 100 standard hours worth of task mastery. The thinking here is that simply "showing up" or putting in "seat time" has nothing to do with the human competence of trainees. Only one thing does—successfully mastering the tasks upon which the program is based.

How it works. To describe how this recommended type of grading system actually works, once again we need to mention the "student performance agreement" you saw part of earlier. Sample 7-5 shows the entire form, which has been filled out to plan the students' work and compute the final grade for the planning period. This particular form was developed at Ridge Vocational-Technical Center in Winter Haven, Florida. It was adapted from a similar instrument developed at the 916 Area Vo-Tech Institute in White Bear

RIDGE VOCATIONAL-TECHNICAL CENTER STUDENT PERFORMANCE AGREEMENT FORM

Name (A) *Ron Askew* Student No. *12-3164* Program *Fash. Merch.* Prog. No. *DE-12* Entry Date *3-2* Exit Date ____

HOURS

Period	FROM	TO	IN SCHOOL HOURS	ACADEMIC HOURS	OTHER	HOURS IN VOC. PROGRAM (HIVP)
1	3-2	3-6	25	— (B)	— (B)	25
2	3-9	4-17	150	18	(K) 12	120
3	4-20	5-29	150	18	12	120

PERFORMANCE AGREEMENT

Period 1

PLANNED: TASK (C)	PLANNED: STD. HOURS (D)	STD. HOURS ACTUALLY ATTAINED (F)
A-01	5	5 BR
A-02	5	5 BR
A-03	4	4 BR
A-04	6	6 BR
B-01	4	4 BR
TOTALS	24 (E)	24 (G)
STUDENT INITIALS	RA	
% (H) 96	GRADE (I) A	
% 100	EMP. SKILLS (J) A	
ABSENCES 0	TARDIES 0	

Period 2

PLANNED: TASK (L)	PLANNED: STD. HOURS	STD. HOURS ACTUALLY ATTAINED (M)
B-02	6	6 BR
B-03	17	17 BR
B-04	20	20 BR
B-05	12	12 BR
B-06	14	14 BR
B-07	5	5 BR
B-08	12	12 BR
D-01	16	16 BR
D-03	12	(9) BR
D-04	5	
D-05	8	
TOTALS	127	114 (N)
STUDENT INITIALS	RA	
% 90	GRADE B	
% 96	EMP. SKILLS A	
ABSENCES 2	TARDIES 1	

Period 3

PLANNED: TASK (O) (P)	PLANNED: STD. HOURS	STD. HOURS ACTUALLY ATTAINED
D-03	3	(3) BR
D-04	5	5 BR
D-05	8	8 BR
D-06	12	12 BR
D-02	15	
C-01	10	
C-02	24	
C-03	20	
F.TRIP	5	5 BR
Store	5	3 BR
Store	5	
DECA	3	
DECA	2	
TOTALS	117	
STUDENT INITIALS	RA	
%	GRADE	
%	EMP. SKILLS	
ABSENCES	TARDIES	

SAMPLE 7-5 Student Performance Agreement (*Source*: Developed at Ridge Vo-Tech Center, Winter Haven, Fla.)

Lake, Minnesota. Let us follow an example to see how this grading system works; you will want to refer back to Sample 7-5 as you go through the example.

EXAMPLE

Ron Askew enrolled in the Fashion Merchandising program at Ridge Vo-Tech Center on March 2. His instructor pulled two blank student performance agreement forms from his desk, inserted a carbon, and began filling it out:

A *The first planning period was from March 2 to March 6—one week. Since Ron entered the program with only one week remaining in a six-week grading period, only one week's worth of work was planned in column 1.*

B *During this week, Ron would be in attendance 25 hours (5 hours a day for 5 days). During this week, he would not be working on anything outside the program, so he would be spending all 25 hours in the vocational program (HIVP).*

C *Together, the instructor and student decided that tasks A-01, A-02, A-03, A-04, and B-01 should be mastered during this first week. Tasks A-01 and A-02 were "orientation" kinds of tasks that take up the first two days for all new students. Task A-03 covered an orientation to the field of fashion merchandising and the program at Ridge in particular.*

D *The standard hours for each task planned was entered under "STD. HOURS" (5 for A-01, 6 for A-04, etc.). Remember that these standard hours are the average time previous students took to master each task.*

E *These were totaled and the student initialed, indicating that he was aware of what he was responsible for during the coming week. Notice that Ron planned to accomplish approximately as many standard hours of mastery (24) as he would be enrolled (25 HIVP).*

F *As each task was mastered, the standard hours for that task was brought over and the instructor initialed it. Notice that someone other than the instructor documented that Ron mastered A-01 and A-02. Since these are two orientation tasks mastered first by all new students ("Complete student forms" and "Use a learning guide to master a task"), the assistant director for curriculum or someone else probably signed-off on these. It is very important that you notice that the standard hours for each task was entered upon mastery—not the actual hours the student worked on the task as is entered on the time card. Since B-01 is worth 4 standard hours, 4 was entered and initialed upon mastery even though Ron may have taken 3 hours or 5 hours on it.*

G *At the end of the grading period (in this case only one week), the standard hours for all the tasks actually attained were totaled. Note that if A-04 had not been mastered, this total would be 18 instead of 24.*

H *The ratio of total standard hours attained to hours in the vocational program (HIVP) was computed by dividing 25 into 24 (I had to use a calculator, too). Ron was responsible for 25 hours worth of standard-hour task attainment and actually attained 24 hours worth—96% of what he was accountable for.*

I *Checking the county-wide grading policy, the instructor (and the student) could see that 96% was an A.*

J *This particular version of the performance agreement also has a place to record the student's grade in "employability skills." At Ridge, students begin each six weeks with 100% of the possible points toward their employability skills grade. Then for each serious infraction in 14 specific areas (such as leaving work area clean, following safety practices, not interfering with others), the student loses a predetermined number of percentage points. During this first week, Ron lost no points and received an A in employability skills. Notice that the employability skills grade is separate and points were not subtracted from the grade that reflected the students "technical" competence.*

K *The process was repeated during the second grading period, which covered a full six weeks (3/9–4/17). One difference was that Ron was scheduled to attend American History class for 18 hours during the coming six weeks ("Academic hours") and received remedial math instruction for 12 ("other"). Ron was held accountable for 120 hours' worth of standard hours of task mastery during the second six-week period (5 hours a day × 5 days a week × 6 weeks = 150 - 18 academic - 12 other = 120 HIVP).*

L *Enough tasks were planned for mastery during the coming six weeks (127 standard hours) to equal the approximate number of hours for which Ron was to be enrolled. Notice that Ron was allowed to work on tasks in duty D after completing the tasks in duties A and B.*

M *Just as before, the standard hours and instructor initials were added each time a task was mastered—not the time spent on each task. This time the six-week grading period ended while Ron was in the middle of learning guide D-03. So that Ron would not be penalized for making progress on but not fully mastering D-03, the instructor awarded him 9 hours of partial credit. Ron showed the instructor that he had completed three of the four enabling objectives for learning guide D-03 or 75% of them, so Ron was given credit for 75% of the 12 standard hours for D-03, or 9 hours.*

N *This time, Ron completed 114 standard hours worth of tasks (regardless of how long he actually worked on the tasks). Dividing 127 into 114 yielded 0.897, or 90%, which was a B in the grading system. During the second six weeks, Ron reached 90% of his "quota." If Ron had mastered more than 127 hours' worth of tasks, say 136, the percentage would be greater than 100—in this case 107%. That is OK; Ron would still get an*

"A" but rather than apply the extra 7% toward the next six weeks' grade, Ron would be allowed to exit early.

O *Tasks planned but not yet mastered during the second grading period were brought forward to the third column. Notice that when D-03 was finally mastered, Ron got only the additional 3 hours of standard hours for D-03 and not all 12, since he had gotten 9 standard hours credit for D-03 during the second six weeks.*

P *During the third grading period, things other than tasks on the task listing were scheduled for Ron. These included an all-day (5 hours) field trip; two 5-hour days working in the campus store and two activities involving the student vocational organization (DECA). As we leave the example, Ron is hard at work on task D-02.*

Advantages. The approach to grading described in this section and the particular grading system shown in this example have several important advantages:

1. Mastery of each task at a high level of proficiency is promoted. The only tasks that count toward the student's grade are those that are mastered at the minimum acceptable level stated in the learning guide for the task (100% at Ridge).
2. Simply showing up, trying hard, expending effort, or having a good attitude counts for *nothing* in the grading system (just like on the job).
3. Absences, tardiness, goofing off, and other nonproductive uses of time all carry a penalty in the grading system.
4. The instructor does not have to worry about figuring weights of various tests, computing separate grades for theory and lab, or averaging grades. When a written and a performance test are required for a task, the written test grade need not be figured in the grading system. Passing the written test is simply a prerequisite for attempting the performance test.
5. Each student can easily compute his or her own grade. The instructor is not burdened with answering questions like: "What grade will I make in here this term?" every few days.
6. It is a simple, straightforward, and practical grading system.
7. There is still a degree of forgiveness in it. Depending on the grading scale decided on, students who do have serious difficulties learning and who master only 70% or 80% of the tasks planned still receive a passing grade. Most important, though, each student is still required to master each task at the same high level before going on to the next task. Some students may not master as many tasks as others, but all tasks mastered will be at the same high level of proficiency.
8. It can be used with a traditional A–F grading system, a pass/fail system, or both. For example, the following percentages resulting from dividing

hours enrolled into hours attained might be used: A = 93-100%; B = 85-92%; C = 74-83%; D = 65-72%. Or, "satisfactory" might be from 74 to 100% and unsatisfactory anything below 74%. Both letter grades and S/U could be used, with students perhaps getting a choice as to which system they are to be graded on.

9. If a student has difficulty mastering a particular task and spends several more hours on the task than standard time, this "lost" time can be regained by spending *less* than standard time on a subsequent task. Spending more or less than standard time on tasks will probably average out over a typical grading period.
10. If a student is out of school for a week or two for good reason, the hours for which the student is being held accountable for can be reduced so that the student's grade will reflect his or her progress while in school.
11. Students who do not apply themselves will flunk *themselves* out of the program. If 70% of standard progress, for example, is your cutoff for making satisfactory progress, students who are not making an honest attempt at the training program will not be able to master a sufficient number of tasks at a high level of mastery to maintain satisfactory progress. Sliders will eventually "slide" right out of the program.
12. Students are held fully accountable for their own actions (or lack thereof). There is no room in this system for coddling students or letting them completely "do their own thing." Students would have a tough time proving that a low grade was based on discrimination or a personality conflict. Standard times and scores for written and performance tests speak for themselves.
13. The system promotes student, instructor, and training program accountability. Each student is responsible for mastering the training tasks and instructors are accountable for certifying the competence of trainees. If a high percentage of students receive unusually low grades, something is wrong. In this system, some objective data are available to begin finding out what it is. Perhaps standard times are too low, maybe students are being given "extracurricular" activities without credit, or perhaps the learning guides or media are not very good.
14. Depending on how long a student is enrolled, a fair grade can be computed for 1 week's work or 6 weeks' work.
15. Such a system is compatible with sound educational practice, is criterion-referenced, can be incorporated into most any system-wide grading policy, is fair, and would probably be endorsed wholeheartedly by most employers.

Using a document such as the student performance agreement shown offers several advantages for planning and monitoring each student's work and computing periodic grades:

1. Planning for an entire 36 weeks or even longer can be accomplished on one form; it could be used front and back.
2. The instructor can keep track of the number of hours each student is scheduled outside the training program.
3. A record of task attainment is generated.
4. By keeping an updated copy, each student knows what tasks have been accomplished and which tasks are planned for the weeks ahead.
5. Projects, field trips, live work, club activities, tutoring other students, and other important learning activities not listed on the task listing can be planned and credited for grading purposes.
6. Adjustments can be made midway through a grading period by erasing, crossing out, or redoing that grading period in the next column.
7. A substitute instructor can tell who is working on what simply by looking at the performance agreement for each student.
8. This one-page document takes the place of weekly or monthly lesson planning forms, a grade book, progress chart, individual student training plans, and grade reports used to prepare report cards or progress reports sent to students.
9. A photocopy of this form can be sent to the central administration for reporting grades, updating transcripts, recording absences, and other uses.
10. It is cheap, handy, quick, easy to use, and *it works.*

Reporting unsatisfactory progress. Another simple form you may find useful is the "progress report" shown in Sample 7-6. This form is used to report and document unsatisfactory progress perhaps midway through a grading period so that the student has ample time to do something about it. It is based on the philosophy that when provided good instruction and enough time for mastery, qualified students who fail to make steady progress in mastering tasks probably fall into two categories:

1. Due to some disability, handicap, disadvantage, or other factor or factors, the student has attempted but *has failed* to master enough tasks at a level high enough for mastery.
2. Due to excessive absences, wasting time, insufficient motivation, or other factors the student has *not tried* to master a sufficient number of tasks at a level high enough for mastery.

This form was designed for the student in the second category. After checking each student's rate of progress midway through a grading period, a form such as Sample 7-6 could be completed for each student who is currently below or just barely making satisfactory progress. By signing the form, the student acknowledges that he or she is aware of the problem. When a "U" or

STUDENT PROGRESS REPORT

Student Jim O'Brien No. 4721 Date 4-19

Program Fire Science Prog. No. FS-763

- Number of hours you have been enrolled in program as of date listed above: 84
- Total standard hours of task mastery attained as of date listed above: 36
- Percentage of "standard progress" you have made as of date listed above: 43%
- According to the "standards of progress" adopted by AVTI, your progress to date in this report period is:

☐ Satisfactory ☒ Unsatisfactory

- Instructor Initials SMK Date 4/20
- Student Initials JB Date 4/22

SAMPLE 7-6 Student Progress Report

an "F" must be issued at the end of a grading period, the instructor can document the fact that the student was warned and given adequate time to correct the problem. The form can also be used as a routine grade report for reporting S/U grades.

Documenting Mastery of Tasks

So far, we have tackled planning each student's work, monitoring progress, assigning grades for each task, and grading students' periodic progress. Now, let us look at ways to document and certify each student's mastery of competencies. Somehow you need to document in an official way which tasks have been mastered by each student. The preceding section showed how mastery of each task was recorded by the instructor on the time card and on the student performance agreement. Both of these instruments might be viewed as being "unofficial" documents. On the time card, performance agreement, or both, the instructor simply records the date of mastery of each task and verifies with his or her initials or signature that each was mastered. The student cannot very well take a stack of weekly time cards or a completed performance agreement to an employer or another school and expect someone to be able to look at it and tell what specific tasks the student has mastered.

Every week or month or at other time intervals, unofficial documentation of tasks mastered should be transferred onto a document that becomes an "official" record of what the student has accomplished. We need something similar to a college transcript. In colleges and universities, even though grades are issued each quarter or semester, the only *official* document recognized that certifies what courses a student has completed is an official transcript.

There are numerous ways to accomplish this in a competency-based program. One way is to record periodically tasks mastered onto a document we will call the "record of tasks mastered." You could call this form a transcript, competency profile, attainment record, or anything else. All it does is provide a permanent record of the specific tasks, by name, that each student has successfully mastered.

Look at Sample 7-7 for an example of the record of tasks mastered form. Notice from the sample that:

1. All important identifying information is on the form, such as name, number, date of the record, etc.
2. This particular form was computer generated. You could develop a similar form that could be completed manually. It might have all the tasks for a particular program preprinted and a copy duplicated for each student. A clerk could then type in "mastered" beside each appropriate task initialed or signed by the instructor on the student time cards or performance agreements for the previous week or month.
3. This particular sample includes provisions for "tested out" for those tasks the student successfully challenged. You might wish to use only "mastered" regardless of whether the student tested out or used the learning guide to master the task.
4. For those tasks *not* yet mastered, symbols such as XX or - - could have been printed by the computer (or clerk) under the "status" heading if the possibility of students tampering with their copy of the record is a concern.
5. The record could be stapled to the student's certificate upon completing the program, issued separately, or it could be reduced photographically and photocopied right on the back of the certificate. To accomplish this, the student's certificate is simply loaded into the paper hopper of a copy machine; the updated record of tasks mastered is placed in the machine as the original; then presto—the record of tasks is copied onto the back of the certificate.
6. The task listing could be preprinted on the back of the program certificate and the instructor's or registrar's signature or other appropriate notation entered beside each task mastered.
7. If desired, the record of tasks mastered could show only the tasks and the status of each without task numbers and standard times. Or it could show

SAMPLE RECORD OF TASKS MASTERED AVTI

STUDENT NAME JOHNSON, CHARLES D. STD.NO. 999-99-9999 DATE 03/02

PROGRAM NAME MOTORCYCLE MECHANICS PROGRAM NO. IND 6249

ENTRY DATE 01/12 EXIT DATE TASKS IN PROG 74 TASKS MSTD 10

TASK NO	STD HRS	TASK	STATUS
DUTY A - ORIENTATION, HAND TOOLS, FASTENERS AND LUBRICANTS			
A-01	3	FILL OUT STUDENT FORMS	MASTERED
A-02	4	USE A LEARNING PACKAGE	MASTERED
A-03	4	USE COMMON HAND TOOLS	TEST OUT
A-04	3	SELECT AND USE FASTENERS	TEST OUT
A-05	2	SELECT AND APPLY LUBRICANTS	MASTERED
A-06	4	DESCRIBE OVERALL OPERATION OF MOTORCYCLE	TEST OUT
DUTY B - SERVICING WHEELS AND BRAKES			
B-01	12	REPAIR TIRES AND TUBES	MASTERED
B-02	22	REMOVE AND REPLACE WHEEL HUBS	
B-03	18	REMOVE AND REPLACE WHEEL BEARINGS	MASTERED
B-04	6	OVERHAUL DRUM BRAKES	TEST OUT
B-05	24	OVERHAUL HYDRAULIC BRAKES	MASTERED
B-06	12	SET UP AND SERVICE NEW MOTORCYCLE	
DUTY C - MAINTAINING AND REPAIRING DRIVE TRAIN			
C-01	18	OVERHAUL PRIMARY DRIVE	
C-02	40	OVERHAUL TRANSMISSION	
C-03	12	REPLACE CHAIN AND SPROCKETS	
C-04	30	OVERHAUL DRIVE SHAFT	
DUTY D - SERVICING FUEL SYSTEM			
D-01	6	IDENTIFY COMP OF FUEL SYS AND DESC OPER	MASTERED
D-02	20	TROUBLESHOOT MALFUNCTIONING CARBURETOR	MASTERED
D-03	4	CLEAN AND REPAIR FUEL TANK AND PETCOCK	TEST OUT
D-04	20	TROUBLESHOOT AND REPAIR SLIDE TYPE CARB	MASTERED
D-05	20	TROUBLESHOOT AND REPAIR C.V. TYPE CARB	MASTERED
D-06	10	TROUBLESHOOT AND REPAIR FIXED VEN CARB	MASTERED

SAMPLE 7-7 Records of Tasks Mastered

not only tasks, task numbers, and standard times, but also the actual number of hours the particular student spent on each task or just the date begun and date mastered or both. These data might be of interest to prospective employers.

8. A student exiting a program early could take the record of tasks mastered to a similar training program and would not be required to repeat instruction in the tasks documented as "mastered" (we hope!).
9. Students graduating from basic training programs and moving into more advanced programs can be given full credit for those tasks already mastered.

Certifying Competence

The last document we will look at is the program certificate, diploma, or other document issued to certify that the trainee has successfully completed the entire training program. Certificates, like all the other components of traditional programs, need some revising to be compatible with the competency-based approach. Let us look at the wording typically found on program certificates or diplomas.

EXAMPLE

This is to certify that
John Doe
has successfully completed the
Accounting Occupations
program
OR
This document certifies that the
student named below has attended
640 hours of the 800 hour
training program in Child-Care Worker.

If you were an employer, a parent, a friend, or anyone else who wanted to know, could you tell from the wording on these two documents *what the student can do*? Do you know what skills the trainee can perform? Do you know what job tasks the student has mastered? I think you see the problem. We need a better way of certifying to those outside the training program *exactly* what it is the student has learned.

EXAMPLES

This certifies that
Roosevelt Williams
has successfully attained the tasks
listed on the reverse side of this document
for the program:
Data Entry Operator
Each task was performed at 100% proficiency at a trainee level.
OR
This certificate attests that the student named above has mastered all required competencies in the major areas of:
Servicing Brakes
Automotive Tune Up
Auto Air Conditioning
and listed on the attached transcript.

These last two examples were taken from program certificates that show very clearly exactly what it is the student has learned. By simply turning the document over or by referring to the student's transcript, the employer can easily see *exactly* what the student has learned—and what the student has *not yet* learned if the certificate is for partial program completion or for completion of a specialized occupation within a broader program.

Putting It All Together

Believe it or not, the strategies and documents shown in this section can actually make the management burden in an individualized program less than or equal to that in a traditional program. In a conventional group-paced program, much of the record-keeping work comes in spurts. Tests for 20 students must be graded and recorded on the same day and detailed lesson plans must be filed periodically. In an individualized program, the record keeping is spread out over time, and students share a lot of the record-keeping responsibilities with you.

If you are serious about implementing a high-quality, competency-based, self-paced training program and want to make efficient use of both your own and your student's time, you should seriously consider carefully designing a management system that serves the function of the following documents described in this section. Of course, this is in addition to a task listing and a well-developed learning guide for each task:

1. Student performance agreement
2. Student time card (with a time clock if at all possible)
3. Record of tasks mastered

Your system can be more or less complex than the one described here, but these three simple instruments—or instruments that do what they do—are a must. They will help you plan each student's work, monitor progress, document task mastery, keep up with attendance and who's working on what, when, and will help you establish accurate standard times.

A word needs to be said about computerizing the record-keeping system. The system described in this section can be effectively handled manually; however, using a computer can reduce the record-keeping burden considerably.

> For about what you would pay for a good 16mm film projector, you can purchase a small computer that can adequately handle the records and data required to manage learning for 20 to 30 students in a competency-based training program.

Instructors who fail to see the importance of developing some kind of computer literacy these days will find themselves very much out of step with education in the near future. If your school or company has a computing system, all you may need is a terminal or perhaps just access to a terminal.

Below are some things you can accomplish with a computer, which is just the tip of the computing iceberg:

1. Standard time for each task can be computed instantly and updated whenever you wish.
2. If you are looking for an advanced student to tutor a beginning student, you (or the student) can find out which students in your class have mastered a certain task, when they mastered it, and what their written and performance test scores were simply by pressing the right buttons.
3. Weekly, biweekly, or monthly "progress graphs" can be generated on a TV screen or in print (or both) for each student. The graph can compare standard progress with each student's actual progress to date and can project which students will make unsatisfactory progress if they continue at their present rate.
4. Test scores can be analyzed to find trends, identify bad test items, compute class averages, and provide a host of other information.
5. Tests and self-checks can actually be given by the computer. Any written test using multiple-choice, true–false, or matching questions or any problem-solving test requiring symbols, circuits, drawings, graphs, or similar graphics can be administered, scored, timed, and recorded by a computer.
6. Instruction can be delivered by computer. Anything that can be typed on paper can be entered into memory. This includes problems, instruction sheets, recipes, tools lists, step-by-step instructions for tasks, and even future learning guides. Many small computers have graphic, color, sound, and other capabilities.

Before going on, complete the following Self-Check.

SELF-CHECK [2]

Check your mastery of ENABLING OBJECTIVE [2] by completing this SELF-CHECK.

1. Why are grading systems that compare each student's performance with other students' *in*appropriate for use in competency-based training programs? ____

   ____

2. List at least two reasons why reporting each student's progress periodically is desirable.

   (a) ______________________________

   (b) ______________________________

3. Which approach to assigning grades for each task is most compatible with the competency-based training philosophy:

   (a) Basing grades on the number of significant accomplishments (such as tutoring other students) beyond a minimum number of tasks mastered

   (b) Basing grades on an equitable weighting of task mastery, attendance, and essential work-related attitudes

   (c) Basing grades on a predetermined set of criteria for varying levels of proficiency in mastering tasks

   (d) Basing grades on the number of tasks successfully mastered during the grading period

4. A considerable amount of evidence indicates that the time it takes most students to master a learning task will be very similar *if* what three conditions exist?

   (a) ______________________________

   (b) ______________________________

   (c) ______________________________

5. Using the grading system proposed in this section and the following grading scale, compute the percentage and letter grade for each student listed below:

Grading Scale

Percent	*High School*	*Adult*
95–100	A	S
90–94	B	S
85–89	C	S
80–84	D	U
Below 80	F	U

Student	Hours Enrolled	Hours Scheduled Outside the Vocational Program	Total Standard Hours Attained	Percent	Grade
(a)	150	0	120	_____	_____
(b)	280	26	262	_____	_____
(c)	50	0	44	_____	_____
(d)	120	20	80	_____	_____
(e)	90	0	84	_____	_____

Compare your responses with those in the Answer Key in the appendix.

ENABLING OBJECTIVE [3]

Manage the Learning Environment

Rearrange the Physical Environment

As you might suspect, the design and layout of classrooms, shops, and laboratories used in traditional training programs are not very well suited for the competency-based approach. Most learning facilities were designed around the conventional, instructor-centered, group-paced model of instruction. Before individualized, self-paced learning can be successfully implemented, certain changes in the physical facility must be made. Since very few instructors or program planners will have the luxury of designing a new facility from scratch or making extensive modifications to existing facilities, this section focuses on making minor yet important changes in traditional facilities already in use. Most of these changes focus on the arrangement of furniture, resources, and other things within the facility.

Most traditional classrooms and labs have been designed and arranged so that the following can take place:

- All students enrolled in the program can be assembled as one group to listen to lectures, watch films, or participate in other group activities in a classroom setting.
- All students enrolled can be directed as a group to engage in some practice or laboratory activity.

Figure 7-1 shows a typical (marine mechanics) classroom and shop designed and arranged for this kind of instruction. First look at the classroom and notice:

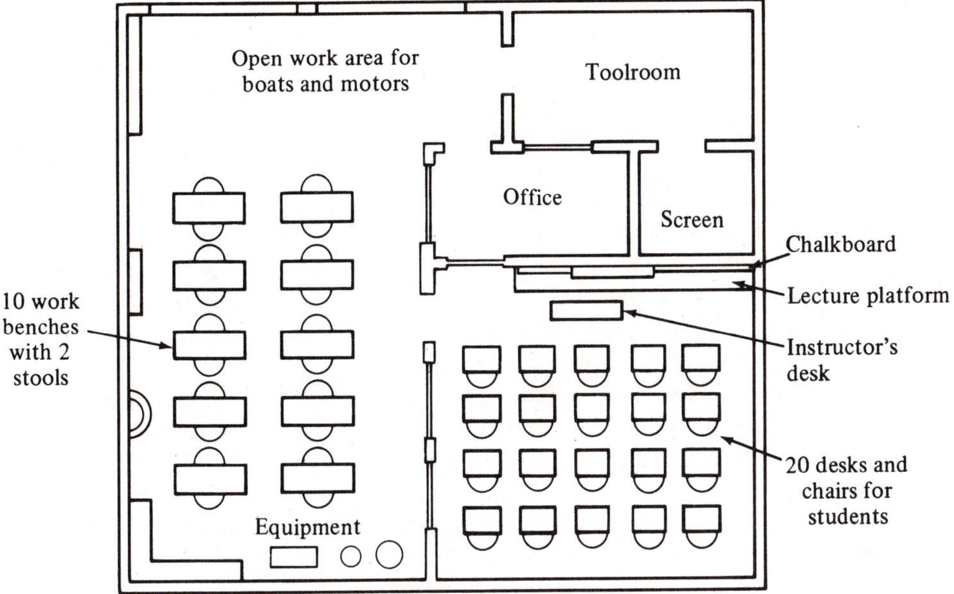

FIGURE 7-1 Traditional Classroom and Shop Layout for *Teaching*

1. All 20 students can be (and usually are) assembled in the classroom for 'theory'' classes.
2. The design of the classroom promotes instructor-centered teaching primarily; notice the raised lecture platform, the chalkboard, and the screen.
3. The layout promotes instructor activity and discourages student activity. Notice how the instructor will be the only one moving around the room. Students will spend most of their time sitting, listening, and watching—not necessarily learning.
4. Notice how this arrangement discourages direct instructor-student contact. Most of the time, the instructor will be addressing the group.
5. Students who have questions must ask them in front of the entire class. The farther back the student sits, the less involved the student is in what is going on.
6. This classroom is arranged for teaching—*not* learning.
7. This arrangement almost *forces* the instructor to cover "theory," concepts, principles, and other knowledge totally removed from skills. It promotes two- and three-hour theory classes (or even longer) in which students have little or no opportunity to apply this knowledge.

Now look at the *shop* area in Figure 7-1 and notice:

1. All 20 students can be assembled in the shop as a group for hands-on activities.
2. The shop is not set up for any instruction whatsoever—only for hands-on activities.
3. There are no *special* places set up for ongoing, planned practice activities in the shop—only some empty work benches. Usually, students will all receive a lecture and/or demonstration in the classroom on some topic, and all the students will proceed to the shop, where an engine or a boat will be repaired by a limited number of students (or perhaps the instructor) while others watch.
4. There are two stools at each bench; students will do all practice work in pairs, with each pair evaluated on its ability to perform some task—not each individual student.

You can see how an arrangement like this does not promote competency-based learning. Now, look at Figure 7-2 and notice the changes that were made in this marine mechanics classroom and shop:

1. It would be difficult for all 20 students to assemble as a group and spend any length of time in either the classroom or the shop. At any given time, some students will be in the classroom and others will be in the shop. Students will be moving back and forth as their learning needs dictate.
2. The platform and screen were removed since very few students will ever need the same group instruction at the same time. A small area of the chalkboard was left exposed for writing announcements and for graphically explaining answers to questions for individuals and small groups.
3. Both the shop and classroom have been rearranged to promote student activity and movement. Students will be moving about within the classroom and shop.
4. The classroom has been turned into a "learning center," housing "stations" for receiving instruction and for practicing.
5. The classroom has been arranged for learning—*not* teaching.
6. The student tables and chairs that were once all lined up in neat rows have been placed around the walls of the room. Plywood partitions were added between tables so that one student will not bother another and the audiovisual equipment used most often has been set up for immediate use.
7. The instructor's desk has been removed completely from the classroom.
8. In the classroom, several stations have been set up for students to perform hands-on practice activities during or after watching A-V presentations or reading print materials.

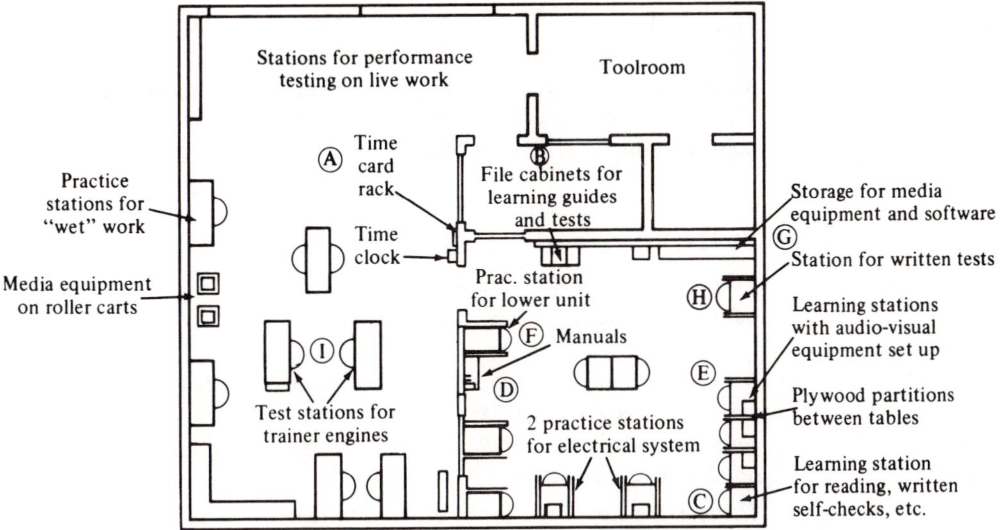

FIGURE 7-2 Layout of Classroom and Shop for Competency-based Learning

9. If oil, grease, or fuel might be spilled, or if an engine will actually be started up, the student will be directed to a work station out in the shop itself. This way, students listening, viewing, reading, or testing in the "classroom" will not be disturbed and the tile floor will not be damaged. Several practice stations with audiovisual equipment have been set up along the walls of the shop.
10. There are separate practice staions for major duty areas (electrical, fuel system, etc.). At each station, the student will find a wide variety of actual parts on which to practice. While completing the learning guide "Check and replace magneto," for example, the student would spend time at one of the two electrical system practice stations. After being shown how magnetos work by reading and viewing learning resources, the student will tear down, rebuild, troubleshoot, repair, and replace several magnetos. Only after sufficient practice at a practice station will the student attempt to check and repair magnetos on working engines owned by the school or on engines brought in by "customers."

Using Figure 7-2, let us follow a student through a typical learning guide to see why the rearrangement of the physical facility is important.

EXAMPLE

A *Susan Mitchell punched in Wednesday morning at 7:45 ready for a new learning guide.*

B *She checked her performance agreement in the file cabinet (she lost her copy) and found that F-12 was the next task for her to work on. She checked the task sequence chart taped to the wall to make sure there were no prerequisite tasks. She pulled a copy of F-12 from the learning* guide file drawer and looked through it. Here are the task and enabling objectives she found on the first page:

Task: Rebuild lower unit.
EO [1]: Describe parts and operation of lower unit.
EO [2]: Remove and inspect lower unit.
EO [3]: Rebuild, install, and test lower unit.

As was her habit, she flipped over to the performance test to see exactly what she was going to have to be able to do to complete the learning guide. She knew she could not already perform the task, so she did not bother trying to test out.

C *The learning steps for EO [1] referred to two different learning resources outside the learning guide as well as an instruction sheet inside the guide. The first resource to be read was the instruction sheet; Susan went to this learning station since no media were needed.*

D *Next, she read the section in a manufacturer's manual indicated by the learning steps in the guide.*

E *A filmstrip without any hands-on activity involved came next, so she sat at this station since it had a filmstrip projector and small screen all set up. Since no one else was waiting to use that station, she remained there to complete the self-check for the first EO. She missed three part names, so she went back to the manual to find out why. Still puzzled by one of the answers on the answer key, she asked a friend working nearby for help.*

F *Enabling objective [2] involved the disassembly of two different types of actual lower units. The guide directed her to the lower unit work station, which was set up for "dry" (without lubricants) practice on lower units. She laid out her learning guide and got comfortable. The guide told her what slide tape unit to watch while disassembling the unit.*

G *She got this unit and a projector from the media cabinet, set it up at station F and got started. This particular commercially produced A-V segment was interactive. After each few frames, the projector would stop, Susan would do precisely what was shown, she would press "start," and the next few frames would advance. She was receiving instruction and practicing all at the same station. The self-check directed her to lay out all the parts, make certain precision measurements, and identify parts she thought should be replaced. After doing this, she called the instructor over to check her work as instructed in the learning guide. She repeated the process for EO [3]. Halfway through EO [3] the day ended and Susan punched out. The next morning after punching in, she went directly to work station F and picked up right where she left off.*

H *The next learning step directed her to take the written test. The instructor unlocked the test file cabinet and gave her written test F-12 and an answer sheet. She sat down at the written test station, completed the test, and took it to the instructor to be corrected. He pulled the answer key from the locked file, checked her responses, congratulated her, and told her to read over the performance test.*

I *The last step in the guide was to take the performance test. Without the use of the learning guide or any other materials, Susan was required to rebuild the lower units on three different makes of engines. Two of the engines were trainers owned by the school and the third was an engine with stripped gears in the lower unit owned by a school employee. After she successfully completed the performance test over the next day and a half, the instructor initialed her time card and recorded her mastery of F-12 on her performance agreement.*

Notice that Susan:

1. Was very active; she moved around within the classroom several times.
2. Moved from one area to another when she was ready.
3. Took responsibility for her own learning. Following the learning guide, she located the resources she needed and used them.
4. Involved the instructor in the learning process at critical times.
5. Practiced the task several times under controlled conditions before attempting to work on an actual engine.
6. Sought help from a fellow student when needed.
7. Began working each morning where she left off the previous day.
8. Enjoyed the benefits of her instructor having developed an effective learning guide with apparently excellent print and nonprint resources.
9. Did not have to "endure" any lecture or "theory" class on how the lower unit works. The first enabling objective in the guide covered this in an appropriate manner and covered it *when* Susan needed to know it.
10. Was heavily involved in the learning process and spent her time *learning*—not being on the receiving end of *teaching*.

Stations

Regardless of how you lay out your facility—and each type of program will be different—you should make sure that you set up some areas within the classroom or lab or both to accommodate three different kinds of student activities.

Learning stations. Some area should be set aside for students to receive instruction for each enabling objective. For reading materials, this can be tables, desks, vacant benches, or any other areas that are quiet, comfortable, and well lit. For nonprint materials, you need carrels, or tables or other areas to set up and view slides, tapes, films, and other materials. You may wish to allow students to move freely to the library, media center, LRC, vacant classrooms, or other areas to receive instruction.

Practice stations. Another area—one often overlooked in setting up traditional facilities—is for practicing in a *controlled* setting what is presented. Applying and checking mastery of knowledge can be accomplished using the same areas used for reading. For practicing skills, however, some sort of *practice station* is essential. An area is needed where the student can lay out tools and materials and fully perform the skill called for. The ideal arrangement is to *combine* the presentation of how to perform the skill with the practice of that skill at the *same* location. This way, as the instruction sheet, slides, or other resource shows the student how to perform each step, it can be performed *right then*. Viewing a film loop showing several steps and remembering those steps while practicing can be difficult. If the "viewing" and the "doing" can be combined into one station (a learning/practice station, I suppose), the loop could be stopped, those few steps performed, and the loop restarted.

Testing stations. You may not need separate areas for testing in all programs, but in many program areas it is essential. Written tests should be taken in quiet, comfortable, well-lit areas that can be monitored periodically. Performance tests may be given in the same areas used for practice or in separate areas. In some occupations such as masonry, carpentry, and plumbing, the performance test for some tasks may have to be given outdoors or even at a remote job site. If you use the same areas for practice and for testing, do not yield to the temptation to skip the practice work. Never have the student jump directly from presentation of instruction in a task to performance of the task to demonstrate mastery. Some students may be able to make the jump but most will not.

Of course, you may not need three separate and distinct areas for presentation, practice/feedback, and testing. Just remember to help students accomplish all three of these activities for each task. The physical layout of the facility will vary considerably depending on the nature of the program. A secretarial program may be housed all in one room with desks and typewriters in one area, transcription machines set up in another, and file cabinets and adding machines in yet another. In a drafting program, the student may be able to receive instruction, practice it, and take the test while never moving from the drawing table. Other programs, such as dental assisting, grocery merchandising, and machine shop, will need to be set up around major pieces of equipment. Although vastly different in appearance, the facilities for each of those programs should be rearranged to accommodate individualized, self-paced, student-centered learning. In each case, a student should be able to begin a new task when ready, find someplace to read print materials or view nonprint materials, and find some area where the knowledge or skill presented can be practiced or applied and then checked. Finally, the student should be directed to some area where the task can be performed in a joblike setting to demonstrate mastery.

Tips

Here are a number of tips you might find helpful as you rearrange your facility:

1. Plan it first; get hold of a copy of the floor plan for your shop and classroom. Draw in those things that cannot be easily rearranged, such as sinks, heavy equipment, closets, air supply lines, and other permanent items. Mark the location of windows, doors, storage shelves, and receptacles. Cut out small cardboard shapes to scale representing desks, chairs, benches, stools, portable equipment, and anything else that can be moved. On your floor plan, try various rearrangements of furniture and equipment. Settle on the best layout you can come up with, rearrange your facility accordingly, and try it out. Let students help you evaluate the new layout for improvements.
2. When you have a choice, order tables instead of desks. Tables can be moved and put together to make learning stations and covered with plywood or a protective cover to make practice stations. Individual student desks are almost useless in competency-based training programs.
3. Carrels to serve as learning stations can be purchased, built, or "adapted" from existing furniture. Small tables can be put together and separated by sheets of paneling or plywood.
4. Set up learning stations using audiovisual equipment near power outlets. Try to get head phones for audiovisual equipment so that students will not interfere with one another's learning.
5. Convert your classroom into a mini-learning resource center. Try to arrange all the print and nonprint resources referred to in your learning guides in an attractive and easy-to-locate manner. You may want to devote particular shelves or cabinets to slide-tape boxes, filmstrips, manuals, reference books, audiovisual equipment, tape cartridges, and other resources. Make sure that all resources are clearly labeled for easy identification and reshelving.
6. If two similar programs, such as nursing and respiratory therapy, have classrooms connected by a portable, folding partition, the partition

can be removed, making one large resource center. This way, students in both programs can share the learning stations, resources, and audio-visual equipment for both programs. One student can serve as a clerk to help check out, set up, and refile media materials for both programs.

7. Do not treat the classroom and lab as two separate rooms—one for theory and one for practice. Treat them as two areas for mastering different kinds of tasks.
8. For industrial programs, a platform or small room can be constructed in the center of a large work area. From this raised, centrally located vantage point, the instructor, foreman, or aide can maintain direct supervision of the use of heavy equipment and, if properly located, will have a clear view into the classroom "learning" center.
9. If needed, you may wish to control slide-tape materials, manuals, expensive reference books, and video tapes as you do tools. Students can check them in and out from a tool room by signing in and out or using tokens or other means.
10. If you are involved in building a new facility or expanding an existing one, insist that the architect and planners visit institutions where individualized instruction has been implemented. Very few architects, planners, trustees, school board members, state department staff, and others heavily involved in facility design have an in-depth understanding of the competency-based approach to training and education.

Create a Positive Learning Environment

Rearranging the facility will help a great deal in successfully implementing the competency-based approach. Another essential is a positive, supportive learning environment. Of course, this is true whether the program is individualized or traditional. A positive environment is more critical in an individualized program, however, because students will be directing their own actions and will have a great deal more freedom and responsibility. This is where the instructor or course manager comes in. The environment you establish will greatly influence the performance of your students. A negative, abrasive, unsupportive learning atmosphere will lead to confrontations, frustration, and failure for some. A supportive, positive atmosphere, on the other hand, can provide the catalyst needed to ensure that the full potential of the competency-based approach is realized. It is largely up to the instructor; his or her outlook, behavior, and expectations will set the stage.

Of course, there is no magic formula for creating this positive kind of atmosphere so important for success. Here are some tips you may want to consider adopting or adapting.

1. Convince students that you are there to help them; give assistance willingly.

2. Try your best to recognize the uniqueness of each individual student. Each has his or her own anxieties, frustrations, hopes, and fears.
3. Let there be no doubt in the students' minds why they are in the program. Make it clear they are there to learn. You will do everything in your power to help them but they must help themselves.
4. Firmly, believe that *every* student can fully master *every* task and you will be amazed at how close they will come.
5. Run your training program in a no-nonsense, businesslike manner. Provide high-quality learning experiences and demand high-quality performance.
6. Provide positive feedback and reinforcement when appropriate but do not overdo it. Try to find out what reinforcers each student responds to best. A pat on the shoulder, a "well done," a smile or wink, or a request to keep a student's work as an example of excellence can make a student feel really good about themselves and their experience in your program.
7. Try to avoid criticizing students; if students mess up—criticize their *actions* or their *work—not them*! "I'm quite upset with your attendance" might have a more positive impact than "I'm upset with *you*."
8. Try to model the kind of behavior and performance you want students to exhibit. If *you* wipe the grease off the fender when you show students how to do a tune up, chances are *they* will, too. When you show up every day, on time, and put in a good day's work, you can expect and more easily get the same from students.
9. Be professional; avoid profanity, off-color jokes, and other behaviors that might be offensive to some students. Remember that a student who *respects* you will learn more from you than one whose respect you have not earned.
10. Establish a few, basic sensible rules for behavior, dress, and the like and enforce them *all* firmly and fairly.

Help Students Complete Learning Packages

Since packaged instruction will be relied on heavily in this approach to training, students who find it difficult to work on and complete learning packages will be at a disadvantage. You may have a small percentage of students who for several reasons just do not feel comfortable using learning packages. These may include:

- It is so different from what they are used to; they may have spent 12 years or so in school with the majority of that time spent sitting and listening.
- Lack of confidence or self-directiveness. Some students may have trouble at first taking the initiative and assuming responsibility for their own learn-

ing. One beauty of relying heavily on packaged and mediated instruction is that the instructor is largely freed from the burden of teaching, so just these kinds of students can be helped along until they get a few tasks under their belts.

- Failure oriented; some students have had one after another failure experience in the traditional system of schooling. These students are the ones for which the conventional approach to education has been least successful. Many have dropped out, or have been pushed out of the system. Some students may think your training program is simply the next in a long history of failures. It is critical that such students be given early success to show them that here is one educational experience that they can not only complete, but one in which they can excel—probably for the first time in their lives.

Here are some strategies you might want to use to help students successfully complete learning packages:

1. Arrange it so that "high-risk" students begin with a series of short, less difficult learning packages for which no prerequisite learning is needed. Try your darndest to *guarantee* the student's success in the first learning package used.
2. Make sure that students are fully oriented as to *what* learning packages are, *why* they are needed, and *how* to use them. You cannot hand new students a packet and expect them all to take off. This is a totally new experience for most of them.
3. Insist that students use the packages as they were designed to be used. Early in the program, new students may come to you with questions obviously answered in the learning resources. Students will find it easier to come to you for information—especially if you give it freely—than locating the resources called for in the learning guides and digging it out themselves. Do *not*—repeat—do *not* yield to this temptation; if you do, you will find yourself swamped with questions all day, with little time left for anything else. Help those who genuinely need it *only* after you are convinced that they used the resources as instructed. If necessary, help the *student* find the answer to his or her question.
4. Let students work together if they wish. That is another advantage of this approach to training. Students can work alone or in small groups. You will find small clusters of students forming who are working on common tasks, especially when a small group enters at the same time. Just make sure that each *individual* student—*alone*—completes the written and performance test required for each learning package.
5. Become familiar with all the resources referred to in each learning guide. Avoid giving answers to questions that conflict with what a manual or instruction sheet says.

6. If a student is having a problem with a learning guide, try to find out exactly what the problem is. Maybe a self-check was skipped, maybe a slide-tape was not viewed or just skimmed over, maybe the student cannot read well enough. It could be anything; find out what the problem is and try to solve it.
7. Be aware of various learning styles. Some students prefer to work in small groups, others like to work alone. Some are very sensitive to noise or other distractions—noise may not affect others. One student may work best only in a well-lighted area, whereas another may not care. Some students need constant interaction and support from the instructor; others may be more independent. Try to key in on what makes each student perform best and, if possible, try to provide that kind of atmosphere.

Before going on, complete the following Self-Check.

SELF-CHECK [3]

Check your mastery of ENABLING OBJECTIVE [3] by completing this SELF-CHECK.

1. In most competency-based training programs, *three* different types of physical areas should be set up for students to use. In this section, these three areas have been referred to as different kinds of "stations." Name each station and briefly describe what is accomplished at each.

   (a) ____________ : ______________________________

   (b) ____________ : ______________________________

   (c) ____________ : ______________________________

2. Why is a positive learning environment more critical in a competency-based program than in a traditional program?

3. List at least two reasons why some students may not feel comfortable using learning packages.

   (a) ____

   (b) ____

Compare your responses with those in the Answer Key in the appendix.

PERFORMANCE TEST FOR TASK 11

TASK 11: Develop System to Manage Learning

DIRECTIONS

When ready, demonstrate your ability to develop a system to manage learning by doing the following:

For one or more competency-based training programs, develop:

1. Instrument(s) to plan and monitor each student's work.
2. A grading system supportive of the competency-based approach.
3. A program certificate/diploma for certifying competence.
4. A detailed drawing of the total learning environment as it will be rearranged to promote competency-based, self-paced learning.

No.	Criteria for evaluating performance; 100% mastery required	Yes	No
	Instrument(s) to Plan and Monitor Each Student's Work		
1.	Does instrument(s) have place for:		
	a. Student's name?		
	b. Student number?		
	c. Program name?		
	d. Program number?		
	e. Time period being planned?		
	f. Task number and name planned for mastery?		
2.	Does instrument have a place to verify if and when each task has been mastered?		
3.	Can the student have a copy of the instrument?		
4.	Is the instrument easy to use and read?		
	Grading System		
5.	Does each student have an *equal* chance to earn each grade possible in the system?		

6. Do students know *exactly* what performance is required for each grade possible?
7. Is the grade *earned* by the student and not given?
8. Does the grading system reflect the actual *competence* of trainees and *not* behaviors such as attendance, attitudes, etc.?

Certificate/Diploma

9. Does the instrument used for certifying competence list or refer to the specific competencies the student has and has not yet mastered?

Layout of Learning Environment

10. Is student activity and movement encouraged by layout?
11. Are large groupings of desks or chairs for lectures avoided?
12. Are well-planned stations or other areas set up for:
    a. Receiving instruction—reading, viewing, etc.?
    b. Practicing what has been presented and getting feedback?
    c. Taking a written test in a quiet and secure area?
    d. Taking performance tests?
13. Are areas set aside to set up the media equipment used most often?
14. Are other media equipment and software stored for quick and easy access?
15. Are references, books, manuals, and related resources kept where students have easy access to them?
16. Are learning packages kept in an easily accessible spot?
17. Has a secure area been reserved for tests?
18. Have the shop, lab, classroom, and other areas been set up to promote individualized, self-paced learning?
19. Has existing furniture been effectively rearranged to enhance learning?
20. Overall, has the learning environment been set up to promote learning and *not* teaching?

When you complete this section, you will be able to:

TASK 12: Implement and Evaluate Training Programs

INTRODUCTION

Developing and implementing competency-based training programs can be a very involved undertaking. Carefully planning for the implementation of programs can save a lot of time and energy and can make the process go a lot smoother. This section shows you how to develop detailed plans to *implement* competency-based training programs. Also, this section describes ways to *evaluate training programs* to determine if existing programs are competency-based and to determine if competency-based programs are effective.

TERMINAL PERFORMANCE OBJECTIVE

To demonstrate mastery of this task, do the following:

For one or more training program, develop plans to implement the competency-based approach to training, develop plans to train the staff, and develop instruments to evaluate programs. Plans and instruments developed should conform to *all* criteria listed in Performance Test 12 at the end of this section.

ENABLING OBJECTIVES

This section is divided into several parts to help you:

[1] *Develop plans to implement competency-based training programs.*
[2] *Plan a staff development program for instructional and support staff.*
[3] *Develop instruments to evaluate competency-based training programs.*

ENABLING OBJECTIVE [1]

Develop Plans to Implement Competency-Based Training Programs

Needed—A Plan

It may seem strange that *planning* is covered in the last section of a book like this; obviously, planning a program should be accomplished before getting under way. Planning was included last so that the reader would have a clear picture of *what* had to be planned. If you had read in Chapter 1 that you needed to plan how competencies were going to be identified, how learning packages were to be put together, and how to plan for effectively managing student learning, it probably would not have made much sense. But now that you are familiar with all the components of a competency-based program, you have a pretty good idea of *what* needs to be accomplished to develop and implement such a program. This section will help you plan for accomplishing this.

Planning and implementing competency-based training programs will usually take place on two different scales:

- *One-program*—you may be an instructor or trainer responsible for a single training program. You may be attempting to install a new program or perhaps restructure an existing one. You may be totally on your own with little or no administrative help or support, or you might find yourself in the enviable position of being a pilot program in a large-scale effort. Or you may be the only instructor in a department or program who is attempting to implement this approach to training.
- *Multiprogram*—You may be part of or even directing a multiprogram implementation effort. Perhaps you are involved in establishing competency-based programs in several loosely related programs or in a particular department or division or perhaps an entire institution, agency, or company. Your task may be to develop new programs, revamp old programs, or both. Your involvement in such a large-scale effort may be as a manager, supervisor, training director, principal, media specialist, instructional designer, or instructor.

So depending on your role and the scope of the program planning effort of which you are a part, you will want to either scale up or scale down the planning process described here. Whether a one-program, 10-program, or 100-program effort, though, the need for careful planning is the same. If you simply strike out listing tasks, throwing together learning packages, and moving furniture around—without a *plan*—you will regret it.

> As with any complex undertaking, there are rewards for carefully planning your work and carefully working your plan.

Seek Support

You would probably agree that implementing a nonconventional approach to training in a very conventional world would be far easier with the support of others, particularly those in authority. If you are a trainer in a large corporation, the support of the vice-president for training and development would be nice. If you are the director of a vocational-technical center, the blessing of the school board or other governing body would prove not only extremely valuable, but essential. So somewhere in your scheme of things you will find a need to drum up support for what you are trying to do.

You should use the usual strategies for gaining the support of others, such as informing, involving, preparing, communicating, and others. Use them to gain support for implementing the competency-based approach just as you would for any other effort. Described below are two strategies for seeking support that may prove helpful, particularly in getting others to buy into the competency-based approach to training.

Apple Pie and CBI Let us say that you are the occupational dean in a state community college. Being from academic backgrounds, the president, trustees, and other decision makers would probably shoot down your proposal to spend substantial dollars to implement competency-based instruction (CBI) in the occupational training programs. However, you might attempt to get the president, the trustees, and others to *publicly* support CBI in *writing* without them knowing it! Sound impossible? I thought so too until I did it. Let us see how an occupational dean at a community college did it.

EXAMPLE

DEAN: *"I appreciate the opportunity to attend this board of trustees' meeting and get your input on what direction the occupational division here at Pleasant Valley Community College should take during the coming years. We've done a lot of soul searching in the division and we realize that a major quality improvement effort is needed. We need to lower our dropout rate, increase placements, better meet the needs of special-needs learners, and improve our curriculum.*

CHAIR: *"Thanks for coming, Dean. I'm glad to see you people in the Vo-Tech Division are concerned about high-quality education like the academic areas are."*

DEAN: *(Trying to control himself) "Knowing how closely the president and the members of the board of trustees keep in touch with the needs and wishes of business, industry, and citizens in the community, I'm coming to you tonight for help. I've developed a short questionnaire that asks a series of very crucial questions (see Figure*

7-3) about our training programs. I'd like your guidance by having each of you fill out the instrument. By your responses, you'll be telling us how you feel our training programs should be set up and operated here at PVCC.

(Two weeks later):

DEAN: "On these two transparencies, you see the results of the survey instrument you completed two weeks ago. I also took the liberty of mailing it to about 65 leaders in business and industry in the local area. You can see from these figures that both the board of trustees and key individuals in business and industry feel very strongly about the way our training programs should be set up in the future. Of the 20 questions on the survey, 16 received a "yes" response by 100% of the 72 individuals completing the survey. Two more were marked "yes" by 90% of the respondents, and the other two questions received a "yes" by 80%. As you can see, to implement the approach to training implied in these 20 questions will require some changes in the way we're presently operating here at Pleasant Valley.

CHAIR: "Do I hear a motion to allow the occupational dean to move ahead with plans to make these changes in the technical programs here at PVCC?"

The beauty of this strategy is that every single item on this survey is based on *common sense* and very, very few people would publicly say "no" to any of them. It would almost be like saying no to motherhood and apple pie.

The dean got the board s unanimous endorsement for the concept without the board really knowing what it was they were endorsing. Notice that the survey form made absolutely *no* mention of any educationese such as "competency-based vocational education" or "self-paced, individualized instruction." In some cases, the worst thing you can do is walk into the director's office and say: "I've decided to implement competency-based instruction in my program; do I have your support?" Proceed with caution! When you mention terms like individualized, open-entry, open-exit, or competency-based, many administrators, supervisors, chairmen, board members, and instructors may:

- Oppose it because they think it is the latest fad in education
- Think it is a fancy term for what they are already doing
- Say they already have "behavioral objectives" written or a V-TECS catalog and that is good enough
- Think it is a pie-in-the-sky, looks-good-on-paper, ideal kind of thing that just will not work in practice
- Be frightened by the apparent complexity and hard work required to implement it

Listed below are several crucial questions regarding the occupational training programs at Pleasant Valley Community College. Base your responses on what you think we *should* be doing at PVCC to *effectively meet the needs of students and business and industry*.

	Yes	No
1. Should each training program be based on the specific job skills (tasks) successful workers actually perform in the occupation?		
2. Should these "job tasks" be listed on a form so that students, employers, and others can see exactly what students will learn?		
3. Should the list of job tasks be verified by workers in the occupation and updated annually?		
4. If certain students only have the ability or desire to prepare for a specialized area (e.g., receptionist) within a training program (secretarial science), should they be allowed to?		
5. Should students successfully master one task *before* going on to the next task?		
6. Should students be able to skip instruction in those tasks they can demonstrate mastery of based on previous learning?		
7. If materials are available and any prerequisites met, should students be able to select their next learning task?		
8. Should efforts be made to provide instruction for each task that is appropriate for the task?		
9. Where possible, should principles, concepts, and other "theory" be learned as a part of the job task for which it is needed?		
10. Should instruction for each job task be presented in a few major parts with time allowed for practice after each?		
11. Should students be allowed to correct their practice of a task before being tested?		
12. If possible, should instruction be designed so that students can slow down, speed up, or repeat instruction as needed to learn?		

FIGURE 7-3 Occupational training programs questionnaire

13. Should the curriculum be designed so that each student receives high-quality instruction and enough time (within reason) to reach mastery of each task?		
14. Should "mastery" of a task be defined as being able to actually perform the task competently at a job-entry level?		
15. Should each student be individually tested for mastery of each essential job task?		
16. If feasible, should a student be allowed to exit with full credit when all job tasks have been mastered?		
17. Should the grading system used be based primarily on successful mastery of job tasks?		
18. Should employers be able to tell *exactly* what skills each graduate can perform?		
19. If feasible, should new students be allowed to enter periodically to fill vacancies?		
20. If possible, should workers already employed in an occupation be allowed to return for instruction in specific, advanced job tasks?		

FIGURE 7-3 (continued)

- Hate it because they tried "it" once and it did not work
- Fly into fits of rage, reel off dozens of reasons why it will not work, and then dare you to try it
- Feel threatened by the inference that what they have been doing all these years might be of questionable quality
- All of the above

So tread cautiously and try to nurture slowly the support of your superiors, colleagues, and those you supervise. Try to avoid debating the issue; avoid pushing someone into saying they oppose the idea before they really understand what it is. Try your best to get others to focus their attention on the *need* for the competency-based approach—not the approach itself. Help them develop ownership in the problems associated with traditional training methods and involve them in helping you come up with solutions.

> Any well-thought-out, *systematic* attempt to make a significant impact on raising the quality of instruction will very closely resemble the competency-based approach.

Show me. Sooner or later you will find yourself confronted with individuals who just cannot be convinced. One reason many still oppose the concept as just another gimmick is because nobody has ever sat down and shown them concrete evidence that it *works* and that it works *better* than the traditional approach. Most people are reasonable and when shown hard data—numbers, figures, facts, and dollar signs—they will begin to come around. Here are some ways in which you can help doubters become convinced:

1. Take them to visit a program, school, or institution that is successfully using the concept. This could be an industry training program, a technical institute, or most any facility. There are a large number of military bases around the country where the "systems approach" to training has been used quite successfully for years. Most large companies have some experience in using "programmed instruction" or "criterion-referenced" instruction. All of these are forms of competency-based training.
2. Let them talk to instructors, trainers, and most important, to students who have used the competency-based approach. Even if only by phone or mail, talking to successful users can often do the trick. Almost without exception, successful users of the concept become outspoken advocates.
3. Take them to professional meetings or seminars. Virtually any state or national gathering devoted to training or education will have several sessions in which competency-based success stories are shared.
4. Have them read journals and other literature. Most professional magazines and journals publish articles describing successful competency-based programs.
5. Most any library can help you scan the literature and find studies, research and development reports, and descriptions of successful competency-based programs implemented in a local setting very similar to yours. There is an impressive amount of evidence mounting that clearly shows the superiority of the competency-based approach. It is just a matter of finding it and presenting it.

Design a Competency-Based System of Learning

Early on, you will be faced with the task of deciding just what your competency-based system of learning will look like. Unfortunately, this book does not contain a model that will fit all situations. Listed in Table 7-2, however, are some crucial questions that you will need to address as you put your system of learning together. No doubt, you will have additional questions beyond those listed in Table 7-2 and perhaps several of those listed may not apply to your particular situation. The point here is to anticipate the questions and problems that will arise and to begin to formulate answers and solutions as early in the program planning process as possible. Thorough planning in the early stages will pay off handsomely.

TABLE 7-2 Questions to Address When Designing a Competency-Based System of Learning

---

WHAT will students learn?

1. What will the outcomes you wish students to master be called—competencies, tasks, skills, goals, or something else?
2. How will student competencies be identified for each training program—observing incumbent workers, using catalogs of tasks, instructor-developed and worker-verified task lists, or other strategies?
3. At what level will competencies be written: at the job task level, subtask level, or broad goal level?
4. How will the student competencies for each program be listed and made available to students and others; what will this list be called?
5. How often—biannually, yearly, or as needed—will the competencies for each program be updated?
6. Will competencies be "fit" into existing program lengths or will program lengths be based on the average time it takes students to master all required competencies successfully?
7. Will competencies be fitted into existing courses or units, or will students simply be enrolled in a "program"?
8. Will all students in a program be trained for the same occupation, or will they be given the option to specialize?
9. Will there be a separate list of competencies for each specialized occupation offered within the program?
10. Will there be a "core" of required competencies for all students regardless of specialization chosen?

WHICH students will be enrolled?

1. Who is the intended student population, and what are their characteristics?
2. How will recruitment, admissions, guidance, and counseling be handled?
3. How will waiting lists for programs be maintained?
4. How often will new students be allowed to enroll—weekly, biweekly, monthly?
5. Will new students be screened for certain essential prerequisites, or will the program focus entirely on *exit* competencies?
6. How will remediation of missing essential prerequisites be handled?
7. How will new students be steered toward training programs for which their chances of success are greatest?
8. How will new students be oriented to the competency-based learning system?
9. Will orientation be done in a central location, in each program area, or both?
10. Will instructor-student ratios be less, the same, or greater than in the traditional approach?

WHEN will students learn each task?

1. Will all students be required to master several basic tasks at the beginning of each program?
2. After the basics are mastered, will there be multiple starting points in those programs where this is feasible?

TABLE 7-2 Questions to Address When Designing a Competency-Based System of Learning (continued)

3. Will all students follow the same sequence of competencies, or will students be able to select the next competency if all prerequisites have been met?
4. How will students be shown multiple starting points, prerequisite tasks, recommended sequences, and multiple exit points?
5. Will students be allowed,encouraged, or required to master one competency before going on to the next?
6. Can a student begin a new task alone, only as a part of a small group, without instructor approval, only on certain days?
7. How will each individual student's training plan be determined and recorded?
8. How will each student's work be planned, how often, and how will it be recorded?
9. How will students be monitored to identify those that are having learning difficulties?
10. Can a student have access to learning materials days, evenings, weekends, holidays?

HOW will students learn?

1. Will the competency-based approach be phased-in, or will your institution jump right in?
2. What approach to curriculum will be taken during the first year or two of operation or transition?
3. Will learning packages be used as the primary means of delivering instruction or as a supplement?
4. Will learning guides, modules, or something else be used to deliver instruction; what will they be called; how will the format be designed?
5. Will one format for learning packages be adopted throughout the entire institution, or can each department or program use its own?
6. Will learning resources be purchased, produced in-house, or both; if several media formats are available, which one will be used; will one type of audiovisual equipment be used in all programs or several?
7. Will separate stations be set up for presentation, practice, and testing; if so, how, where, and when?
8. Will students each get a copy of each learning package, or will only a limited number be produced; will students purchase the learning packages, or will they be furnished?
9. Will media, materials, and equipment be housed in each program area, in each wing of the facility, or in a central location?
10. Will classrooms be converted to learning centers? If so, how and when?

IF students have mastered tasks?

1. Will "mastery" be defined as being competent in performing a task at a high level of proficiency, or will "minimum competence" be acceptable?
2. Can each program establish its own minimum criteria for mastery of tasks, or will the criteria level be the same throughout the institution; will 100% mastery be required?

TABLE 7-2 Questions to Address When Designing a Competency-Based System of Learning (continued)

3. How will unsatisfactory progress be defined and reported; what are the consequences?
4. Will students be allowed to test out of packages; if so, how will this be handled and recorded?
5. Will a pretest be developed for each task, or will post-tests be used?
6. Will grades be issued; if so, how and when?
7. How many times and how frequently will students be required to perform each competency to be considered competent?
8. Will written tests be "graded" or simply be a prerequisite for taking the performance test?
9. How will mastery of competencies be evaluated, certified, and documented?
10. How will employers and others be shown exactly what competencies each trainee has and has not yet mastered?

WHO will provide the instructor with the training, curriculum, administrative, and technical support needed?

1. Who will be the driving force behind the effort; who will be willing to publicly support the competency-based approach; who will provide the overall leadership for directing the implementation effort; whose support will be sought, and how?
2. Who will assume the day-to-day responsibility for supervising the development of learning packages; will that person(s) be freed from normal administrative/supervisory chores to focus entirely on curriculum?
3. Who will train the instructional and support staff to develop and use learning packages?
4. Who outside the program and institution will be involved in program development; will advisory committees, steering committees, curriculum review committees, or others be involved?
5. Who will be required to develop learning packages—volunteers, lead instructors, or everyone; what about those who refuse to or are not capable of developing learning packages?
6. On whose time will instructors develop learning packages and resources—the instructors', the schools', or both; will instructors be paid extra—if so, how much, and from what source; who will own the learning packages and supporting media?
7. Who will see to it that rules, policies, procedures, schedules, fees, records, publications, management strategies, budgets, forms, reports, and related components all support competency-based learning?
8. Who will field-test, evaluate, and revise learning packages; when and how; who will evaluate existing and newly developed programs and by what criteria?
9. Who will do the typing, editing, drawing, filing, copying, photographing, and other activities needed to support the development of learning guides and media?
10. Who will provide technical assistance for developing media, materials, learning packages, task listings, rearranging facilities, and developing management strategies?

PROGRAM DEVELOPMENT OBJECTIVE NO. 3		Develop, verify, and revise task listing for each program.											
	Accomplishments	Aug	Sep	Oct	Nov	Dec	Jan	Feb	Mar	Apr	May	Jun	Jul
a.	Define role of tasks and task listings in programs.												
b.	Conduct search for previously developed task listings.												
c.	Conduct task listing development workshops for instructors.												
d.	Mail out task lists for verification by business and industry.												
e.	Revise and finalize task listing for each program area.												

	To Begin	To Complete	Person Responsible	Est. Cost	Comments
a.	Aug. 2	Aug. 27	Dir. G. H. Wright	0	
b.	Sep. 1	Nov. 25	Asst. Dir. M. Jones	$ 500	Go back only five years
c.	Dec. 3	Jan. 26	Asst. Dir. P. Nelson	$2000	3 separate workshops 12/6, 12/13, 1/6
d.	Jan. 3	Feb. 28	Asst. Dir. M. Jones	$ 750	Reviewed by M.J. before mailing out
e.	Mar. 1	Apr. 30	Asst. Dir. M. Jones	$ 250	

FIGURE 7-4 Part of a Local Plan of Action

Developing some sort of flowchart showing the relationship among key components in the system may be of help. Also, a flowchart showing key events in the instructional process may help out. Such a chart might begin with the student determining the next task to be mastered, locating the learning guide for that task and ending, perhaps, with the student successfully completing the performance test and the loop repeating for the next task.

Develop a Plan of Action

Whether a one-program or a 50-program planning effort, a detailed plan of action is essential. You need to pin down *what* needs to be done, *when* it needs to be accomplished, *who* is responsible for seeing that it gets done, and *how much* it is going to cost. Without a well-thought-out local plan of action, a lot of time, energy, and money can be wasted. Figure 7-4 shows a portion of a local plan of action. Local plans of action can be constructed using several formats, such as time lines, PERT charts, and others. The key is to tie down as best you can the what, when, who, and how much.

You might want to develop a time line similar to that of Figure 7-4 for each major component of the competency-based system being developed or for each major goal in the implementation process. Those major components might look something like those shown below. Remember: for each component, specific activities or accomplishments are needed, with dates, who is responsible, cost, and any other information necessary to carry them out.

EXAMPLES

Goal 1: *Conceptualize and describe competency-based vocational education at Mid-State Skills Center.*

Goal 2: *Develop competency list(s) for each program.*

Goal 3: *Design a student learning guide format and curriculum delivery system.*

Goal 4: *Develop grading system and certificate(s).*

Goal 5: *Develop instruments and strategies to manage competency-based learning.*

Goal 6: *Develop and conduct a teacher training program.*

Before going any further, see if you can develop plans for implementing competency-based programs by completing the following Self-Check.

SELF-CHECK [1]

Check your mastery of ENABLING OBJECTIVE [1] by completing this SELF-CHECK.

1. When seeking the support of others for implementing competency-based training programs, why is it a good idea to avoid the mention of terms such as "competency-based" or "individualized"?

____

____

2. Rather than pushing the competency-based approach as a solution, what should you first try to get others to focus their attention on?

____

____

3. Assume that you have been charged with the responsibility of directing the transition from conventional programs to competency-based programs in a large training institution (select your own if possible). Refer to Table 7-2 and select at least *five* critical questions from each area (what, which, when, how, if, and who). Develop well-thought-out, specific answers to each question.

4. For the situation described in question 3, select one major component of the competency-based system of learning or one major goal to be accomplished in the program implementation process. Develop a detailed local plan of action for that area.

Compare your responses with those in the Answer Key in the appendix.

ENABLING OBJECTIVE [2]

Plan a Staff Development Program for the Instructional and Support Staff

The Staff—Key to Successful Programs

As with any education or training program, the instructional and support staff is the real key to making a competency-based training program succeed. Of course, the facility, tools, equipment, curriculum, training aids, and other resources are important, but it is the instructors, trainers, program managers, and backup staff who make it work. The most elaborate training facility, the most sophisticated training aids, and the most carefully developed learning materials are of little use without a competent training staff. Unfortunately, we spend millions and millions of dollars building and expanding training facilities and too often, not a nickel on training the instructional and support staff in skills needed to ensure that a high percentage of trainees become highly competent workers.

If you are directing or involved in a large-scale competency-based program development effort such as converting an entire school from the traditional to the competency-based approach, do not underestimate the critical need for and potential rewards of a well-thought-out and carefully implemented staff development effort. If you are attempting to implement competency-based instruction on a large scale *without* the benefit of a carefully developed, formalized staff training component you may as well save yourself the effort, because the odds are heavily against you. Asking instructors and trainers to develop, implement, and manage competency-based, self-paced instructional programs without the benefit of specialized training is like asking a meat cutter to perform surgery. The meat cutter might become proficient at surgery with enough practice, but we would lose an awful lot of patients in the process.

Practice What You Preach

If you make the decision to develop a formalized staff development program to equip the staff with the skills needed to develop and operate competency-based training programs, you will be faced with a number of decisions about the instructor training program itself. How long should it be, what materials will be used, what kind of format will it follow, and a host of other questions. One suggestion is offered that should make those decisions a lot easier to make.

> The instructor training program developed to equip instructors with the skills needed to implement competency-based training programs successfully should also be designed, developed, and implemented using the competency-based approach.

If the competency-based approach to training is an appropriate strategy for training students, why would it not also be appropriate for training instructors? Putting your instructor training program together in a format *other* than one that is competency-based would be very confusing for the instructors being trained and would waste a golden opportunity. Developing the instructor training program following the competency-based approach has two very important advantages (besides being more effective):

- If instructors (particularly those who come from traditional teaching assignments) participate *successfully* in a competency-based instructor training program, chances are they will have a positive attitude toward the competency-based approach. They will see, firsthand, that it works better than the conventional approach and that students prefer it.

- After having gone through a competency-based instructor training program, instructors will be knowledgeable of and see the need for each major component of a competency-based program. They will see the benefit of having the competencies listed and given to them the first day and they will see the necessity for packaged learning materials. They will quickly appreciate the criterion-referenced approach to testing and grading.

Lecturing to instructors on the benefits of individualized instruction is probably not a good idea. Talking to a large group of teachers for several days on how to develop learning packages is really not practicing what you are preaching. If your goal is to equip your instructional and support staff with skills needed to implement competency-based training programs, put your instructor training program together the same way. A well-planned and delivered staff development program is critical for successfully implementing the competency-based approach because:

- The whole concept may be new and unfamiliar to most instructors.
- Most instructors have developed their own personal "system" of instruction over the years by trial and error (mostly error).
- Instructors are people just like you and me, and we are all resistant to change.
- The competency-based approach will require experienced instructors to give up a role they have become comfortable with—presenters of instruction—and assume a new and unfamiliar role—managers of learning.

Identify Instructor Competencies

As you recall from Chapter 3 one of the first steps in developing a competency-based program is to identify the competencies or tasks you want students to master. The same holds true for developing a competency-based *instructor* training program. Once your competency-based system of learning for students has been designed, you need to pin down the skills that instructors will need to implement the system in their respective program areas. The list of instructor competencies you develop might look very similar to the competencies around which this book was developed. Chapters 2 through 7 are based on several instructor "tasks" (competencies) which are listed at the beginning of each section. The number of instructor competencies you identify upon which to build your instructor training program will depend on how complex your competency-based system of learning is and other factors, such as how experienced the instructors are and the nature of their training programs.

It is a good idea to try and verify the instructor competencies just as each instructor will verify the job tasks upon which each training program will be built. You may have some difficulty doing this because you will find very few instructors who have experience in actually using the competency-based approach. Try and find several instructors who have used this approach successfully and ask them to verify your instructor competencies upon which you will base your instructor training program.

As with any competency-based program, the competencies should then be analyzed, terminal performance objectives written, and appropriate written and performance tests developed. Develop objectives and written and performance tests for the instructor competencies using the *same* precision and format you want the instructors to use in developing their own objectives and tests for their programs.

Plan the Instructor Training Program

Now that you know *what* it is you want your instructors to learn, you can begin to plan a staff development program to help them get there. There are a variety of approaches you might take. You might plan and develop the program in-house or you might call in consultants to help or both. Factors to consider in planning the instructor training program include:

1. How many instructors will be involved? Will there be five or fifty?
2. How much experience do they have with competency-based instruction?
3. Are they a newly formed team of instructors, or have they taught together before?
4. Do they represent closely related training areas, or everything from floral merchandising to electromechanical technology?
5. Generally, what kind of attitudes do the instructors have toward the competency-based approach? Do they even know what it is; are they suspicious or even outright hostile? Have they, perhaps, tried it once and failed?
6. What about the lead instructors, department chairpersons, supervisors, and administrators involved? Do they support it, are they involved willingly, or have they been "drafted?"
7. What shape are the instructional programs in now? Are these new programs beginning from scratch, or are existing programs being converted? If existing programs, how much and what is the quality of the learning materials now in use?
8. Will instructors be able to devote their full-time efforts to the training program for several weeks or months, or will their involvement be in addition to a regular teaching assignment?
9. Do special arrangements need to be made with the local governing board, nearby college or university, or the state department of education to sanction the program for teacher certification or college credit?

10. Who will be responsible for designing, developing, implementing, and evaluating the training program; will this be done by an experienced instructor who fully understands the competency-based approach to training?
11. Have any of the instructors been recruited directly from business and industry with no previous professional training whatsoever?
12. How many of the instructors are experienced and have taught a number of years in more traditional programs?
13. What are the instructors' main concerns about this new, unfamiliar approach and how it will affect them; are they concerned with the time, the extra work, perhaps failing, trying something new, managing it, whether it really works?
14. What kinds of rewards will each instructor respond to best to continue to expend the effort required; is it money, praise, seeing his or her name in print, acknowledgment before peers, a job well done, or what?

Develop the Program

If at all possible, put the instructor training program together just like you want the instructors to put together their training programs for students. List the instructor competencies on the same task listing form that instructors will use for their task listings. Develop a program map or sequence of tasks or other document that indicates which instructor competency must be mastered before another, just as instructors will do for their own programs. Develop a terminal objective for each instructor task just as you want instructors to do for each of their job tasks.

Most important, use the *same* format for the curriculum in the instructor training program that instructors will be using in their programs. If you decide that learning guides will be used to deliver the bulk of the routine instruction in each task for students, use learning guides to do the same for instructors. This will get the instructors accustomed to learning guides, and very important, it will show them through personal experience that learning guides work.

If you have made the decision that 35mm slides and audio cassettes will be the predominant form of audiovisual instruction in the training programs throughout the department or institution, use 35mm slides and cassettes in the instructor training program.

> Use the instructor training program to model successfully the instructor competencies you want instructors to perform in their new role as learning managers in their particular programs.

If you want instructors to spend less time teaching and more time moving about the classroom and lab helping students learn, the teacher trainers who deliver your instructor training program should do the same. Do not ask instructors to do anything that you and your teacher trainers have not done themselves.

Tips

Below are some suggestions for designing, developing, and implementing your staff development program.

1. Allow enough time for the instructional staff to acquire the skills needed to implement competency-based programs successfully. If you think, for example, that four weeks or six weeks or two months is needed to train the staff of a large vo-tech center, insist that time and funds be allocated to support a training program of that length.
2. Try your best to operate the program as a truly competency-based training program. Try to give each instructor enough time to acquire each skill before going on to the next. Use criterion-referenced evaluation for assessing each instructor's competence. Use detailed performance tests to evaluate task listings, media, and learning guides developed during the program.
3. Devote time early in the program to convince instructors that the competency-based approach is not just another way but the *best* way. *Show* them why its better—do not just tell them. Present facts and figures and reliable data showing why this approach is superior.
4. You may want to demonstrate the superiority of packaged and mediated instruction over instructor-centered methods. One way to do this is to select a task from a program area that most of the instructors will be unfamiliar with. Have a well-constructed, mediated learning guide developed for the task. Split the instructors randomly into two groups. Give one group copies of the learning guide and access to the media. Have someone (or yourself) prepare and deliver a traditional lecture/demonstration for the same task to the other group. Give everyone the same post-test and compare scores. Usually, the scores of those instructors using the learning guides will be higher and there will be less spread in the individual scores. Even if the scores of the "traditional" and the "competency-based" groups are similar, you can show how training time was saved in the competency-based group by having each instructor record and then report exactly how much time was spent on the learning guide.
5. You may want to implement the teacher training program in two or more phases. The first phase might last several weeks and might focus

on convincing instructors that the competency-based approach is better, helping them to develop a tentative task listing, and aiding them in developing several learning packages. Later phases might cover verifying tasks, managing competency-based learning, and continuing the development of learning packages.

6. Remember that during an instructor training program of several weeks in length, only a limited number of learning packages can be developed. Be sure to show new instructors how to teach effectively using traditional teaching methods while gearing up for competency-based instruction.
7. Emphasize to instructors that until all learning packages are completed, which may be several years, they will have to deliver some instruction traditionally. Regardless of which teaching method is used, however, explain the critical importance of following a task listing. Stress the importance of capturing instructor-delivered demonstrations on slides or tape for use as a resource for future learning packages.
8. You may want to prepare a file folder for each task on the task listing for each program. Instructors can be encouraged to place in the appropriate folder all handouts, lecture notes, demonstration outlines, job sheets, tests, references, and other materials used to teach each task in a traditional manner until learning packages are developed. As time permits, the instructor can then use all the material collected in each folder to develop learning packages.
9. Try to use several resource people in your instructor training sessions who are currently using the competency-based approach successfully. There is nothing like hearing it from the horse's mouth.
10. Make sure that each participant thoroughly understands the role that learning packages and media play in competency-based learning. Provide instructors with a "model" learning package that has been very carefully constructed, tested, and checked for errors. Encourage them to follow this model very closely as they write their first several learning packages.
11. Involve all key personnel in the training sessions—particularly the administrative head of the training site. Do not limit participation to instructors or trainers. Involve guidance and counseling personnel, media specialists, instructional designers, supervisors, administrators—anyone who will have direct involvement in the operation of the training programs once they are developed and implemented.
12. Insist on high-quality products developed during the training program. Once you accept a task listing with poorly worded task statements or a learning package of questionable soundness, you have set the standard for materials developed later. If you only have three days for a training session and it takes the full three days just to get a good, tentative task listing developed, that is fine—at least you have that much accomplished.

13. Make sure that you package and mediate as much of the program as possible. As new instructors, supervisors, or staff members are added, they can use the instructor training materials on a self-paced basis. This is, of course, the same approach as you are preparing instructors to use.
14. Your training sessions may consist of individual, small-group, or large-group activities. Sessions may be one hour a day after school, six solid weeks before a new institution opens, or other planned times. Formats might be workshops, seminars, courses, or other arrangements.
15. Adopt a common learning guide format throughout the entire company, school, or district! Make sure the format has been carefully designed and field tested and then stick to it. Letting each instructor or department develop and use its own format will lead to wasted time and chaos. Using a *common* format will assist your typists, clerks, resource persons, media specialists, curriculum developers, and test writers in working with any and every instructor without first having to decipher his or her system. It will also encourage sharing and cooperative development of materials for wide usage throughout the institution.

Now, see if you can plan an instructor training program for implementing competency-based programs by completing the following Self-Check.

SELF-CHECK [2]

Check your mastery of ENABLING OBJECTIVE [2] by completing this SELF-CHECK.

1. List two advantages of designing the staff development program for equipping instructors with skills needed to implement competency-based programs using the same competency-based approach.

   (a) ______________________________

   (b) ______________________________

2. What format should be followed when putting the instructor training materials together, and why?

   ____

   ____

Assume that you are putting together a formal instructor-training program for preparing the instructional and support staff of a large new training site for the implementation of competency-based instruction.

3. List the instructor competencies upon which you would build the instructor training program.

4. Assume that at least three but no more than six weeks will be devoted to the program. Develop a detailed agenda for the program. Include length, sequence of instructor competencies, and average time devoted to each.

Compare your responses with those in the Answer Key in the appendix.

ENABLING OBJECTIVE [3]

Develop Instruments to Evaluate Competency-Based Training Programs

When to Evaluate

Although you may find yourself involved with evaluating competency-based training programs at various times, two particular occasions should be mentioned. One occasion calling for the evaluation of a program or programs is during the transition from traditional to competency-based. During such a switchover you are certain to encounter instructors who absolutely insist that their current training programs are *already* competency-based, and therefore they do not need to go to all the effort of identifying tasks and developing learning guides.

Another occasion when a program should be evaluated is after a newly implemented competency-based program has been in operation for a year or two and again, periodically. First, let us look at evaluating an existing program during the transition period to determine if it is already competency-based.

Evaluating Existing Programs

If you happen to be a director or supervisor charged when the responsibility of changing over a number of programs from the traditional to the competency-based approach you had better prepare yourself for this situation because it is certain to happen sooner or later—probably sooner. You no sooner announce your intentions to the instructional staff when several instructors arrive in your office insisting that their programs are not only competency-based already but have been for years. To avoid being placed in the no-win situation of having to make a judgment on such programs you need some means of objectively and fairly—yet critically—evaluating such programs to determine if they are, in fact, competency-based. You just cannot afford to take someone's word for it. If a program is already completely or largely competency-based, that is great—just one less program you will have to worry about converting.

Figure 7-5 shows an instrument for evaluating programs to determine how close to being "competency-based" they really are. You might want to develop a similar instrument. Of course, your instrument would reflect the philosophy of the training site and the design of the competency-based system of learning in use. A program considered competency-based at site A may not be at site B. It depends on each site's definition of "competency-based." An evaluation instrument will help you formulate your local "definition" and will allow you to evaluate each program objectively using the same criteria. Such an instrument may also come in handy in checking periodic progress in each program as it moves from traditional to competency-based.

You may also find yourself faced with instructors who insist that the curriculum materials they are currently using are just as good as learning packages. Again, an objective instrument for evaluating their current materials can be very helpful in pointing out weaknesses. Showing an instructor that his training modules do not measure up on 12 out of 25 criteria would be a lot easier to swallow than "your stuff is no good." Figure 7-6 shows such an instrument that might be used to evaluate various learning packages or modules instructors may be using. Such an instrument may also come in handy when reviewing commercially available materials that are being promoted as "self-paced" or "individualized" or for putting out bids for materials to be purchased. It can also be adapted for use as a checklist for instructors to use as they write learning packages and for curriculum specialists to use in reviewing drafts of newly developed packages.

Evaluating New Programs

Even though a newly implemented program may have been carefully designed, developed, and operated as a truly competency-based program, that is no guarantee the program is operating as it should. Two areas we might take a look at are how the program is operating (*process*) and the results of the training program (*product*). After a year or two of operation, it is a good idea to take a good, hard look at both the *program* and the finished *product*.

A newly implemented training program can be evaluated just as an existing program can. Instruments similar to those shown in Figures 7-5 and 7-6 might be used to evaluate how the training program has been set up and the learning packages being used. You might want to use the *same* instruments for evaluating newly developed programs as you do for evaluating existing programs. This way all programs will be judged by the same standard.

	Yes	No
1. Are the desired outcomes (competencies) of the training program:		
a. Based on the actual skills (tasks) performed on the job?		
b. Specific, precisely stated, and in writing?		
c. Listed and made available to each new student?		
d. Updated at least annually?		
e. Primarily *skills* resulting in a product or service for which someone would be willing to pay?		
2. Can a student choose to master *only* those *specific* competencies required for employment in a *specialized* occupation offered within the program?		
3. Can students skip instruction in those competencies for which they can demonstrate mastery?		
4. For competencies that are *not* sequential, can a student select which competency to work on next?		
5. Is there a well-developed terminal performance objective written for each competency that clearly spells out:		
a. Under what specific *conditions* the trainee must perform the competency to demonstrate mastery?		
b. Exactly what *performance* is required for mastery?		
c. The specific *criteria* by which mastery will be determined?		
6. Is each *individual* student required to actually demonstrate mastery of *each* competency?		
7. Is the *primary* method of testing *performance* testing requiring the trainee to perform each task in a joblike setting?		
8. Is *mastery* of each task defined as being able to actually perform the task at a *high level* (90 to 100%) of competence?		
9. Is each student *required* and *allowed* to spend enough time on each task to reach a *high level* of mastery *before* being allowed or forced to move on to the next task?		
10. Is the bulk of the routine instruction for each task packaged in some way that:		

FIGURE 7-5 Instrument for determining if a program is competency-based

a. Provides high-quality instruction?

b. Allows each student to spend as much time on each task as needed to reach mastery?

c. Allows each student to speed up, slow down, skip over, or repeat parts of instruction as needed?

d. Presents instruction in only a part of the task at a time rather than in the entire task at once?

e. Provides for practice of what was presented?

f. Provides for immediate feedback on performance after each practice?

g. Incorrect practice is detected and corrected?

h. Allows the student to practice the task correctly before being evaluated?

11. Are learning resources and materials that actually deliver instruction:

a. Effective?

b. Appropriate for the task?

c. Appropriate for the student?

d. Efficient?

12. Is a physical learning environment provided that:

a. Promotes student movement and activity?

b. Provides easy access to all learning resources needed for mastering tasks?

c. Provides a place where each task can be practiced under supervised, controlled conditions?

d. Enhances learning?

13. On any given day, are students working on several different tasks either individually or in small groups?

14. Is frequent instruction in large groups avoided?

15. If grades are given, are they based solely on mastery of competencies?

16. Does the instructor devote most of his or her time each day to helping individual students learn, rather than teaching?

17. Are facts, concepts, principles, and other knowledge learned as an integral part of the job tasks for which this knowledge is needed?

FIGURE 7-5 Instrument for determining if a program is competency-based (continued)

Program ______________________ Evaluator ______________________ Package No. ______ Title ______________ Date __________ Source __________		
	Yes	No
1. Is the overall appearance of the learning package attractive?		
2. Can the student easily determine *exactly what competency* the learning package covers?		
3. Is the competency covered in the package not too *broad* and not too *narrow*; can it *stand* alone and *have meaning* to the student as a *separate* unit of learning?		
4. Can the student easily determine what *prerequisite* competency (if any) is required *before* this one?		
5. Can the learning package be easily *identified* for locating, refiling, storing, etc.?		
6. Is some means provided of *motivating* the student to want to learn the competency?		
7. Is a well-written *performance objective* included that is *based on the task* and includes *conditions* under which student must perform, exact *performance* required, and *how well* it must be performed for mastery?		
8. Does the package *present* instruction in the task in *several phases* rather than the entire task at once?		
9. If needed, are any *prerequisite* background, facts, or concepts relating specifically to this task taught early in the package?		
10. Is each manipulative step that is required to *perform* the task presented sequentially, clearly, and accurately?		
11. Is the *knowledge* essential to performing each step safely and accurately taught *right along with* the steps in doing the task?		
12. Are the learning activities called for in the package *appropriate* for the task?		
13. Are alternative learning activities provided to accommodate students' differences in learning styles (reading, viewing, etc.)?		

FIGURE 7-6 Learning package evaluation form

14. Is the student provided with *hands-on* practice of the task or each portion of the task immediately after it is presented?		
15. Is some means of *immediate feedback* provided so that students can determine the success of this practice?		
16. If any instruction sheets, job sheets, drawings, etc., are included, are they *appropriate*, clearly worded, easy to read, and technically complete and accurate?		
17. Is the *instructor* called for in the learning process to evaluate, answer questions, etc.?		
18. If external resources are required, is the student told *exactly* what portion of each resource is called for?		
19. If appropriate, is the student *tested* on the knowledge and concepts essential to performing the task competently?		
20. Is a detailed, comprehensive *performance test* included that indicates *exactly* how the student will be evaluated?		
21. Overall, is the learning package largely *self-instructional*?		
22. Does the package make *efficient* use of paper, time, and other resources and materials?		
23. Does the package provide adequate *guidance* to the student throughout the learning process?		
24. Is the package effective in helping the student *transfer* this learning to different settings on the job?		
25. Overall, does the learning package do a good job of aiding the student in reaching mastery of the task?		

FIGURE 7-6 Learning package evaluation form (continued)

It is a little more difficult to evaluate the *outcomes* of training programs since the finished product has (hopefully) been placed into the occupation for which training was received. An excellent way to evaluate the effectiveness of a training program is to locate a number of program completers and early leavers and find out how they are doing. You may want to contact former students one year, five years, and even ten years after leaving the training program and finding out such things as:

- How many are presently employed in the field for which they were trained

- How long it took each former student to secure initial employment
- What their starting, first year, fifth year, and tenth year wages were
- If they left early, why
- How many job changes they have made and why
- What serious accidents they have had on the job, if any
- What promotions they have received
- What difficulties they had making the transition from training to working
- What about the training program they found most and least helpful
- Other important information that will aid in improving the training program

Of course, some of the questions should be asked of very recent graduates and other asked of graduates who have been on the job a number of years.

One question you certainly want answered is:

Just how competent are program graduates?

Looking at starting salaries, raises, and similar data can only give you a general feeling for the competence of former students. To be able to revise the portions of your training program that need it, you must find out how competent graduates are in specific tasks. One way to do this is to send a modified version of your task listing to recent program graduates *and* to their immediate supervisors. On this survey form, you will ask your former students and their supervisors to identify any competencies for which your students were not adequately trained.

If a number of survey forms like this come back saying that a sizable percentage of graduates were not adequately trained in how to "ventilate a building using mechanical means" or how to "apply fertilizer to greens" or how to "slip-stitch a hem by hand" the instructor, trainer, or program manager can *do something* about it. The learning guides for those tasks can be upgraded, added to, or revised as needed or even scrapped and rewritten completely.

Before going on, see if you can develop instruments to evaluate competency-based training programs by completing the following Self-Check.

SELF-CHECK [3]

Check your mastery of ENABLING OBJECTIVE [3] by completing this SELF-CHECK.

1. Identify two occasions when competency-based training programs may need to be evaluated.

   (a) ______________________________

   (b) ______________________________

2. What two things are we looking for when a training program is evaluated?

   (a) ______________________________

   (b) ______________________________

3. What is the value of finding out how adequately students were trained in *specific* tasks?

4. Develop an evaluation instrument to be used to determine if an existing training program is already competency-based. Include at least 10 specific criteria that would distinguish a program that is compentency-based from one that is not.

5. Select an actual training program (your own if possible) and evaluate the program using the instrument you develop for problem 4 above.

Compare your responses with those in the Answer Key in the appendix.

Continue with the following performance test.

PERFORMANCE TEST FOR TASK 12

TASK 12: Implement and Evaluate Training Programs

DIRECTIONS

When ready, demonstrate your ability to implement and evaluate training programs by doing the following:

For one or more competency-based training programs:

1. Design a competency-based system of learning by answering each applicable question (narrative or graphically) listed in Table 7-2.
2. Develop a plan of action similar to Figure 7-4 for each major component of the implementation effort.
3. Plan a staff development program, including competencies, agenda, and materials format.
4. Develop instruments to assess if existing programs are competency-based, current curriculum materials are suitable, and if graduates received adequate training in each program task.

No.	Criteria for evaluating performance; 100% mastery required	Yes	No
	Competency-Based System of Learning		
1.	Were all questions concerning *what* students will learn addressed in a manner that will promote the human competence of trainees on the job?		
2.	Were all questions concerning *which* students will be enrolled addressed in a manner that will maximize each student's chance of success?		
3.	Were all questions concerning *when* students will learn each task addressed in a manner that will ensure that each student receives sufficient time for mastery?		
4.	Were all questions concerning *how* students will learn each task addressed in a manner that will provide high-quality, self-paced, individualized, effective, and efficient learning?		

5. Were all questions concerning *if* students mastered tasks addressed in a manner that will reflect each individual's actual competence?

6. Were all questions concerning *who* will support the effort addressed in a manner that will provide the needed administrative, supervisory, and technical support?

Plan of Action

7. Does the local plan of action cover the implementation effort in a comprehensive manner?

8. Does the local plan of action address each of the following for each major component of the implementation effort?
   a. Exactly what is to be accomplished to successfully implement the competency-based program?
   b. Specific beginning and ending dates for each activity to be accomplished?
   c. Who is responsible for each activity?
   d. Estimated cost for each activity?

Staff Development Program

9. Were instructor competencies identified in at least the following areas?
   a. Specifying the competencies upon which each training program will be based?
   b. Developing objectives for each competency?
   c. Sequencing competencies and/or objectives?
   d. Developing tests?
   e. Developing learning packages, media, and other learning materials?
   f. Effectively managing programs?

10. Is the planned length of the staff development program sufficient to equip instructors with the necessary skills to implement competency-based programs?

11. Are instructor training materials put together using the same format for learning packages that instructors will be using?

12. Is the instructor training program designed and developed as a *competency-based* program?

	Evaluation Instruments		
13.	Has an instrument been developed that will objectively distinguish between programs that are competency-based and those that are not?		
14.	Has an instrument been developed that will distinguish between curriculum materials that are suitable for competency-based programs and those that are not?		
15.	Has an instrument been developed that will give feedback on how adequately the program trained students in each *specific* task?		

Appendix

Answer Keys to Self-Checks

CHAPTER 2, TASK 1, ANSWER KEY [1]

Your responses to SELF-CHECK [1] should agree with those given below.

1. Any three of the following or other valid reasons:
   (a) Program focuses on training for actual occupations.
   (b) Some students may only have the time, interest, or ability for training in a specialized area.
   (c) Students would not be forced to go through the entire program.
   (d) Dropout rate may go down.
   (e) Employed students can return and enter specialized training program(s).
   (f) Special-needs students can be served better.
   (g) Programs can respond quicker to changes.
   (h) Specialized training needs of specific employers can be met.
   (i) Recruitment might be enhanced.
   (j) Some programs might be made portable.

2. Any four of the following or other valid criteria:
   (a) Is formal training needed?
   (b) Allowed or authorized?
   (c) Employment demand?
   (d) Student interest?
   (e) Entry-level occupation?
   (f) Instructor(s) qualified?
   (g) Facility adequate?
   (h) Demand for additional graduates adequate?

3. The following or other appropriate job titles:
   (a) Seamstress, tailor, garment maker, alterationist, custom drape maker, or other specific titles related to the area of sewing.
   (b) Finish carpenter, rough carpenter, cabinet maker, form builder, mill carpenter, or other specific titles related to the area of carpentry.

(c) File clerk, payroll clerk, auditing clerk, clerk/typist, or other specific titles related to the clerical area.

If you missed any, go back and review pages 31-38.

CHAPTER 2, TASK 1, ANSWER KEY [2]

Your responses to SELF-CHECK [2] should agree with those given below.

1. Any five of the following or other appropriate individuals or groups:

   (a) Anyone who is developing a competency-based training program

   (b) Prospective and actual students

   (c) Guidance personnel

   (d) New instructors

   (e) Parents and the public

   (f) Advisory committee members

   (g) The administration or supervisors

   (h) Governing bodies or agencies

   (i) Employers

2. Any of the following or other appropriate information:

   (a) Kinds of activities performed

   (b) Working conditions

   (c) Equipment or instruments used

   (d) Special abilities, aptitudes, or traits needed

   (e) Level of training needed

   (f) Opportunities for advancement

   (g) Special restrictions or license needed

3. Carefully review your job description and determine if it:

	Yes	No
(a) Fully describes the activities performed on the job?		
(b) Describes the occupation as it is in the world of work?		
If appropriate, does it describe:		
(c) Working conditions if extreme or unusual?		
(d) Equipment or instruments used?		
(e) Special abilities needed?		
(f) Level of training needed?		
(g) Advancement opportunities?		
(h) Restrictions or licenses needed?		

If you missed any, go back and review pages 39-41.

CHAPTER 2, TASK 2, ANSWER KEY [1]

Your responses to SELF-CHECK [1] should agree with those given below.

1. (a) Any measurable physical trait, such as full use of both arms, two legs, 20/20 vision, etc.
   (b) Any precisely defined skill, such as safe use of a radial saw, ability to make a "tee" weld, etc.
   (c) Any easily measurable knowledge, such as the ability to solve problems using trigonometry, ability to convert English units of measurement to metric, etc.
   (d) Any attitude that could be assessed objectively by observation, checking with previous instructors, completing an attitude assessment instrument, or other means. Examples might be "working cooperatively with others," "punctuality," etc.

2. Any of the following or any other benefit of identifying prerequisites:

   (a) Guidance personnel can steer prospective students to appropriate programs.

(b) Students' chances of success in the program are maximized when essential prerequisites have been met.

If you missed any, go back and review pages 44-47.

CHAPTER 2, TASK 2, ANSWER KEY [2]

Your responses to SELF-CHECK [2] should agree with those below.

1. Since we do not know too much about the driver's education course or the students enrolled, it is difficult to say which prerequisites are valid. However, the following assessment of these prerequisites serves to reinforce the points made in this section:

(a) *Not valid.* Securing learners' permits for students would probably be one of the major objectives of a driver's education course. Since students would be aided in getting a permit while enrolled in the course, this certainly would not be a valid prerequisite.

(b) *Not valid.* Although good vision is essential to safe driving, 20/20 vision is, perhaps, too stringent. Something like "20/40" or "vision corrected to pass eye test" might be a more appropriate level.

(c) *Valid.* Looks like a legitimate prerequisite; handicapped students who are still physically capable of operating special controls would not be excluded.

(d) *Not valid.* This is a tough one. Certainly, a tenth-grade reading level is not required to pass a driving test or to operate a motor vehicle safely. Perhaps this prerequisite was set with a textbook or other reading material in mind. Anyway, it seems unreasonably high for a driver's education course.

2. Your tentative prerequisites should conform to the criteria listed below.

	Yes	No
(a) Was the number of prerequisites held to an absolute minimum?		
(b) Is each prerequisite stated precisely?		
(c) Is each prerequisite essential to successful performance in the program or on the job?		
(d) Is each prerequisite set at a level *low* enough so that qualified students may enroll but *high* enough to match job requirements?		

If you missed any, go back and review pages 48-52.

CHAPTER 3, TASK 3, ANSWER KEY [1]

Your responses to SELF-CHECK [1] should agree with those given below.

1. Your responses could be anything that results in a finished product or a service the employer or customer would pay for.

   (a) Police officer: write a ticket, patrol, write accident report, etc.

   (b) Mason: build a wall, build a foundation, lay a sidewalk, etc.

   (c) Electrician: install meter, pull wires, repair motor, etc.

   (d) Tailor: alter suit, taper pants, make a coat, etc.

   (e) Bank teller: issue certificates of deposit, issue cashier's checks, process deposits, etc.

2. Your responses could be any of the following or other sound reasons.

   (a) Students know what will be learned.

   (b) Advisory committee and others can see what is taught.

   (c) A better argument can be made for getting resources needed to learn specific tasks.

   (d) Articulation is enhanced.

   (e) Instructors and students can focus on tasks.

   (f) Individualized training programs can be developed for students.

   (g) Tasks serve as common language among instructors, students, and employers.

   (h) Selection of tools, media, etc., can be based on tasks.

   (i) Students become more task oriented.

   (j) Student evaluation can focus on actual performance of tasks.

   (k) Transcripts can reflect tasks mastered.

   (l) Task listing can be continually updated.

   (m) Program will be based on valid tasks—not solely on the instructor.

   (n) Program curriculum can then be based on tasks.

If you missed any, go back and review pages 56-68.

CHAPTER 3, TASK 3, ANSWER KEY [2]

Your responses to SELF-CHECK [2] should agree with those given below.

1. (a) *Correct.* This is a broad category of specific tasks performed on the job; correctly worded.

   (b) *Incorrect.* This seems to be a single *task* for a law enforcement program.

   (c) *Incorrect.* Although "repairing radios" is probably an appropriate duty for a radio repair program, the "knowing how" part is not needed.

   (d) *Incorrect.* This statement is nothing more than an overall goal of a program; it says nothing about tasks performed on the job.

   (e) *Correct.* Begins with "ing" form of action verb and is of appropriate scope to be a major duty.

   (f) *Incorrect.* Although a typical unit in most programs, the statement does not describe actual *tasks* performed for which the worker is paid.

   (g) *Incorrect.* A broad area of knowledge—not a category of tasks done on the job.

2. Carefully evaluate each duty statement using the criteria listed below.

	Yes	No
(a) Describes a broad category of tasks actually performed on the job?		
(b) Begins with "ing" form of action verb?		
(c) Is it clear what *kind* of tasks are included in each duty?		

If you missed any, go back and review pages 69-75.

CHAPTER 3, TASK 3, ANSWER KEY [3]

Your responses to SELF-CHECK [3] should agree with those given below.

1. (a) *Correct.* Well-worded task statement; typical job assignment, has meaning for student, should be learned as a single unit of instruction.

(b) *Incorrect.* Much too general; seems to be a broad category of tasks.

(c) *Incorrect.* Too specific; would make little sense for students to learn this by itself; probably is a single *step* in a task, such as "set up oxy-acetylene welding equipment."

(d) *Incorrect.* Too broad; this really could describe the *entire* electromechanical technician occupation.

(e) *Incorrect.* Too general and does not begin with an action verb.

(f) *Correct.* Begins with an action verb, has definite beginning and ending, and has procedural steps.

(g) *Incorrect.* No verb; should read something like "take fingerprints."

(h) *Incorrect.* Has no action verb; is only a "topic," and only describes knowledge.

(i) *Incorrect.* Although this is a skill, it is not really a valuable accomplishment for which someone is willing to pay. "Drill and tap holes" is.

2. (a) Pan-fry meats.
   (b) Install bumper.
   (c) Remove and replace vent window.

3. Carefully evaluate each task statement using the criteria below.

Tasks	Yes	No
(a) Is each a complete unit of work or separate job activity?		
(b) Does each have a definite beginning and ending point?		
(c) Can each be broken down into steps?		
(d) Is each a job assignment or service?		
(e) Does each result in a finished product or service or change in work environment for which someone is willing to pay?		
(f) Does each have meaning for trainees to want to learn?		
(g) Can each be learned as a separate unit of learning?		

(h) Is each short and concise?

(i) Can each be learned in about 6 to 30 hours?

(j) Does each describe exactly what the trainee will do?

(k) Does each begin with an action verb in the present tense?

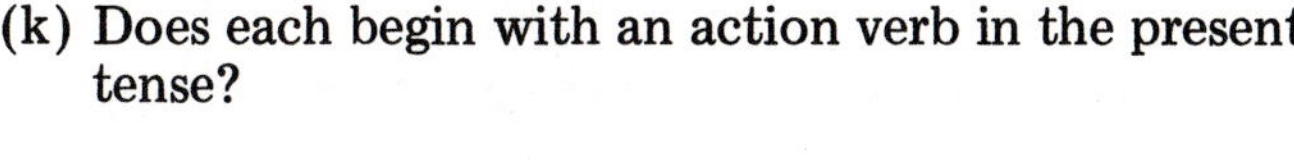

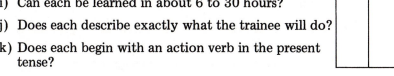

If you missed any, go back and review pages 76-85.

CHAPTER 3, TASK 3, ANSWER KEY [4]

Your responses to SELF-CHECK [4] should agree with those given below.

1. Tasks should be verified to ensure the accuracy and need for each.

2. Your responses could include these or any other valid criteria:

   (a) Importance to the worker on the job

   (b) Frequency of performance

   (c) How critical the task is

   (d) Percentage of entry-level workers needing it

   (e) Whether the task could be learned easier after employment

   (f) Whether the task is a prerequisite for others

   (g) How much time is available

If you missed any, go back and review pages 86-90.

CHAPTER 3, TASK 4, ANSWER KEY [1]

Your responses to SELF-CHECK [1] should agree with those given below.

1. These or any other practical uses:

   (a) Becomes the basis of planning learning activities and materials.

   (b) Is used to identify any specialized tools and materials needed to perform the task so they may be learned along with the task.

   (c) Aids in tying together the skills, knowledges, and attitudes required to perform the task.

   (d) Produces an outline for needed audiovisual materials.

(e) Helps to spot complex or dangerous steps.

(f) Makes sequencing of tasks easier.

(g) Makes developing tests easier.

2. Evaluate your completed task analyses using the criteria below.

(a) Steps and Technical Knowledge	Yes	No
1. Are steps listed as they would be performed on the job?		
2. Is the task analyzed from start to finish?		
3. Does each step begin with an action verb?		
4. Are trivial or obvious steps omitted?		
5. Is great detail avoided on complex steps?		
6. Is all essential technical knowledge needed to perform each step correctly and safely included?		
7. Is all nonessential knowledge omitted?		
8. Are cautions and danger points noted?		
9. Is only one method of performing the task included in the analysis?		
10. Has analysis avoided mention of how the task might be taught?		
(b) Are any *specialized* tools, equipment, instruments, supplies, or materials *unique to the task* listed?		
(c) Are related knowledges needed to perform the task listed; including:		
1. Math skills?		
2. Science concepts?		
3. Background information?		
4. Other?		
(d) Are all critical safety skills and facts listed?		
(e) Are all attitudes for performing the task competently on the job listed?		

If you missed any, go back and review pages 93-103.

CHAPTER 3, TASK 4, ANSWER KEY [2]

Your responses to SELF-CHECK [2] should agree with those given below.

1. Your responses should agree with these:
   (a) *Incorrect.* "Understand" is very vague; should have used "describe" or "explain."
   (b) *Incorrect.* "Demonstrate the ability to" is not needed.
   (c) *Correct.* Looks OK; precisely worded.
   (d) *Incorrect.* Just a topic statement; need an action verb such as "define," "describe," etc.
   (e) *Correct.* Worded OK; looks like a knowledge task written at a *high* level.

2. Evaluate your major units of knowledge using the criteria below.

	Yes	No
(a) Is each a broad, major unit of knowledge cutting across many tasks?		
(b) Can each be learned as a single unit of instruction?		
(c) Does each begin with action verb in the present tense?		
(d) Does each describe exactly what the trainee will do to demonstrate mastery of the knowledge?		

If you missed any, go back and review pages 104-114.

CHAPTER 4, TASK 5, ANSWER KEY [1]

Your responses to SELF-CHECK [1] should agree with those given below.

1. Terminal performance objectives are very helpful in completing the following steps in the program planning process:
   (a) Developing materials, media, activities, and other learning resources students will use to master the program tasks.

(b) Developing evaluation instruments and devising testing situations to determine if students have mastered tasks.

2. Your response could be any five of the following or other valid reasons:

   (a) The wording of the tasks can be double-checked.

   (b) Students know exactly what is expected of them.

   (c) Appropriate learning activities can be developed.

   (d) Appropriate testing situations are revealed.

   (e) Learning resources needed for learning the task are indicated.

   (f) Prerequisite tasks may be determined.

   (g) A sound argument for additional resources needed can be made.

   (h) Everyone tends to stay more task-oriented.

   (i) Objectives can be used to evaluate program effectiveness.

   (j) Research indicates use of objectives enhances learning.

   (k) Lends precision to the learning process.

   (l) Objectives can be refined to enhance learning.

If you missed any, go back and review pages 120-124.

CHAPTER 4, TASK 5, ANSWER KEY [2]

Your responses to SELF-CHECK [2] should agree with those given below.

1. *Incorrect*. OK, except too many trivial items (paper, pencil) mentioned in the condition.
2. *Incorrect*. No criteria specified; also, no need to say "the student will be able to."
3. *Incorrect*. All three components have a problem. The condition specifies a *learning* activity; 'learn" is very vague and the criteria component for the objective is fuzzy.
4. *Correct*. All three components are written correctly.
5. *Incorrect*. The condition looks too restrictive, procedure probably the same for any kind of engine; also, looks like too many verbs in-

cluded in the performance—perhaps "grind" would have been sufficient (implies locate, remove, etc.). Also, "correctly" is not needed.

6. *Correct.* OK as it is.

If you missed any, go back and review pages 124-130.

CHAPTER 4, TASK 5, ANSWER KEY [3]

Your responses to SELF-CHECK [3] should agree with those given below.

1. Your terminal objectives should look something like these:

   (a) Given tools, materials, and a pump, pressure-test the water supply of a building. All leaks must be detected and pressure readings must agree with instructor's.

   (b) Given merchandise, props, and materials, set up window display. Display must exhibit all basic elements of design, be structurally and electrically safe, and have no fire hazards.

   (c) When shown pictures or samples of 15 types of common nails, identify each by name and describe the purpose of each. Thirteen must be identified and described correctly.

2. Your TPOs should conform to the criteria listed below.

TPOs for Skill Tasks	Yes	No
(a) Does the *condition* describe what the student will be provided with during the testing situation?		
(b) Is a long list of, or obvious tools, equipment, etc., avoided in the condition?		
(c) Is the condition general enough to avoid being too restrictive?		
(d) Are things the student should *not* be given *not* listed in the condition?		
(e) Does the condition closely resemble the setting in which the task is performed on the job?		
(f) Are references to learning resources avoided in the condition?		

	Yes	No
(g) Does the *performance* state *exactly* what the trainee should be able to do at the *end* of the learning process?		
(h) Is instructor performance *not* mentioned?		
(i) Is the performance based on the task statement?		
(j) Are phrases such as "the student will," "fully," "correctly," etc., avoided?		
(k) Does the *criteria* component specify how well the task must be performed?		
(l) Are criteria at a high-enough level to ensure competence but still be attainable?		
(m) Are the major indicators of competence included in the criteria?		
(n) Are vague criteria such as "to the instructor's satisfaction" avoided?		
(o) Is mention of learning resources avoided in the criteria?		
(p) If criteria are not included in the TPO, is a minimum score on a performance test included?		
TPOs for Knowledge Tasks		
(a) If the objective has a *condition*, does it describe a problem or testing situation?		
(b) Does *performance* indicate exactly what the student must do to demonstrate mastery of the task?		
(c) Do the criteria (if included) specify a minimum acceptable level of performance?		
(d) If criteria are not included, is a minimum score on a written test included?		

If you missed any, go back and review pages 131-133.

CHAPTER 4, TASK 6, ANSWER KEY [1]

Your responses to SELF-CHECK [1] should agree with those given below.

1. The following or other benefits:

   (a) Attendance and tardiness problems decrease.

(b) Student motivation is easier to develop and maintain.

(c) Students have more incentive for success.

(d) Students' chances of success are enhanced.

(e) Students can begin the next task with a more positive attitude.

2. Your sequence of duties should have looked something like the following:

(a) *Homemaker*

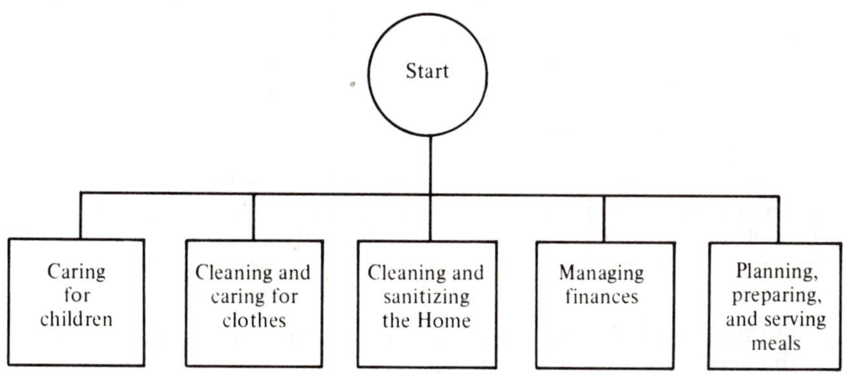

It looks as if the tasks in these five duties are independent of one another. For example, a trainee in a homemaking training program would not need to master the tasks dealing with "caring for children" before beginning the tasks involved in "cleaning and caring for clothes." Therefore, the sequence of duties is very wide horizontally, meaning that a student can begin the duties in any sequence.

(b) *Nurse's Aide*

In this example, the tasks in several duties seem to be prerequisites for tasks in other duties. "Maintaining a clean and safe environment" probably includes "washing hands" and other related tasks, so this duty should probably be the first tackled by trainees. It also seems reasonable that the trainee would need to know how to move the patient around physically before mastering the tasks involving assisting with nutrition and elimination needs and caring for personal needs. Perhaps the tasks involved in medical treatments could be learned after the student has learned how to maintain a clean and safe environment. Of course, your sequence might not look exactly like this one. The point here was for you to place any duty *you* felt was a prerequisite for another duty *before* the duty for which it is pre-

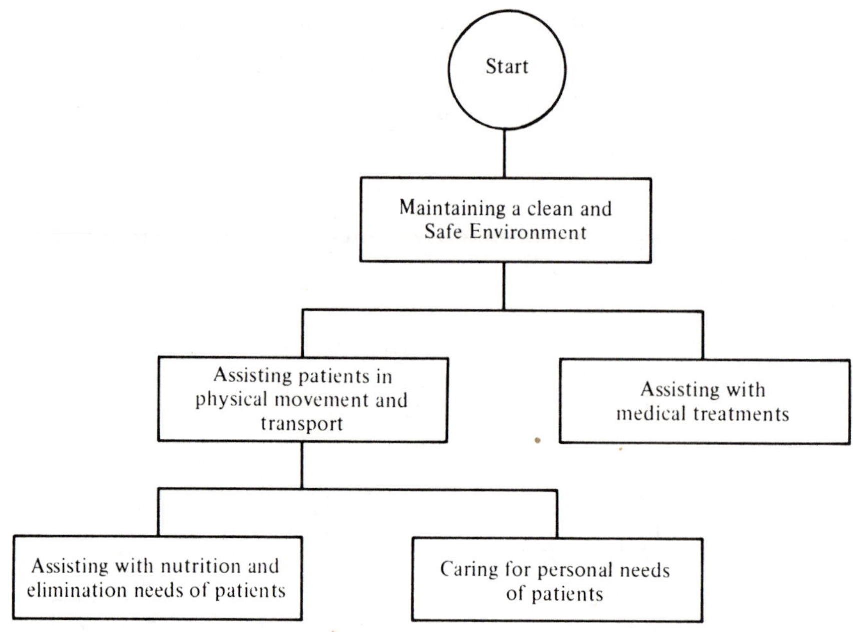

requisite and also to *avoid* a definite sequence for those duties that you felt were independent.

If you missed any, go back and review pages 139-144.

CHAPTER 4, TASK 6, ANSWER KEY [2]

Your responses to SELF-CHECK [2] should agree with those below.

1. Based on the sequence of tasks shown, your responses should be:
   (a) Students may begin with 01 *or* 02.
   (b) Tasks 03, 04, and 05 can be completed in any order since they are all on the same level.
   (c) Tasks 01 through 05 must be completed before 06 since they are all above 06.
   (d) Task 09 may be begun after completing tasks 01 through 06.

2. Based on the tasks described, your sequence of tasks should show the following relationship among tasks:

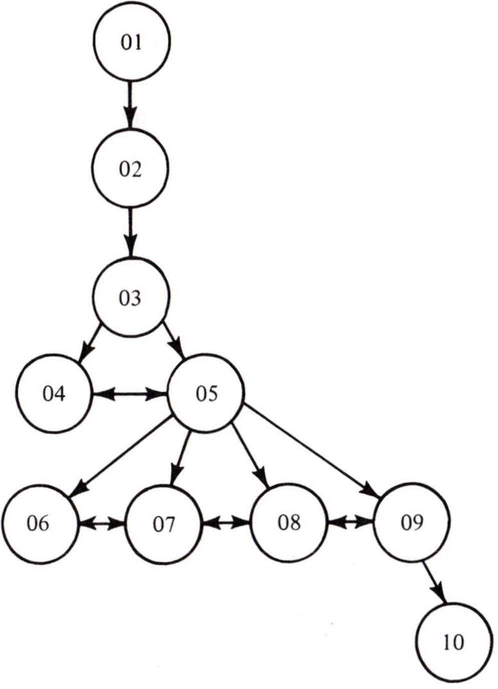

If you missed any, go back and review pages 145-149.

CHAPTER 5, TASK 7, ANSWER KEY [1]

Your responses to SELF-CHECK [1] should agree with those given below.

1. The following or other valid benefits:

   (a) Students do not need to learn from a particular resource.

   (b) Resources can be selected that teach the task as it is assessed on the test.

   (c) If the test is comprehensive and developed first, we will be more likely to select or develop learning materials that effectively teach the entire task.

   (d) How students learn the task can be independent of how they are tested. A variety of learning materials can be selected as long as each prepares the student to succeed on the test.

(e) If tests are developed before instructional materials, they will focus more on the task as it should be performed on the job.

(f) We are more likely to develop learning materials that teach the task fully but that teach only what is needed for task mastery if we develop the test first and then develop materials to ensure that students will pass the test.

2. (a) Providing feedback
   (b) Evaluating training materials
   (c) Diagnostic
   (d) Assessing mastery

If you missed any, go back and review pages 154-158.

CHAPTER 5, TASK 7, ANSWER KEY [2]

Your responses to SELF-CHECK [2] should agree with those given below.

1. (a) To report which students scored at the minimum criteria level.
   (b) Criteria are fixed—determined before testing occurs and based on level required to be competent.
   (c) Encouraged; students may take a test several times; reaching mastery is the goal.
   (d) Competition among students is reduced.
   (e) Mastery or nonmastery; time it takes to reach mastery.

2. (a) Not much choice here; trainee must actually type manuscript from a written draft or other source.
   (b) Student must diagnose problems in the cooling system of an actual vehicle. Troubleshooting a "bugged" trainer would be OK, but an actual vehicle would be better. A written test may also be needed, but alone it is not enough.
   (c) Not only must the trainee correctly operate the device (whatever it is), it must be set up as well.
   (d) The student should be required to test actual samples of urine for sugar and acetone content.
   (e) A written test would assess this task; however, the test questions must be beyond simple recall of facts or terms. The stu-

dent, by his or her answers, must demonstrate mastery of the principles underlying the operation of a four-cycle engine.

If you missed any, go back and review pages 160-163.

CHAPTER 5, TASK 7, ANSWER KEY [3]

Your responses to SELF-CHECK [3] should agree with those given below.

1. *Process*. Wording OK except that "the student" is not needed; should begin with a verb in the past tense.

2. *Process* (unless this could be observed by the position of the valve when student is finished). Worded correctly.

3. *Product*. Very subjective; "correctly" needs to be defined, such as ±0.01 in., etc. Also, "were" should probably be replaced by "are," since the finished product exists now.

4. *Process*. Not worded very clearly. Would make more sense beginning with a verb, such as "Was clean oil used?" "Was sterilizer set at 320°?" should be a separate test item.

5. *Process* (or may be product if assessment can be made by observing the completed work). Vague—how much is "enough"?

If you missed any, go back and review pages 164-174.

CHAPTER 5, TASK 8, ANSWER KEY [1]

Your responses to SELF-CHECK [1] should agree with those given below.

1. ___(a)
___(b)
_X_(c)
_X_(d)
___(e)
_X_(f)

2. Any four of the following or other valid advantages:
   (a) Students can respond to the items quickly.
   (b) There is only one correct answer.
   (c) The items can be graded quickly.
   (d) They can be graded by a clerk.
   (e) Grading is very objective.
   (f) They can evaluate basic knowledge as well as higher-level learning.

3. d; Item a requires only a general knowledge of the concept of board feet; item b can be answered by memorizing the formula; item c can be guessed at with a 50% chance of accuracy; item d has enough choices to discourage guessing; and since the possible choices each represent various answers resulting from common mistakes made when computing board feet, the student must be able to compute it correctly.

If you missed any, go back and review pages 179-182.

CHAPTER 5, TASK 8, ANSWER KEY [2]

Your responses to SELF-CHECK [2] should agree with those given below.

1. • "Because of" should have been in stem—not in each alternative.
   • Choice (3) was much longer than others; may unfairly influence student to pick (or not pick) choice (3) as answer.
   • Capital letters would be much easier to respond to and keep track of instead of (1), (2), (3), and (4).
   • Choice (3) contains two complete thoughts.

2. • Stem is too short and incomplete; perhaps should read "electricity could be defined as."
   • There is really no *one* right answer.
   • B contains two thoughts and is longer than others.
   • C is not a plausible distractor.

- There are only three alternatives, which results in 50% chance of guessing after C is eliminated.
- No punctuation after stem.

3. • Stem is very confusing; do we mean cubic feet, lineal feet, or *board* feet?
   - Alternatives should be on separate lines.
   - Alternatives should be arranged in ascending or descending order.
   - Stem should be punctuated with a question mark.

If you missed any, go back and review pages 183-186.

CHAPTER 6, TASK 9, ANSWER KEY [1]

Your responses to SELF-CHECK [1] should agree with those given below.

1. (a) Effectiveness (how well it works).
   (b) Efficiency (how much it costs).

2. Any five of these or other valid characteristics:
   (a) Keep student mastery as the overriding concern.
   (b) Allow each student enough time to reach mastery.
   (c) Break each learning task down into smaller segments.
   (d) Provide instruction appropriate for the task and student.
   (e) Allow students to speed up or slow down their learning pace.
   (f) Tell students exactly what they are to learn.
   (g) Help students when and where needed.
   (h) Allow students to spend most of their time engaged in learning.
   (i) Provide feedback on performance and help correct performance if needed.
   (j) Ensure mastery of early prerequisite tasks.

3. Any two of these or other valid reasons:
   (a) Student outcomes are very vague.
   (b) Relies on instructor-centered, group-paced instructional methods.
   (c) Forces many students to move on to the next task before they are ready.

4. Any four of these or other valid reasons:
   (a) Providing a variety of appropriate learning resources and activities.
   (b) Providing self-paced learning materials when students need them.
   (c) Providing needed structure.
   (d) Organizing the program by task.
   (e) Can help improve the quality of instruction.
   (f) Including built-in checkpoints for checking progress.
   (g) Is a system that students prefer.
   (h) Ensures that each student receives the same instruction initially.

If you missed any, go back and review pages 192-196.

CHAPTER 6, TASK 9, ANSWER KEY [2]

Your responses to SELF-CHECK [2] should agree with those given below.

Your responses should agree with those given below.

	Advantages	Disadvantages
1.	e	c
2.	b, h, i	
3.	g	a, d, f

f, g 4.

h 5.

i 6.

j 7.

c 8.

d, e 9.

d, e 10.

a, b 11.

If you missed any, go back and review pages 197-212.

CHAPTER 6, TASK 9, ANSWER KEY [3]

Your responses to SELF-CHECK [3] should agree with those given below.

	Yes	No
1. Evaluate your enabling objectives (EOs) using the items below.		
(a) Is each EO numbered, specific, and observable?		
(b) Does each begin with an action verb in the present tense?		
(c) Does each EO have meaning for the student?		
(d) Is each EO narrow enough that students can remember what was presented while practicing?		
(e) Do the EOs for each task enable the student to perform the task?		
(f) Is each EO something new the student will learn?		
2. Evaluate each cover page using the items below.		
(a) Is the task stated just as it is on the task listing?		

(b) Does the introduction tell the student specifically why it is important to learn the task?

(c) Does the TPO clearly describe what the student must do to demonstrate mastery?

(d) Does each enabling objective conform to items 1a–f above?

3. Evaluate the learning steps developed for each enabling objective using the items below.

   (a) Are the learning steps clear and concise?

   (b) Is one or more learning step included that presents instruction that is appropriate for the enabling objective?

   (c) If needed, is more than one learning step for presenting instruction included?

   (d) Is one or more appropriate learning step included that guides the student through practice or application of the performance called for in the EO?

   (e) Is one or more appropriate learning step included that gives the student feedback on performance?

   (f) Are learning steps included telling the student when to attempt the written and performance test?

If you missed any, go back and review pages 215-227.

CHAPTER 6, TASK 9, ANSWER KEY [4]

Your responses to SELF-CHECK [4] should agree with those given below.

1. Practice
2. Present
3. Feedback
4. Feedback
5. Present

6. Practice

7. Present

8. Feedback

9. Feedback

10. Present

11. Evaluate the learning resources you selected and developed using the items below.

Resources for Presenting Instruction	Yes	No
(a) Does each resource actually present the student performance called for in the enabling objective?		
(b) Is the type of resource appropriate for the kind of performance called for in the enabling objective?		
(c) Is the resource appropriate for the level of students?		
(d) Is each resource the least costly available that will effectively teach the performance called for in the enabling objective?		
(e) Is each resource technically complete and accurate?		
(f) Is the student directed to *specific* slides, pages, frames, etc.?		
(g) Is each instruction sheet easy to follow and illustrated if needed?		
Resources for Practice and Feedback		
(h) For *knowledge*-enabling objectives, is the student called upon to apply or use the knowledge presented?		
(i) Do knowledge self-checks provide an opportunity to apply what was presented?		
(j) Is an answer key or some other means provided to give the student immediate feedback on how well the knowledge was mastered?		

(k) For *skill*-enabling objectives, is the student called upon to actually perform the skill presented?

(l) Are any special resources needed for practice (such as materials or equipment) mentioned in the learning steps?

(m) Is some means provided for the student to compare the practice performance with correct performance?

(n) Do skill self-checks list specific, observable criteria by which to check the process or product?

If you missed any, go back and review pages 228-245.

CHAPTER 6, TASK 10, ANSWER KEY [1]

Your responses to SELF-CHECK [1] should agree with those given below.

1. (a) The purpose of the initial tryout is simply to see if students can follow the steps and resources used in the learning guide.

   (b) The purpose of the field test is to find out how well the learning guide actually works in helping students master the task.

2. d

3. d

4. c

5. Evaluate your initial tryout using the items below.

	Yes	No
(a) Were all necessary components of each learning guide included?		
(b) Was the rough draft legible?		
(c) Were learning resources in their normal locations?		
(d) Were one or two average or above-average students used in the tryout?		
(e) Were the students oriented?		
(f) Did the instructor observe each student and make note of any problems or questions?		

(g) Was constructive criticism from students encouraged?

(h) Was the rough draft corrected as needed?

If you missed any, go back and review pages 251-253.

CHAPTER 6, TASK 10, ANSWER KEY [2]

Your responses to SELF-CHECK [2] should agree with those given below.

1. d

2. a

3. Evaluate your field testing using the items below.

	Yes	No
(a) Did each guide have an initial tryout?		
(b) Was each guide field-tested with three to five students?		
(c) Was little said to the field-test students about the guides being tested?		
(d) Was the instructor involved only as dictated by the learning guide?		
(e) Was constructive criticism encouraged from each field-test student?		
(f) Were needed changes in the learning guide made based on the results of the field test?		

If you missed any, go back and review pages 254-256.

CHAPTER 7, TASK 11, ANSWER KEY [1]

Your responses to SELF-CHECK [1] should agree with those given below.

1. Instruction or teaching

2. Learning

3. Any five of the following or other valid factors:
   (a) Students enter at various times throughout the year.
   (b) Students may be training for different occupations.
   (c) Students move to the next task only after mastery of the current task.
   (d) Students progress at their own rate.
   (e) Students are tested when ready to demonstrate mastery.
   (f) Immediate student feedback is given at critical points.
   (g) The instructor may have to answer questions on many tasks on a given day.
   (h) Retesting is encouraged.
   (i) Learning materials for several tasks must be readied each day.
   (j) Student enrollment remains near program capacity.
   (k) A wide variety of media and materials must be managed each day.
   (l) The program usually operates year-round.
   (m) Day and evening programs may have access to all learning materials.
   (n) If possible, students may determine the sequence of tasks.

4. Any three of the following or other important pieces of information:
   (a) All necessary identifying information—name number, program, etc.
   (b) The period of time being planned for—beginning and ending dates.
   (c) The task numbers planned for mastery.
   (d) The task names planned for mastery.
   (e) The recommended sequence for mastering the task.
   (f) The student's signature verifying that he or she is aware of what tasks are planned for mastery.

5. Any three of the following or other valid benefits:
   (a) Students can be held responsible for filling out their own time cards.
   (b) A lot of valuable data can be collected, including absences, tardiness, time spent on tasks, etc.

(c) Students gain experience punching a time clock.

(d) Students get valuable experience keeping accurate records and managing their own affairs.

(e) The training program is more businesslike.

If you missed any, go back and review pages 263-274.

CHAPTER 7, TASK 11, ANSWER KEY [2]

Your responses to SELF-CHECK [2] should agree with those given below.

1. Such norm-referenced grading systems do not reflect what each student has actually learned.

2. Any two of the following or other appropriate reasons:

   (a) Learning is enhanced

   (b) Excellence is encouraged

   (c) Necessary for accountability

   (d) Instruction can be evaluated

   (e) It is just good sense

3. d

4. (a) If students desire to learn the task

   (b) If students possess the necessary prerequisite learning

   (c) If students receive high-quality instruction

5.

Student	*Percent*	*Grade*
(a)	80	D or U
(b)	131	A or S
(c)	85	C or S
(d)	80	D or U
(e)	93	B or S

If you missed any, go back and review pages 277-296.

CHAPTER 7, TASK 11, ANSWER KEY [3]

Your responses to SELF-CHECK [3] should agree with those given below.

1. (a) *Learning stations*: Here students *receive instruction* in knowledge or skill for each enabling objective.

   (b) *Practice stations*: Here students actually *practice* the performance of skills. They may also receive instruction here while practicing.

   (c) *Testing stations*: Here students take written or performance *tests*. Tests may be given in the same place as practice.

2. Students have a great deal of freedom.

3. Any two of the following or other valid reasons:

   (a) Using learning guides is so different from what they are used to.

   (b) Some students may lack confidence or self-directiveness.

   (c) Some students may have a long history of failure in school.

If you missed any, go back and review pages 298-309.

CHAPTER 7, TASK 12, ANSWER KEY [1]

Your responses to SELF-CHECK [1] should agree with those given below.

1. Many instructors, trainers, supervisors, administrators, and others sometimes have negative preconceived ideas about "competency-based, self-paced, individualized, open-entry/open-exit programs."

2. It might be good to first get your colleagues involved in focusing on the *need* for an approach to training that will produce better results than the traditional approach.

3. Responses for each question:

   (a) Is each response specific?

   (b) Does each response support the competency-based approach to training?

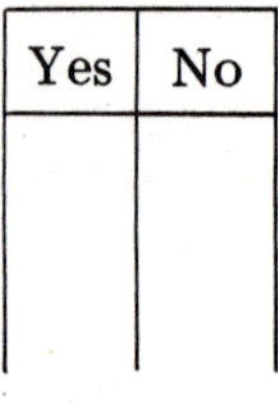

Yes	No

4. Does the local plan of action specify:

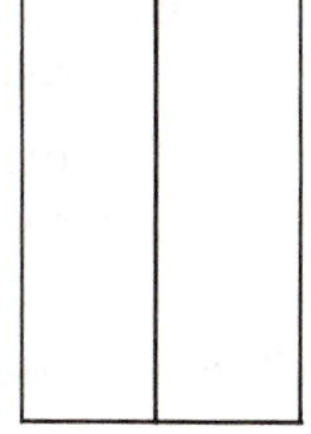

(a) Exactly what is to be accomplished?

(b) Beginning and ending dates?

(c) Who is responsible?

(d) Approximate cost?

If you missed any, go back and review pages 313-323.

CHAPTER 7, TASK 12, ANSWER KEY [2]

Your responses to SELF-CHECK [2] should agree with those given below.

1. Any two of the following or other valid reasons:

   (a) Chances are, it will be more effective.

   (b) If successful, instructors will develop a positive attitude toward the competency-based approach.

   (c) Instructors will be familiar with and will see the need for each component of a competency-based program.

2. The instructor training materials should be developed using the same learning guide format that instructors are being trained to use in their programs. This will help instructors become familiar with the format and will show them that learning packages are effective.

3. The list of instructor competencies:

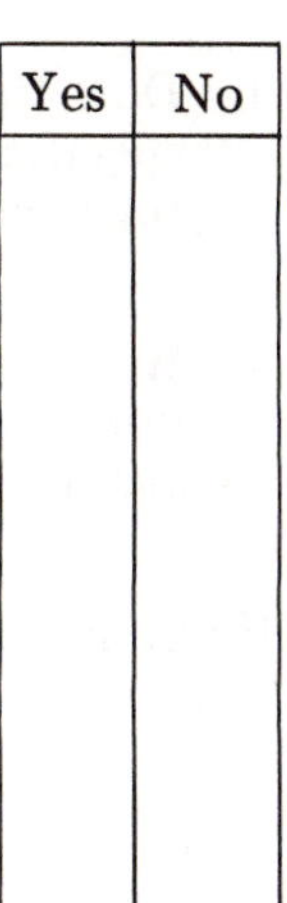

	Yes	No
(a) Does the list include the major skills needed to develop and implement a competency-based program?		
(b) Are the competencies specific and precise?		
(c) Are they listed on a form similar to the task listing form to be used by instructors?		

4. The agenda for the instructor training program:

   (a) Does the program include all the instructor competencies?

(b) Are the competencies addressed in an apparent logical sequence?

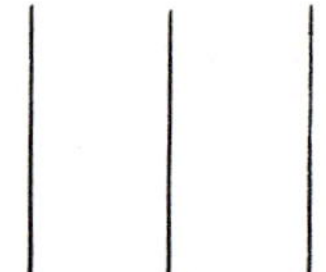

(c) Does it appear that realistic times have been attached to each competency?

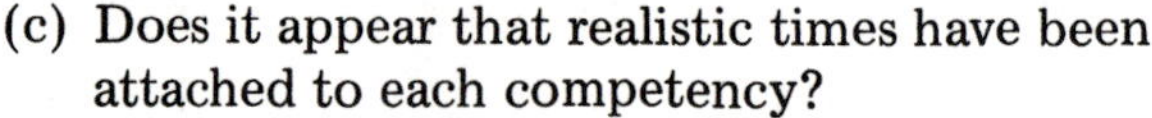

If you missed any, go back and review pages 324-331.

CHAPTER 7, TASK 12, ANSWER KEY [3]

Your responses to SELF-CHECK [3] should agree with those given below.

1. Competency-based programs may need to be evaluated:

   (a) During the transition from traditional to competency-based to determine which are already competency-based

   (b) After newly developed programs have been in operation for several years

2. Two things looked for are:

   (a) How the program is set up and operating (process)

   (b) How effective the program (product) is

3. When the effectiveness of a training program can be determined task by task, learning packages for those tasks graduates were not adequately trained in can be improved.

	Yes	No
4. Does the evaluation instrument contain objective, specific criteria that distinguish between competency-based and traditional programs?		
5. Were elements of the actual training program that were *not* competency-based identified and noted on the evaluation instrument?		

If you missed any, go back and review pages 332-338.

Index